GODLY READING

This innovative study explores the history of puritanism and the history of reading in the long seventeenth century. Drawing on a wide range of significant but understudied source materials, it seeks to advance our understanding of puritan or 'godly' culture by examining the place of reading within that culture between c.1580 and 1720. In contrast to long-standing claims about the connections between advanced Protestantism and emergent individualism and interiority, the book demonstrates the importance of communal and public forms of reading in the practice of godly piety. Andrew Cambers employs a novel framework, based around the spaces and places of early modern reading, to offer a revised understanding of the nature of puritanism and of the practice and representation of reading during the period. Moving beyond existing interpretations, *Godly Reading* opens up fresh discussions and debates about the nature of early modern reading and religion.

ANDREW CAMBERS has taught at the Universities of Oxford, Exeter and Lancaster and is editor of *The Life of John Rastrick, 1650–1727*, Camden Fifth Series, Volume 36 (2010).

CAMBRIDGE STUDIES IN EARLY MODERN
BRITISH HISTORY

SERIES EDITORS

JOHN MORRILL, *Professor of British and Irish History,
University of Cambridge, and Fellow, Selwyn College*
ETHAN SHAGAN, *Associate Professor of History,
University of California, Berkeley*
ALEXANDRA WALSHAM, *Professor of Reformation History,
University of Exeter*

This is a series of monographs and studies covering many aspects of the
history of the British Isles between the late fifteenth century and the early
eighteenth century. It includes the work of established scholars and
pioneering work by a new generation of scholars. It includes both reviews
and revisions of major topics and books, which open up new historical terrain
or which reveal startling new perspectives on familiar subjects. All the
volumes set detailed research into our broader perspectives, and the books
are intended for the use of students as well as of their teachers.

For a list of titles in the series go to
www.cambridge.org/earlymodernbritishhistory

GODLY READING

*Print, Manuscript and Puritanism
in England, 1580–1720*

ANDREW CAMBERS

CAMBRIDGE
UNIVERSITY PRESS

CAMBRIDGE UNIVERSITY PRESS
Cambridge, New York, Melbourne, Madrid, Cape Town, Singapore,
São Paulo, Delhi, Dubai, Tokyo, Mexico City

Cambridge University Press
The Edinburgh Building, Cambridge CB2 8RU, UK

Published in the United States of America by Cambridge University Press, New York

www.cambridge.org
Information on this title: www.cambridge.org/9780521764896

First published 2011

Printed in the United Kingdom at the University Press, Cambridge

A catalogue record for this publication is available from the British Library

Library of Congress Cataloging-in-Publication Data
Cambers, Andrew, 1977–
Godly reading : print, manuscript and puritanism in England, 1580–1720 / Andrew Cambers.
p.   cm. – (Cambridge studies in early modern British history)
Includes bibliographical references and index.
ISBN 978-0-521-76489-6 (Hardback)
1. Reading–England–History.   2. England–Religious life and customs.
3. Books and reading–England–History.   4. Puritans–England–History.
5. England–Church history.   I. Title.
BR756.C36 2011
274.2′06–dc22
2010037679

ISBN 978-0-521-76489-6 Hardback

For Alice and Jack

Contents

Illustrations

Abbreviations

BL   British Library, London

ODNB   *The Oxford Dictionary of National Biography* ed. H. C. G. Matthew and Brian Harrison (60 vols., Oxford, 2004)

Actes and Monuments (1583)   John Foxe, *Actes and Monuments of Matters most Speciall and Memorable, Happenyng in the Church, with an Uniuersall History of the same* (London, 1583)

HEHL   Henry E. Huntington Library, San Marino, CA

TNA, PRO   The National Archives, Public Record Office, London

The Life of John Rastrick   Andrew Cambers (ed.), *The Life of John Rastrick, 1650–1727*, Camden 5th series, vol. 36 (Cambridge, 2010)

Heywood, *Diaries*   J. H. Turner (ed.), *The Rev. Oliver Heywood, B.A. 1630–1702, his Autobiography, Diaries, Anecdote and Event Books, Illustrating the General and Family History of Yorkshire and Lancashire* (4 vols., Brighouse, 1881–5)

STC   A. W. Pollard and G. R. Redgrave, *A Short-Title Catalogue of Books Printed in England, Scotland, and Ireland and of English Books Printed Abroad 1473–1640* (2nd edn, London, 1976–91)

Wing   Donald Wing, *Short-Title Catalogue of Books Printed in England, Scotland, Ireland, Wales and British America and of English Books Printed in Other Countries 1641–1700* (2nd edn, New York, 1972–88)

Conventions

Original spelling has been retained in quotations, except in the cases of 'i' and 'j' and 'u' and 'v', which have been modernized. Punctuation and capitalization have generally been left in early modern style, saving a few instances where the absence of punctuation renders long quotations unreadable. Standard contractions have been silently expanded. Dates before September 1752 are in the Old Style, except that the year is taken to begin on 1 January. Emphases in quotations and extracts are in all cases as they appear in the original.

Acknowledgements

It is a pleasure to be able to thank those whose advice, encouragement and support have helped me to write this book.

First and foremost, Bill Sheils was an exemplary doctoral supervisor, generous to a fault with his time and ideas – this book can only be a small token of thanks for his unstinting support. At the University of York, I was fortunate to work among a flourishing and friendly group of early modernists. As friends, fellow students or esteemed colleagues, I learned much from Wolfgang Behringer, John Bossy, Stuart Carroll, Simon Ditchfield, Liz Evenden, Mark Jenner, Jason Scott-Warren, Jim Sharpe, Helen Smith and Michelle Wolfe. I have vivid memories of Alex Walsham and Mark Jenner's examination of the thesis and thank them both for helping me to think about how to turn it into a book.

Since finishing the dissertation, chopping and changing between temporary posts and only finishing the book in a period of gainful unemployment, things have not always been settled or easy. Nevertheless, I have learned much from cohorts of students at Keble College, Oxford; Oxford Brookes University; and the Universities of Exeter and Lancaster and I count it as my good fortune to have worked alongside so many stimulating colleagues. Among them, I must thank Ian Archer, Jonathan Barry, Henry French, Maria Fusaro, Sandy Grant, Alison Kay, Andrew Spicer, James Taylor and Alex Walsham. I would also like to acknowledge the collegiality of seminars at the Institute of Historical Research and all that I have learned at them, especially at Ken Fincham and Nicholas Tyacke's seminar on the Religious History of Britain. Many others have sent me their work, provided good counsel or just encouraged me to get on with it, especially David Como, David Cressy, Lori Anne Ferrell, Tom Freeman, Arnold Hunt, Alex Lumbers, Catherine Molineux, Bill Sherman, Tracey Sowerby and Sam Thomas. I owe particular thanks to Bill Sherman, Sam Thomas and Alex Walsham, who gave up their time to read drafts of the whole book. Their advice has improved it immeasurably.

xii

Numerous librarians and archivists have helped along the way, especially the staff at York Minster Library, the British Library and the Huntington Library. No less important has been the financial support that has supported my research, from the University of York, the Huntington Library, and the Bibliographical Society. I am also grateful to a grant from the Scouloudi Foundation in association with the Institute of Historical Research, which has made publication of the illustrations possible.

Some of the ideas and arguments expressed in this book were first aired in seminar papers at the Universities of Cambridge, Exeter, Oxford and York, as well as at the Institute of Historical Research, and have benefited from the probing questions and lively discussions on those occasions. Although this book has been conceived and written as a whole, short passages of Chapters 2 and 3 have been anticipated in my articles: 'Reading, Family Religion, and Evangelical Identity in Late Stuart England', *Historical Journal*, 47 (2004), pp. 875–96 (© Cambridge University Press); 'Reading, the Godly, and Self-Writing in England, circa 1580–1720', *Journal of British Studies*, 46 (2007), pp. 796–825 (© The North American Conference on British Studies); and 'Demonic Possession, Literacy and "Superstition" in Early Modern England', *Past and Present*, 202 (2009), pp. 3–35 (© The Past and Present Society). I am grateful for permission to reprint excepts from them here.

I would also like to thank everyone at Cambridge University Press for their help, especially Michael Watson, Liz Friend-Smith and Gillian Dadd.

Finally, I would not have been able to write this book without the love, support and encouragement of my family: my parents and brothers, my wife Alice and my son Jack.

London, June 2010

CHAPTER I

Reading and puritanism in the long seventeenth century

INTRODUCTION

This book is about the intersection of the culture of puritanism and the history of reading in the long seventeenth century. It seeks to advance our understanding of puritanism by examining the place of reading within this religious culture and argues that by intertwining these two strands of study – reading and religious culture – we emerge with a deeper under-standing of both and of their place within early modern English society.

Writing his *Book of Martyrs* – a book which would become one of the key works of puritan culture – in the middle of the sixteenth century, John Foxe looked back on printing as an invention inspired not so much by Gutenberg as by God. The year 1450, he wrote, had been 'famous and memorable, for the divine and miraculous invention of printing'. 'God himselfe was the ordayner and disposer' of this invention and it was no coincidence that it was revealed just as the Church was trying to persecute as heretics those who struggled to reveal God's truth. Against the worldly power of the Roman Antichrist, God sought 'with Printing, writing, and reading to convince darkenes by light, errour by truth, ignorance by learning'. By the time Foxe wrote, the invention had wrought such a religious transformation – its effects were such that 'knowledge groweth, judgement increaseth, books are dispersed, the Scripture is seene, the Doctours be read, stories be opened, times compared, truth decerned, falshod detected'. Western culture was at a juncture at which 'eyther the pope must abolish printing, or he must seek a new world to raygne over: for els, as this world standeth, printing doubtles will abolish hym'. Foxe described a technology which was intrinsically democratic: 'through the light of printing, the worlde beginneth nowe to have eyes to see, and heades to judge'. The pitch of his invective became higher as he described how

By this printing, as by the gift of tongues, and as by the singular organe of the holy Ghost, the doctrine of the Gospell soundeth to all nations and countryes under heaven: and what God revealeth to one man, is dispersed to many and what is knowne in one nation, is opened to all.

Printing was intrinsically connected with Protestantism and the activities which it furthered worked against the power of the papacy. 'Now nothing doth debilitate and shake the high spire of his Papacie', wrote Foxe, 'so much as reading, preaching, knowledge & judgement, that is to say, the fruit of printing'. In this providential world view, in which technology facilitated the rediscovery of religious truth, it was as if 'the penne of Luther ... hath set the triple crown so awry on the popes head, that it is like never to be set streight agayne'.[1]

Foxe's description evokes a familiar image not only of the allegedly inevitable link between the development of the printing press and the growth of Protestantism – a connection between two religious and technological revolutions – but also of some of the imperatives of reformed religious practice. Bible-reading was a vital component of the practice of Protestantism, a means by which to channel the Holy Spirit into the soul of the reader. Reformation theology and iconography frequently described and depicted faith as if it came through the printed book, as if God spoke to the believer directly through the pages of the Bible. The association was particularly strong for puritans because the believer was denied recourse to the wider material and sacramental repertoire open to Catholics and, to a lesser extent, mainstream Protestants. Puritans were everywhere depicted with their books open before them, or clutched in their hands: pious reading was represented as their favourite religious activity. Indeed, the echoes of Foxe's description can be heard reverberating through the words of the historians who have followed in his footsteps, connecting printing and Protestantism at the hip and figuring

---

[1] *Actes and Monuments* (1583), pp. 707–8. It is rarely observed that the reformers also argued that the Devil as well as the pope acted against the press. Cotton Mather, the great historian of early American puritanism, for example, argued that the Devil hindered the invention of printing and spectacles, by which scripture could be spread and seen: and that the Devil would 'with all his heart make one huge Bonefire of all the Bibles in the world'. See Cotton Mather, *The Wonders of the Invisible World: Being an Account of the Tryals of Several Witches Lately Executed in New-England* (repr. of 1693 edn, London, 1862), pp. 52, 182. The subject of attitudes towards printing will be greatly advanced by Elizabeth Eisenstein's forthcoming *Divine Art, Infernal Machine: The Reception of Printing in the West from First Impressions to the Sense of an Ending*. For the importance of Foxe to studies of the history of the book, see especially John N. King, *Foxe's* Book of Martyrs *and Early Modern Print Culture* (Cambridge, 2006); and Elizabeth Evenden and Thomas S. Freeman, *Religion and the Book in Early Modern England: The Making of John Foxe's 'Book of Martyrs'* (Cambridge, forthcoming).

private religious reading as perhaps the defining characteristic of reformed individual religious belief.[2]

The realities of religious practice and of religious belief frequently strayed some distance from these idealized models. Such was the diversity of Protestant uses of the Bible that in 1695 an obscure Devon rector called John Rost drew the remarkable comparison between Muslim respect for the sacred book and Christian defilement of its once sacred pages. Rost recalled an ambassador's observation of the Turks that

> when they were at their Solemn devotions, and he observed that when in reading the Alcaron, (which is their Bible) or of their Prayers, the Priest pronounced the name of *Mahomet* they all bowed themselves very low, but when he pronounced the name of God they fell flat upon their Faces to the Ground. And he says that they are exceedingly careful to preserve Paper from any filth or Defilement, and that if they chance to see any lie scattered on the ground, they presently take it up, wipe it, and put it into some safe place; and the reason they give for it is this that for ought they know, the name of God hath been, or is written upon it. And if any one doth tread, or sit upon the Alcaron, they esteem it an unpardonable Crime: Because they look upon it as a contempt cast upon that Book, in which the name of God is so often written.[3]

Instead of having such reverence for the sacred space of the page, Protestants *used* their books, dog-earing pages, underlining passages and writing in their margins. The uses of Bibles – let alone other books – were nothing if not varied and they show us how the book carried an importance not only as a sacred text (however much it was scribbled upon) but also as an object which had a particular cultural resonance. In particular, Bibles assumed great significance for the godly – a term I use interchangeably with puritan – whether they were presented as gifts, lent to fellow believers, passed through families, or held aloft as symbols of the faith.[4] When a widow of an old acquaintance came to beg the charity of the

---

[2] This theme of the reformers has been triumphant in scores of influential historical studies, including A. G. Dickens, *Reformation and Society in Sixteenth-Century Europe* (London, 1966); Elizabeth L. Eisenstein, *The Printing Press as an Agent of Change: Communications and Cultural Transformations in Early Modern Europe* (2 vols., Cambridge, 1979); Mark U. Edwards Jr, *Printing, Propaganda, and Martin Luther* (Berkeley, CA, 1994); and David Daniell, *The Bible in English: Its History and Influence* (New Haven, CT, 2003). The association has been effectively challenged by, among others, Richard Gawthrop and Gerald Strauss, 'Protestantism and Literacy in Early Modern Germany', *Past and Present*, 104 (1984), pp. 31–55; and Alexandra Walsham, '"Domme Preachers"?: Post-Reformation English Catholicism and the Culture of Print', *Past and Present* 168 (2000), pp. 72–123.

[3] John Rost, *The Swearer's Doom; Or, A Discourse Setting Forth the Great Sinfulness and Danger of Rash and Vain Swearing* (London, 1695), pp. 20–1.

[4] For definitions of puritanism, see pp. 10–16 below.

puritan intelligencer Roger Morrice in 1685, too poor to feed and clothe her children or herself, Morrice gave her five pounds, and she held up her Bible, entreating him to be 'obedient to the contents of this booke'.[5] In such moments, the Bible was simultaneously a holy object and a sacred text, as it had been in the Civil War when parliamentarians marched under banners in which books testified to the religious significance of their political allegiance. Their banners bore images of the Bible, rousing mottoes like 'For Reformation', 'Antichrist must downe' and 'Pray and fight', together with stirring quotations from the Psalms.[6] Following the same logic, albeit more precariously, in a religious dispute in New England in the 1630s – in which the opponents styled themselves 'Scots' and 'English' – the 'Scots' marched with a Geneva Bible strapped to a pole to signify their religious allegiance.[7] The troubled years of the mid-seventeenth century offer many similar examples which testify to the importance to puritans of Bibles both as objects and as religious texts, as well as many hostile descriptions which claimed they were religious vandals who treated the holy book with disrespect. A particularly imaginative graphic example of this (see Figure 1) can be seen in a woodcut illustrating the title page of the Royalist water-poet John Taylor's *Religions Enemies* (1641), in which an Anabaptist, a Brownist, a Familist, and a Papist held the corner of a blanket and used it to toss the truth of religion – which was represented by a large Bible – around in the air.

Furthermore, the Bible had a range of more official physical uses, which offer us further evidence of the key role it played in social relations. These included some uses which remain familiar today, like swearing an oath on the Bible in court, as well as others which are rather more unfamiliar, such as the ceremony for degrading a clergyman from the priesthood, which began with the cleric being handed a Bible which was then taken away from him, before his cap, girdle and gown were formally removed by the authorities.[8] Even more alien to us was the widespread use

---

[5] Mark Goldie et al. (eds.), *The Entring Book of Roger Morrice 1677–1691* (6 vols., Woodbridge, 2007), vol. III, p. 47.

[6] See Ian Gentles, 'The Iconography of Revolution: England 1642–1649', in Ian Gentles, John Morrill and Blair Worden (eds.), *Soldiers, Writers, and Statesmen of the English Revolution* (Cambridge, 1998), pp. 98, 103.

[7] See David Cressy, 'Books as Totems in Seventeenth-Century England and New England', *Journal of Library History*, 21 (1986), pp. 94–6. The account is related in Thomas Lechford, *New-Englands Advice to Old-England* ([London], 1644).

[8] If we are to judge from Roger Morrice's account of the degrading of the pamphleteer and Whig clergyman Samuel Johnson in November 1686, which was part of his punishment for inciting the army to mutiny in his *An Humble and Hearty Address to all the English Protestants in the Present Army* (1686). See Goldie et al., *The Entring Book of Roger Morrice*, vol. III, p. 304.

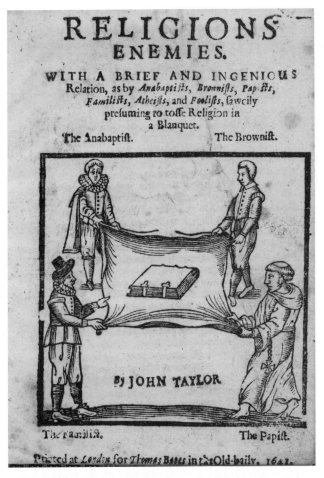

Figure 1. John Taylor, *Religions Enemies With A Brief And Ingenious Relation, as by Anabaptists, Brownists, Papists, Familists, Atheists, and Foolists, sawcily presuming to tosse Religion in a Blanquet* (London, 1641), title page. By permission of the Huntington Library, San Marino, California.

of the Bible as an object with quasi-magical properties, to protect homes from demons and to expel them when they afflicted families: practices which retained their power in the reformed world.[9]

---

[9] For which see Andrew Cambers, 'Demonic Possession, Literacy and "Superstition" in Early Modern England', *Past and Present*, 202 (2009), pp. 3–35.

Such uses of books – which remind us that many Protestants frequently drew upon methods of religiosity more reminiscent of those practised by Catholics – together with more straightforward modes of reading provide the material upon which this book is based. They offer evidence of how people encountered, read and used books in the past. The range of uses suggested above is important, for this is not just a book about what kind of books were read by puritans as part of their religious practice – although that subject will be covered – but rather it is an examination of the place of reading in puritan culture, of how the godly read and used books, and of how and why reading mattered so much in their lives. As such, my analysis seeks to cast light upon the religious and cultural history of early modern England more generally.

THE ARGUMENT

It is no surprise that books were central to godly culture. The image of the puritan was intrinsically linked to that of the book, so much so that literacy was often presented as a key skill in the religious repertoire of those who hoped that God had set them on the path to salvation. Some godly readers rejoiced as if picking up their Bibles established a hotline to God. To adapt the phrase of David Hall, they appear to have believed that the very presence of the Bible was akin to having God next to the reader.[10] But for others the presence of a text with which they could not engage merely confirmed their reprobation. This stark realization was perhaps particularly clear to those who came from outside Christian culture and were disappointed that the Word of God did not speak to them through their Bibles. As the curious and heartfelt comment inscribed in the margin of a Bible owned by a Christian Indian in Martha's Vineyard in New England read, 'I am forever a pitiful person in the world. I am not able clearly to read this, this book.'[11] But in seeking to reconstruct godly

---

[10] David D. Hall, *Worlds of Wonder, Days of Judgment: Popular Religious Belief in Early New England* (New York, 1989), p. 26.

[11] Cited in Jill Lepore, *The Name of War: King Philip's War and the Origins of American Identity* (New York, 1998), p. 31. Others expressed similar bewilderment. In his autobiography of 1789, Olaudah Equiano wrote, 'I had often seen my master and Dick employed in reading; and I had a great curiosity to talk to the books, as I thought they did; and so to learn how all things had a beginning: for that purpose I have often taken up a book, and have talked to it, and then put my ears to it, when alone, in hopes it would answer me; and I have been very much concerned when I found it remained silent.' Olaudah Equiano, *The Interesting Narrative and Other Writings*, ed. Vincent Carretta (Penguin Classics revised edn, London, 2003), p. 68. The notes detail a series of similar examples, pp. 254–5.

devotional reading and place it in a series of contexts – domestic, urban, political and so on – this book probes deeper beneath the surface of reading practices, observing and analysing the ways in which puritans read and used their books and using this reconstruction to refine our understanding of both the nature of puritanism and the practice and representation of reading in the seventeenth century.

Treating reading capaciously and employing a broad definition of the book (including manuscripts and ephemeral matter alongside printed books), I argue that reading was vital to the practice of puritanism. Reading was a crucial strand of puritan self-identity. As a social practice, it both bound the godly together and helped to set them apart from their non-godly neighbours. It offered a practical way of channelling the Holy Spirit as well as an accessible means of testing one's salvation: it was one of the methods by which the godly examined themselves for signs of election. At the same time, unravelling the ways in which the godly read draws attention to the areas of convergence between godly, mainstream Protestant and traditional modes and styles of piety. Of particular importance here is communal reading. In contrast to much of the historiography, I argue the case for the special importance of collective, social and public reading to the godly, demonstrating how far reading aloud and in company was a vital strand in the fabric of puritan piety. The godly read in this way not because they (or the majority of them) did not have the ability to read silently or privately – although it must be admitted that the collectivity of this reading made the practice of their religiosity more accessible (at least in theory) to those without fully articulated reading skills – but because the sociability of reading in this way was interwoven with other aspects of the style of puritan religiosity, such as their word-centred piety, which oscillated between extempore prayer and set text; their willingness to encapsulate the doctrine of predestination by self-consciously using their social practices to set themselves apart from their non-godly neighbours; and their stress on voluntarism as a means of expressing their devotion.[12] Such reading, although hardly exclusive to

---

[12] For these characteristics as those salient to the definition of puritanism, see Peter Lake, 'Defining Puritanism – Again?', in Francis J. Bremer (ed.), *Puritanism: Transatlantic Perspectives on a Seventeenth-Century Anglo-American Faith* (Boston, MA, 1993), pp. 3–29. Although the prevalence of social and oral reading in the practice of puritanism might be latched upon by those wanting to argue (in a revisionist vein) that puritanism was diluted in practice and thus 'unpopular', or (in a different vein) that such modes of piety made puritanism more accessible and thus 'popular' than is usually thought, both urges should be resisted. The point is that the godly self-consciously adopted a mode of social reading as part of their practice of puritanism.

puritans and not the *only* kind of reading they did – the godly were both oral and silent readers – intersected with, and was intimately related to, other crucial components of godly religiosity, such as listening to sermons, writing and praying.[13] It was at the heart of modes of evangelical piety from the early days of the Reformation in the sixteenth century to the stirrings of evangelicalism in the early eighteenth century. This reading was not only a practical way of spreading the word, but also, as it had been since the days of the Lollards – who probably got their name because of the sound made by their reading of the scriptures in the vernacular – an outward sign of religious allegiance and identity.[14]

In what follows I trace these styles of piety across the seventeenth century, establishing connections between the religiosity of early Stuart puritans and post-Restoration nonconformists which are rarely examined in any depth by historians. In part, I argue that the disjuncture between these separate historiographies has been a consequence of an artificial periodization which has parcelled the seventeenth century into three self-contained and sealed packages: before the Civil War; the era of Civil War, Commonwealth and Protectorate; and the era of the Restoration and the later seventeenth century. Despite all the upheavals of the century and the importance of these key moments of history, it makes sense to study the history of religious practice over the whole century, to think about continuity and change over the long seventeenth century. This approach recognizes that religious practices did not necessarily change quickly and neither did the books people read. It highlights the importance of studying old books, of thinking about their reception long after their first publication, as they were digested by their readers, sold and resold, as they passed through families and religious communities, and as they found new audiences in changed circumstances. Thinking of the century as a relatively coherent period in English religious history allows the long-term influence of key works – including Foxe's *Actes and Monuments* and Samuel Clarke's numerous collections, in which the lives of the godly were pickled and preserved, both reflecting and shaping puritan identities – to be drawn out. The reverberations of godly books across the century are vital to understanding the nature of religious identity.

---

[13] For the interplay of orality and literacy in the period more generally, see Adam Fox, *Oral and Literate Culture in England, 1500–1700* (Oxford, 2000).

[14] For these continuities, see Andrew Cambers and Michelle Wolfe, 'Reading, Family Religion, and Evangelical Identity in Late Stuart England', *Historical Journal*, 47 (2004), pp. 875–96.

We need only turn to the most famous examples of life-writing to see the need to trace such developments. In the spiritual autobiographies and diaries that characterize much of the culture of puritanism in the seventeenth century, we see the echoes of key works, whether they were written by the humblest, long-forgotten puritans or by the most famous worthies of the age. In his printed autobiography, *Grace Abounding* (1666), John Bunyan recalled that his wife had inherited from her father few worldly goods saving two invaluable tokens of early Stuart piety: Arthur Dent's *The plaine mans path-way to heaven* (1601) and Lewis Bayly's *The Practise of Pietie* (1612). In the context of his own experiences in the Civil War, it was the reading of these works of early Stuart puritanism that helped to bring about the spiritual transformation of the man who became the most famous late Stuart dissenter.[15]

In interweaving the histories of the book and reading with those of religious belief and practice, the book makes three essential claims. First, that godly reading was a style of religious engagement with texts which was frequently oral and communal: to read among fellow believers was a key sign of evangelical religious identity. Second, such reading lends itself to a model of early modern religion in which 'belief' was primarily socially constructed and maintained, thus casting doubt on the common assumption that the Reformation ushered in an era of individualization and interiorization. Third, that focusing on the practice of reading draws attention to the complexity of godly culture, simultaneously showing how reading was a social practice which provided cohesion within the godly community and revealing how it operated as a kind of 'ritual of separation' which helped to set the godly apart from their neighbours, despite the fact that the practices of reading themselves highlighted many of the areas of convergence and overlap between godly, mainstream Protestant and 'traditional' religious cultures.[16] As such, the book also offers a way of engaging with the continued debates on the success of the 'long Reformation' from a novel and challenging perspective since it provides an assessment of how far the devotional reading practices of the godly, whom we might expect to have reacted most positively to the reformed message, lived up to the ideals

---

[15] John Bunyan, *Grace Abounding: with Other Spiritual Autobiographies*, ed. John Stachniewski with Anita Pacheco (Oxford, 1998), p. 9.

[16] For 'rituals of separation', see Mary Douglas, *Purity and Danger: An Analysis of Concepts of Pollution and Taboo* (London, 1966), Chapter 1; and the brilliant exposition in John Bossy, *The English Catholic Community 1570–1850* (London, 1975), pp. 108–48, esp. pp. 108–9.

prescribed by reformed writers.[17] Historiographically, the book draws on the insights of the work of scholars of post-Reformation religion such as Peter Lake, Margo Todd and Alex Walsham and seeks to intertwine them with work on reading, print and literacy by Adam Fox, Roger Chartier and Adrian Johns. Its impact upon these fields is explored further below.

DEFINING PURITANISM AND GODLY CULTURE

In exploring the nature of the reading, the book also advances our understanding of the nature of puritanism. Whatever the sympathies and prejudices of its authors, who have themselves spanned a full spectrum of religious positions (from Laudian polemicists to noncon-formists and secularists) as well as political standpoints (Marxist, Whig and Conservative), the history of puritanism has traditionally been written with particular emphasis placed upon doctrine – especially upon the single issue of predestination – and the religious programme which they advocated has been located in the context of its relation to politics. In part, of course, such an emphasis is very proper. Historians have to define puritanism and since it is deeply problematic to follow those hostile contemporaries for whom 'puritan' was a catch-all term of abuse, they have focused on the tangible. Principally, this has meant figuring puritans as those who thought that the Reformation of the sixteenth century had not gone far enough and who thus advocated further reform of church and state, based not on what they saw as the compromised halfway house of Lutheran theology but upon the further and more clearly articulated theology of Calvin and Beza, in which the doctrine of predestination was paramount. Although the wider impact of puritanism is frequently noted, its definition in doctrinal terms has tended to result in political histories which have charted the godly proposals for further reform and assessed their success both in the Elizabethan period and in the run-up to the Civil Wars of the mid-seventeenth century.

---

[17] On the long Reformation, see Nicholas Tyacke (ed.), *England's Long Reformation 1500–1800* (London, 1998). A parallel story might also be told of the history of Catholic devotional reading, one which places renewed emphasis on the comparisons between post-Reformation Catholicism and nonconformity. Although some such comparisons are drawn in what follows, they are meant as preliminary and speculative and more research might be done in this area. For a rich and suggestive essay towards such a study, see Walsham, '"Domme Preachers"?'.

This political history of puritanism has undergone a series of developments in the last sixty years or so.[18] Its modern historiography began with
Christopher Hill's efforts to see puritanism as an ideology opposed to the
alliance of church and state: a dissenting minority who pushed events
onward towards a 'bourgeois' revolution.[19] Fraught with difficulties, this
interpretation could not survive a wave of revisionism which emerged out
of Patrick Collinson's *The Elizabethan Puritan Movement* and culminated
in his *The Religion of Protestants*. Collinson, together with Peter Lake and
Nicholas Tyacke, demonstrated that far from being a radical minority,
puritans were at the heart of the late Elizabethan and Jacobean religio-
political (Calvinist) establishment.[20] A third overlapping phase, with
many of the same participants, sought to pay further attention to exactly
what puritanism was and in particular the relative degree to which it was
either radical or conservative. Faced with attempts to reinvent puritanism
as a radical Calvinist cadre that wrested control from the mainstream of
the English church, Patrick Collinson, Kenneth Fincham, Peter Lake and
Nicholas Tyacke all insisted that puritans were the most active proponents
of the Calvinist consensus that had come to dominate the church.[21] They
diverged, however, when it came to the radicalism of this group. Where
Collinson and Tyacke essentially viewed puritans as hardly distinguish-
able from the Calvinist bedrock of the church; others – notably Fincham,
Lake and Tom Webster – argued for puritanism's rightful position as a
more distinct grouping that, while it operated within the religious establishment, was not simply a subset of it, and contained a series of positions
that ranged from the moderate to the more radical.[22]

---

[18] For a concise survey of the shifting approaches to puritanism, see Peter Lake, 'The Historiography
of Puritanism', in John Coffey and Paul C. H. Lim (eds.), *The Cambridge Companion to Puritanism*
(Cambridge, 2008), pp. 346–71.

[19] The approach is encapsulated in Christopher Hill, *Society and Puritanism in Pre-Revolutionary
England* (London, 1964).

[20] Patrick Collinson, *The Elizabethan Puritan Movement* (London, 1967); Patrick Collinson, *The
Religion of Protestants: The Church in English Society, 1559–1625* (Oxford, 1982); Nicholas Tyacke,
Anti-Calvinists: The Rise of English Arminianism, c.1590–1640 (Oxford, 1987); Peter Lake, *Moderate
Puritans and the Elizabethan Church* (Cambridge, 1982).

[21] For puritanism as a destabilizing force, see George Bernard, 'The Church of England, c.1529–
c.1642', *History*, 75 (1990), pp. 183–206; Kevin Sharpe, *The Personal Rule of Charles I* (New Haven,
CT, 1993). For positions relating to a Calvinist consensus, see note 20 above.

[22] See Kenneth Fincham, *Prelate as Pastor: The Episcopate of James I* (Oxford, 1990); Lake, 'Defining
Puritanism – Again?'; Peter Lake, 'Moving the Goal Posts? Modified Subscription and the
Construction of Conformity in the Early Stuart Church', in Peter Lake and Michael Questier
(eds.), *Conformity and Orthodoxy in the English Church, c.1560–1660* (Woodbridge, 2000), pp. 179–
205; Tom Webster, *Godly Clergy in Early Stuart England: The Caroline Puritan Movement c.1620–
1643* (Cambridge, 1997).

For all the importance of such work, its relatively narrow definition of puritanism has made for a series of limitations. In particular, the privileging of predestination has meant that it is the puritanism of those who articulated their religious positions in theological treatises and sermons which has been given most attention. Yet puritanism, imagined and real, was more than doctrine. Although Ben Jonson's satirical characters 'Zeal-of-the-land Busy' and 'Tribulation Wholesome' in *Bartholomew Fair* (1614) and *The Alchemist* (1610) are the best remembered,[23] it was not only on the stage that puritans gave their children distinctive names. In practice, many of the baptismal registers of the late sixteenth century include names which speak of the zealotry of their parents, including: Fear-not, Praise-God, Mercy, Thankful, Sin-deny and indeed Zealous.[24] Likewise, the puritan sermon (like other sermons) was a social event: puritans did not just listen to sermons, they met other members of the godly there and socialized with them; sometimes, they would travel for miles gadding to hear famous preachers; and they would take notes of sermons and repeat them at home in the family. Similarly, fasting, praying and exercising moral and religious discipline in the community were part of what it meant to be a puritan. Even aspects of gesture might be pertinent to what puritanism meant in practice, at least if we are to take any meaning from the satirical image of puritans as those who turned up the whites of their eyes in prayer.[25] It is with such considerations in mind that recent years have seen the evolution of a history of puritanism as a form of religious culture. Such work – by Nicholas Tyacke, Patrick Collinson and especially Peter Lake – has located puritanism in a broader analytical

[23] On Jonson's representations of puritans, see Peter Lake with Michael Questier, *The Antichrist's Lewd Hat: Protestants, Papists, and Players in Post-Reformation England* (New Haven, CT, 2002), pp. 579–620.

[24] See Nicholas Tyacke, 'Popular Puritan Mentality in Late Elizabethan England', in Peter Clark, Alan Smith and Nicholas Tyacke (eds.), *The English Commonwealth 1547–1640: Essays in Politics and Society Presented to Joel Hurstfield* (Leicester, 1979), pp. 77–92, 229–33. It should be noted that this essay was openly framed as a way of unpacking puritan culture.

[25] As encapsulated by the stage direction for the behaviour of the puritan in *Two Wise Men and All the Rest Fooles: or A Comicall Morall, Censuring the Follies of this Age* (London, 1619) – 'She openeth her Bible, and makes shew to reade, and many times turnes her eyes with the white upward'. Cited in William P. Holden, *Anti-Puritan Satire 1572–1642* (New Haven, CT, 1954), p. 119. On this and other aspects of the character of the stage puritan, see Patrick Collinson, 'Ecclesiastical Vitriol: Religious Satire in the 1590s and the Invention of Puritanism', in John Guy (ed.), *The Reign of Elizabeth I: Court and Culture in the Last Decade* (Cambridge, 1995), pp. 150–70; and his 'The Theatre Constructs Puritanism', in David L. Smith, Richard Strier and David Bevington (eds.), *The Theatrical City: Culture, Theatre and Politics in London, 1576–1649* (Cambridge, 1995), pp. 157–69. For gesture more generally, see Michael J. Braddick (ed.), *The Politics of Gesture: Historical Perspectives* (*Past and Present* supplement no. 4, Oxford, 2009).

framework which combines an understanding of ecclesiology, theology and politics with those aspects of the puritan style of religiosity noted above.[26] Not only does such an approach broaden our understanding of puritanism – by thinking about religious practice and the ways it was represented, the approach highlights the questions of what it meant to be a puritan, how puritans saw themselves and how they were perceived by others – it has also led to a reassessment of the politics of puritanism. In particular through the work of David Como and Peter Lake, it has alerted us more than ever to the fact that puritanism was at once composed of different and in some ways competing strands which contained the potential to undermine both religious unity and the social order.[27]

While acknowledging the complexities of the term in both contemporary discourse and subsequent debate, therefore, this book defines puritanism as a way of characterizing that strand of reformed Protestantism which is best known for its expression of dissatisfaction with the prevailing theological and ecclesiological state of the English church and for desiring its reform in line with the precepts of Calvinist theology. It argues that this desire for reform was rooted in a series of cultural practices which were used by the godly to deliberately set themselves apart from the majority of the population and to confirm them in their status as a persecuted minority. While their general outlook can thus be defined as encompassing a hostility towards popery, a fondness for Calvinist divinity and an obsession for word-centred piety, my definition of puritanism rests more specifically upon a series of shared self-consciously evangelical cultural practices. The most readily identified of these practices included

---

[26] See, for example, Tyacke, 'Popular Puritan Mentality in Late Elizabethan England'; Nicholas Tyacke, *The Fortunes of English Puritanism, 1603–1640* (London, 1990); Patrick Collinson, 'Elizabethan and Jacobean Puritanism as Forms of Popular Religious Culture', in Christopher Durston and Jacqueline Eales (eds.), *The Culture of English Puritanism, 1560–1700* (Basingstoke, 1996), pp. 32–57, and the other essays in that collection; Lake, *The Antichrist's Lewd Hat*. See also Margo Todd, *The Culture of Protestantism in Early Modern Scotland* (New Haven, CT, 2002).

[27] Tyacke, *The Fortunes of English Puritanism*; Collinson, 'Elizabethan and Jacobean Puritanism as Forms of Popular Religious Culture'; Peter Lake and David Como, '"Orthodoxy" and its Discontents: Dispute Settlement and the Production of "Consensus" in the London (Puritan) "Underground"', *Journal of British Studies*, 39 (2000), pp. 34–70; David Como and Peter Lake, 'Puritans, Antinomians, and Laudians in Caroline London: The Strange Case of Peter Shaw and Its Contexts', *Journal of Ecclesiastical History*, 50 (1999), pp. 684–715; Ian Atherton and David Como, 'The Burning of Edward Wightman: Puritanism, Prelacy and the Politics of Heresy in Early Modern England', *English Historical Review*, 120 (2005), pp. 1215–1250; Peter Lake, *The Boxmaker's Revenge: 'Orthodoxy', 'Heterodoxy' and the Politics of the Parish in Early Stuart London* (Manchester, 2001); Lake, *The Antichrist's Lewd Hat*; David R. Como, *Blown by the Spirit: Puritanism and the Emergence of an Antinomian Underground in Pre-Civil-War England* (Stanford, CA, 2004).

modes of fasting and prayer, Bible-reading, Psalm-singing, meditation, sermon-gadding, strict sabbatarianism, and a strong commitment to moral discipline and spiritual self-examination, but there were doubtless other outward signs of puritan distinction which have made a less visible impression upon the historical record. These practices were not in and of themselves puritan, but were used by the godly to set themselves apart from the spiritually alien and lacklustre majority. My book, therefore, while drawing on previous general studies of puritan culture, takes the next step and subjects to scrutiny one specific cultural practice – reading – as a means of understanding puritan or godly culture more deeply.[28]

Although previous studies have dealt with the question at best indirectly, any analysis of puritan culture calls for some precision as to the meaning of the term 'culture', certainly if it is to be used in a less nebulous fashion than 'society', that other historical catch-all. The term is here employed relatively loosely in an anthropological sense, whereby 'religious culture' refers to a series of interrelated signs and sets of assumptions with which people understood their place in the world. This standpoint allows me to use the sources to observe early modern practices from the inside out, to try to understand what people meant by doing and saying things, and to evaluate and scrutinize contemporary perceptions of these actions and words.[29] Of course, it would be as foolish to assume that anthropologists share a uniform definition of culture as it would be to imagine that historians agree upon the definition of puritanism. Although it would be tedious to explore the full range of definitions, it is worth making the distinction between those who use 'culture' to refer to a uniform and relatively static system of meaning for large areas like countries and those who prefer to think of cultures in the plural, of competing and contesting sets of symbols used by people within a broader unit of society.[30] In fact, to the historian of

---

[28] Throughout this book, the terms 'godly' and 'puritan' are used interchangeably. Since the mid-1990s, most scholars, including Patrick Collinson and Peter Lake, have used the terms 'puritan' and 'godly' in this way and with much more freedom than had previously been the case. This freedom is itself a product of treating puritanism as religious culture. For recent examples, see Francis J. Bremer, *John Winthrop: America's Forgotten Founding Father* (Oxford, 2003), pp. xvi–xviii; and Lake, *Antichrist's Lewd Hat.*

[29] Clifford Geertz, *The Interpretation of Cultures: Selected Essays* (London, 1973), esp. Chapter 4, 'Religion as a Cultural System'. Of course, anthropologists dispute exactly what is meant by 'culture'. The assumption that symbols are shared and carry meaning to those who use them is, however, common across the discipline. It should be noted that I am not suggesting, along the lines of the history of the Annales school, that culture is somehow the product of economics and demography, nor am I assuming that a quantitative approach is the best way of understanding it.

[30] For which, see Michel de Certeau, *Culture in the Plural*, ed. Luce Giard, trans. Tom Conley (Minneapolis, MN, 1997).

early modern England, both ways of conceptualizing culture are useful and throughout this book I utilize a stratified definition of culture, in which puritanism is conceived as a broad religious culture, within which there were a range of subcultures that, although still recognizably and meaningfully puritan, sometimes pulled in different directions – clearly the politics of puritanism, as already noted, which manifested itself in both conservatism and political radicalism, sits neatly within such a framework. To talk of such layers of puritan culture is to find a way to match the instantly familiar facets of an overarching godly culture – the puritan stereotype of turning up the whites of the eyes, moral hypocrisy, novel naming patterns, sermongadding, shared religious and social practices, as well as theological texts and so on – with those based for instance on locality, landscape or the personal charisma of a particular individual, which can only be understood with a greater focus on context. Thus a puritan in the outer reaches of Yorkshire, or in the Channel Islands, would share much with a puritan in Dorchester or Cambridge, but they might also be distinct, depending on individuals, the proximity of centres of intellectual and cultural exchange, forms of local government and their interaction with national policies. Thinking of a plurality of godly cultures within a wider umbrella of a more general culture also allows for an understanding of transformation and an analysis of change over time.[31]

Defining puritanism as a religious culture, rather than simply as doctrine and ideology, also offers a more fruitful way not only of understanding the impact and experience of puritans but also of getting to grips with those other forms of cultural activity which have traditionally been grafted onto the rise of puritanism. A wide range of developments have ridden on the back of Max Weber's claims about the connections between puritanism and the 'spirit of capitalism' and the emergence of modern Western culture.[32] But whereas historians of puritanism have long been sceptical of Weber's claims, those in adjacent fields – in particular sociology, literature and cultural studies – have continued to rely on his

---

[31] It is a symptom of many works – including the very best examples – which adopt an anthropological approach to history that they often present rather static characterizations of society. See, for instance, Rhys Isaac, *The Transformation of Virginia, 1740–1790* (Chapel Hill, NC, 1982); and Keith Thomas, *Religion and the Decline of Magic: Studies in Popular Beliefs in Sixteenth- and Seventeenth-Century England* (revised edn, London, 1973).

[32] Max Weber, *The Protestant Ethic and the Spirit of Capitalism*, trans. Talcott Parsons (1930) (London, 1992); William Haller, *The Rise of Puritanism* (New York, 1938); Edmund S. Morgan, *The Puritan Family: Religion and Domestic Relations in Seventeenth-Century New England* (New York, 1966).

model for their groundwork on puritanism. Thus Robert K. Merton used a Weberian definition of puritanism in his much-disputed thesis that there was a connection between puritanism and the rise of experimental science.[33] More problematically, some scholars have continued to assert connections between aspects of self-writing (notably diary-keeping) and puritanism as if they were self-evident, while others have clung on to the notion that puritanism was somehow crucial in the rise of silent reading and the development of interior religious belief and even of the self.[34] Taking a broad approach to the study of the culture of puritanism allows for a critique of some of these positions. It allows me to show how the role of puritanism in the development of silent reading has been overstated, and to challenge assumptions about the connections between puritanism and the rise of private, interior religiosity by showing how the godly frequently read collectively and socially as part of their religious culture.

PURITAN ATTITUDES TOWARDS BIBLE-READING

While we have already seen some examples of the godly championing Bible-reading, we should be wary of assuming that all puritans granted the practice pride of place in their religious culture or of supposing that they did so for identical reasons. Thus while some puritans used Bible-reading as a distinctly experimental means of channelling the Holy Spirit, for others its appeal seems to have resided as much in its function of upholding the patriarchal bonds of the domestic and social order as in its more experimental guise. And we should not forget the suspicion, hostility and outright rejection of Bible-reading which was evident at (and beyond) the boundaries of puritan culture throughout the seventeenth century, particularly in the heady days of the Civil War and when hierarchical and social breakdown met with more extreme sorts of religious fervour.

---

[33] For the Merton thesis, see I. Bernard Cohen (ed.), *Puritanism and the Rise of Modern Science: The Merton Thesis* (New Brunswick, NJ, 1990); and, for a famous deployment, Charles Webster, *The Great Instauration: Science, Medicine and Reform, 1626–1660* (London, 1975). For sensible reviews of the relevance of the Merton thesis, see Roy Porter and Mikuláš Teich, *The Scientific Revolution in National Context* (Cambridge, 1992), Chapter 7; and William Lamont, *Puritanism and Historical Controversy* (London, 1996), Chapter 9.

[34] For a review of these arguments, see my comments in Andrew Cambers, 'Reading, the Godly, and Self-Writing in England, circa 1580–1720', *Journal of British Studies*, 46 (2007), pp. 796–825. For some claims based on Weberian understandings of puritanism, see, for example, John Stachniewski, *The Persecutory Imagination: English Puritanism and the Literature of Religious Despair* (Oxford, 1991); Michael Mascuch, *Origins of the Individualist Self: Autobiography and Self-Identity in England, 1591–1791* (Cambridge, 1997).

A significant strand in the religious positions of many sectaries – perhaps the most obvious thing that divorced them from mainstream puritans – was the rejection of Bible-reading as a sort of idolatry, or creature-worship. Examples abound of mid-century rejection of Bible-reading and they testify to its importance, despite being drawn from a relatively narrow seam of source material.

This position is most easily seen in the work of those outraged authors who swiftly condemned the irreligious sectaries. For many of these authors, the most obvious product of the sectaries' belief that the spirit lay within the believer was their subsequent rejection of the authority of the Bible. John Holland, for example, described the Ranters' views of the spirit: 'There was one of them said in my hearing that he need not read the Scripture, nor heare Sermons, for the Father, the Son, and the Spirit were all three in him'.[35] Such positions were also set out by radicals themselves. The radical Army chaplain William Dell proclaimed that 'the *Believer*, is the onely *Book*, in which *God* writes his *New Testament*', while the Ranter Jacob Bauthumley announced, 'The Bible without is but a shadow of the Bible which is within'.[36] Although it would be foolish to smooth over the lumps and bumps in the landscape of radical thought, there were two main justifications for this rejection of Bible-reading. The first, common to radicals from sixteenth-century members of the Family of Love through to the Ranters and Quakers of the mid-seventeenth century, denied that the Bible was the literal truth and instead figured these stories as allegories to be interpreted by each individual. The second, in part a product of the first, rejected the absolute truth of the Bible by subjecting it to close textual scrutiny. The scriptures could not claim to be the divinely inspired truth when man had so variously translated, edited and adapted them over the centuries.[37] The rejection of Bible-reading by

[35] See John Holland, *The Smoke of the Bottomlesse Pit or, A More True and Fuller Discovery of the Doctrine of Those Men which Call Themselves Ranters: or, The Mad Crew* (London, 1651), p. 3.

[36] See William Dell, *The Tryal of Spirits both in Teachers and Hearers. Wherein is held forth the Clear Discovery, and Certain Downfal of the Carnal and Antichristian Clergie of these Nations* (London, 1653), p. 20; Jacob Bauthumley, *The Light and Dark Sides of God or A Plain and Brief Discourse, of the Light Side God, Heaven and Earth, the Dark Side Devill, Sin, and Hell. As also of the Resurrection and Scripture. All which are Set Forth in their Severall Natures and Beings, according to the Spirituality of the Scripture* (London, 1650), pp. 76–7. For the radical rejection of Bible-reading, see esp. Christopher Hill, *The World Turned Upside Down: Radical Ideas during the English Revolution* (revised edn, London, 1975), pp. 261–8; and Nigel Smith, *Perfection Proclaimed: Language and Literature in English Radical Religion, 1640–1660* (Oxford, 1989), Chapter 7.

[37] On these approaches, see Hill, *The World Turned Upside Down*, pp. 261–3; and (for an approach which acknowledges critical approaches beyond the heterodox) Ariel Hessayon and Nicholas Keene (eds.), *Scripture and Scholarship in Early Modern England* (Aldershot, 2006).

the early Quakers is particularly intriguing since they attached to the reading of their own works something like the significance the godly gave to reading the scriptures – they read their own works as a means of revealing the spirit within themselves. They argued that the scriptures had originally been inspired by the same Holy Spirit which was now moving the Quakers to write their tracts, but where their own tracts displayed the immediacy of this religious revelation, translations and textual interventions into the text of the Bible rendered it useless in helping to reveal the light within. In short, Quakers claimed to be writing the Word of God – a claim which makes more understandable the abject horror their views were met with by their opponents – while downgrading the scriptures from their conventional status as the Word to merely the 'letter', or the apostles' representation of their encounters with the Holy Spirit.[38]

On the level of practice, evidence of unambiguous rejection of Bible-reading is thinner on the ground. Most of those whose words appear to signal rejection of the Bible – like John Gawler, a Dorset man who was hauled before the church courts in 1622 for disrespecting the clergy and calling the Bible 'a book of lies' – were blasphemers whose ill-considered words got them into trouble, not separatists elucidating anything like a fully formed position.[39] Even the very occasional instances of godly people apparently rejecting the reading of the Bible – the Somerset man, up before the ecclesiastical courts in 1628, who declared that 'the reading of the Word . . . is worth nothing nor to be respected' or the Northamptonshire puritan who told a court in 1615 that 'the reading the word of God cannot beget faith' – should be taken with a large pinch of salt. Such comments were usually made in the context of disputes about the use of the Book of Common Prayer or when the godly objected to preachers *simply* reading out from the Bible, when they should have been moved by the spirit in their sermons.[40] Of course, small groups of separatists did indeed reject Bible-reading as a necessary step on the path to salvation. The Familists traced by Christopher Marsh in sixteenth-century Wisbech, for example, were adamant that the scriptures were a set of allegories rather than a literal truth, however much their own collective reading of the works of

---

[38] See Kate Peters, *Print Culture and the Early Quakers* (Cambridge, 2005), esp. pp. 34–5; and Geoffrey Nuttall, *The Holy Spirit in Puritan Faith and Experience* (revised edn, Chicago, 1992).

[39] See Christopher Haigh, *The Plain Man's Pathways to Heaven: Kinds of Christianity in Post-Reformation England, 1570–1640* (Oxford, 2007), pp. 55, 168.

[40] See Haigh, *The Plain Man's Pathways to Heaven*, pp. 104, 18.

Hendrik Niclaes resembled the social practices of the godly.[41] The same holds true for the followers of those antinomian preachers like John Everarde in the 1620s and 1630s, or at least those who put such distinctly heterodox ideas into daily practice.[42] Interestingly, Everarde's radical interpretation of scripture – that the Bible was not the Word of God, that the scriptures were mysteries to be interpreted, and that its stories were constantly re-enacted in the believer – was positioned polemically directly against the practices of the godly: he went out of his way to condemn those who were satisfied with their reading of scripture both in church and in the family, however learned they might be, without transforming such reading into a true internal spiritual experience.[43]

The sceptical may have some doubts as to how successful Everarde was in his mission to transform the spiritual lives of his hearers in Kensington and it is only after the social breakdown of the Civil War that we can see anything like widespread evidence of how a spiritual community dealt with more significant numbers of people who put into effect a reasoned rejection of the efficacy of Bible-reading. We can certainly see consternation in the well-known records of the Baptist church at Fenstanton in the 1650s, where the church struggled with members who expressed outright separatist ideas, dismissing conventional notions of sin, maintaining that the Bible was an allegory and refusing to be guided by the scriptures.[44] But even in such stirring times, public displays of rejection of the Bible brought little support. When 'the Lord' told the prophet Thomas Tany to burn his possessions in December 1654, he lit a fire in Lambeth and consigned his Bible, along with his other books and his saddle, sword, musket and pistols, to the flames. Tany explicitly rejected the Bible as an

---

[41] Christopher W. Marsh, *The Family of Love in English Society, 1550–1630* (Cambridge, 1994), pp. 30, 39, 268. Although this comparison seems justified, it would be wise to allow room for the prejudices of the questioners to be taken into account here: they asked about Bible-reading to help to determine whether they were dealing with separatists rather than those whose practices had strayed into heterodoxy but might be brought back into the fold.

[42] For Everarde's treatment of scripture, see Como, *Blown by the Spirit*, pp. 219–65, esp. pp. 233–4. Como, of course, argues persuasively that such ideas emerged from within puritanism rather than against it.

[43] 'Thou saist thou *readest* in the Church, and in thy family twice a day ... *thou doest well*, it is good in *its place*: but *what good* doth it convey *to thy soul*? ... what *manner of people are these*, that so champ the *Letter* between their teeth, and *roul it on their tongues*? what are they in their lives? have they got *any vertue* from Christ by being so *conversant* with him? are they transformed and *made new Creatures*? do they live *the inward and spiritual life* of the Word?' John Everard, *Some Gospel-Treasures Opened: Or, The Holiest of all Unvailing* (London, 1653), pp. 329–30, cited in Como, *Blown by the Spirit*, pp. 243–4.

[44] See *Records of the Churches of Christ, Gathered at Fenstanton, Warboys and Hexham. 1644–1720*, ed. Edward Bean Underhill (Hanserd Knollys Society, London, 1854), p. 8 and *passim*.

idol, an unholy creation of man, while asserting that the true Word of God was incombustible and written in his soul. His reasons for doing so, it was subsequently reported, were 'because the people say it is the Word of God, and it is not'.[45] Perhaps as evident as Tany's rejection of the Bible, however, was the frosty reception his behaviour received: Tany hastily withdrew to the Thames, sword drawn (he had another one, presumably), and was stoned by a crowd while he was rowed to safety.[46]

The focus of this book will be, for the most part, on the godly who did not turn in such directions and who held fast to the belief that the Bible was indeed the word of God and that they needed to read it in their religious practice. Nevertheless, the questioning of its authority, particularly in the middle of the seventeenth century, has had some consequences which remain relevant to any study of puritanism. First (historiographically), the rejection of the authority of the Bible from a 'rational'/critical textual perspective has long been a key element in the association of puritanism with modernity. But we should remember that it was not only radicals who approached the study of the Bible in this way and recall the other less 'rational' elements in the cosmologies of these radicals.[47] They ascribed to their own books the same properties other Protestants attached to their Bibles: Quaker works, for example, were prized 'as specific instruments of "convincement"', while Familists treated with reverence the writings of Hendrik Niclaes, reading them aloud collectively in search of spiritual illumination.[48] Second, this challenge to the exalted place of the Bible accentuated a paradox which had been festering within godly culture since the late sixteenth century. As Nigel Smith puts it, 'they stressed the spontaneity and immediacy of inspired speech as the Holy

---

[45] See Arise Evans, *To the Most High and Mighty Prince, Charles the II. By the Grace of God, King of Great Britain, France and Ireland, Defender of the Faith, &c. An Epistle Written and Humbly Presented for His Majesties Use, and Enlightning of the Nation* (London, 1660), p. 51.

[46] See Thomas Tany, *My Edict Royal* ([London], 1655?) and Ariel Hessayon, *'Gold Tried in the Fire': The Prophet TheaurauJohn Tany and the English Revolution* (Aldershot, 2007), pp. 373–4. Although it is easy to see the unhinged elements in Tany's behaviour, it would be a mistake to doubt his sincerity or to deny the puritan roots of his later sectarianism. As Ariel Hessayon asserts, Tany's experiences were rooted in a faith that might be called puritan and he appears to have been deeply engaged in 'frequent scriptural reading' in his youth. See Hessayon, *'Gold Tried in the Fire'*, pp. 7, 81.

[47] For a useful corrective, see Hessayon and Keene (eds.), *Scripture and Scholarship*. For the non-'rational' elements of radical practice, see the examples gathered in Thomas, *Religion and the Decline of Magic*.

[48] See Peters, *Print Culture and the Early Quakers*, p. 32; Marsh, *The Family of Love in English Society*, p. 268.

Spirit moved them, but most of them accepted the printed Bible as the record of divine truth'.[49] Although this tension remained fairly benign in the years before the Civil War – where godly rejection of printed authority was in effect funnelled into hostility towards the prayer book – it became more problematic after the Restoration. Thereafter, with most noncon-formists desperate to avoid the stench of separatism and with many of them still hopeful for comprehension within the Church of England, Bible-reading became even more significant to the practice of their piety. Indeed, many of the more experimental aspects of their religiosity took place in the context of Bible-reading, a framework which was easy to pass off as orthodox religious practice.

PURITAN STRATEGIES OF ALIENATION AND RITUALS OF SEPARATION

Writing his autobiography in the mid-1660s, the prolific puritan writer Richard Baxter (1615–91) intertwined the narrative of his own spiritual life with the unfolding of the nation's traumatic religious and political his-tory. The fissures which would tear apart the body politic in the 1640s, thought Baxter, were certainly evident in the culture of the Shropshire village in which he grew up in the 1620s. On Sundays, after a service which consisted of little more than a cursory reading of the prayer book, the parish would divide into those who gathered to spend the rest of the day dancing and those who stayed at home to read the scriptures. These cultural activities were used as evidence of religious allegiance: Baxter's father – a Bible-reader, of course – was branded a puritan for this aspect of his spirituality. While Baxter's autobiography, which was published post-humously, was far from uncontroversial and drew venomous responses, the language such issues were framed in is instructive. 'We could not read the Scripture in our Family', reflected Baxter, 'without the great disturb-ance of the Tabor and Pipe and Noise in the Street!' The very young Baxter was, he admitted, entranced by the revellers and 'inclined to be among them', but his subsequent comment is particularly telling, for it reveals something not only about the cultural divisions of village life but

---

[49] See Nigel Smith, 'Non-Conformist Voices and Books', in John Barnard and D. F. McKenzie (eds.), *The Cambridge History of the Book in Britain* (7 vols., Cambridge, 1999–), vol. IV, *1557–1695* (2002), p. 413.

also about the importance the godly placed on processes and strategies of spiritual alienation and cultural separation:

> But when I heard them call my Father *Puritan*, it did much to cure me and alienate me from them: for I consider'd that my Father's Exercise of Reading the Scripture, was better than theirs, and would surely be better thought on by all men at the last; and I considered what it was for that he and others were thus derided.

All this convinced Baxter that 'Godly people were the best, and those that despised them and lived in Sin and Pleasure, were a malignant unhappy sort of People: and this kept me out of their Company'.[50]

In Baxter's account, the godly were passive victims in this process of identification – after all, it was a sign of the truth of their religion that they were persecuted – but throughout this book I reveal some of the ways in which the godly deliberately set themselves apart, not simply through their theology but in particular through their cultural choices. Among these strategies of alienation – strategies which, it should be reiterated, were not themselves exclusively or necessarily puritan but which were used by the godly to set themselves apart from the spiritually lacklustre or openly hostile – were, as we have already seen, the distinctive naming practices adopted by the godly, alongside a wider range of cultural practices, which while they might seem theologically indifferent and socially harmless, in fact possessed considerable cultural power in separating the godly from their neighbours. Alongside collective reading, they included gadding to sermons and repeating them in the household, styles of fasting and prayer – not only an insistence upon extempore prayer but also a refusal to kneel to take communion, which was the embodiment of their doctrinal objection to the Book of Common Prayer – aspects of gesture such as turning up the whites of their eyes, strictness in keeping the sabbath holy, taking godly boarders and young graduates into the household, the practice of spiritual diary-keeping, their manner of speaking, and even styles of dress.[51]

Although it has often been tempting to some to view such cultural phenomena as not 'religious' in the usual sense of that term, or as being of interest merely in revealing some of the ways puritanism was perceived

---

[50] *Reliquiæ Baxterianæ: or, Mr. Richard Baxter's Narrative of the Most Memorable Passages of his Life and Times*, ed. Matthew Sylvester (London, 1696), pp. 2–3. For responses to the publication of Baxter's autobiography, see esp. Samuel Young, *Vindiciæ Anti-Baxterianæ: or Some Animadversions on a Book, Intutuled Religuæ Baxterianæ; or The Life of Mr. Richard Baxter* (London, 1696).

[51] Most of these aspects of puritan culture can be traced through the essays in Durston and Eales, *The Culture of English Puritanism*. See also the comments in John Spurr, *English Puritanism, 1603–1689* (Basingstoke, 1998), Chapter 3, esp. pp. 40–1. For godly boarding (which deserves a fuller study), see Tom Webster, *Godly Clergy in Early Stuart England*, Chapter 1.

(they were important parts of the puritan stereotype), when we think harder about how the godly used them as a means of setting themselves apart, they take on added significance. Some obstacles remain. While we are used to thinking about the implications of the cultural and social separation of Catholics from the rest of early modern society[52] – perhaps to the detriment of understanding the ways in which they integrated and engaged with the populace at large – the strength of Patrick Collinson's arguments about puritanism as a theological movement which operated within the Church of England, rather than as a radical sect which operated outside it, has made it difficult to think about a distinctive culture of puritanism. The legacy of Collinson's argument – which has resulted in a near pathological obsession with precise theological defin-itions of puritanism – has been to leave issues of culture as almost necessarily secondary to those of doctrine. Those who have examined puritan culture have tended to do so in the shadow of Collinson's work. Thus the questions about puritan culture appear to have been designed with the explicit purpose of either reinforcing or challenging Collinson's argument: how far can puritan culture be said to have actually existed? Can any practice be deemed puritan? To what extent did puritanism draw upon 'popular' culture, or was it antagonistic to such culture?[53] With the weight of such historiography pressing down upon them, few have taken the trouble first to unpick the practices at the heart of puritan culture and then to work outwards from there to establish their significance.[54]

However, once we accept that puritans actually did things – and few could dispute that reading (although not limited to the godly) was a practice which was right at the heart of the experience of puritanism, whether seen from inside or out – thinking from an anthropological perspective about 'rituals of separation' helps to problematize and make

---

[52] The classic analysis of post-Reformation Catholicism as held together by a set of rituals of separation is Bossy, *The English Catholic Community*. It is regrettable that, while many other aspects of Bossy's argument have been subjected to close scrutiny, few have extended this discussion or discussed its significance to puritanism.

[53] It must be said that Collinson's own work on puritanism and popular culture, while essentially framed in these terms, has been typically rich and suggestive. See his 'Elizabethan and Jacobean Puritanism as Forms of Popular Religious Culture', in Durston and Eales, *The Culture of English Puritanism*, pp. 32–57, 280–8; and his 'Ecclesiastical Vitriol: Religious Satire in the 1590s and the Invention of Puritanism', in Guy, *The Reign of Elizabeth I*, pp. 150–70. There is a useful review of the issues in Alexandra Walsham, 'The Godly and Popular Culture', in Coffey and Lim, *The Cambridge Companion to Puritanism*, pp. 277–93.

[54] Notable exceptions include Peter Lake, '"A Charitable Christian Hatred": The Godly and Their Enemies in the 1630s', in Durston and Eales, *The Culture of English Puritanism*, pp. 145–83, 301–7; and Lake, *The Antichrist's Lewd Hat*.

more interesting the study of puritan culture.[55] In particular, the analysis of such rituals helps us to move beyond interpretations of culture based on polarities, to discover the richness of these cultural practices and to think much harder about why they matter – to think about the effects and meaning of practices as much as the practices themselves. We know from the evidence of church courts, libels and the like that there were considerable tensions between the godly and their enemies over the long seventeenth century and that communities were very often divided as a result. But we know much less about the processes by which these groups – in this case the godly – used aspects of their religiosity to actively set themselves apart. Thus to examine collective Bible-reading as a ritual of separation is to see it as a facet of their everyday religiosity which was also a strategy of cultural separation. Such reading served key purposes for the godly. It was at the heart of their faith, both individually and communally, and while it was for some a conduit for experimental forms of religiosity and a lightning-conductor for radicalism, it could equally well be presented as the most orthodox of household religious practices. This ambiguity will emerge time and again throughout this book, as godly reading divided puritans from the spiritually lukewarm and hostile yet was also defended rigorously as merely enthusiastic conformity. Such reading was, therefore, one of the means by which the godly as a religious subculture perceived their own collective identity in opposition to the mass of the population.[56]

THE HISTORY OF READING

Who shall tell what may be the effect of writing? If it happens to have been cut in stone, though it lie face downmost for ages on a forsaken beach, or 'rest quietly under the drums and tramplings of many conquests,' it may end by letting us into the secret of usurpations and other scandals gossiped about long empires ago: – this world being apparently a huge whispering-gallery. Such conditions are often minutely represented in our petty lifetimes. As the stone which has been kicked by generations of clowns may come by curious little links of effect under the eyes of a scholar, through whose labours it may at last fix the date of invasions and unlock religions, so a bit of ink and paper which has long been an innocent

---

[55] For 'rituals of separation', see Douglas, *Purity and Danger*, Chapter 1 and Bossy, *The English Catholic Community*, pp. 108–48.

[56] I am not, of course, arguing that the godly and their enemies were entirely distinct or that areas of overlap between puritan and non-puritan cultures are without interest. Rather, I am suggesting that those areas of convergence, like those of distinction, need to be subjected to closer scrutiny.

wrapping of stop-gap may at last be laid open under the one pair of eyes which have knowledge enough to turn it into the opening of a catastrophe.[57]

George Eliot's description of the importance of writing would strike a chord among historians as the essence of their craft: the reconstruction of the truth of the past through the encounter with the written word. Although most historians work in archives rather than on forsaken beaches, the potential for such a discovery is what keeps many a historian sifting through papers for that which others have overlooked. But Eliot's description also tells of another history: a story of the encounter of the individual with the textual fragment across the ages, as generations read and misread the piece of evidence. Although such questions were long neglected, over the past generation a range of critical theorists, literary critics and historians have drawn attention to the questions of how readers approached the text and proclaimed the importance of the reader in the construction of meaning. That these questions have permeated more mainstream understandings of the past can be seen in their place in a range of contemporary fiction, from Italo Calvino's novel about the reader reading a novel, to Umberto Eco's rendering of a library as a labyrinth, and Henning Mankell's opening of a crime novel in which an annotated Bible is found next to a headless corpse.[58]

Although hardly linear in development and lacking agreement on central issues, a series of important works has sought to draw out the reader in texts and in history. These have ranged from those theoretical studies, like those of Wolfgang Iser and Stanley Fish, which have hunted for the reader in the text and have attempted to unravel his (or her) importance in the shaping of the text,[59] to work on the more general conditions of print culture, inspired more by social history than by bibliography, which has included landmark studies by Marshall McLuhan, Richard Altick, Henri-Jean Martin, Elizabeth Eisenstein and Adrian Johns.[60] Parallel to much of this work

[57] George Eliot, *Middlemarch: A Study of Provincial Life* (Edinburgh and London, 1871–2), Chapter xli.

[58] Italo Calvino, *If on a Winter's Night a Traveller*, trans. William Weaver (London, 1983); Umberto Eco, *The Name of the Rose*, trans. William Weaver (London, 1983); Henning Mankell, *Before the Frost*, trans. Ebba Segerberg (London, 2005).

[59] Wolfgang Iser, *The Act of Reading: A Theory of Aesthetic Response* (Baltimore, MD, 1978); Wolfgang Iser, *The Implied Reader: Patterns of Communication in Prose Fiction from Bunyan to Beckett* (Baltimore, MD, 1980); Stanley Fish, *Is There a Text in this Class? The Authority of Interpretive Communities* (Cambridge, MA, 1980).

[60] Marshall McLuhan, *The Gutenberg Galaxy: The Making of Typographic Man* (Toronto, 1962); Richard Altick, *The English Common Reader: A Social History of the Mass Reading Public 1800–1900* (Chicago, 1957); Lucien Febvre and Henri-Jean Martin, *L'Apparition du livre* (Paris, 1971), trans. David Gerard as *The Coming of the Book: The Impact of Printing 1450–1800* (London, 1976); Eisenstein, *The Printing Press as an Agent of Change*; Adrian Johns, *The Nature of the Book: Print and Knowledge in the Making* (Chicago, 1998).

on print culture has been a strand of work more focused on the reader than on the more general availability of print and the conditions of the marketplace. Much of this work – again written as social history – is concerned with the nineteenth and twentieth centuries and the reading habits of the working classes, and stretches from Richard Hoggart's pioneering work on *The Uses of Literacy* (1957) to Jonathan Rose's *The Intellectual Life of the British Working Classes* (2001).[61]

These works continue to inspire great tomes, from vast multi-volume synoptic histories of the book, such as those on England, France, America, Scotland and other countries, to massive works on print culture, often based on publishers' records and focused on the eighteenth century.[62] They have also prompted Ian Green's important study of *Print and Protestantism in Early Modern England* (2000), a work which sets out to explore Protestant best- and steady-sellers between 1530 and 1720.[63] My book, however, takes its inspiration from a different strand of scholarship, which has endeavoured to unravel the importance of the methods in which readers read books and to explore this reading to reconstruct their mental landscape. Such work – again dovetailing with a desire to uncover the history of ordinary people and to understand what they made of the world around them, but much more focused on the sixteenth and seventeenth centuries than on studies of print culture – has included pioneering microhistories like Carlo Ginzburg's *The Cheese and the Worms*, together with innovative studies by Robert Darnton and others.[64] Using a rather different base of evidence, they have tried to offer examples of how people read and to work outwards from there to show why this mattered.

[61] Richard Hoggart, *The Uses of Literacy: Aspects of Working-Class Life with Special Reference to Publications and Entertainments* (London, 1957); Jonathan Rose, *The Intellectual Life of the British Working Classes* (New Haven, CT, 2001).

[62] See, among others, D. F. McKenzie, David McKitterick and I. R. Willison (eds.), *The Cambridge History of the Book in Britain* (7 vols., Cambridge, 1999–); Roger Chartier and Henri-Jean Martin, *Histoire de l'édition française* (4 vols., Paris, 1982–6); David D. Hall (ed.), *A History of the Book in America* (5 vols., Cambridge, 2000–); Bill Bell, David Finkelstein and Alistair McCleery (eds.), *The Edinburgh History of the Book in Scotland* (4 vols., Edinburgh, 2007). There are, of course, other national studies. For the eighteenth century, see Richard B. Sher, *The Enlightenment and the Book: Scottish Authors and Their Publishers in Eighteenth-Century Britain, Ireland and America* (Chicago, 2006); William St Clair, *The Reading Nation in the Romantic Period* (Cambridge, 2004).

[63] Ian Green, *Print and Protestantism in Early Modern England* (Oxford, 2000).

[64] Carlo Ginzburg, *The Cheese and the Worms: The Cosmos of a Sixteenth-Century Miller*, trans. John and Anne Tedeschi (London, 1980); Robert Darnton, 'Readers Respond to Rousseau: The Fabrication of Romantic Sensitivity', in his *The Great Cat Massacre: And Other Episodes in French Cultural History* (New York, 1984), pp. 215–56.

Looking in more detail at this large body of literature, it is worth paying closer attention to some of the types of study there have been in the history of early modern reading, the evidence upon which they have been based and the various models of reading which have been proposed as a result. In large part, the history of reading as it was experienced in the past (rather than the reader as imagined in works of fiction) has been written from the sources upwards but, since the sources for such a history are extremely varied, the results produced have been starkly divergent. Historians have often clung onto fragments of information about reading, in particular those snippets of information about what readers read contained in diaries, letters and autobiographies. Where no other evidence has existed about a reader, such information has had to do, but it needs to be used cautiously. Fragmentary information of this sort often has the advantage of placing reading within a broader context of a range of experiences, emotions and intellectual and social practices, but it is also beset with pitfalls. To take one example, in 1873 Karl Marx sent Charles Darwin an inscribed copy of the second edition of *Das Kapital* expressing his admiration for Darwin's work. The correspondence surrounding this moment of textual exchange tells us one story – that Darwin wrote back politely thanking Marx for the gift of his book – which might be used to suggest that he indeed read, and perhaps approved of, Marx's work. But the physical book tells another – that Darwin had only cut the first 105 pages of a book of more than eight hundred pages.[65] In this case, the physical evidence seems to outweigh the more anecdotal evidence.[66] Nevertheless, anecdotal evidence is better than none and when it has been used carefully, evidence of reading contained in diaries and autobiographies has resulted in path-breaking studies, notably that of Jonathan Rose.[67]

In other cases, historians have come across a range of archival sources with which to write the history of reading. Some such sources, like those

[65] See I. Bernard Cohen, *Revolution in Science* (Cambridge, MA, 1985), pp. 344–5. The presentation copy remains at Darwin's house, Down House in Kent.

[66] For a stern rebuttal of the use of anecdotal evidence – and a rather old-fashioned belief in quantitative evidence – in the history of reading, see St Clair, *The Reading Nation in the Romantic Period*, p. 5: 'Reports of individual responses to reading as recorded in letters, diaries, or other documents can help us to break out of the closed circle implicit in exclusively text-based approaches. For that purpose they are invaluable. But anecdotal information raises methodological difficulties of other kinds. When records are plentiful, it is easy to slip into the belief that they are a reliable record of actual acts of reception. It is easy to forget, however many of such reports are found and collected, that they can never be, at best, anything beyond a tiny, randomly surviving, and perhaps highly unrepresentative, sample of the far larger total acts of reception which were never even turned into words in the mind of the reader let alone recorded in writing.'

[67] Rose, *The Intellectual Life of the British Working Classes*.

based on library catalogues and personal book-lists, frequently reveal more about the collection and organization of knowledge than about reading as such, but they are certainly suggestive.[68] Others have attempted to use the records of publishers, sometimes with spectacular results, such as those promised by the business records of the Société typographique de Neuchâtel, the Swiss publishing house whose vast archives allow a general reconstruction of the production and dissemination of books in the later eighteenth century.[69] The sheer size of such resources, however, has inclined this kind of research towards studies of print culture rather than towards studies focused on readers. And the accumulation of materials about reading tends to flatten out the history. Ian Green's study of *Print and Protestantism*, for example, is predicated upon a methodology – the classification as steady-sellers of works which went through five editions or more in thirty years and, more problematically, the desire to classify broad swathes of literature and look for shared positions – which irons out the eccentricities and radicalism of religious books and thus charts a history of print and Protestantism which, through its methodological choices as well as its style of analysis, collapses Protestantism into a theologically benign 'Anglicanism'.[70] Green's study has attracted considerable criticism for the arguments it presents about Protestantism in early modern England, much of it justified, but rather less credit than it deserves for attempting to ask questions about the relationship between print and Protestantism in the period. In fact, even after the excellent books on pamphlet culture by Peter Lake and Joad Raymond, both of which are sensitive to ambiguity and wary of smoothing out rough edges, we still need more studies which focus on the reception and readership of print in early modern England.[71]

One way in which histories of reading have moved beyond the essential groundwork provided by the more general histories of literacy and of print culture[72] is by focusing on the surviving evidence pertaining to the

[68] For instance, R. J. Fehrenbach and E. S. Leedham-Green (eds.), *Private Libraries in Renaissance England* (Binghamton, NY, 1992–).

[69] See Simon Burrows's AHRC-funded project, The French Book Trade in Enlightenment Europe, 1769–1787.

[70] Green, *Print and Protestantism in Early Modern England*. In what follows, I make the case for a much more distinctive godly book culture – as approached from the perspective of the reader – than that proposed by Green.

[71] For some of the flaws in Green's work, see Patrick Collinson, 'Books of the People', *Times Literary Supplement*, 29 June 2001; and for a more strident criticism, Lake, *The Antichrist's Lewd Hat*, esp. pp. 315–31; Joad Raymond, *Pamphlets and Pamphleteering in Early Modern Britain* (Cambridge, 2003).

[72] Key works are David Cressy, *Literacy and the Social Order: Reading and Writing in Tudor and Stuart England* (Cambridge, 1980); and Fox, *Oral and Literate Culture in England, 1500–1700*.

use of books, in particular the material, copy-specific evidence of manuscript marginal annotations, underlinings and those other forms of encounter with the text which have left their mark in the historical record, from stitches to traces of food.[73] A string of works, comprising articles and fully fledged monographs, has explored reading practices through an analysis of such annotations and (less frequently) marks. They have included essays on single readers of single books; important case studies of readers like John Dee, William Drake and Gabriel Harvey; and examinations of all the extant copies of single works – like Owen Gingerich's analysis of the reception of Nicolaus Copernicus's *De Revolutionibus* and Ann Blair's work on the reception of Jean Bodin's *De Natura Universalis Theatrum*.[74] Recently, there have been attempts to pull some of this work together, whether in studies of female reading, in more general interpretations of marginalia or in work which is starting to restore the breadth of early modern understandings of reading and book use.[75] Necessarily diverse, these studies cover an impressive range of subjects, although the neglect of heavily annotated legal and medical books means there is still much potential for future work and, given the sheer number of sixteenth- and seventeenth-century religious books, it might be observed that there are relatively few studies there too.[76]

Although their conclusions have often been flatly contradictory, this string of case studies has led to some more general models about how people read in the past, frequently making use of the earlier theoretical

[73] For a discussion of material traces on the text including stitches and food, as well as writing, see William H. Sherman, *Used Books: Marking Readers in Renaissance England* (Philadelphia, PA, 2008).

[74] See, among others, Fred Schurink, 'Like a Hand in the Margine of a Booke': William Blount's Marginalia and the Politics of Sidney's Arcadia', *Review of English Studies*, 59 (2008), pp. 1–24; Lisa Jardine and Anthony Grafton, '"Studied for Action": How Gabriel Harvey Read his Livy', *Past and Present*, 129 (1990), pp. 30–78; William H. Sherman, *John Dee: The Politics of Reading and Writing in the English Renaissance* (Amherst, MA, 1995); Kevin Sharpe, *Reading Revolutions: The Politics of Reading in Early Modern England* (New Haven, CT, 2000); Owen Gingerich, *The Book Nobody Read: Chasing the Revolutions of Nicolaus Copernicus* (New York, 2004); Ann Blair, *The Theater of Nature: Jean Bodin and Renaissance Science* (Princeton, NJ, 1997). Incidentally, in 2008 Copernicus's remains were positively identified by matching the DNA of the skeleton with that of hair found in a book in the portion of Copernicus's library which remains at Uppsala University in Sweden. *The Guardian*, 21 November 2008.

[75] Heidi Brayman Hackel, *Reading Material in Early Modern England: Print, Gender, and Literacy* (Cambridge, 2005); H. J. Jackson, *Marginalia: Readers Writing in Books* (New Haven, CT, 2001); H. J. Jackson, *Romantic Readers: The Evidence of Marginalia* (New Haven, CT, 2005); Sherman, *Used Books*.

[76] Valuable studies on Bibles and prayer books include Sherman, *Used Books*, Chapters 4–5; and Eamon Duffy, *Marking the Hours: English People and their Prayers, 1240–1570* (New Haven, CT, 2006).

work on reader-response theory. The boldest model, which actually pre-dates most of the work on individual readers and is based on a very slim body of evidence, was proposed by Rolf Engelsing in 1974. He suggested that before about 1750, people read a small number of books (Bibles, devotional works and so on) 'intensively' – that is, over and over – often aloud and in company. In contrast, he claimed that this mode of reading was transformed by 1800, by which time readers read 'extensively', hun-grily getting hold of the latest newspaper or novel, reading it once and not returning to it again.[77] Unsurprisingly, such a rigid model snaps when pressure is applied. This 'revolution' in reading, even in the most general of terms, was hardly straightforward and, although most readers probably had access to many more books after 1800, many of which were more ephemeral than edifying, it is still possible to find numerous examples of 'intensive' and/or collective reading of the old style, whether as a deliber-ate evocation of a mode of Romantic sensibility or, more obviously, as a form of religiosity.[78]

Amongst this array of 'object' studies (where the focus is on numerous readers of one book), 'impact' studies (where the focus is on a single reader) and more general studies of readership, one particular interpretation of reading has been given prominence: that early modern readers were 'active' readers who 'appropriated' texts. In this model, which owes a debt to Michel de Certeau's theoretical work which figured reading as a potentially subversive, creative process of 'poaching', as well as to post-modernist theories of appropriation and to Pierre Bourdieu's insights into both cultural production and cultural distinction, early modern readers approached books for the use they could get out of them.[79] They read in

---

[77] Rolf Engelsing, *Der Bürger als Leser: Lesergeschichte in Deutschland 1500–1800* (Stuttgart, 1974).

[78] Aspects of Engelsing's thesis are effectively complicated by Darnton, 'Readers Respond to Rousseau'; by Rose, *The Intellectual Life of the British Working Classes*; and by any understanding of the readership of religious books. Nevertheless, the general shift has some truth to it, and is affirmed in David D. Hall, 'The Uses of Literacy in New England, 1600–1850', in his *Cultures of Print: Essays in the History of the Book* (Amherst, MA, 1996), pp. 36–78. Certainly by the nineteenth century there was (for some) a perception that repetitive reading (by others) in search of some sort of edification was an outdated practice, perhaps as a defence against auto-didacticism. One thinks of the combination of social conservatism and repetitive reading (in this case, somewhat comically, of *Robinson Crusoe*) by Gabriel Betteredge, the house-steward in Wilkie Collins's *The Moonstone* (London, 1868).

[79] Michel de Certeau, 'Reading as Poaching', in his *The Practice of Everyday Life*, trans. Steven Rendall (Los Angeles, CA, 1984), pp. 165–76; Pierre Bourdieu, *The Field of Cultural Production*, ed. Randal Johnson (Cambridge, 1993); Pierre Bourdieu, *Distinction: A Social Critique of the Judgement of Taste* (London, 1984); Pierre Bourdieu and Roger Chartier, 'La Lecture: Une pratique culturelle', in Roger Chartier (ed.), *Pratiques de la lecture* (Marseille, 1985). For 'appropriation' see Roger Chartier, 'Culture as Appropriation: Popular Cultural Uses in Early Modern France', in S. Kaplan

an alarmingly non-linear fashion, flicking backwards and forwards for information which they might then extract and use elsewhere. Certainly such a model ties in well with many of the traces of early modern reading, in particular the thematically arranged pages of commonplace books and, of course, marginalia. The model of active reading has been particularly important in the path-breaking case studies of Gabriel Harvey, John Dee and William Drake.[80] Subsequent works have followed these studies in attempting to categorize readers as being of a particular type, rather than thinking about individuals who might adopt different styles of reading based on the context in which they read. At the same time, another strand of work, which intersects with Stephen Greenblatt's work about the containment of radicalism in early modern culture, has probed the relationship between the reader who constructed and reconstructed meaning and those people (authors, compositors and printers) who, and those features of the text (including everything from the size of the font to pagination, marginal notes and indexes) which, attempted to direct, control and restrict interpretations. Although this work – in particular that of Roger Chartier – has been attacked for suggesting that the text was capable of being interpreted in a limitless number of ways by the reader, it nevertheless reminds us that early modern reading was a creative and active process, subject to transformation and fluctuating in different social and cultural contexts: in short, that reading has a history.[81]

Work which has focused on texts themselves, as opposed to the activities of readers, has generated a range of alternative interpretations of early modern reading. Some of this work, particularly that built upon our understanding of what D. F. McKenzie called 'the sociology of texts' and the reciprocal relationships between speech, manuscript and print (rather than a linear transition culminating in print) usefully provides a

---

(ed.), *Understanding Popular Culture* (Berlin, 1984), pp. 229–53. For useful essays on the implications of these theories in the history of the book, see Peter D. McDonald, 'Implicit Structures and Explicit Interactions: Pierre Bourdieu and the History of the Book', *The Library*, 6th ser., 19 (1997), pp. 105–21; Roger Chartier, '*The Order of Books* Revisited', *Modern Intellectual History*, 4 (2007), pp. 509–19.

80 See Jardine and Grafton, '"Studied for Action"'; Sherman, *John Dee*, and Sharpe, *Reading Revolutions*. It might also be noted that these models of reconstructing readership highlight the *political* context above others. The same theoretical impulses also helped to shape Roger Chartier, *The Order of Books: Readers, Authors, and Libraries in Europe between the Fourteenth and Eighteenth Centuries*, trans. Lydia G. Cochrane (Stanford, CA, 1994).

81 William W. E. Slights, *Managing Readers: Printed Marginalia in English Renaissance Books* (Ann Arbor, MI, 2001); Chartier, *The Order of Books*.

context for our understanding of reading.[82] However, rather more work
has used an internalist reading of texts to sustain models of early modern
reading, with remarkably few references to real readers. A large body of
work has used literary works and a smattering of historical references –
usually starting with Augustine's *Confessions*[83] – to chart a linear development from a medieval model of widespread communal and social reading
to an early modern model, bolstered by Reformation rhetoric, of internalized belief and of private and silent reading.[84] These arguments have
usually been attached to other master narratives of the early modern
period, especially the birth of the 'self' and the rise of 'privacy'.[85] Such
works tend to restrict our understanding of the practice of reading by
placing it within a series of inflexible, linear transitions as well as by trying
to characterize reading as a whole – again, they aim to show that early
modern reading was private and that communal or oral readers were
somehow relics of the past, rather than trying to think about the full
variety of styles of reading that an individual might engage in, depending
on context.[86]

Although many of the works on private reading and interiority have
grappled with religion, in fact the history of devotional reading has been
one area in the history of reading which has suffered relative neglect, at least
when compared to the profusion of sixteenth- and seventeenth-century
religious books. A prime example is Heidi Brayman Hackel's otherwise
excellent study of the reading of Frances Bridgewater, which excludes religious books on the basis that they raise separate issues to other books.[87]

---

[82] D. F. McKenzie, *Bibliography and the Sociology of Texts* (London, 1986); and D. F. McKenzie,
'Speech – Manuscript – Print', in D. Oliphant and R. Bradford (eds.), *New Directions in Textual
Studies* (Austin, TX, 1990), pp. 86–109; Harold Love, *Scribal Publication in Seventeenth-Century
England* (Oxford, 1993).

[83] St Augustine, *Confessions*, trans. Henry Chadwick (Oxford, 1992), p. 93, describes St Ambrose's
unusual habit of silent reading. Augustine figures largely in many general works on the history of
reading such as Alberto Manguel, *A History of Reading* (London, 1996).

[84] On silent reading, see Paul Saenger, 'Silent Reading: Its Impact on Late Medieval Script and
Society', *Viator*, 13 (1982), pp. 367–414; and his *Space between Words: The Origins of Silent Reading*
(Stanford, CA, 1997). Many studies of early modern reading cite Saenger as evidence that they need
not discuss reading aloud in the early modern era.

[85] See, among many others, Cecile M. Jagodzinski, *Privacy and Print: Reading and Writing in
Seventeenth-Century England* (Charlottesville, VA, 1999); Jennifer Bryan, *Looking Inward:
Devotional Reading and the Private Self in Late Medieval England* (Philadelphia, PA, 2008). I am
not arguing that such works have no value, rather that they present a distinctly one-sided portrait of
reading practices in this period.

[86] For a rare example of sensitive analysis of types of reading which nevertheless retains these general
paradigms, see Brian Stock, *After Augustine: The Meditative Reader and the Text* (Philadelphia, PA,
2001), Chapter 1, esp. his comments at pp. 22–3.

[87] For this rationale, see Brayman Hackel, *Reading Material in Early Modern England*, p. 15.

There have, of course, been studies of the readership of the Bible and of Books of Hours,[88] but the breadth of studies on the history of early modern devotional reading is relatively slight. Despite the innovative work of Margaret Spufford, there is little to compare to Mary Erler's study of late medieval devotional reading, or to studies of Ireland and early America by Raymond Gillespie, David D. Hall and Matthew P. Brown.[89] Instead, most of the work which marries an interest in book history with that of early modern piety – in particular that by Tessa Watt, Alexandra Walsham and Ian Green – has been focused on print culture, rather than on readers as such.[90] It is the aim of this book to extend that work by thinking about the place of reading in the practice of early modern piety. It does so by employing a relatively strict framework, basing an analysis of types of early modern godly reading around the spaces and places in which such reading was performed.

STRUCTURE AND METHODOLOGY: THE SPACES OF READING

When faced with such a broad and frankly contradictory set of interpretations about the nature of early modern reading, some choices have to be made. To avoid the problems associated with focusing on an individual reader or on a particular book or type of book, this book draws on the 'spatial turn' of much work in cultural geography, architecture, social and cultural history, and literary criticism over the past decade. Building on this work, the book analyses godly reading in a series of places and spaces in the early modern environment, from the most seemingly private of spaces – the closet – through to the other spaces of the household, before confronting reading in more obviously public spaces like the church and

---

[88] See Sherman, *Used Books*, Chapters 4–5; Peter Stallybrass, 'Books and Scrolls: Navigating the Bible', in Jennifer Anderson and Elizabeth Sauer (eds.), *Books and Readers in Early Modern England: Material Studies* (Philadelphia, PA, 2002), pp. 42–79; and Duffy, *Marking the Hours*.

[89] See Margaret Spufford, *Small Books and Pleasant Histories: Popular Fiction and Its Readership in Seventeenth-Century England* (London, 1981), esp. Chapter 8; Mary C. Erler, *Women, Reading and Piety in Late Medieval England* (Cambridge, 2002); Raymond Gillespie, *Reading Ireland: Print, Reading and Social Change in Early Modern Ireland* (Manchester, 2005), Chapter 6; Hall, *Worlds of Wonder, Days of Judgment*; Matthew P. Brown, *The Pilgrim and the Bee: Reading Rituals and Book Culture in Early New England* (Philadelphia, PA, 2007).

[90] See Tessa Watt, *Cheap Print and Popular Piety, 1550–1640* (Cambridge, 1991); Alexandra Walsham, *Providence in Early Modern England* (Oxford, 1999); Green, *Print and Protestantism in Early Modern England* (Oxford, 2000). Green has a short discussion of types of reader on pp. 24–41, but the discussion is effectively preliminary. A much larger body of work deals effectively with printing and the Reformation. See, among others, Jean-François Gilmont (ed.), *The Reformation and the Book*, trans. Karin Maag (Aldershot, 1998).

the coffee house. This spatial framework allows much of the diversity and complexity of early modern reading to be drawn out.[91]

The physical environment in which reading was set clearly had an impact upon the manner in which reading was performed, as it does today; reading is conditioned by its context: on the train, in the study, in the library, at the coffee shop and so on. Historians of reading have shown an awareness that the place of reading made a difference as to how reading was done. Making a brief passing comment about images of reading, Robert Darnton noted, 'The "where" of reading is more important than one might think, because placing the reader in his setting can provide hints about the nature of his experience.'[92] Some have started to take up the challenge, considering reading as it was practised in a range of places. Heidi Brayman Hackel, for example, has written about reading in closets, while Sasha Roberts has explored reading in the early modern bedchamber.[93] But few have thought about a wider range of places, with the notable exception of Harold Love, who attempted to chart some of the social uses of scribally published texts by looking at a series of sites of reading: the country house, the coffee house, the court, and the inns of court and universities.[94] Although Love was ultimately downbeat about the possibility of writing a history of reading in which styles of reading were viewed through the spaces in which they took place – he thought the evidence too fragmentary[95] – the approach is in many ways very promising. It allows us to make sense of the variety of models of reading surveyed above and to move forward without privileging one model – for instance private reading – over all the others. Crucially it shifts the focus away from trying to characterize any particular reader as being of a particular type and instead shows how individuals could adopt a range of styles of reading

---

[91] The turn towards space is now a well-established interdisciplinary field. For some excellent examples with an early modern focus, see Cynthia Wall, *The Literary and Cultural Spaces of Restoration London* (Cambridge, 1998); Alice Friedman, *House and Household in Elizabethan England: Wollaton Hall and the Willoughby Family* (Chicago, 1989); Paul Griffiths and Mark S. R. Jenner (eds.), *Londinopolis: Essays in the Cultural and Social History of Early Modern London* (Manchester, 2000); Amanda Flather, *Gender and Space in Early Modern England* (Woodbridge, 2007); Lena Cowen Orlin, *Locating Privacy in Tudor London* (Oxford, 2007); and David A. Postles, *Social Geographies in England (1200–1640)* (Washington, DC, 2007).

[92] Robert Darnton, *The Kiss of Lamourette: Reflections in Cultural History* (London, 1990), p. 167.

[93] Brayman Hackel, *Reading Material in Early Modern England*, pp. 34–43; Sasha Roberts, 'Shakespeare "Creepes into the Womens Closets about Bedtime": Women Reading in a Room of Their Own', in Gordon McMullan (ed.), *Renaissance Configurations: Voices/Bodies/Spaces, 1580–1690* (New York, 1998), pp. 30–63.

[94] Love, *Scribal Publication in Seventeenth-Century England*, pp. 195–230.

[95] Ibid., pp. 196–7, 229.

depending on the context in which they read. If this leads to the possibility of repetition, it also pays more attention to the range of textual experiences among individuals and communities in early modern England and it helps us to make connections between individual readers and the broader 'imagined communities' of readers.[96]

The chapters analyse in turn a variety of spaces in which godly reading took place. Starting with those seemingly 'private' spaces of the household – the closet, the bedchamber and the study – which are usually given pride of place in studies of reading and the self, the book moves on to the more public spaces of the household, venues which offered outlets for more familial, communal reading: the household hall, the parlour and kitchen, and gardens. Beyond the household, reading is evaluated in a series of public spaces, from personal libraries to the more public libraries of the parish, town, school and college, before attention is turned to reading in church, in the pulpit, at the coffee house and in the bookshop. The final space of reading considered is that which occurred in the prison, a place which encompassed many types of reading, including communal spiritual reading, but which was also a key venue in the development of the godly stereotype of the solitary reformed reader.

The approach allows for a consideration of how people read in different ways, depending on the spaces in which that reading took place. This is designed not to fragment reading into an infinite range of contexts, but instead to help to sharpen the focus on context and on some of the connections between readers that would be lost in a totalizing model of readerly experience based on the accumulation of examples. In common with David Hall's work on early American reading, the approach helps to forefront reading communities and a series of 'cultures of print'.[97] Such a formulation is particularly useful in discussing religious reading, where the style of reading was often deliberately chosen (by individuals and groups) as a means of effecting a specific style of piety.

These various styles and practices of reading – for which there was a much richer and more nuanced vocabulary than exists today[98] – are brought to life using a wide range of source materials, from readers' marginalia (which some contemporaries described as a practice particularly

---

[96] For which see Benedict Anderson, *Imagined Communities: Reflections on the Origin and Spread of Nationalism* (London, 1983).

[97] See Hall, *Cultures of Print*, esp. ch. 6.

[98] For this problem, see Sherman, *Used Books*, xvi and Chapter 1.

prevalent among puritans[99]) and physical evidence of textual exchange to book-lists and descriptions of reading preserved in histories of the godly. However, special attention is given to accounts of reading drawn from diaries and spiritual biographies and autobiographies. Although such sources might be rejected as the basis for a study on the grounds of typicality, they provide perhaps the richest of all material for the history of reading and they do so within a broader social framework which often allows for an assessment of the place of reading in the practice of everyday life. Such sources have figured prominently in important studies of reading, from Margaret Spufford's work on humble seventeenth-century readers to Jonathan Rose's examination of nineteenth-century working-class readers.[100] Spiritual autobiographies in particular provide a wealth of information about the spaces in which reading took place that simply cannot be mined from other sources. Of course, there will always be questions about these sources: about the nature of this strand of source material as a whole; about the typicality of one particular individual's reflections upon their spiritual condition; and about the pathology of those whose intense, soul-searching spirituality drove them to record in minute detail not only what they read but also how and where they did so. If such a base of source material still seems narrow, it is worth remembering not only that the coherence of the body of evidence lends sharpness to the overall picture of godly culture, but also that these books themselves were absolutely central to the religious culture of the godly. Needless to say, I have tried to use as wide a range as possible of such sources and to think about them critically – as books which were read, circulated, exchanged, edited

---

[99] Puritans were described as having little reverence for the book as a clean object. John Manningham, that colourful if not necessarily trustworthy commentator, recalled that his cousin told him 'what dissembling hypocrites these Puritanes be, and howe slightly they regard an oath: Ravens having a book brought unto him by a puritane to have his opinion of it, the booke being written by B. Bilson, Ravens as he reade it would needes be shewing his foolish witt in the margent, in scoffing at the booke'. Likewise, John Favour praised Tobie Matthew, the archbishop of York, in his *Antiquitie Triumphing Over Noveltie*, for allowing him access to his books, which he had 'not onely read . . . with a dilligent eye, but . . . also noted . . . with a judicious pen . . . and made continuall use of them in his sermons'. Another godly preacher, Elkanah Wales, described his own Bible in which he had written 'many profitable annotacions and references'. See John Bruce (ed.), *Diary of John Manningham, of the Middle Temple, and of Bradbourne, Kent, Barrister-At-Law, 1602–1603* (Camden Society, old ser., 99) (London, 1868), pp. 110–11; John Favour, *Antiquitie Triumphing Over Noveltie* (London, 1619), sig. A3v; and J. A. Newton, 'Puritanism in the Diocese of York (excluding Nottinghamshire) 1603–1640' (unpublished DPhil thesis, University of London, 1955), p. 347.

[100] Margaret Spufford, 'First Steps in Literacy: The Reading and Writing Experiences of the Humblest Seventeenth-Century Spiritual Autobiographers', *Social History*, 4 (1979), pp. 407–35; Margaret Spufford, *Small Books and Pleasant Histories*; Rose, *The Intellectual Life of the British Working Classes*.

and preserved for posterity as well as used in everyday spirituality – rather than to treat them uncritically, as has often been the case, as clear windows into the early modern world.[101] In fact, it is worth pointing out directly that it is my innovative use of these materials – applying a methodology drawn from the history of reading to such seemingly well-known sources, thinking about them as books which were read, circulated and exchanged – which allows me to sustain much of my argument about the nature of the culture of puritanism. Every type of source has its problems for the historian, but in combination they certainly have the potential to tell us much about the history of reading. Since some sources are particularly valuable, we will return to particular individuals – people like Nehemiah Wallington, Ralph Josselin and John Rastrick – with some regularity over the course of the book. I hope that this does not seem repetitive but that it instead reinforces the point that the same individuals could adopt different styles of reading depending on the context in which they read.

My aim in this book is to use these materials to write the history of reading and its place within puritan culture from the inside out, rather than thinking about the problem from above or from below. Other difficulties of course remain. Historians of books and of reading are necessarily in the curious position of relying for information about their subject on both books and their own practices of reading, a situation which can lead to some circularity. At times, too, in places within this book, much will be said about London as the centre of the English book trade. If this seems to favour the capital over other areas, it should be noted that I have drawn material from across the country where relevant and those sections which seem London-centred are so because London was particularly important in that context, especially as a venue for booksellers, coffee houses, and prisons. Finally, some attention needs to be drawn to the issue of change over time. I have already explained the rationale of thinking about the long seventeenth century in the history of puritanism and although this is explicitly a thematically arranged book, I have no wish to present a static picture of either puritanism or reading practices.[102] Having said that, some instances of godly reading drawn from the end of the period might seem practically identical to those

---

[101] For further remarks upon the typicality of diarists and autobiographers and comments upon the value of such sources, see pp. 40–2 below. For a critical use of diaries and autobiographies along these lines, see Cambers, 'Reading, the Godly, and Self-Writing'.

[102] There is certainly some continuity in reading practices over the period, as is argued by Brown, *The Pilgrim and the Bee*, p. 18.

described at its start. But this does not just tell us that reading practices evolved slowly, it also demonstrates that people of a particular religious disposition would adopt modes and methods of reading and religiosity which identified strongly with the past. These styles of reading and their transformations over the century will be considered in the chapters that follow.

CHAPTER 2

Domestic spaces and private reading

INTRODUCTION

Reading was an essential strand of the religious and cultural identity of godly people. Although the practical skills of literacy were not strictly necessary for salvation, it was consistently acknowledged that the path was more easily travelled with a working knowledge of the Bible. In the majority of cases, this knowledge came through reading. A select few – such as 'old Robert', a servant in the godly household of John Bruen in Cheshire, who used 'a strange girdle ... of leather, long and large', in which he placed a series of knots to help him remember the chapters and verses of the Bible without actually reading – might be held up as examples of godliness achieved without such skills, but they were few and far between. Contemporaries used such examples as exceptions to prove a general rule, not as illustrations to engage with modern historiographical discussions of the scope of the reading public.[1]

This chapter and the one that follows provide an examination of the scope, importance and meaning of reading in the godly household, first apparently private and then more communal. Rather surprisingly, given the often-quoted assertion that the Bible was 'the religion of protestants', very little work has probed the nature of godly reading and attempted to assess the practical importance of reading in their religious lives.[2] Instead,

[1] William Hinde, *A Faithfull Remonstrance of the Holy Life and Happy Death, of John Bruen of Bruen Stapleford* (London, 1641), pp. 56–8. Many discussions of cultural literacy, notably Adam Fox, *Oral and Literate Culture in England, 1500–1700* (Oxford, 2000), appropriate this sort of evidence as supporting the idea of a 'literate environment'. While this has certainly broadened our understanding it tends towards taking anecdotal evidence out of context. See Keith Thomas, 'The Meaning of Literacy in Early Modern England', in Gerd Baumann (ed.), *The Written Word: Literacy in Transition* (Oxford, 1986), pp. 97–131.

[2] In fact, Chillingworth's assertion 'The BIBLE, I say, The BIBLE only is the religion of protestants!' was part of an argument that just as the Catholic world revolved around the Council of Trent, so all Protestants shared the truth of the Bible. William Chillingworth, *The Religion of Protestants a Safe Way to Salvation* (Oxford, 1638), p. 375.

most studies have fed readers with a diet of quotations that relate to ideal
readerly praxis, drawn from sermons and how-to books, rather than with
accounts of reading as it was actually practised and experienced. In part,
this is because such models had crystallized before the history of the book
and the history of reading had emerged to ask new questions of old
sources. But it is also because the traditional assumptions of the emergence of interior piety and individualized religious belief dovetail both
with modern understandings of reading and with received wisdom about
the Protestant Reformation. But as these models are being dismantled,
and as the extent to which they rest upon the flimsy foundations of
Reformation mythology is established, so the ideal Reformation reader,
often assumed to be a model of internalization and interiority, is overdue
reassessment.[3]

In exploring the nature of individual readerly praxis among the godly,
the chapter also asks questions about the historiography of the self.
Reading appears to offer a rich vein of source material to be mined for
evidence of selfhood, interiority and internalization. But to tackle individual reading poses numerous difficulties, some of which extend from
the problematic nature of the sources available to examine the experience
of reading. The key problem is how far can we use evidence of writing –
from seemingly immediate marginalia to sophisticated stylized narratives –
as evidence of reading. As we have already seen, such issues are complex,
and the problems would only multiply if an attempt were made to form a
homogenized picture of what the godly read, working outwards from
book-lists and library catalogues towards mentalities. Such an attempt
would be likely to provide as misleading a picture of godly reading as Ian
Green's survey does of Protestant writing.[4] Instead, this chapter uses a
single slice of writings – spiritual diaries and life-writings – to unravel the
complexities of godly reading practices. A microscopic analysis of reading
as it is revealed in a relatively small number of such sources expands and
refines our understanding of godly reading, allowing its intricacies to
emerge: we will see individuals reading in different ways because of the
situation which confronted them, the time of the day or the space where
they read. Providing a thick description of such reading highlights the
contingencies of intellectual activity, while warning against any desire

---

[3] For a deconstruction of the Weberian model at the heart of key historical works like Keith Thomas,
*Religion and the Decline of Magic: Studies in Popular Beliefs in Sixteenth- and Seventeenth-Century
England* (revised edn, London, 1973), see Alexandra Walsham, 'The Reformation and "The
Disenchantment of the World" Reassessed', *Historical Journal*, 51 (2008), pp. 497–528.
[4] Ian Green, *Print and Protestantism in Early Modern England* (Oxford, 2000).

to arrive at a typology of godly reading. Catholics and mainstream Protestants, as well as puritans, read as part of their religious activity. Reading was thus a crucial, but not by itself a defining, component of godly identity.[5]

It might be objected that to focus on the navel-gazing diarists and autobiographers of the early modern world is likely to uphold exactly those models of modernity that the chapter seeks to qualify. Nevertheless, diaries and autobiographies provide evidence of reading practices that is unparalleled by other textual sources. While fragmentary narratives are more problematic, the many books that survive intact allow us some insight into the importance individuals placed upon reading in their religious life and often significant information on how and in what contexts they performed this reading. And although the question of the typicality of any one diarist should always be kept in mind, it should also be noted that this book is about precisely those kinds of godly people who did keep diaries, rather than about a more mainstream current which ran beneath early modern society. In fact, diarists and autobiographers appear to have been broadly typical of the godly – they just seem unusual because relatively few of their writings survive.[6] Therefore, when we handle such materials carefully and approach them not as texts that transport us into early modern minds, but as books that were read, exchanged and cherished in godly families and communities, they become doubly useful in the history of reading.

The social reading which emerges from these sources certainly reinforces the overarching argument of this book – that godly reading was shaped through communal and familial forms of piety. But the usage and readership of these cultural artefacts also allows for refinement to the historiography of selfhood. As I have argued elsewhere, carefully disentangling the history of reading from the history of selfhood tends to leave discussion of early modern selfhood, which is usually at the core of

---

[5] Recent work on the culture of puritanism has helpfully avoided claiming that any particular set of practices were distinctive marks of puritanism. Such work is clearly suggesting that no practices are likely to be exclusive to the godly, rather that identity is built up through associations: of people, networks, technologies and practices. For recent research on the contexts of Catholic reading, see Eamon Duffy, *Marking the Hours: English People and Their Prayers, 1240–1570* (New Haven, CT, 2006); and Alexandra Walsham, '"Domme Preachers"? Post-Reformation English Catholicism and the Culture of Print', *Past and Present*, 168 (2000), pp. 72–123.

[6] It is clear that the survival rate of diaries and associated writings is patchy and problematic. Certainly those who wrote collections of godly lives had access to a range of self-writings which no longer exists. See, for instance, Samuel Clarke, *The Lives of Thirty-Two English Divines Famous in their Generations for Learning and Piety, and most of them Sufferers in the Cause of Christ etc.* (London, 1677).

discussions of both diaristic writing and puritanism, with little in the way of textual evidential foundations.[7] In part this is down to a huge reliance on Max Weber's paradigm of modernity. At the heart of Weber's 'spirit of capitalism' was puritanism, an ascetic of self-control founded on 'inner loneliness' and 'the inner isolation of the individual'. This was sustained by the spiritual diary and only the 'Reformed Christian', in Weber's telling phrase, 'felt his pulse with its aid'.[8] But when they are seen for what they really were, diaries and autobiographies blow up in the faces of Weber's followers. The spiritual autobiography in context, as used, read, and circulated, renders obsolete the arguments of those like John Stachniewski who have suggested that 'the autobiography sharply defines the alienated individual'.[9]

The focus on these diaries and autobiographies in context also enables a critical realignment of current work on the culture of puritanism. A microhistorical perspective avoids the pitfalls associated with collapsing godly Protestantism into a more or less harmonious and homogeneous Protestantism,[10] and allows me to engage with a body of work which is starting to characterize puritanism as a culture which encouraged radicalism as well as conformity.[11] Although it is frequently written off as a

---

[7] Andrew Cambers, 'Reading, the Godly, and Self-Writing in England, ca. 1580–1720', *Journal of British Studies*, 46 (2007), pp. 796–825. There is, of course, much sensible contextualized work on godly diaries and autobiographies. See, for instance, Patrick Collinson, '"A Magazine of Religious Patterns": An Erasmian Topic Transposed in English Protestantism', in his *Godly People: Essays on English Protestantism and Puritanism* (London, 1983), pp. 499–525; Margo Todd, 'Puritan Self-Fashioning: The Diary of Samuel Ward,' *Journal of British Studies*, 31 (1992), pp. 236–64; Tom Webster, 'Writing to Redundancy: Approaches to Spiritual Journals and Early Modern Spirituality,' *Historical Journal*, 39 (1996), pp. 33–56; and (for commonplace books) Peter Lake, *Moderate Puritans and the Elizabethan Church* (Cambridge, 1982), pp. 116–68. For recent studies, see D. Bruce Hindmarsh, *The Evangelical Conversion Narrative: Spiritual Autobiography in Early Modern England* (Oxford, 2005); and David George Mullan, *Narratives of the Religious Self in Early-Modern Scotland* (Aldershot, 2010).

[8] Max Weber, *The Protestant Ethic and the Spirit of Capitalism*, trans. Talcott Parsons (1930) (London, 1992), pp. 104, 105, 124 and *passim*.

[9] John Stachniewski, *The Persecutory Imagination: English Puritanism and the Literature of Religious Despair* (Oxford, 1991), p. 115. I discuss the implications of such reading in Cambers, 'Reading, the Godly, and Self-Writing', but it is worth stressing that a focus on the reading of self-writing provides an added dimension to those histories of reading written from autobiographical accounts, notably Jonathan Rose's *The Intellectual Life of the British Working Classes* (New Haven, CT, 2001).

[10] Green, *Print and Protestantism in Early Modern England*. This line of criticism is made most forcefully in Peter Lake with Michael Questier, *The Antichrist's Lewd Hat: Protestants, Papists and Players in Post-Reformation England* (New Haven, CT, 2002), pp. 215–331.

[11] This has been the drift of the last decade of work on puritanism. It is asserted most stridently in David R. Como, *Blown by the Spirit: The Emergence of an Antinomian Underground in Pre-Civil-War England* (Stanford, CA, 2004); but also in Peter Lake, *The Boxmaker's Revenge: 'Orthodoxy', 'Heterodoxy' and the Politics of the Parish in Early Stuart London* (Manchester, 2001).

harmless domestic activity, considered broadly, communal reading will be shown to have encouraged a strong strain of radical religiosity.[12] Of this the authorities were well aware. From Elizabeth I's fury about prophesyings to Restoration frenzy about conventicles, they saw a conjunction between communal reading and spiritual activity and the undermining of the authority of the state and its church.

This chapter thus explores reading in three domestic spaces where we might expect the most private and internalized forms of reading to occur: the closet, the bedchamber and the study. Was godly reading in these domestic spaces silent and solitary? Does it bolster arguments that godly religious belief was internal and interiorized? Or does such reading, using these sources, overlap with social, exterior and collective practices?

THE CLOSET

Although it could be used in a general sense of any small room or cupboard, by the early seventeenth century the closet was recognized as a small room earmarked for devotional activity. Often adjoining the bedchamber, and sometimes enveloped by it, the closet was a notable feature of aristocratic and socially aspiring households.[13] These were devotional spaces: rooms for prayer, reading, writing and meditation. John Collinges (1623/4–1691), the presbyterian chaplain to Sir John and Lady Frances Hobart, was certain. Reflecting upon the life of Lady Hobart, he recalled that

---

[12] It should be stressed that modern Western culture tends only to render Christian communal reading as harmless. By contrast, it tends to render communal reading among the young in Islamic schools as radical indoctrination.

[13] For closets, see Mark Girouard, *Life in the English Country House: A Social and Architectural History* (New Haven, CT, 1978), esp. pp. 56, 129, 169 and 173–4. While Girouard (and others) present the closet as a space of privacy – 'The closet ... was essentially a private room ... it was perhaps the only room in which its occupant could be entirely on his own' (p. 56) – others have provided more nuanced accounts of closets as spaces of both privacy and sociability. See especially Alan Stewart, 'The Early Modern Closet Discovered', *Representations*, 50 (1995), pp. 76–100; and Lena Cowen Orlin, *Locating Privacy in Tudor London* (Oxford, 2007), Chapter 8. Although closets had long been associated with the devotional lives of the pious aristocracy of pre-Reformation Europe, after the Reformation they became more closely associated with reading. For medieval parallels, see Andrew Taylor, 'Into His Secret Chamber: Reading and Privacy in Late Medieval England', in James Raven, Helen Small and Naomi Tadmor (eds.), *The Practice and Representation of Reading in England* (Cambridge, 1996), pp. 41–61; and Mary C. Erler, *Women, Reading, and Piety in Late Medieval England* (Cambridge, 2002). See also Amanda Vickery, *Behind Closed Doors: At Home in Georgian England* (New Haven, CT, 2009).

when she came from her closet, it was easie for us who conversed with her, to judge what she had been doing: she was much in prayer, much in tears, much in reading the holy Scriptures, in reading over good books, and notes of Sermons.[14]

As devotional spaces, closets transcended post-Reformation religious allegiances. In the King James Bible, they were recommended as places for private prayer: 'But thou, when thou prayest enter into thy closet: and when thou hast shut thy door, pray to thy Father which is in secret; and thy Father which seeth in secret, shall reward thee openly.'[15] But, although Catholics and conformist Protestants also used closets as devotional spaces, they were particularly associated with godly women.[16]

Closets, seemingly private spaces for interior reflection, have been discussed enthusiastically by those interested in the history of privacy and selfhood. Scholars such as Richard Rambuss equate the appearance of the closet in the seventeenth century with the emergence of the modern self.[17] Such socially privileged sites were tied up with a change in the meaning of the word 'private' from roughly 'domestic' to more clearly 'individual'. As such, they offer grist to the mill of those who argue that it was the experience of reading which helped to foster the development of the private self in the seventeenth century.[18] While many cultural historians continue to view the closet as *the* space of privacy and selfhood, those who have opened the door of the closet and examined what went on there get us nearer to its true importance. As Alan Stewart in particular has argued, the closet was first and foremost a 'transactive' space, a place for a range of textual and social activities. It is not helpfully positioned in a private sphere which is sharply differentiated from more public arenas.[19]

Although Alan Stewart and Heidi Brayman Hackel have profitably examined closet readers, they have both focused on the limitations of the public/private and community/self distinctions.[20] What follows here

---

[14] J[ohn] C[ollinges], *Par Nobile. Two Treatises. The One, Concerning the Excellent Woman, ... the Lady Frances Hobart ... The Other,... the Lady Katharine Courten ...* (London, 1669), p. 268.

[15] Matthew 6:6. This translation superseded the usual 'chamber' and is likely to have reflected, as well as shaped, contemporary practice.

[16] See, for example, William Palmes, *The Life of Mrs Dorothy Lawson, of St Anthony's, near Newcastle-on-Tyne* (London, 1855), p. 39.

[17] Richard Rambuss, *Closet Devotions* (Durham, NC, 1998).

[18] Cecile Jagodinski, *Privacy and Print: Reading and Writing in Seventeenth-Century England* (Charlottesville, VA, 1999).

[19] Alan Stewart, *Close Readers: Humanism and Sodomy in Early Modern England* (Princeton, NJ, 1997), pp. 161–87, quotation at p. 163. See also Lena Cowen Orlin, *Locating Privacy in Tudor London*, Chapter 8.

[20] Stewart, *Close Readers*, pp. 161–87; Heidi Brayman Hackel, *Reading Material in Early Modern England: Print, Gender, and Literacy* (Cambridge, 2005), pp. 34–43.

extends their analysis by thinking about the devotional dimensions of closet reading. It considers the styles of reading that the godly practised in their closets and probes the connections between this reading and prayer. As an activity that could involve books, objects, voice and thought, prayer helpfully delineates the otherwise blurred boundary between non-textual and textual activity. Many writers, outlining the shape of godly devotion, noted that the closet was explicitly a space for prayer. John Bruen's closets, for example, were described as prayer venues, although he would also pray in his study, his bedchamber and his gardens and orchards.[21] In the household of the puritan clergyman and post-Restoration nonconformist John Angier (1605–77) in Lancashire, prayer in the closet set the tone for the round of sabbath devotions. As Oliver Heywood, the great nonconformist minister and autobiographer who was also Angier's son-in-law, described it, 'Lords day was thus spent; after private devotions in their closets, in the Family, near Eight a Clock a Chapter was read, a Psalm sung, then he went to prayer.' Closet prayer thus preceded family prayer, reading and devotion before the family set off for the service and a day of sermon repetition and further prayer.[22] Diarists also remarked upon praying in their closets. Lady Margaret Hoby adopted a particular mode of individual piety for the closet. It was there that her 'privat praier' took place and she noted unambiguously that she 'praied ... privatly in my Closett'. Occasionally, she lets us share in the fluidity of closet activity. For 10 December 1600, her diary recorded her 'privat medetation and praier' in her closet. The following days the two activities were 'privat readinge and praier'.[23] So prayer might encompass, or be connected with, a variety of activities, but we must show some caution. Lady Hoby's closet prayer, as Alan Stewart has argued, was not quite as private as it appears. Writing of it in her diary was to publicly enact the withdrawal into the private closet.[24]

As a venue for prayer, much of which was of course oral and never recorded, the closet naturally keeps many of its secrets. To explore further the mode of piety within closets, which informed the practice of reading there, requires recourse to the literature of invocation. Oliver Heywood's

---

[21] Hinde, *A Faithfull Remonstrance of the Holy Life and Happy Death, of John Bruen*, p. 156.

[22] [Oliver Heywood], *A Narrative of the Holy Life and Happy Death of That Reverend, Faithful and Zealous Man of God, and Minister of the Gospel of Jesus Christ, Mr John Angier* (London, 1683), p. 60.

[23] Joanna Moody (ed.), *The Private Life of an Elizabethan Lady: The Diary of Lady Margaret Hoby, 1599–1605* (Stroud, 1998), pp. 17, 128.

[24] Stewart, *Close Readers*, p. 168.

Closet-Prayer helps to identify the strands of this piety. Conventionally, Heywood distinguished private closet prayer from a more public form of family prayer. A duty for men, women and children, closet prayer required practitioners first to shut the closet door and then to kneel or lie down. These prayers were explicitly 'secret' but not private – they involved a noisy outpouring of the heart, 'including of the voice as well as the body'. The use of the voice was to be preferred because it provided 'an example to his family'. Closet prayer thus mirrored forms of communal prayer and intersected with family piety.[25] And, as we will see, leading nonconformist divines like Philip Henry made clear that closet prayer and family religion were two central and interwoven strands of godly religiosity.[26]

The method of reading in the closet in many ways mirrors the methods of praying. This is not surprising because, as we have seen, prayer might involve reading and there was a fine line between devotional reading and prayer. Indeed, for all he advocated the closet as a venue of prayer, Oliver Heywood often made use of his for scriptural reading. Heywood wrote of days when he was involved in 'secret prayer' in the closet, but such prayer was explicitly associated with devotional scriptural reading. Furthermore, he urged himself to do it more. Making a covenant in 1672, he sought God's assurance that he would make daily scripture reading part of his 'closet work'.[27] That daily reading of scriptures formed part of self-examination for Heywood is indicative of the mutability of prayer, scriptural reading and meditation in the godly devotional routine. Certainly Heywood's closet reading contrasts in both substance and style with his reading in other parts of the house, be it his family reading as part of household devotion or his more professional reading in his study.[28]

---

[25] Oliver Heywood, *Closet-Prayer, a Christian Duty: Or a Treatise upon Mat. vi. 6* (London, 1671), pp. 5, 10, 21, 86, 110. Other works on closet prayer include Thomas Brookes, *The Privie Key of Heaven; or, Twenty Arguments for Closet-Prayer: in a Select Discourse on that Subject* (London, 1665); Nathaniel Resbury, *Of Closet-Prayer. A Sermon* [on Matthew 6:6] *Preach'd before the Queen at White-Hall, on Sunday, Aug. 27. 1693* (London, 1693); Edward Wetenhall, *Enter into thy Closet* (London, 1666); Thomas Comber, *A Companion to the Temple and Closet* (London, 1672); Samuel Slater, *A Discourse of Closet, or Secret Prayer* (London, 1691).

[26] *An Account Of The Life and Death Of Mr Philip Henry, Minister of the Gospell, near Whitchurch in Shropshire. Who Dyed June 24; 1696 in the Sixty fifth Year of his Age. With Dr Bates's Dedication.* (2nd edn, London, 1699), p. 50.

[27] Heywood, *Diaries*, vol. I, pp. 237, 307–9.

[28] It should be noted that there are both gendered and professional distinctions to be made. Those such as Ralph Josselin, a cleric who had both closet and study, used the closet solely for prayer, while devotional reading was confined to the study. See Alan Macfarlane (ed.), *The Diary of Ralph Josselin, 1616–1683* (Oxford, 1976), pp. 386, 596.

Although the evidence is fragmentary and often capable of multiple interpretations, the pieces which survive offer the outline of a more rounded picture of closet reading. Certain features of this reading are particularly noticeable. First and most obvious, closet reading, much like closet prayer, was an early morning activity. Early in the morning, long before breakfast and family prayers, the godly resorted to their closets to engage in cycles of prayer and devotional reading. Second, this kind of reading in the closet was a heavily gendered activity. While men might perform a similar style of devotional reading in their studies, it was women who would do so in the closet, sometimes with their children in tow. Of course, this was also partly because wives were frequently denied access to their husband's studies, especially in clerical families but also in large godly households.[29] Far from being a neutral division of space, the near confinement of individual female reading to the closet coloured what was read and how it was done: although it might encompass semi-canonical godly authors like William Perkins, closet reading was predominantly scriptural and it was a piecemeal, daily and cyclical activity. This was reading as part of devotional duty and thus removed from historiographical portraits of goal-orientated reading.[30]

This is not to say that female godly closet reading is without interest as a mode of performance. Closet reading was an identifiable mode of devotional reading. Not only did godly women read over the scriptures, they also did so in a particular manner. This reading was generally individual, laced with emotion, and rarely silent. In her autobiography, the godly Northamptonshire gentlewoman Elizabeth Isham (1609–54) detailed her sins as a young child, which included stealing liquorice from her mother's cupboard and (imitating St Augustine) hiding pears which her father had forbidden her to eat in her closet. She was full of fear of the judgement of God at her sins but, as she recalled, the Lord gave her comfort in 'reading & praiying' with 'the Bookes which I had in my closet'. The practice was individual yet oral, and it intersected with her writing notes out of her New Testament.[31] Just as Lady Hobart read with tears, Sarah Savage's closet reading involved an outpouring of her heart. Like prayer, such scriptural reading was almost necessarily noisy. The closet was also a venue for cyclical, repetitive reading. Again Sarah Savage alludes to how the reading

---

[29] On this issue I am indebted to the unpublished paper of Michelle Wolfe, '"Sacred Imployments": Gendering Spiritual Space and Labour in the Clerical Household'.

[30] Lisa Jardine and Anthony Grafton, '"Studied for Action": How Gabriel Harvey Read His Livy', *Past and Present*, 129 (1990), pp. 30–78.

[31] Princeton University Library, MS RTC01 (no. 62) (Elizabeth Isham, 'My Booke of Rememberance'), fo. 10r.

was performed, noting that she read Acts 'in course in secret'.[32] Likewise, Susannah Stubbs read scripture privately in her closet, a mode which contrasted with her collective reading aloud of printed sermons in the household of her cousin Ralph Thoresby in Leeds in the 1680s.[33]

The voluminous manuscript diaries of Mary Rich, Countess of Warwick, offer considerable evidence of the material the godly might read in their closets and of how they performed it. Rich apparently turned to the godly life after a misspent youth, in which she had wasted her time 'reading romances ... seeing and reading playes ... dressing and adorning [her] wild body and ... lookeing in Glasses to sett [her] selfe out'.[34] Seeing the error of her ways, she turned to the godly life with considerable zeal – she could no longer understand those 'who would seem devout at Church, could laugh at others for being serious out on't, and burlesque the very Bible, and turn Religion into Ridicule' – and set out a record of her spiritual life in painstaking detail in a series of diaries.[35] Although some of her writings do not survive, in particular the occasional meditations she wrote, scrubbed out and rewrote in her table book, these diaries reveal the importance of reading in her daily spiritual life.[36]

---

[32] Cheshire Record Office, Z D/Basten/8 (Diary of Sarah Savage, 1686–1688), fo. 4r. Savage's extensive diaries record such reading in some detail. For other instances of her reading 'in course', see *Memoirs of the Life and Character of Sarah Savage*, ed. J.B. Williams (London, 1821), pp. 140, 144, 177, 179.

[33] York Minster Archives, Add MS 214 (Diary of Henry Stubbs, 1678). The latter part of this diary was written by Henry Stubbs's daughter-in-law, Susannah Stubbs, who presented the manuscript in turn to her cousin, Ralph Thoresby.

[34] BL, Additional MSS 27351-5 (Diaries of Mary Rich, Countess of Warwick, 5 vols., 1666–77), vol. II, fo. 256v.

[35] BL, Additional MSS 27351-5 (Diaries of Mary Rich, Countess of Warwick, 5 vols., 1666–77). Rich's diaries are important for a variety of reasons, not least for being so extensive – few diarists carried on so extensive a record of their spiritual lives for so long – and they are also interesting textually. They were begun in earnest after conference with two 'soul-friends'. She began to write them every evening, but soon wrote them the following morning instead. See Anthony Walker, *Eureka, Eureka. The Virtuous Woman Found her Loss Bewailed, and Character Exemplified in a Sermon Preached at Felsted in Essex, April, 30, 1678. At the Funeral of that most Excellent Lady ... Mary, Countess Dowager of Warwick* (London, 1678), p. 59, which includes the comment about those who mistreated the Bible. The diaries include many corrections, elaborations, summaries and textual interventions made by Thomas Woodroofe, the chaplain to the Earl of Warwick. And intriguingly, Rich might well have taken inspiration from the encouragement towards diary-keeping promoted by John Beadle, whose sermons she heard and which later became the most extensive how-to guide on diary-keeping in the seventeenth century. See John Beadle, *The Journal or Diary of a Thankful Christian. Presented in Some Meditations upon Numb. 33. 2* (London, 1656). For examples of people being inspired by Beadle's book to keep diaries, see Tom Webster, 'Writing to Redundancy', p. 38.

[36] For a rare mention of the erasable qualities of table books, see BL, Additional MSS 27351-5 (Diaries of Mary Rich, Countess of Warwick, 5 vols., 1666–77), vol. I, fo. 117r: 'as sone as up I retired and red over som ocasionale meditations of my own and whilst I was readeing one of them which was upon washing out of a littell table booke a great deale of writeing with the helpe of a littell water and cleaneing the table booke as cleane as if there had neaver bene any writeing in it'.

A typical entry simply began with a dry record that she had, after getting up, gone into her closet to read and pray.[37] At other times, she provided more detailed information on her closet reading. For 23 September 1666, she noted:

Sunday morneing. I rose very early and went into my Clossett, and red in the worde and upon reading that passage of Scripture, of Christes askeing Peter wether he loved him, and St Peter's answering that he knew he loved him, god was pleased to melt my heart exceedingly, and to make me with abundance of teares say, as he did, that he knew I loved him better then all thinges in heaven or earth.

This bout of intense spiritual reading served to help her in her subsequent meditation.[38] Although such scriptural closet reading appears to have been a solitary undertaking, we should not assume that it was silent. From time to time, she noted how God had been so pleased with her closet reading that he made tears stream down her face. And, as Anthony Walker confirmed in her funeral sermon, 'her *sighs* and *groans* would eccho from her Closet at good distance'.[39] That her closet was not solely a private space is also confirmed by the fact that she frequently recorded receiving godly preachers – and in particular those ministers who had been deprived in 1662 – there and reading and praying with them.[40] It was also where she dealt with business surrounding her servants.[41]

Such scriptural closet reading undoubtedly played an important part in Mary Rich's spirituality, whether as usual in the morning or on occasion in the afternoon, when she might read from her own meditations and scripture reflections.[42] But the closet also played host to a considerable amount of extra-biblical reading. This reading is particularly interesting since it shows how Rich read from a broader canon of godly literature to effect the same sort of spiritual transformation provided by the Bible. On

---

[37] Ibid., vol. I, fo. 17v.   [38] Ibid., vol. I, fo. 27r.

[39] Ibid., vol. I, fos. 58v–59r (Feb 1666/7); Walker, *Eureka, Eureka*, p. 61.

[40] See, for example, BL, Additional MSS 27351–5 (Diaries of Mary Rich, Countess of Warwick, 5 vols., 1666–77), vol. I, fos. 9v, 26v. It is noteworthy that those ministers whom she had pray in her closet were almost exclusively those that had been deprived in 1662.

[41] Walker, *Eureka, Eureka*, p. 109.

[42] BL, Additional MSS 27351–5 (Diaries of Mary Rich, Countess of Warwick, 5 vols., 1666–77), vol. I, fo. 45r.

one occasion, she noted that her heart was softened by reading the godly Essex minister Jeremiah Dyke's 'book of the Sacrement'.[43] Although she seems to have held a high regard for books like Abraham Caley's *Glimpse of Eternity* (London, 1677),[44] Rich singled out the works of Richard Baxter for particular praise, reading them in much the same way as she read the scripture. On one occasion, in March 1667, she noted:

In the morning ris very early, and then reatired and red in the word of god, with which my heart was affected, then red in Mr Baxtres Saintes rest, and whilst I was reading of the Joyes of heaven God was pleased much to ravisch my heart with thinkeing of it ...

At another time:

in the morneing as sone as drest went into my clossett red in Mr Baxteres booke of being crusefide to the world by the crosse of christ, God was pleased whilst I was reading much to move my heart and to make me shed many tears, after I had done readeing I meditated upon what I had red and God was pleased to affect my heart much by this passage ...[45]

These books played a key part in her piety. She noted that reading his *The Saints Everlasting Rest* (London, 1649), for example, 'did mightily draw out the strength of [her] affections after God' and even used Baxter's books as a template for judging her own spiritual state when she withdrew and examined herself 'by some markes of Mr Baxters'.[46] Rich appears to have accorded Baxter's practical godly books the same importance that she gave scripture and she read them much in the same way, as if the place and situation conditioned her manner of reading.

This style of closet reading and piety deliberately evoked (and tapped into) a strand of religiosity which had long been crucial to godly women. Lady Margaret Hoby, as we have already seen, used her closet as a devotional space for prayer. She recorded in her diary several instances in which she went into her closet to pray. But her closet was not simply an empty, undecorated space for puritan prayer. By her own admission, she occasionally set aside time in which to order the things in her closet and to

[43] Ibid., vol. I, fo. 26r. This was Jeremiah Dyke, *A Worthy Communicant: or, A Treatise, Shewing the Due Order of Receiving the Sacrament of the Lords Supper. By Jer. Dyke, Minister of Epping, in Essex* (London, 1636), a hefty godly guide to preparing for the sacrament which was frequently reprinted throughout the seventeenth century.

[44] BL, Additional MSS 27351–5 (Diaries of Mary Rich, Countess of Warwick, 5 vols., 1666–77), vol. I, fos. 43v, 77v, 282r.

[45] Ibid., vol. I, fos. 67v–68r, 38v.   [46] Ibid., vol. I, fos. 172v, 87v and *passim*.

sort papers.[47] She 'dressed up' her closet and was 'busie' there.[48] By and large, the closet was a space for prayer and 'privat examenation'.[49] She appears to have used her closet in the morning as a devotional space and it is probable that it was the usual venue for her diary-writing. However, a careful reading of the diary suggests that she used her closet more frequently and for a wider range of tasks than it initially reveals. Taking a closer look at the diary entries which specifically mention her closet, it is striking how they are, without exception, records of its *unusual* use. She mentions the closet when she used it for prayers at irregular times, or when she used it for unusual activities, such as sorting through all her papers there, recording its contents or for making oil.[50] In fact, it is likely that she used her closet each morning – a suggestion that is reinforced by her retrospective entry for 23–26 December 1600 in which she recalled that she remained in her chamber for these four days, because she had a cold, and 'went not in to my clositt'.[51] Instructively, there are no daily entries for these days, which points towards the closet being her usual venue for writing her diary.

For Margaret Hoby, the closet was a space given over to the interconnected tasks of morning prayer, self-examination and devotional reading. The overlap between her writing and devotional reading here is particularly instructive because the two were at the heart of her experience of reading. Lady Hoby appears to have read in her closet after private prayer and before having breakfast. This reading, excepting the occasions when she was ill, confined to her bedchamber, or on her travels, was exclusively scriptural: either from her Bible or Testament.[52] On the few occasions where the evidence is inconclusive – for instance when she simply noted 'I went to my booke' or that she read 'a while' – we might assume this was also scriptural.[53]

The place that Margaret Hoby's closet reading occupied in her wider devotional life can be analysed further by carefully using the diary to show

[47] Moody, *The Private Life of an Elizabethan Lady*, p. 95. For reflections on Hoby's reading practices in her diary, see Mary Ellen Lamb, 'Margaret Hoby's Diary: Women's Reading Practices and the Gendered Reformation Subject', in Sigrid King (ed.), *Pilgrimage for Love: Essays in Honor of Josephine A. Roberts* (Tempe, AZ, 1999), pp. 63–94; Mary Ellen Lamb, 'The Sociability of Margaret Hoby's Reading Practices and the Representation of Reformation Interiority', *Critical Survey*, 12(2) (2000), pp. 17–32.

[48] Moody, *The Private Life of an Elizabethan Lady*, pp. 56, 55.   [49] Ibid., p. 46.

[50] Ibid., pp. 17, 46, 55, 56, 99–100, 145, 165, 181 (for prayer), 95 (papers), 115 (inventory), 101 (making oil).

[51] Ibid., p. 132.

[52] Ibid., *passim*. Throughout, Hoby distinguishes the Bible from the (New) Testament.

[53] Ibid., pp. 120, 54.

how this reading was done. The timing of the reading, taking place directly after what Lady Hoby described as 'private' – that is, individual – prayer, is the first suggestion. It hints at an intimate connection between this scriptural reading and the vocal and emotional practice of closet prayer that we have already described. If the 'private' nature of the reading mirrored that of the prayer, then we need not assume that it was silent, rather that it was placed in contrast with more communal forms of family reading. It was also performed with pen close at hand, more like a scholarly exercise than typical understandings of the practice of piety. Lady Hoby had no reverence for the sacred space of the printed pages of scripture. Instead, her diary entries constantly testify that she marked her texts: 'I wrett notes in my bible' and 'I wrett notes in my testament' are just two of scores of examples of her written engagement with scriptural reading.[54] Each instance is frustratingly brief but the multiplication of examples displays how both note-taking and scriptural reading formed part of the larger whole of self-examination.

Although there is a conspicuous absence of non-canonical authors in her descriptions of closet reading, it would be wrong to view it as an entirely separate practice. Instead, it is certainly suggestive that at other times of day she used her Testament to record the heads of sermons by Stephen Egerton and notes of the sermon she heard the previous night, and at other times that she was prompted after hearing the sermon to make notes in both her Testament and in Perkins.[55] Such annotation highlights that the practice of godly reading extended beyond its theoretical function as a conduit to channel the Holy Spirit into the soul. In practice, this reading was a comparative textual process, which overlapped with the art of hearing and the act of writing. Indeed, Lady Hoby's own marginal annotations on her surviving volumes now in York Minster Library reveal a very significant intertextual engagement with the printed text. In her copy of Philip du Plessis Mornay's *Fowre Books, of the institution, use and doctrine of the holy sacrament* (London, 1600), she extracted key information into the blank margin, digesting the text for future reference and readings, perhaps to serve as a resource for the religion of her household.[56] The diary

---

[54] Ibid., pp. 47, 12.   [55] Ibid., pp. 127, 15, 59.

[56] For a full discussion of this marginalia, see Andrew Cambers, 'Print, Manuscript, and Godly Cultures in the North of England, c. 1600–1650' (unpublished DPhil thesis, University of York, 2003), pp. 86–118, and for her reading more generally pp. 41–119. See also Andrew Cambers, 'Readers' Marks and Religious Practice: Margaret Hoby's Marginalia', in John N. King (ed.), *Tudor Books and Readers: Materiality and the Construction of Meaning* (Cambridge, 2010), pp. 211–31; and Julie Crawford, 'Reconsidering Early Modern Women's Reading, or, How Margaret Hoby Read Her de Mornay', *Huntington Library Quarterly*, 73 (2010), pp. 193–223.

establishes that her reading, writing and diary-writing formed part of her self-examination: the closet was the venue for her search for marks of election and as a practice this encompassed the written and the spoken word, the practice of reading, the art of hearing and the discipline of writing. Such reading was a key part of a dynamic and multi-dimensional godly religiosity.

This evidence certainly adds complexity to, rather than turns upside down, those accounts that see closet activity as part and parcel of an emerging culture of privacy and selfhood. However, where the evidence allows it, glimpses can be snatched of closet reading being a distinctly oral and communal activity. These insights suggest that the closet functioned simultaneously as a self-consciously devotional space and as a plausible venue for communal reading that stretched beyond the devotional. Although difficult to evaluate, a credible scene of such reading is afforded in *Titus Andronicus*, where Titus addresses Lavinia and Marcus, apparently proposing some family reading in the closet:

> Lavinia, go with me
> I'll to thy closet and go read with thee
> Sad stories chanced in the times of old.
> Come, boy, and go with me. Thy sight is young,
> And thou shalt read when mine begin to dazzle.[57]

Although such images should be treated with caution, the scenario is clearly not meant to be funny: the audience accepts that closets could function as venues for family reading. Offstage, Lady Anne Clifford, whose own closet was evidently large enough for her to 'set up a great many of the Books' she inherited on her mother's death, alludes to the closet as a venue of communal activity.[58] In the fragmentary eighteenth-century transcript of one of her diaries, there are two references to communal closet reading. In an entry for 9 January 1617 she noted that she 'went up to see the things in the closet & began to have Mr Sandy's Book read to me about the Government of the Turks, my Lord sitting the most part of the Day reading in his closet'. Again, in April 1617 she recorded sitting in her husband's closet and reading 'much in the Turkish History and Chaucer'.[59] Necessarily fragmentary, such evidence suggests

---

[57] William Shakespeare, *Titus Andronicus* (1594), III. ii. 81–5.
[58] D. J. H. Clifford (ed.), *The Diaries of Lady Anne Clifford* (revised edn, Stroud, 2003), p. 59; on Clifford's reading more generally, see Mary Ellen Lamb, 'The Agency of the Split Subject: Lady Anne Clifford and the Uses of Reading', *English Literary Renaissance*, 22 (1992), pp. 347–68; Brayman Hackel, *Reading Material in Early Modern England*, esp. pp. 221–41.
[59] Clifford (ed.), *The Diaries of Lady Anne Clifford*, pp. 47, 58.

that closets could be used for communal as well as individual reading and that such reading could stretch from the devotional to works of literature and history. The godly closet was certainly a space for individual prayer and devotional reading but we should not assume that it was always a solitary, or a silent, experience.

THE BEDCHAMBER

In 1646, at the age of nineteen, the future clergyman Henry Newcome craved time alone. To this end, and no doubt to continue the edifying work of preparing to take his degree at Cambridge, Newcome 'made a candlestick of a piece of a box-lid (of fir deale board) & a socket of velome' which he 'had nailed to my beds head, & set a candle in it, to read in bed'. Writing of this in his diary, and later copying noteworthy chunks of the diary into a composite volume for his family, he recalled the hand that providence had taken in his individual night-time activity. He recalled that he had fallen asleep, only to wake in the morning to find 'the candle burnt quite away & the socket shrivelled but the fir wood catched not & the candle fell not into the bed'.[60] Such a providential escape raises a series of questions about the nature of reading for the godly. Was the bedchamber reading of the godly silent and solitary, an interior and a private practice? What was read there? And how was it done?

The literature on reading in bed and in the bedchamber, like that on reading in the closet, is usually framed in terms of private and public and draws its evidence from fictional representations.[61] And yet, both bed and bedchamber were frequent sites of reading, not least for the godly. Although there was naturally some overlap with the style of reading performed in closets (and it is notable that those without a closet would do their devotional reading in the bedchamber), the godly frequently read in their bedchambers. They were venues for a wider range of reading material and reading styles. These appear to have fluctuated depending both upon social status – where poorer families read in crowded bed-chambers, that reading was almost necessarily communal – and upon the age of the reader. By following reading through the stages of the life cycle,

---

[60] Chetham's Library, MS A.3.123 ('Autobiography, or the abstract of diary, of Henry Newcome (1627–1695)'), p. II (contemporary pagination). This seems to confirm Harold Love's assertion: 'Reading in bed seems to have been regarded as anti-social and a fire-risk.' See Harold Love, *Scribal Publication in Seventeenth-Century England* (Oxford, 1993), p. 196.

[61] Stewart, *Close Readers*; Brayman Hackel, *Reading Material in Early Modern England*.

we can see the range of modes of reading that occurred in the bed-chamber: from the first steps in literacy as a child, to youth, adulthood and old age.

A significant how-to literature emerged in the seventeenth century crammed with advice for parents unsure of how to teach their children to read. Then, as now, the process of learning involved a process of interaction – of speaking, looking and repeating – between an adult and child. The most common tool for teaching children to read was the Bible and the most common domestic venue was the bedchamber, which offered a friendlier forum than the household hall and an arena more attuned to concentration than the family parlour. Alice Thornton, who remained steadfastly within the Church of England but cultivated godly styles of piety, taught her son Robert to read in her bedchamber. For Alice, this was a supremely emotional experience, as she collapsed into bed after brief sessions of teaching.[62] Others recalled their own experiences of learning to read and frequently cited godly works as great inspirational tools. Philip Henry was far from alone in learning both how to read and how to be godly from William Perkins's *Six Principles*, a work with which his learned and pious mother encouraged the instruction of her young son.[63]

Reading in the bedchamber in childhood was a consistently communal, social and interactive activity. This persisted through childhood and encouraged particular styles of devotion. In 1660, the ten-year-old John Rastrick (1650–1727) found himself without a schoolmaster. In the absence of a teacher, he kept himself busy by collecting prayers from the Psalms and other parts of the Bible and by 'Reading and conferring the Bible and other good books'. This devotional reading spanned the Bible and godly works. Although he had been bought and 'learned' the *School of Vertue* and Cotton's *Milk for Boston Babes* – the latter characteris-tically troubling him because he thought it was exclusively for those born in Boston, Lincolnshire[64] – Rastrick, who spent twenty-three years as a

---

[62] *The Autobiography of Mrs Alice Thornton, of East Newton, co. York*, Surtees Society, 62 (Durham, 1875 for 1873), p. 260.

[63] *An Account of the Life and Death of Mr Philip Henry*, p. 3; William Perkins, *The Foundation of Christian Religion Gathered into Sixe Principles* (London, 1591) was consistently re-published throughout the seventeenth century and appears to have become known popularly as the Six Principles.

[64] F[rancis] S[eagar], *The Schoole of Vertue and Booke of Good Nurture* (London, 1557). It is likely that Rastrick read the revised edition which first appeared in 1582 and was reissued many times in the seventeenth century; John Cotton, *Milk for Babes. Drawn out of the Breasts of both Testaments. Chiefly, for the Spirituall Nourishment of Boston Babes in Either England: But May be of Like Use for*

clergyman within the Church of England before leaving and serving another thirty-nine years as a presbyterian minister, recalled the influence of two classics of early seventeenth-century piety:

> We had in our Family Dyke's Deceitfulness of Man's Heart and Dent's Plain man's path way to H.— Old books: These I delighted to reade and they much affected me. O what would I have given if I had had it that Dent's Plain Man's Pathway had been perfect, for it was torn and much of it gone

Until this spiritual epiphany, Rastrick's bedtime reading, like that of Philip Henry, had involved answering his father 'in repeating some part of Perkin's catechism, the 6 Principles; when we were in Bed'. But charged with evangelical fervour, Rastrick took control of night-time devotion. During the day he extracted prayers from Dyke and Dent 'to say at nights, when we were in Bed, (for we used not to pray before <we were in bed> and we lay all in a room)'.[65] Reading in the bedchamber thus interacted with reading in the wider household: it was oral, communal and, although not scriptural, performed as part of a routine of devotional activity. It was properly familial and firmly catechistical.

Even in youth, when from our modern perspective we might expect godly piety to be at its most internalized, there is much to suggest that reading provided a communal bond between evangelical teenagers. Of course, much of the evidence here, at times of spiritual conversion, tends to contrast the desires of individuals against the conservative impulses of their parents. As a young girl, Elizabeth Cary, Lady Falkland (1585–1639), the aristocrat who would become notorious for her conversion to Catholicism during the reign of Charles I, 'spent her whole time in reading, to which she gave herself so much that she frequently redd all night'. Her mother attempted to foil this nocturnal reading by forbidding the servants from giving her candles – as it happened to no avail, as the servants saw the opportunity to make a handsome profit by selling the candles to Elizabeth at half a crown a piece, 'so was she bent to reading', and she had soon amassed a debt of one hundred pounds, which equates

---

any Children (London, 1646). For Rastrick's doubts on its applicability, see *The Life of John Rastrick*, p. 33: 'I remember before this he had bought me the School of Vertue, about youth's behaviour wher I was taught to put Lord Protector instead of King in one of the Prayers: and he brought me from Boston once a small catechism of Mr Cotton's called Milk for Boston Babes when I was so young and childish as to be troubled that it was not for Heckington babes, and thought it was not for me'.

[65] *The Life of John Rastrick*, p. 33. Arthur Dent, *The plaine mans path-way to heaven* (London, 1601); Daniel Dyke, *The Mystery of Self-Deceiving. Or a Discourse . . . of the Deceitfulnesse of Man's Heart* (London, 1615).

to eight hundred candles.[66] Likewise, Christopher Love, the presbyterian clergyman who was executed in 1651 for conspiring with royalists, stressed the strength of his youthful devotion, despite the presence of a father uneasy at the pitch of his son's fervour. Inevitably, this led to conflict. With a charismatic puritan preacher in town and fearing the worst, Love's father locked Christopher in the attic. Nevertheless, Christopher 'ventured his life by tying a cord to the window sliding downe by it' and hurried to the sermon regardless.[67] In a similar vein, in his autobiography Richard Baxter looked back on his own intimate spiritual friendship with a young man while he was a teenage pupil of Richard Wickstead in Ludlow: 'We walk'd together, we read together, we prayed together, and when we could we lay together', wrote Baxter. Despite the friend's subsequent departure from the path of godliness – he succumbed to drink – Baxter reminisced fondly about the friend who was 'a daily Watchman over [his] soul' and who was 'unwearied in reading all serious Practical Books of Divinity; especially *Perkins, Bolton, Dr. Preston, Elton, Dr. Taylor, Whately, Harris,* &c.'.[68] Such anecdotes might suggest that we would be right to contrast the communal sermon experience with the interior and solitary experience of reading. But this should be resisted. Even with such a father, Christopher Love engaged in rounds of nocturnal Bible-reading and prayer in his bedchamber with a godly friend after dark.[69] Secret piety might be neither individual nor internal, merely contrasted against the wishes of parents or authority.

But social reading in the youthful bedchamber could also reinforce authority. This is particularly clear among the godly at the start of the seventeenth century, when several possessed teenagers, their bodies and souls torn in a conflict between God and the Devil, were read to as part of a routine of semi-legitimate measures to perform a godly exorcism. In such cases the bedchamber, or the parlour turned into a kind of sickroom with a bed in it, could serve as a public venue for communal

[66] See *Elizabeth Cary Lady Falkland: Life and Letters*, ed. Heather Wolfe (Cambridge, 2001), p. 108. Although Cary famously converted to Catholicism – and her life is explicitly framed within the parameters of conversion – she was brought up as a Calvinist. In this instance, however, feeding the youth with Calvinist theology backfired. Elizabeth found numerous faults in the text when her father gave her a copy of Calvin's *Institutes* at the age of twelve (so many that he said she had 'a spirit averse from Calvin'). And later, at the age of twenty, it was her reading of Hooker's *Laws of Ecclesiastical Polity* which prompted her first doubts as to the truth of Protestantism, doubts which would later lead to her conversion to Catholicism. Ibid., pp. 108, 110–11.
[67] BL, Sloane MS 3945 ('The Life of Mr. Christopher Love'), fo. 80r.
[68] See *Reliquiæ Baxterianæ: or, Mr. Richard Baxter's Narrative of the Most Memorable Passages of his Life and Times*, ed. Matthew Sylvester (London, 1696), part i, p. 4.
[69] BL, Sloane MS 3945 ('The Life of Mr. Christopher Love'), fo. 81v.

reading.[70] Thus the fourteen-year-old Mary Glover, who hailed from a godly family in the parish of St Helen's, Bishopsgate, and who suffered spectacular fits of possession in 1602, was cured through rounds of communal prayer and communal reading. On 14 December 1602, a group of twenty-four people, including six preachers, met early in the morning at the house of one Mistriss Ratcliff in Shoreditch. Mary Glover made her own way into the parlour, which was furnished with a small settle and a bed next to the fireside, and sat down. Armed with a Bible, she turned to the chapters the preachers prescribed and was an active participant in the communal reading designed to alleviate her condition. Her participation in the shared reading of the sacred text was crucial both in giving the occasion legitimacy in the godly community and in the eventual cure. As one of the godly accounts of the case recalled:

if she at any time failed, either by greife of body, or infirmity of mynde, or meditation, or by fayling of sight (which seemed sometimes so to be, by the rubbinge of her eyes with her hand) then a woman sittinge by, was ready alwayes in that behalfe to helpe her, especially at the instance of the Preachers, who directinge their speaches many times to her by name, would call uppon her to turne to the place alleaged, and so would stay till she had found it.

The example shows the importance of communal reading in the bed-chamber, while also illustrating the textuality of exorcism, a point under-scored when, at the very moment the devil left Mary, she repeated the words that her martyred grandfather had used at the stake and which were preserved in Foxe's *Book of Martyrs*.[71]

On the cusp of adulthood and independence, reading in the bedcham-ber continued to be a fusion of individual and communal experiences. At university, chamber-fellows struck up bookish relationships, discussing authors and texts together in their bedchambers. John Rastrick profited much from the inquisitiveness of his chamber-fellow at Trinity College, Cambridge. He introduced Rastrick to Clarke's *Martyrology* and *Lives*, which he had borrowed from the college library, and frequently engaged in discussion of the merits of godly books.[72] Such discussion might be the

---

[70] Further instances of reading and possession in the context of textual activity in the parlour are discussed in Chapter 3 below.

[71] See John Swan, *A True and Breife Report, of Mary Glovers Vexation, and of her Deliverance by the Meanes of Fastinge and Prayer* (London, 1603), pp. 8–10, 47 and *passim*; for more detailed discussion of communal reading and demonic possession, see Andrew Cambers, 'Demonic Possession, Literacy, and "Superstition" in Early Modern England', *Past and Present*, 202 (2009), pp. 3–35.

[72] Samuel Clarke, *A Generall Martyrology ... Whereunto are Added, The Lives of Sundry Modern Divines etc* (London, 1651).

precursor to silent, individual reading, but the chamber could also provide a venue for explicitly communal reading, usually of scripture. Rastrick repeated sermon notes in his tutor's chamber on Sunday evenings, to the derision of his fellow students.[73] Such communal reading in a semi-private space was indicative of the experience for the godly at university. Oliver Heywood was a regular participant in the communal reading of lectures and prayers with his fellow students and tutor in his tutor's rooms at night.[74] As a practice, it appears to have been voluntary, and thus to have attracted the scorn of outsiders. It is in character with what we know about the informal education at those Cambridge colleges associated with early Stuart puritanism, such as Emmanuel and Sidney Sussex, dubbed by William Laud 'the nurseries of puritanism', but attracted special attention after the Restoration when to outsiders it smacked of illegal conventicling.[75]

In adulthood, reading in the bedchamber continued to be both individual and communal. At first glance, many diaristic and autobiographical accounts seem to confirm our modern notions of bedchamber reading being a solitary and nocturnal experience. Edmund Harrold, the melancholic Manchester wigmaker and enthusiastic part-time book-trader best known to historians for his remarks about his heavy drinking and rampant sex life, also read over religious books and sermons, bit by bit, at night before he went to bed. These works spanned a range of ecclesiastical positions, and their authors ranged from trenchant Anglicans to die-hard nonconformists, but Harrold read most often books of a moderate religious position, whichever side of the conformist divide they happened to be on. Perhaps because it reminded him that the fruits of religion were ultimately sweeter than the pleasures of the flesh, he appears to have drawn particular comfort at night from reading William Sherlock's *A practical discourse concerning death*, a massive popular treatise on death which focused on dealing with the fear of death.[76] On one occasion, scolded by his wife for coming to bed drunk and unable to settle down, Harrold got up and read an edifying sermon by John Norris (1657–1712).[77]

---

[73] *The Life of John Rastrick*, pp. 51, 58.   [74] Heywood, *Diaries*, vol. I, p. 159.

[75] See Sarah Bendall, Christopher Brooke and Patrick Collinson (eds.), *A History of Emmanuel College, Cambridge* (Woodbridge, 2000), esp. pp. 56–90, 177–226; David Reynolds (ed.), *Christ's: A Cambridge College over Five Centuries* (London, 2005); Tom Webster, *Godly Clergy in Early Stuart England: The Caroline Puritan Movement c.1620–1643* (Cambridge, 1997).

[76] Heywood, *Diaries, passim*; Craig Horner (ed.), *The Diary of Edmund Harrold, Wigmaker of Manchester 1712–15* (Aldershot, 2008), pp. 10, 18, 23, 26, 27, 28, 30, 31, 33. William Sherlock, *A Practical Discourse Concerning Death* (London, 1689, and many later editions).

[77] Horner, *The Diary of Edmund Harrold*, pp. 43–4.

Others, like Henry Newcome, whose nocturnal reading we have already mentioned, read in bed. For John Rastrick, returning home to Lincolnshire after taking his degree, and now with a room of his own, bed provided the most welcome venue to engage in scholarly reading, and he would read there until three or four o'clock in the morning.[78] Taking up his first post as curate at Fosdyke, Lincolnshire, in 1671, he continued the practice, devoting evenings to 'private and undisturbed Studys' in his bedchamber. This literally gave Rastrick cold feet – the bedchamber lacked a fire – but he was warmed by the refuge the room provided from the lazy divine there who simply urged him to read his sermons out of standard works.[79] And perhaps especially for godly clergy, the bedchamber would remain a reserved place of reading as well as sleeping throughout their lives. Foremost among the long-lived members of the godly – and an advert for a sober lifestyle – was the figurehead Laurence Chaderton (c.1536–1640), who even in his final years was able to read for many hours at a time, untroubled by fatigue and without the need for spectacles.[80]

There are, of course, several accounts of recreational bedchamber reading. Sir Kenelm Digby perused *Religio Medici* in bed,[81] while Henry Newcome read over some of Robert Wild's 'comedy of the benefice' and his verses on Calamy's imprisonment,[82] together with Samuel Butler's *Hudibras*.[83] But such reading, for the godly, could often lead to trouble. Richard Bovet, for instance, included in his *Pandaemonium* the story of a Dorset falconer who was 'very fond of a Book by night', especially

---

[78] *The Life of John Rastrick*, p. 69.   [79] *The Life of John Rastrick*, p. 81.

[80] As Samuel Clarke related, 'A little before his death, an old Servant of his came to see him, and found him reading in a Book'. Chaderton took a moment to notice the servant's entrance but upon asking the time – it was eleven o'clock in the evening – he said 'I have … here got a Book that I have been reading of ever since eight a Clock'. Such feats of reading were evidence of the heroic faith of the godly and, wrote Clarke, all the more remarkable because Chaderton had 'all that time … read without Spectacles'. See Clarke, *The Lives of Thirty-Two English Divines*, p. 147.

[81] Digby noted reading in bed in his *Observations Upon Religio Medici* (London, 1643), cited in Steven N. Zwicker, 'Habits of Reading and Early Modern Literary Culture', in David Loewenstein and Janel Mueller (eds.), *The Cambridge History of Early Modern English Literature* (Cambridge, 2002), p. 175, which also contains other examples of bedchamber reading.

[82] Robert Wild, *The Benefice: A Comedy* (London, 1689); Robert Wild, *A Poem upon the Imprisonment of Mr. Calamy* (London, 1663).

[83] Thomas Heywood (ed.), *The Diary of the Rev. Henry Newcome, from September 30, 1661, to September 29, 1663*, Chetham Society, 1st ser., 18 (Manchester, 1849), pp. 160, 157; Samuel Butler, *Hudibras* (London, 1663). Newcome disliked the 'senseless poem Hudibras. He would be wicked but is without wit'. Interestingly, he read both Butler and Wild in the piecemeal fashion in which he read godly works, and he interspersed his reading of these works with the usual rounds of godly reading. For Wild's poetry as an intervention in the religious politics of the Restoration, see George Southcombe, 'The Responses of Nonconformists to the Restoration in England' (unpublished DPhil thesis, Oxford University, 2005), pp. 44–99.

'because he seldom found the other, who was his Bedfellow, in a humour to discourse'. One night, neglecting conversation with his drunken room-mate, the falconer 'betook himself to a certain Book he had got out of the Chaplain's Chamber, who used to lend him one at times, to incourage him in reading'. Unfortunately it was 'the wrong sort for the poor Falconer' and he had barely started reading in it when he caught a glimpse of a creature by the side of his bed which would only depart when the chaplain returned. The moral, wrote Bovet, was that 'Some People, by perusing unlawful Studies, have put themselves in the power of Evil Spirits'.[84] Likewise, Bovet related another insight into bedchamber reading when telling the story 'Of divers strange Appearances of Spirits in a Noblemans House in the West'. While visiting this house, which had once been a nunnery – quite to the opposite of his intentions, Bovet's stories have the narrative flair and ghoulish settings of later gothic novels – Bovet shared a bedroom with the nobleman's steward. The two, who were evidently early to retire to bed, made use of the roaring fire in the chamber by sitting up reading. After they were in bed and the candles out, and with the room at least partially illuminated by moonlight, the two had a bet as to whether 'it was possible to read written hand by that light upon the Bed where we lay'. Bovet swiftly took a manuscript out of his pocket and the steward read it, winning the bet. But such reading was far from harmless. It seems to have prompted the appearance in their room (although it was locked) of a procession of 'five … lovely Women', dressed as nuns. The first came right up to Bovet and struck him on his left arm which had been hanging out of the bed. Shocked, Bovet grabbed the steward but as soon as he asked him whether he also saw them, the apparitions disappeared. Determined to prove that he was indeed seeing things, Bovet stayed in the same room the following night. Bovet 'ordered a Bible, and another Book to be laid in the Room', and read by the fire until he felt himself falling asleep shortly after one o'clock in the morning. No sooner had he got into bed than he heard what he thought was 'like a Woman with a Tabby Gown trailing about the Room'. Alarmed at this rustling sound, Bovet got up, opened the curtains and opened the door of the adjoining closet, where he saw the groaning apparition dragging a large chair and 'turn[ing] over the leaves of a large Folio' until the morning.[85] Although hardly describing an everyday event, Bovet certainly provides an

---

[84] Richard Bovet, *Pandaemonium: or, The Devil's Cloyster. Being a Further Blow to Modern Sadduceism, Proving the Existence of Witches and Spirits* (London, 1684), pp. 197–8.
[85] Ibid., pp. 202–6.

insight into night-time reading and perhaps too the tricks played by the imagination as the firelight flickered across the pages of a book. Whatever unwelcome guests might emerge in the process, reading in bed was obviously a form of textual activity with which seventeenth-century people were familiar.

But the staple of the bedchamber was the scriptural text and the godly sermon. And although many diarists recorded reading such edifying literature in the bedchamber, the precise nature of this reading is often hard to discern. In the middle of the night, it could be the meditative, godly equivalent of counting sheep. When he lay awake in the night, the prominent puritan preacher William Gouge 'used in his thoughts to run through divers Chapters of the Scripture in order, as if he had heard them read to him; and by this means he deceived the tediousness of his waking'.[86] Likewise, the martyr John Bradford, whose exemplary life was preserved for the godly in Foxe's *Actes and Monuments*, 'slept not commonly above foure houres in the night: & in his bedde till sleep came, his booke went not out of his hand'.[87] But for others, reading in the bedchamber could be social. Such reading clearly had precedents in the activities of those early Protestants whose lives the godly returned to again and again in the pages of Foxe. The remarkable table of early Protestant readers in Lincolnshire in 1521, which appeared in *Actes and Monuments*, paid testimony to the excitement of such night-time reading. John and Richard Butler, along with W. King, 'sate up all the night in the house . . . reading all the night of a Booke of Scripture'.[88] And for generations of godly readers, reading in the bedchamber continued to be a social activity. Henry Newcome, for example, read in Mr Illingworth's chamber, which was lined with books.[89] And the boundaries of such reading are frequently unclear. Particular caution needs to be taken with those who recorded reading 'alone'. This could mean solitary practice but it could also be used to signify reading in small groups. Matthew Henry, for example, differentiated between reading 'alone' – that is, with his wife – and reading with his wider family.[90]

Reading in the bedchamber was not without its dangers. Henry Newcome almost burnt his house down, John Rastrick caught a chill, and Simon Patrick sat up reading so late that it 'brought upon . . . a sore

[86] Clarke, *The Lives of Thirty-Two English Divines*, p. 235.
[87] *Actes and Monuments* (1583), p. 1604.   [88] Ibid., p. 824.
[89] Heywood (ed.), *The Diary of the Rev. Henry Newcome*, pp. 82, 133.
[90] See Matthew Henry Lee (ed.), *Diaries and Letters of Philip Henry of Broad Oak, Flintshire, 1631–1696* (London, 1882), p. 103, for this distinction.

disease, the haemorrhoids, with which I was so afflicted, that I was forced to lay aside my books, and wholly mind my health'.[91] However, the bedchamber was also frequently a venue for reading to the sick. Whether in the hope of medical remedy, or spiritual alleviation, such reading provides an important, if not an everyday, example of how adult reading in the bedchamber could be oral and communal. Certainly, reading to heal the sick was advised in godly how-to literature and sermons. Gilbert Freville, of Bishop Middleham, County Durham, for example, noted those parts of scripture which his preacher had recommended be read by (or to) the sick, including Luke 22:23, Psalms 29, 42, 51 and 143, John 14, Revelation 7, and I Corinthians 15.[92] And many did indeed read appropriate texts while ill. The manner of this reading is illuminating. For some, especially the clergy, reading while ill or recovering from illness was simply the only spiritual work that could be done. Laid up with pleurisy, Henry Newcome 'lay in bed & read the reasons against Toleration of Popery'.[93] For Oliver Heywood, who read Richard Baxter's *Gildas Salvianus* (London, 1656) while ill in the late 1650s, this reading seems to have formed part of an internal and personal programme of spiritual recovery.[94] Likewise, when her husband's fits of pain and suffering disrupted her spiritual routine, Mary Rich simply adapted it to meet the circumstances. In her diary entry for 14 October 1667, for example, she noted:

in the morneing as sone as upe I retired and meditated but my Lord being still full of violent paine I had not so much time as usuall for my devotiones, but in prayer my heart did breath after God in the afternoone stirr'd not from my Lord but whilst he slept I red in the word, and whilst I was readeing of Hesekias message . . . my heart was much affected to thinke if I had such a message sent me how I should be prepared for it.[95]

While she occasionally read aloud to her husband from works of history, her usual method of reading in the bedchamber was to wait until he went to sleep and to get on with her own scriptural or quasi-scriptural reading

[91] Alexander Taylor (ed.), *The Works Of Symon Patrick, D.D. Sometime Bishop of Ely, Including His Autobiography* (9 vols., Oxford, 1858), vol. IX., p. 427.

[92] BL, Egerton MS 2877 (Commonplace-Book of Gilbert Freville), fo. 89r.

[93] Heywood (ed.), *The Diary of the Rev. Henry Newcome*, p. 170.

[94] Heywood, *Diaries*, vol. I, p. 177; vol. II, p. 142; more generally, see Roy Porter, 'Reading: A Health Warning', in Robin Myers and Michael Harris (eds.), *Medicine, Mortality and the Book Trade* (Folkestone, 1998), pp. 131–52.

[95] BL, Additional MSS 27351-5 (Diaries of Mary Rich, Countess of Warwick, 5 vols., 1666–77), vol. I, fo. 145r.

which the severity of his illness had obviously disrupted.[96] Such reading contrasts with those for whom sickbed reading was distinctly communal and designed specifically to aid recovery. Henry Newcome recounted in his abstract the story of one Mrs Hallows, who, suffering from breast cancer in 1695, was visited by a Mr Heyward. On his arrival Mrs Hallows 'betook herself to her bible, and diverted her pain by shewing him the texts that comforted her'.[97]

In the majority of cases, the character of reading in the bedchamber during illness was recognizably communal and social. The example from the earliest surviving diary of Anne Clifford – whose aristocratic reading was characteristically presented as 'work'[98] – brings the experience to life. In October 1619, Anne caught a severe chill that kept her confined to her bedchamber until March 1620. Although the severity of this illness makes it more likely that the diary entries covering this period were in fact written after she had recovered, the communal nature of reading in the bedchamber is conspicuous. Sir Francis Slingsby visited Anne and read from 'the Sea Papers about my Father's Voyages'.[99] Listening to others reading about histories and sea voyages was likely to have been a welcome distraction for Anne: the recreational nature of such reading is evident when she was read to while games were played in the bedchamber.[100] Nevertheless, these rounds of oral reading were also both educational and devotional. A servant read 'Leicester's Commonwealth' to her, and she was struck by the description which it related of the fate of Mary Queen of Scots, even if she did not comment on its (admittedly dated) ideological positioning. And the same servant read to her from Josephus.[101] Even Mary Rich, who otherwise soldiered on with her reading while she had severe headaches, had people read aloud to her in her bedchamber. On 30 August 1673, for example, she had Simon Patrick's *The Hearts Ease*, fittingly a volume explicitly designed 'to prevent immoderate grief for the death of our friends', read to her while she was ill.[102] What is striking

---

[96] Ibid., vol. 1, fo. 282v. For an instance of her reading Baxter while he slept, see vol. 2, fo. 14v: 'whilst he slept I had time to read in Mr Baxters booke of the Saintes rest, with which my heart was much affected'.

[97] R. Parkinson (ed.), *The Autobiography of Henry Newcome*, Chetham Society, 26, 27, (2 vols., paged continuously, Manchester, 1852), p. 284.

[98] Clifford, *The Diaries of Lady Anne Clifford*, p. 43.

[99] Ibid., p. 86.   [100] Ibid., p. 87.

[101] Ibid., pp. 86–7; see also Dwight C. Peck (ed.), *Leicester's Commonwealth: The Copy of a Letter Written by a Master of Art at Cambridge (1584) and Related Documents* (Athens, OH, 1985).

[102] BL, Additional MSS 27351–5 (Diaries of Mary Rich, Countess of Warwick, 5 vols., 1666–77), vol. II, fo. 83r; vol. III, fo. 217v, and for further examples, see vol. IV, fo. 7r; Simon Patrick, *The Hearts Ease, or A Remedy against all Troubles. To which is Added a Consolatory Discourse against the Loss of our Friends and those that are Dear unto us* (London, 1660).

about this reading is that it confirms the bedchamber as a semi-public space in which communal reading could occur.

Elizabeth Isham's autobiography provides ample evidence of the reading that was performed while her mother and later her sister were ill. Indeed, so sharp is her focus on detailing this reading that we can assume that it played a particularly important part in her style of puritan piety. Such reading was distinctly familial and a key component of the culture of puritanism. When Elizabeth was eight years old and her mother sick, her grandmother read 'good books' to her mother in her bedchamber 'wherein they rejoyced together' before God. Elizabeth learned that such reading alleviated the symptoms of spiritual illness. When her mother fell ill again, this time troubled by melancholy and assaulted by Satan, Psalms were read aloud to her, often long into the night. The illness kept her mother confined in her chamber for an extended period of time and expert advice was sought, in the form of the godly guru John Dod, who was a regular visitor to the household and a key influence on the Ishams' familial piety. Dod, who had 'a singuler gift in comforting afflicted consciences', prescribed a spiritual cure. As Elizabeth explained, 'Mr. Dod appointed my selfe Sister & Brother to read 2 chapters a day the one in the Old Testament in the morning & the other in the New at night'. The puritan leader recommended communal reading to cure the sick, and Elizabeth noted that she would sometimes select particularly suitable chapters for her mother's condition, at which her mother was moved, sometimes wanting them said 'in her eare'. This same pattern of reading occurred when Elizabeth's sister was troubled with 'the mother', the medical condition in which the womb was displaced and which was frequently accompanied by severe fits. This condition was exacerbated by their mother's death and compounded by the assaults of Satan, 'her spirituall adversary'. But by now Elizabeth had learned how to calm such spiritual illness. As she recalled, 'I perceved her spirits was much raised with reading to her those Bookes or places wherein she delighted'.[103]

Likewise, after suffering a prolonged bout of severe toothache in March 1600, and being fed with 'diverse medesons that did litle profett', Lady Margaret Hoby began to recover when she implored 'Mr Hoby to read

[103] Princeton University Library, MS RTC01 (no. 62) (Elizabeth Isham, 'My Booke of Rememberance'), fos. 4r, 11r, 11v, 12r, 22r.

some of perkines to me'.[104] In part, textual healing substituted for the
traditional therapeutic repertoire provided by sacramentals which was no
longer available to the godly.[105] It also overlapped with individual reading
while recovering from illness. Immediately after her husband had read to
her, Lady Hoby read (perhaps aloud) 'as Longe as I coulde my selfe'.[106]
The link between reading and illness was explicit, with Lady Hoby noting
in her diary, for instance, that she 'did read for a whill for beinge not
well'.[107] Such reading was sometimes individual and sometimes not, often
depending on the severity of the illness. In particularly bad cases, she was
always read to, either by her husband, by one of her godly boarders or by
her chaplain, Richard Rhodes.[108] Such reading was invariably in Lady
Hoby's bedchamber. When others in the household were ill, she recipro-
cated with rounds of religious reading, as she did on 24 May 1601 when
she 'reed, tell church time, to a sicke maid in my house'.[109]

The communal nature of reading in Lady Hoby's bedchamber might
be extended to several entries from her diary in which she appears to have
described how she read scriptural and godly texts to cure herself of the
temptations of Satan. Lady Hoby wrote of suffering 'satan … his buffets'
and 'satan buffetts' in her entries for 18 July and 1 August 1602.[110] Many of
her entries and the notes made alongside them chronicled the temptations
made to her by the Devil. Plagued by temptation, she often plunged
herself into charitable and religious activity – dressing her patients, talking
with neighbours and reading, writing letters or making notes in her
sermon book.[111] Particularly tormented in January 1600, Lady Hoby
appears to have used reading to drive away Satan. After suffering devilish
discomfort, she 'reed in perkins tell I went againe to the Church, wher
I found the Lord to assisst me most graciously from the malice of my
enemie'. A round of communal reading followed on her return, including
Thomas Hoby reading from Cartwright and, the following day, Richard
Rhodes reading to her from a book 'against some newe sprange herisies'.
Such reading, of course, alerts us to the areas of overlap between godly
and traditional practices, however they manifested themselves, but also to

[104] Moody, *The Private Life of an Elizabethan Lady*, p. 65. For an extended analysis of Lady Hoby's
   reading and illness, see Cambers, 'Print, Manuscript and Godly Cultures', pp. 78–82.
[105] For a parallel process for the ways women in childbirth dealt with the loss of recourse to the Virgin
   Mary, see Mary E. Fissel, *Vernacular Bodies: The Politics of Reproduction in Early Modern England*
   (Oxford, 2004), Chapter 1.
[106] Moody, *The Private Life of an Elizabethan Lady*, p. 65.   [107] Ibid., p. 31.
[108] Ibid., pp. 47, 59–60, 135 and *passim*.   [109] Ibid., p. 148.   [110] Ibid., p. 182.
[111] Ibid., p. 62.

the quasi-scriptural qualities of the godly canon – it was by reading and hearing Perkins and Cartwright that relief was gained.[112]

In old age, communal reading in the bedchamber became more pronounced. Just as Titus wanted his family to read to him in his closet, because his son's eyes were better than his, so others were read to at the bedside by those better able to perform the task. Those in search of spiritual solace often lacked energy and, in the final stages of life, perfect eyesight. Of course, many had put up with bad eyesight throughout their lives and spectacles with convex lenses to alleviate far-sightedness were only available to those with at least moderate levels of disposable income.[113] Although there are notable instances of the godly encouraging the old to read, most memorably that of Samuel Fairclough, who 'when the sight of old people was decayed . . . would furnish them with Bibles of a larger print' and who 'gave an incredible number of spectacles away (for their help)', elderly readers seldom mentioned using spectacles to read.[114] And the technology available meant that spectacles could not help many who would have needed them – James Ussher, for one, could get no help with his failing eyesight in his final weeks, so he had people read books aloud to him instead.[115] Ussher, of course, as an archbishop who was deferential to royal authority, can hardly stand for the godly as a whole, but in old age many of them did indeed continue with the devotional modes of communal reading we have seen elsewhere. Anne Clifford's reading in the last few months of her life mirrored that of her own godly upbringing in its record of communal devotional reading. Every Wednesday and Sunday, the parson Samuel Grasty visited and, usually after being

---

[112] Ibid., p. 54.

[113] See Andrew Pettegree, *Reformation and the Culture of Persuasion* (Cambridge, 2005), pp. 107–9; for an overview on spectacles, see Alan Macfarlane and Gerry Martin, *The Glass Bathyscape: How Glass Changed the World* (London, 2002), Chapter 8, 'Spectacles and Predicaments', pp. 144–74. Spectacles were probably cheaper than Pettegree suggests, judging by the evidence of the inventory of the Foster bookshop in York in 1616, whose unsold stock included twenty-one pairs of 'Christall Spectacles', valued at 10 s, and forty pairs 'of green glass', valued at 9 s. See Robert Davies, *A Memoir of the York Press: with Notices of Authors, Printers, and Stationers, in the Sixteenth, Seventeenth, and Eighteenth Centuries* (Facsimile reprint, York, 1988; original edn Westminster, 1868), pp. 370–1.

[114] Samuel Clarke, *The Lives of Sundry Eminent Persons in this Latter Age* (London, 1683), p. 180. It is possible that there was a certain stigma attached to wearing spectacles, presumably because they tampered with God's design for life. On the stage, they were frequently associated with the Devil, poisoners, Jesuits and the frivolous elite. See, for example, Robert Davenport, *A Pleasant and Witty Comedy: Called, A New Tricke to Cheat the Divell* (London, 1639); John Webster, *The White Devil* (London, 1612); Thomas Middleton, *A Game at Chæss* (London, 1625). For the epistemology of vision and its connection with the demonic, see Stuart Clark, *Vanities of the Eye: Vision in Early Modern European Culture* (Oxford, 2007), esp. pp. 123–60.

[115] Clarke, *The Lives of Thirty-Two English Divines*, p. 298.

fed, would withdraw to Anne's bedchamber with her family and any visitors and would there read aloud from the Book of Common Prayer, then read a chapter of the Bible, and finally sing a Psalm. The entries in Anne's diary described communal scripture reading as routine: 'there dined here also Mr Samuel Grasty, our parson, and after dinner he came into my chamber and said Common Prayers (as usuall upon Wednesdays) and read a Chapter to mee and them and my family'.[116] Although routinized, such entries suggest the extent of communal reading, the interplay between the written and the spoken word and the overlap between such reading and the practice of prayer. They also anticipate the more obvious forms of familial reading which will be examined in the next chapter.

A final form of bedchamber reading was that which occurred around the godly deathbed. Communal reading appears to have been an intrinsic element of the Calvinist take on the *ars moriendi* and, although modern commentators have had little to say about the nature of this reading, they certainly acknowledge its existence and it was a familiar enough practice to be depicted in godly ballads.[117] A woodcut illustrating the popular 'A hundred godly lessons that a mother on her death-bed gave to her children' presented the dying mother in a moment which combined communal reading and family prayer.[118] The image of communal prayer and reading, presumably from the Bible, was repeated in the woodcuts illustrating other godly ballads like 'The clarke of Bodnam', which is described by Tessa Watt. Although Watt argues that the words of such ballads are hardly theologically distinctive, and notably silent on issues of election and predestination, it is suggestive that the woodcuts used to illustrate them closely resemble the descriptions of communal family reading and prayer at the heart of the godly experience. It is also instructive that the image is a reproduction of one used earlier in the seventeenth

[116] Clifford, *The Diaries of Lady Anne Clifford*, p. 272. For other examples, see pp. 243, 244, 246, and 239–80.

[117] Ralph Houlbrooke, for instance, notes but does not describe the nature of the scriptural reading that happened around the deathbed. See Ralph Houlbrooke, *Death, Religion, and the Family in England, 1480–1750* (Oxford, 1998), p. 192. For Calvinism's translation of the Ars Moriendi, see M. Claire Cross, 'The Third Earl of Huntingdon's Death-Bed: A Calvinist Example of the "Ars Moriendi"', *Northern History*, 21 (1985), pp. 80–107. The longevity of such forms of deathbed behaviour is rarely discussed but there are clear continuities among evangelicals across the seventeenth century and beyond. See Richard Bell, '"Our People Die Well": Deathbed Scenes in John Wesley's Arminian Magazine', *Mortality*, 10 (2005), pp. 210–23.

[118] *A Hundred Godly Lessons. That a Mother on her Death-Bed Gave to her Children, whereby They may Know how to Guide Themselves towards God and Man, to the Benefit of the Common-Wealth, Joy of their Parents, and Good of Themselves* (London, c. 1674–9).

century, thus underscoring the continuities in styles of godly piety over the long seventeenth century.[119]

Such prayers at the deathbed were not always spontaneous and personal. Sometimes, they were based on models from books and were used communally around the deathbed. Alice Thornton's affectionate description of her mother's death blends extempore prayer and communal reading. She recalled how her mother frequently repeated the 71st Psalm in the days before death and chose both the preacher and the texts (Revelation 14:13) for her funeral. Like many others, her mother used prayer as a means to speed the process along, singing 'all that Friday night ... "*Come, Lord Jesus, come quickly*"'. But she also made her servant 'pray with her that praier of Dr Smith made in his booke for a person at the point to die; and tooke great notice of each pettition, praing with zeale and ardency'.[120] Such examples show how prayer at the deathbed could intersect with non-scriptural communal reading.

Other texts might also be demanded on the deathbed. For some of the godly, the fact that they were dying could not be allowed to interrupt their work. The influential puritan scholar and preacher Thomas Gataker (1574–1654), for example, after telling those friends who visited him and hoped he would recover 'not to expect Miracles', got back to his proper work – checking over drafts for Richard Baxter.[121] Intriguingly, others asked for their diaries. The Welsh baptist Vavasor Powell, in a sickness he feared would be his last, wished to consult his diary, presumably to judge the state of his soul. Although he might have wanted this to be an individual encounter, it was not, because he had 'lent it to a Christian Friend that was far distant'.[122] Such lending tempers opinions that puritan diaries were purely personal but it also shows that in their final hours many were preoccupied with the sins committed in their lifetime. Reading over such records provided spiritual comfort. At the very end of his life, Henry Newcome read over a volume in which he had made an abstract of his previous diaries. Though he knew his own life was ending, his rereading gave him comfort. He recorded the rereading in his diary:

---

[119] See Tessa Watt, *Cheap Print and Popular Piety, 1550–1640* (Cambridge, 1991), pp. 101–2, 104–9. Watt argues that (the words of) these ballads are not theologically distinctive, and do not deal with predestination, or mention the elect, yet the images closely resemble those described by more obviously godly families.

[120] *The Autobiography of Mrs Alice Thornton*, pp. 100–16, quotation at p. 109.

[121] Clarke, *The Lives of Thirty-Two English Divines*, pp. 258–9. This reading was clearly part of the wider godly pattern of continuing to work until the moment of death.

[122] Edward Bagshaw, *The Life and Death of Mr Vavasor Powell* (London, 1671), p. 12.

Aug 25 1695, I read in the abstract of my Diary some things that might be of use to me, from what I found of God's love in the days of old: and he is the same, and his compassions fail not. Decline I do sensibly.[123]

That this was not entirely private is suggested by the fact that his son Henry transcribed his final entries into the abstract. Certainly, the interpretative waters are rather murky when evidence that can be used as internal and individual (in its words) can simultaneously be thought of as social and communal (in its use).

But by far the most common of the books read at the deathbed was the Bible. Of course, many such moments were individual, or at least appear as such, mediated as they are through sources which privilege the individual's life story and autonomy, such as diaries, biographies, and funeral sermons. For many of the godly, to read the Bible was the essential preparation for a good death. The strongly Protestant Lady Elizabeth Jobson, half-sister of Robert Dudley and wife to Sir Francis Jobson, the Lord lieutenant of the Tower, was treated by the queen's physicians as she lay dying in 1569 so that she could prolong her devotional life for just a few more days. Sound in mind, she spent the additional time tied to her book. According to the imprisoned merchant and amateur chemist Clement Draper (c.1541–1620), who was told of her treatment by her son and remarked upon it in his notebooks, this gave her opportunity for 'muche Comfortable talke' before she 'died, her booke in her handes, and was readinge'.[124] For those who were beset with spiritual doubts, the Bible could be a supremely emotional object, as well as text. Katherine Brettergh, the sister of John Bruen who gained fame for the intensity of her godly deathbed temptations, could not bear to have it near her, so much did it confirm to her the gravity of her own sins. She threw it away from her, saying 'it was indeede the booke of life, but she had read the same unprofitably, and therefore feared it was to become to her the booke of death'.[125] The Bible, read aloud, was ultimately crucial in her triumph over these devilish doubts and it gave others, like Henry Hastings, the puritan Earl of Huntingdon, comfort when attending clergy read and prayed.[126] Such reading was clearly an oral and communal experience for the family as well as for the dying, as they were bound together by the text.

[123] Parkinson, *The Autobiography of Henry Newcome*, p. 286.
[124] The incident is sketched in Deborah E. Harkness, *The Jewel House: Elizabethan London and the Scientific Revolution* (New Haven, CT, 2007), pp. 199–200. For the quotation from Draper's account, see BL, MS Sloane 3690, fo. 88r–v.
[125] *A Brief Discourse of the Christian Life and Death, of Mistris Katherine Brettergh* (London, 1602), p. 12.
[126] Cross, 'The Third Earl of Huntingdon's Death-Bed'.

A particularly clear example can be seen in the Stockton household in Suffolk, and interestingly this transcends distinctions between individual and collective spirituality and textuality. Thus, in the hours before their eighteen-year-old daughter Elizabeth died in June 1677, the nonconformist minister Owen Stockton, his wife Elianor, and Elizabeth herself all gained succour from biblical texts. Uniquely, both mother and father recorded the incident in independent diaries and their diary entries reveal that although all three gained solace from the Bible, they did so through different passages. Although we may feel uneasy eavesdropping on a family and their grief, the moment encapsulates how Bible-reading in the bedchamber at death could be both individual and communal.[127]

THE STUDY

Further evidence of the reading of godly diarists can be seen in their activities in the study. This was a space apart, frequently given over to reading and writing.[128] As the Czech polymath Comenius put it in his influential textbook:

The Study is a place where a *Student*, a part from men, sitteth alone, addicted to his *Studies*, whilst he readeth *Books*, which being within his reach, he layeth open upon *a Desk* and picketh all the best things out of them into his own *Manual*, or marketh them in them with a dash, or *a little star*, in the *Margent*.[129]

For many, like Oliver Heywood, the study was a space for storing and using books and the majority of his book collection appears to have been permanently housed in the study. They might include borrowed books, as the godly clergyman and diarist Ralph Josselin noted in March 1657/8: 'I have parted with all the books out of my studdy that were borrowed of my friends, and am now left to my own stocke.'[130] Such recording, usually in diaries, appears to have been a kind of audit but it also lets us see inside the study and speculate on its use. Adam Eyre, the Yorkshire puritan

---

[127] The death is recorded in the diary of Owen Stockton, Dr Williams's Library, London, MS 24.7, p. 91; and in Elianor Stockton's diary, Dr Williams's Library, MS 24.8, fo. 18. For the Stocktons, I am indebted to Jeremy Schildt, '"God Put it into his Heart to Record it": Domestic Encounters with Scripture in Post-Restoration England', paper given at the Institute of Historical Research, London, 29 June 2006.

[128] For an excellent survey of the study, focused on the Italian 'studio' but with relevance to the early modern study more generally, see Dora Thornton, *The Scholar in His Study: Ownership and Experience in Renaissance Italy* (New Haven, CT, 1997).

[129] Joannes Amos Comenius, *Orbis sensualium pictus*, ed. James Bowen (Sydney, 1967), pp. 200–1. Cited in Love, *Scribal Publication in Seventeenth-Century England*, p. 222.

[130] Macfarlane, *The Diary of Ralph Josselin*, p. 420.

yeoman who had served in the parliamentarian army, provides an example, noting in his diary:

There are two books on my study bord which are none of myne, viz. Bateman upon Bartholomew, which is Oliver Roberts'; and the 3d volume of Crisp's Sermons, which is Mary Greaves' of Smallshaw, who hath two books of myne, one is Saltmarshes' Smoke in the Temple, and other things therewith bound up, and Mr Dell's Sermons; allso a little book or pamphlett, lying between the others, of Archer's of the Millenaryes, is Edward Smithe's. All the rest are my owne.[131]

Since the study was simultaneously a venue for reading and writing, it contained both furniture and the tools of the trade. Adam Eyre kept a box in his study and Ralph Josselin kept several, which appear to have been used to organize his writings and in particular to keep safe precious documents and papers, notably all the papers and witness statements which related to land disputes and his 'writings of Mallories' and his diary.[132] Oliver Heywood organized the notes of his own sermons which he had not already had stitched up into books into six thematically arranged bundles in March 1686 and placed them in 'the fir-deel box, under my desk in my study'. Heywood's study contained candles to work at night, together with pens, inks, paper and other materials.[133] A particularly important feature for this reading and writing space was the desk, which affords us some insight into how the study was used. Adam Eyre probably wrote his diary there, since he referred to his diary in his will as the 'long narrow booke lying on my study board'.[134] Furnishing their studies with desks and the materials of reading and writing, seventeenth-century readers appear recognizably modern, at least to scholarly models of reading. But such an image would be misleading. In particular, studies sometimes contained several desks which meant that the space could be one for communal reading and education. The London puritan artisan and prolific diarist Nehemiah Wallington gave his daughter Sarah a reading desk in his study at the age of fourteen and Philip Henry appears

[131] Adam Eyre, 'A Dyurnall, or Catalogue of all my Accions and Expences from the 1st of January, 1646–[7]', in *Yorkshire Diaries and Autobiographies in the Seventeenth and Eighteenth Centuries*, Surtees Society, 65 (Durham, 1875), pp. 23–4.
[132] Eyre, 'A Dyurnall, or Catalogue of all my Accions and Expences', pp. 62, 69; Macfarlane, *The Diary of Ralph Josselin*, p. 70. Thornton, *The Scholar in His Study*, notes the many functions of the study, from a place to hold an individual's books to a place to store family papers and to display collections of pictures.
[133] Heywood, *Diaries*, vol. II, p. 225; vol. I, p. 285.
[134] Eyre, 'A Dyurnall, or Catalogue of all my Accions and Expences', pp. 23, 355.

to have taught his children Hebrew in his study.[135] As much as the furniture suggests individual reading, and although the study was a space to which women often had only limited access, it is clear that studies served educational and communal purposes.[136]

Setting aside the aristocracy, for whom it might serve as an estate office, the study tended to be a relatively small and distinctly masculine room, especially common in the houses of the clergy. For them, it became both an essential space for the cultivation of a particularly intense and scholarly form of religiosity and a professional space, set apart and placed above the rest of the household and given over to the reading that their vocation demanded, notably that required for the composition of sermons. Studies were also found in the houses of the middling sort who aspired to a life of bookish devotion. Thus Nehemiah Wallington made space for a study, even though it involved utilizing a precarious loft space perched above the bedchamber.[137]

The demands of everyday life placed studies at the mercy of contingency. Thus Oliver Heywood, in a recognizably modern moment of interior rearrangement, transformed his son's chamber into a study on his departure to Frankland's Academy.[138] Few outside the very wealthy or childless could afford to sacrifice such valuable rooms. Instead they made do. Studies were commonly located above bedrooms, probably in attic spaces. This physical separation made them ideal spaces in which to cultivate godly piety. Nehemiah Wallington recalled such a Sunday routine: 'I did get up between three & foure a clocke in the morning & went up into my study to wrestle with the Lord (in holy prayr) as Jaakob

---

[135] See Wolfe, '"Sacred Imployments": Gendering Spiritual Space and Labour in the Clerical Household'. The presence of girls in their fathers' studies complicates the portrayal of the study as a strictly gendered space. Thornton, *The Scholar in His Study*, pp. 90, 94, argues that the study was an overwhelmingly masculine space and cites (at p. 96) the example of Edward Dering, who appears to have invited his wife into his study 'at chosen times' as a rare and unusual exception. See N. Krivatsky and L. Yeandle, 'Books of Sir Edward Dering of Kent, 1598–1644', in R. J. Fehrenbach and E. Leedham-Green (eds.), *Private Libraries in Renaissance England: A Collection and Catalogue of Tudor and Early Stuart Book-Lists, vol. 1: PLRE 1–4* (Binghamton, NY, 1992), p. 145.

[136] For Lady Margaret Hoby's caution over entering her husband's study, see Sir Erskine Perry (ed.), *The Van den Bempde Papers. The Bibliographical and Historical Miscellanies of the Philobiblion Society*, vol. XII (London, 1868–9), pp. 17–18.

[137] Thornton, *The Scholar in His Study*, p. 77, observes how studies were often found on mezzanine floors, on landings next to staircases. Those with less spacious houses made do with more precarious spaces above bedchambers and in attics.

[138] Heywood, *Diaries*, vol. II, p. 222. For further rearrangement, see *An Account Of The Life and Death Of Mr Philip Henry*, p. 50, which records that 'upon the removing of his Closet but from one Room in the House to another', Henry noted in his diary, 'this day ... my new Closet was *Consecrated*, if I may so say, with this Prayer; *That all the Prayers that ever should be made in it according to the Will of God, Morning, Evening and at Noon-Day, ordinary or extraordinary, might be accepted of God and obtain a gracious Answer, Amen and Amen*'.

did, and putting my mouth in the dust if so be their might be hope.'[139] This position, as a rather makeshift space above the bedchamber, appears to have been the norm. Ralph Josselin's study was an upper room, though this made it vulnerable to fires lit in the room below as well as to the elements.[140] Henry Newcome registered his surprise when rain started falling into his study, but this must have been a common enough experience for those who used an upper chamber for their books.[141] And, as Michelle Wolfe has argued, the position of the study served to stratify clerical marital arrangements, with the manly world of books and study set above the domestic, female and familial.[142]

Studies were central to godly identity. As Nehemiah Wallington fell asleep, it loomed large in his vision of the predicament of the godly: Wallington dreamt that as he opened his 'study doore for to go to praye, there was a thing like a man all in blacke ready to destroy me'.[143] But usually the connection between godly identity and the study was a positive one. John Rastrick recalled the sight of his local minister's study at the age of fifteen as a key stage in the development of his own godly and ministerial ambitions and identity:

Once (I remember) I got a Sight of his Study; and seeing so many Books, and papers lying on the Table with pen and ink, Reading Glass, and other studying furniture and a Library so great (as I then thought it was) that took up one Side of a Wall: The Thoughts of his delightful Study and Pleasant Conversation among his Books so delighted me ever after and had such a pleasing relish in my mind, that I wished, and extremely desired that I might have but the <such> same, and (methought) could not but rejoyce in the Hopes thereof.[144]

It seems important that Rastrick did not connect the clerical study with silent reading and interior piety but with conversation and spiritual fellowship. Such associations were reinforced when he recollected his experience as he prepared to go to university and was under the tutorship of Mr Walker, the minister of Great Hale. Rastrick recalled:

He lent me Books: (viz good English books of Piety as well as learning;) and when he was out of the way; I would often be getting into his Study (which was at the end of the Chimney in the Hall, and always stood open) which was a great delight and help to me; and he was not angry that I should Pore amongst his Books. Here amongst others I met with Mr Bolton's Works which I extremely liked, and they

[139] BL, MS Add 40883 (Nehemiah Wallington, 'The Growth of a Christian'), fo. 126r.
[140] Macfarlane, *The Diary of Ralph Josselin*, pp. 56, 111.
[141] Heywood (ed.), *The Diary of the Rev. Henry Newcome*, p. 141.
[142] Wolfe, '"Sacred Imployments": Gendering Spiritual Space and Labour in the Clerical Household'.
[143] BL, MS Add 40883 (Nehemiah Wallington, 'The Growth of a Christian'), fo. 9v.
[144] *The Life of John Rastrick*, p. 40.

wrought much upon me: amongst other things, looking (I remember) into Mr Bolton's Life (having never seen any Minister's Lives before) I was so taken with that little I could get time to read in it, that it mightily excited my endeavours and raised my desires after the Ministry . . .[145]

Such an association between studies and godliness also worked the other way around, at least for Rastrick, who condemned the spiritual negligence of the rector of Fosdyke, whom he served as curate, because he would not allow him access to the clerical study and because he urged him against composing his own sermons, instead suggesting that he read aloud from translations. In part, this was because Rastrick was eager to get his hands on Baxter's *Confession of his Faith*, which the rector owned but would not part with because, as he said, 'if you read nothing but what is good in the Knaves you will fall in Love with them', and lent him 'a Virulent Pamphlet against Dr Owen' instead.[146]

Such stories and fond recollections alert us to the extent to which studies were spaces for sociability as well as individual scholarship, reading and piety.[147] Allowing the faithful into one's study, to read, talk or borrow books, was a sign of godly fellowship, particularly for the clergy. Nehemiah Wallington, in a period of despair, burst into the study of Henry Roborough, the curate of St Leonard's, Eastcheap, while he was writing a sermon, in search of spiritual succour. Roborough, who had learned to deal with Wallington's anxieties as far as he could, tried to soothe him by telling him to go to the church, although he subsequently went home and his father sat down by his bedside and read to him until he had calmed down.[148] For the godly, the study was a venue of special interest when they visited each other's houses. Oliver Heywood, for example, rooted through the books in Thomas Jollie's study when he visited him and Ralph Josselin viewed the books of Mrs Rose Church and registered his surprise that such a godly woman should own a comedy. His surprise was double because it included his oversight: he had not seen it despite the fact that he 'often viewed the books'.[149]

---

[145] Ibid., pp. 42–3.

[146] Ibid., p. 80; Richard Baxter, *Rich: Baxter's Confesssion* [sic] *of his Faith* (London, 1655).

[147] For the study as a social space in an Italian context (and particularly among the wealthy), see Thornton, *The Scholar in His Study*, pp. 120–3. Thornton, however, argues that those studies which served such sociable purposes tended *not* to house an individual's collection of books but rather functioned as elaborate waiting rooms which housed collections of pictures and curiosities.

[148] Guildhall Library, MS 204 (Nehemiah Wallington, 'A Record of the Mercies of God; or, a Thankefull Remembrance'), p. 8.

[149] Heywood, *Diaries*, vol. I, p. 276; Macfarlane, *The Diary of Ralph Josselin*, p. 319. The study as an apparently 'private' space which in practice functioned in a range of modes, from the personal to the distinctly social, bears comparison with William Sherman's portrait of the so-called 'private' library. See William H. Sherman, *John Dee: The Politics of Reading and Writing in the English Renaissance* (Amherst, MA, 1995), pp. 45–50.

In fact, the study as a locus of godly sociability is made clear in that it could be a venue for communal prayer. Oliver Heywood recalled how a group of the godly held a 'private day for seeking the Lord in prayer' in June 1664 'in the roome which was my father Angier's study'.[150] And yet, for all that our other seemingly private spaces have yielded up numerous instances and styles of communal reading, the evidence for communal reading in studies is very slight indeed. Perhaps the rooms were too small, too full, or too inconvenient, or maybe a book selected from the study would be taken to one of the more communal spaces of the house. The evidence for individual reading in the study is far more extensive and allows some insight into both what and how the godly read there.

Although it is a little schematic, I think there are four elements of this reading, or four reading styles, which deserve discussion: devotional reading, reading that necessitated writing, professional reading and lay godly reading. First, and most obviously, the godly, conjuring up the quintessential Reformation image of the religious reader alone at work in the study, used the space as a venue for self-consciously private devotion. Such reading frequently included prayer and provided not only edification but also religious refreshment. It also has echoes of closet reading and devotion. Although studies as spaces would be the venue for much wider reading too, it would be a mistake to neglect the study as a place for scriptural reading. Diaries and associated materials provide some information on how this reading, which was primarily a masculine form of piety, was performed. This style of reading would take place early in the morning. Oliver Heywood was reading the Bible in his study by five o'clock in the morning,[151] while, as we have already seen, Nehemiah Wallington would rise even earlier: 'between three & foure a clocke ... to wrestle with the Lord (in holy prayr) as Jaakob did'. Wallington's recollection signals the overlap this reading had with prayer and also the echoes it had of biblical exemplars. It was individual reading but not necessarily silent and it frequently involved tears. This reading blurred the boundaries between intellectual and spiritual or emotional activity not only in the inclusion of penitential tears but also in its overlap with meditation. The godly would pause over a reading of a particular chapter or verse and meditate upon it in the hope that God would strengthen their faith through a spiritualized method of reading.

---

[150] Heywood, *Diaries*, vol. I, p. 189.   [151] Ibid., vol. III, p. 314.

Such reading might mirror their spiritual state. Feeling himself 'dead & dry' and hard of heart, Wallington was moved to read 'concerning the dead and dry bones' in Ezekiel 37:4. Reading it, his faith was strengthened in his subsequent prayer 'which melted my hard heart and the Lord with his holy spirit breathed life in my dry & dead soule'.[152]

This was reading 'in course'.[153] It was a repetitive formula which was evidently vital to the religious identity of many of the godly, whether it was performed in the closet, bedchamber or study. In the study, it could be distinctly formulaic. Oliver Heywood prescribed himself a cycle of semi-devotional study reading, which included two chapters from Genesis every morning, and different books, such as Proverbs and Matthew, for the afternoon and evening.[154] It mirrors those who advised that the best way to deal with the Bible was to read chapters in course and shows that this form of godly piety, reading and prayer was far more stylized than it was charismatic.

Reading, praying and meditating appear to take us some distance away from the models of 'goal-oriented' reading posited by Grafton and Jardine. Obviously, there was a goal to scriptural reading – salvation – but this was not to be achieved on earth, however often the steps towards it were retraced over the course of a lifetime. Nevertheless, reading based in the study was frequently undertaken in a style close to the 'goal-oriented' model, notably in the kinds of godly reading done there which required writing. The study was a space in which much of the reading done was with pen in hand, whether it was excerpting passages into a diary or commonplace book, taking notes, or writing in the book itself. Such reading was perhaps particularly prevalent among the clergy, for whom the composition of a sermon was frequently a duty which encompassed both writing and reading. Although some, such as Wallington, would write while engaged in the devotional style of study reading, others less pathologically attached to their pens were only likely to pick them up for a broader style of reading which had different and more varied purposes.[155]

---

[152] BL, Add MS 40883 (Nehemiah Wallington, 'The Growth of a Christian'), fos. 126r, 126v, 128r, 82r. It should be noted that reading and prayer that took place very early in the morning was most likely performed in the interval between periods of sleep. On patterns of sleep in the early modern period, see Roger A. Ekirch, 'Sleep We Have Lost: Pre-industrial Slumber in the British Isles', *American Historical Review*, 106 (2001), pp. 343–86.

[153] Macfarlane, *The Diary of Ralph Josselin*, p. 623.   [154] Heywood, *Diaries*, vol. I, p. 222.

[155] Guildhall Library, MS 204 (Nehemiah Wallington, 'A Record of the Mercies of God; or, a Thankfull Remembrance'), p. 405.

Henry Newcome's study was a key venue for both reading and annotating his books.[156] This reading was broad in content, including reading plays and poetry alongside devotional material and it was certainly common for godly clergy to read Catholic works in their studies in order to refute them in their sermons and publications. Such reading was unlikely to have been acceptable if it were practised in a semi-public household space because such spaces were recognized as places for devotion. But in the study they could be used for godly purposes, either to extract snippets of helpful information or in order to refute or ridicule their authors. This confirms suspicions that we are dealing with a kind of goal-oriented reading, rather than with a more Cartesian style in which the book is read on its own terms within the mental world it constructs.

Reading and writing together in the study also alerts us to the extent to which the study was a venue for professional reading. Among the godly, this was likely to mean the clergy, rather than lawyers or medics, and for the clergy to withdraw themselves to a space above and a space apart within the household was to cultivate a pastoral ideal.[157] Memoirs and diaries reveal the study as a convenient and practical location for the professional reading of the clergy. They read there because education was a continual part of their vocation, and because such reading no doubt interested them, but first and foremost because it was a practical venue in which to perform a task which intersected in obvious ways with the routine composition of sermons and perhaps the writing of their own polemical works. Reading with such ends in mind had a fairly distinctive style. As with so many other modes of reading it was done 'in course' over a period of days or weeks. Occasionally, such reading would be interspersed with reading chunks of other books; that such instances are relatively rare, however, suggests that we should temper initial enthusiasm at finding apparent examples of reading 'for action' and maintain a healthy suspicion of the reality of comparative reading, especially as it was sometimes represented in the form of the book-wheel.[158] In fact, care was the keynote of such reading and knowing the whole of an argument

---

[156] Heywood (ed.), *The Diary of the Rev. Henry Newcome*, p. 141.

[157] More generally, however, there is reason to suspect that other professionals used their studies for similar styles of reading, certainly if we are to judge by the extent of marginalia on professional books.

[158] Book-wheels are – and probably were – extremely rare. Surviving examples include that in the Bibliotheca Thysiana at Leiden, acquired by Johannes Thysius (1622–53) in 1648. A comic representation of the book-wheel appears at the start of *The Three Musketeers*, dir. Richard Lester (1973).

was particularly important in getting to grips with religious polemic; cutting and pasting would not do for the pious divine or the would-be polemicist. John Angier advised the ejected clergyman Adam Martindale that, when undertaking 'a great piece of work', he thought it crucial

> to read over endways all the considerable authors I could get for and against Presbyterianism and Independencie, and to write out all the concessions I could meet with from either partie, and by comparing them under every head, to try whether men of peaceable spirits of both persuasions might not hold communions sweetly together, notwithstanding their different apprehensions in some notionall principles; and to this purpose lent me a great number of bookes, to which I added many more by the helpe of my purse and friends.[159]

Although Martindale did not publish the treatise which Angier egged him on to write, such advice strongly suggests the folly of assuming that more modern scholarly approaches to early modern reading were entirely absent.

This mode of reading for the godly bore a remarkable resemblance to modern scholarly reading. The clergy read in their studies to prepare the gist of, or to write out, their sermons. Of course, such sermons were far from necessarily polemical and need not have strayed from a biblical text or two, but clerical readers were frequently glossing the latest interpretation of arguments and noting passages as they read in their studies. It was in this context that Henry Newcome kept an index of his reading, while a particularly clear example of a clergyman annotating his library with the specific purpose of extracting information for sermons can be seen in the surviving collection of Archbishop Tobie Matthew of York.[160]

In addition, the study was also a venue for wider lay godly reading. Such reading was no doubt nothing if not various, and our records of it are less than they might be, but in interesting ways this reading among the godly resembled that of their godly clergy. Another diarist, Adam Eyre, reflected on how it was done. Eyre read in his study and recorded the practice in his diary which he wrote there too. He read works by John Saltmarsh, Nathaniel Ward, Henry Lawrence, William Dell, William Lyly, John Foxe, Walter Raleigh, Erasmus and others on subjects ranging from history and politics to religion and astrology. Such reading was

---

[159] Richard Parkinson (ed.), *The Life of Adam Martindale, Written by Himself, and now First Printed from the Original Manuscript in the British Museum*, Chetham Society, 1st ser., 4 (Manchester, 1855).

[160] Parkinson, *The Autobiography of Henry Newcome*, pp. 285–6; Tobie Matthew's library is preserved at York Minster Library.

clearly practised in course: he spent three cold days in the winter of 1647 reviewing the 'Arguments for Independency' presented in John Salt-marsh's *The Divine Right of Presbyterie* (1646), while Foxe required his more or less sustained attention over at least two months.[161] Again the study was a place for simultaneous writing and reading, and Eyre made notes in his books as he went along, recording for instance of his reading of Nathaniel Ward's *The Simple Cobler of Aggavvam in America* (1647), 'I writt in the margent as far as I went'.[162] Likewise, it was in the study that Nehemiah Wallington organized and recorded his knowledge. Here he copied chunks of his own notes, diaries, and letters into other books and compiled indexes to his reading. In fact, Wallington provides an example of the variety of uses to which the godly study was put, from the devotional to the academic.

CONCLUSION

Although it has focused on the apparently private spaces in the seven-teenth-century household, where we might expect what evidence there is of reading to be individual and/or silent, this chapter has highlighted the variety of reading practices in closets, bedchambers and studies. For the godly, reading was a central part of devotional practice and remained so throughout the seventeenth century. As such, it was predominantly oral and social, a shared practice that bound the family in their religious identity. Of course, not everyone kept a diary or memoir, but the fact that those who did so tended to record social reading practices suggests that the pattern might be representative of godly religiosity in general. Historians see such diarists as thoroughly modern, their internalization recognizably so, yet the evidence suggests that their reading was far from silent and solitary. And on the relatively rare occasions when they recorded private or silent reading, they did so as a self-consciously private devotional mode, which, rather than betraying its normality, was unusual enough to need to be externalized through writing.

When examined in some detail, this reading clarifies several issues. Most obviously, it shows the essential overlap, in both performance and understanding, between styles of prayer and styles of reading. Both were oral, social and overwhelmingly emotional. The godly read the Bible as part of their devotional practice, and we might note that the book was

---

[161] Eyre, 'A Dyurnall, or Catalogue of all my Accions and Expences', pp. 10, 70–9.
[162] Ibid., p. 42.

close to the centre of what they understood as prayer. But the style adopted to read the sacred book was also extended to other literature, and became a method of reading that could be used, with profit, to approach almost any text in a godly fashion. As such this has consequences for the predominant historiographical model which describes reading as goal-oriented.

Not only does all this evidence rectify the assumptions of those who have taken for granted that reading in private spaces was a modern, silent, and solitary enterprise, it also alerts us more strongly to the atmosphere of godly reading and how its communality formed part of what it meant to be one of the faithful. This communality becomes clearer when we move to the more public spaces of the household.

CHAPTER 3

Reading the family

INTRODUCTION

Godly reading was a social practice conducted in the godly family. Amid copious diaristic reflections and frequent spiritual anxieties, Philip Henry

was careful and faithful in making good his solemn Vow at his ordination, that *he and his House would serve the Lord.* He would often say, *That we are really which we are relatively. It is not so much what we are at Church, as what we are in our* Families. Religion in the Power of it will be *Family Religion.*[1]

As Henry's biography and many other works explained, reading was at the heart of this religious culture. This chapter explores the intricacies of reading with and within the family. Where the previous chapter set out to examine individual readerly praxis but found numerous points of overlap between individual and communal reading even in the most seemingly private spaces in the household, this chapter unravels the complexities of communal reading in the more public spaces of the godly household and highlights the importance of such reading in shaping and maintaining godly religious culture. Whereas the 'private' and 'secret' reading described by contemporaries does not correspond to our understanding of such concepts, exploring 'family reading', a term occasionally used by contemporaries, poses fewer problems.[2] And where secret reading sits uneasily with modern understandings of self and individuality, family reading reflects a wider social and interactive practice. As well as unpicking several important threads in the fabric of godly culture, the focus on communal

---

[1] *An Account Of The Life and Death Of Mr Philip Henry, Minister of the Gospell, near Whitchurch in Shropshire. Who Dyed June 24; 1696 in the Sixty fifth Year of his Age. With Dr Bates's Dedication* (2nd edn, London, 1699), p. 50.
[2] Matthew Henry explicitly distinguished 'secret' and 'family' reading. See Matthew Henry, *A Sermon Concerning the Catechizing of Youth* (London, 1713), p. 17.

reading in the family serves to reconnect the historiography of puritanism with the historiographies of the family and of intellectual culture.

It is worth pausing over this historiographical disjuncture. Forty years ago, it would have been obvious that the histories of the family, intellectual culture and puritanism were interwoven: readers were presented with a clear vision of the detail and texture of the fabric of seventeenth-century culture. There was the pioneering work of the Shakespearean scholar Levin Schücking, Christopher Hill's penetrating study of the spiritualization of the Protestant household, and Edmund Morgan's sparkling book on the puritan family.[3] Today the associations between the histories of puritanism and of the family are either ignored or left at the level of the infuriatingly vague or hopelessly banal. In large part, this has been an unfortunate by-product of the rerooting of puritanism in its theological context, which has left little space for discussion of family or culture.[4]

While the history of puritanism was becoming framed more insistently in theological terms, in the era of personal computers historians of the family began to move away from cultural perspectives which encompassed religion and towards more measurable questions about family, household and social relations.[5] At the same time, the established framework of the history of the family – which was essentially the history of women as seen through (often puritan) conduct books – was challenged and undermined. As the discipline became more academically rigorous and took an archival turn, based more on court records than on conduct books and (latterly) focused upon gender relations and not just upon women, the history of the puritan family – so long part of the established narrative – was dropped from the picture.[6] Nevertheless, more recent sophisticated

---

[3] L. L. Schücking, *Die Familie im Puritanismus. Studien über Familie und Literatur in England im 16. 17. und 18. Jahrhundert* (Leipzig and Berlin, 1929); English edition: Levin L. Schücking, *The Puritan Family: A Social Study from the Literary Sources*, trans. Brian Battershaw (London, 1969); Christopher Hill, 'The Spiritualization of the Household', in his *Society and Puritanism in Pre-Revolutionary England* (London, 1964); Edmund S. Morgan, *The Puritan Family: Religion and Domestic Relations in Seventeenth-Century New England* (revised edn, New York, 1966) (first published Boston, MA, 1944).

[4] For which, see above, pp. 10–16.

[5] Some social histories in this era did engage with religion. See Margaret Spufford, *Contrasting Communities: English Villagers in the Sixteenth and Seventeenth Centuries* (Cambridge, 1974); Keith Wrightson and David Levine, *Poverty and Piety in an English Village: Terling, 1525–1700* (New York, 1979).

[6] Even the seminal works in this historiography are too numerous to list here. But for an influential overview in the late 1980s, see Judith M. Bennett, 'Feminism and History', *Gender and History*, 1 (1989), pp. 251–72; for some of the new directions in gender history, see Karen Harvey and Alexandra Shepard, 'What Have Historians Done with Masculinity? Reflections on Five Centuries of British History, circa 1500–1950', *Journal of British Studies*, 44 (2005), pp. 274–80.

histories of the family and household, from Lyndal Roper's path-breaking *The Holy Household* to Naomi Tadmor's *Family and Friends*, have paved the way for a reconciliation of the historiographies of puritanism and the family.[7]

The broad lack of understanding and dialogue between historians of puritanism and of the family has had serious consequences which have bred considerable misunderstanding. In the context of this book, this misunderstanding has been further complicated by lack of dialogue with historians of the book and of reading. And yet, as this chapter shows, the three historiographies can be usefully intertwined to reveal the importance of communal reading in the godly family. Despite historiographical neglect, such reading was a key part of godly identity. But before thinking about the complexities of communal reading in the godly household, two related concepts need to be clarified.

THE FAMILY AND 'FAMILY RELIGION'

In the seventeenth century the most basic unit of society was the household. As a generation of social and economic historians have shown, such households contained not the extended family of the romantic imagination, but the nuclear family consisting of married parents and their children.[8] For all the basic truth of this picture, it tends to conceal as much as it exposes. As contemporaries understood it, the term 'family' included those linked to the household through ties other than those of kinship, such as servants and boarders and even overnight guests. Likewise, the language of house and home informed the ways in which contemporaries described and imagined political institutions, the practice of government and the economy.[9]

The importance of this broad definition of the family is rarely touched upon by historians of religious practice. Yet it challenges how we think

---

[7] Lyndal Roper, *The Holy Household: Women and Morals in Reformation Augsburg* (Oxford, 1989), esp. Chapter 7; Naomi Tadmor, *Family and Friends in Eighteenth-Century England: Household, Kinship, and Patronage* (Cambridge, 2001). It is important that historians of gender acknowledge further the important work on the family done by historians of puritanism, such as Jacqueline Eales, *Puritans and Roundheads: The Harleys of Brampton Bryan and the Outbreak of the English Civil War* (Cambridge, 1990).

[8] For household structure, see P. Laslett and R. Wall (eds.), *Household and Family in Past Time* (Cambridge, 1972); Ralph Houlbrooke, *The English Family, 1450–1700* (London, 1984).

[9] For a brief discussion of household patterns, see Keith Wrightson, *Earthly Necessities: Economic Lives in Early Modern Britain* (New Haven, CT, 2000), Chapter 1, esp. pp. 30–4. For a fuller discussion, see N. Tadmor, 'The Concept of the Household-Family in Eighteenth-Century England', *Past and Present*, 151 (1996), pp. 111–40; and her *Family and Friends in Eighteenth-Century England, passim*.

about religion in the post-Reformation. In particular, it stresses the importance of the 'spiritualized household' and widens its impact. Following in the footsteps of Durkheim, John Bossy memorably described one of the seismic shifts in early modern religion as the plates of religion and society gradually moving apart. In this rupture, Christianity moved from meaning 'a body of people' to a 'body of beliefs'. As I argued in the introduction, Protestantism (and particularly puritanism) is usually described and defined in terms of the beliefs of its individuals. But when we focus on the godly household, we see a world in which religion is simultaneously defined as being rooted in both people and beliefs. Indeed, it becomes clear that it was religious practices which bound together groups of people.[10]

'Family religion' was a key strand of evangelical piety in the seventeenth century and one which helps us to reconnect the Restoration period with its early Stuart past.[11] It came to prominence after the Restoration, when many preachers feared that it was passing out of fashion, and as a concept it illustrates particularly clearly how the histories of the family and religious practice were intertwined. Family religion was promoted in the pulpit and in print from the 1650s until the end of the seventeenth century and beyond. Although it only entered common currency in the middle of the century, its first title, *Family-Religion revived*, aptly describes how it evoked a style of piety rooted in the past, notably in the key works of late Elizabethan and early Stuart piety by Daniel Dyke and Arthur Dent.[12] A series of titles appeared to promote this practice, including works by William Payne, John Tillotson, Samuel Slater, John Shower and Matthew Henry.[13]

---

[10] John Bossy, *Christianity in the West, 1400–1700* (Oxford, 1985), pp. 170–1.

[11] Andrew Cambers and Michelle Wolfe, 'Reading, Family Religion, and Evangelical Identity in Late Stuart England', *Historical Journal*, 47 (2004), pp. 875–96.

[12] Philip Goodwin, *Religio Domestica Rediviva: or, Family-Religion Revived. Or A Treatise as to Discover the Good Old Way of Serving God in Private Houses: so to Recover the Pious Practice of those Precious Duties unto their Primitive Platform* (London, 1655); Arthur Dent, *The plaine mans path-way to heaven* (London, 1601); Daniel Dyke, *The Mystery of Self-Deceiving* (London, 1615).

[13] William Payne, *Family Religion: Or, The Duty of Taking Care of Religion in Families, And the Means of Doing it. Recommended in A Sermon Preached at Guild-Hall Chappel Before the Lord Mayor And Court of Aldermen, On Sunday February 22th 1690/91* (London, 1691); John Tillotson, *Six Sermons, I. Of Steadfastness in Religion. II. Of Family-Religion. III. IV. V. Of Education of Children. VI. Of The Advantages of an Early Piety* (London, 1694); Samuel Slater, *An Earnest Call to Family-Religion, or, A Discourse Concerning Family Worship being the Substance of Eighteen Sermons* (London, 1694); John Shower, *Family Religion in Three Letters to a Friend* (London, 1694); Thomas Bray, *An Appendix to the Discourse upon the Doctrine of our Baptismal Covenant being a Method of Family Religion* (London, 1699); Matthew Henry, *A Church in the House. A Sermon Concerning Family-Religion* (London, 1704).

Such titles struck a chord with many other volumes, such as the biographies of John Angier and Philip Henry, as well as numerous works by Richard Baxter.[14]

Although family religion was, according to Archbishop Tillotson, 'strangely overlook'd and neglected in this loose and degenerate Age', contemporaries were left in no doubt of what it comprised.[15] Alongside family prayer, family religion consisted of communal reading in the godly household. As David Jones explained, 'The chief things which *Family-Duties* consist of, are *Reading the Scripture, Praying and Catechizing.*'[16] Such reading extended beyond the reading of scripture to include godly books and catechisms,[17] where the family would repeat aloud the answers to questions central to their faith.[18] It is likely that, for many, from Isaac Archer's mention of his delight at his accidental stumbling across his father's 'old written book of experiences of God to him' in 1670 to those who passed their accounts from hand to hand, it included the communal reading of the lives and memoirs of their godly predecessors, which further betrays our misunderstanding of such works when we see them as evidence of interior spirituality.[19] In short, this communal reading was a key part of godly identity in the seventeenth century. This chapter explores the importance of such reading and unravels some of its complexities in some of the more public spaces in the godly household: the hall, the household parlour or kitchen, and out of doors. Avoiding the usual assumption that communal and oral reading is at best a second-rate activity, practised by the semi-literate who aspired to private silent reading, it examines such reading as a self-consciously pious form of godly social activity.

---

[14] For fuller details, see Cambers and Wolfe, 'Reading, Family Religion, and Evangelical Identity in Late Stuart England.'

[15] Tillotson, *Six Sermons*, p. 50.

[16] David Jones, *A Sermon Of the Absolute Necessity of Family-Duties* (London, 1692), p. 34.

[17] Tillotson, *Six Sermons*, p. 54.

[18] See Chetham's Library, MS A.2.125 (Matthew Henry, 'Catechistical Instructions of Sabbath Evenings'); Ian Green, *The Christian's ABC: Catechisms and Catechizing in England c. 1530–1740* (Oxford, 1996).

[19] See Andrew Cambers, 'Reading, the Godly and Self-Writing in England, circa 1580–1720', *Journal of British Studies*, 46 (2007), pp. 796–825. For Isaac Archer, see Cambridge University Library, MS Add 8499, fo. 134. Archer was clearly surprised at stumbling over his father's diary and comforted by the similarity of their religious experiences: 'And I find Satan got the better of him in the same sort of sins as he did of me ... who would think that the same vain, filthy, lewd thoughts should be in both of us'. Archer was the son of a dissenting minister but became a Church of England clergyman, albeit one who maintained strong ties with local dissenters.

THE HALL

Perhaps the most recognizable image of communal reading in the early modern period is the formal picture of the family reading in the household hall. The father, sitting at the head of a great table, would read from the Bible to instruct his family and servants. His family might take some part in the reading, either by answering questions, recalling passages or even reading when the great book was passed around the family seated at the table. It is an image of patriarchy in practice, sustained through the communal reading of the Bible or semi-canonical works like Foxe's *Book of Martyrs*. Such reading was rigidly orthodox and it reflected the realities of the patriarchal world at large.

Although Roger Chartier has suggested that descriptions of such seigneurial reading were probably more the result of mythical portrayals of idealized notions of rural society than of actual practice, the evidence from England not only reveals the prevalence of such practices but also suggests a much more nuanced and potentially more radical picture of household reading and piety than of simple patriarchalism.[20] Asking a series of simple but fundamental questions transforms how we think about this reading: what book are the family reading? Is it the Bible and if so which edition are the family using? Is it just the Bible, or are they also using other texts? How far are the family involved? Are they actively contributing to the reading by making notes or suggesting changes? And perhaps most importantly, are they the rigid nuclear family, or a more fluid group, known to contemporaries as 'family', but consisting of servants, visitors and boarders as well as the mother, father and children? Considered in this way, the picture has the outline of the most conformist, patriarchal scene but all the detail of a potentially radical religious meeting: a conventicle.

The two pictures can be overlaid in our examination of communal reading in the godly household hall. Certainly the lines between the image of the conformist patriarch and the radical conventicle might be blurred, and contemporaries were able to suggest that the latter was simply a harmless version of the former. Thinking about the communal reading of the godly as both patriarchal and radical or subversive raises several questions: what was this reading like – was it scriptural, catechistical or dependent on a broader godly canon? What part did this sociable reading

---

[20] Roger Chartier, *The Cultural Uses of Print in Early Modern France*, trans. Lydia G. Cochrane (Princeton, NJ, 1987), p. 228.

play in godly identity? Does it reinforce our picture of a sociable and externalized religious culture? And does it help us to think about the links between general godly practice and outright radical separatism?

In the large household, the hall was a formal and semi-public space. It was the natural venue for gatherings of the entire family as well as an arena for entertaining visitors. In this, the hall of the godly household resembled that of any other. But it differed in its use. Where many a household would use the hall as a space for entertainment which would include drinking and gaming, among the godly it was a space in which to inform and to educate, a space to be the public face of the puritan household. In the hall of the Bruen household, the most famous of the Cheshire puritan families, we can see the constructive side of the culture of puritanism. John Bruen, who in addition to his own family, had several servants and up to twenty-one godly boarders or 'tablers' in his 'family', banned his family from playing cards, dice and games. At this, according to his biographer, 'hee began to think of a wiser, and better course ... To which end hee brought in, and set up upon a deske, both in his Hall, and in his Parlour, two goodly faire Bibles of the best Edition, and the largest volume'. He put them there to become 'continuall residentiaries' so that those 'of good minds might exercise themselves in reading, and hearing the Word of God'.[21] The placing of Bibles in public spaces for communal reading was at the heart of their family piety and godly identity, and was praised as such by William Perkins.[22] And when this reading was with the culturally understood 'family' – rather than its narrower biologically defined core – it takes on a wider significance in godly identity. Mary Rich, for example, was especially active in attending to the spiritual needs of her servants in such spaces within her household. She took care

In scattering good Books in all the common Rooms and places of attendance, that those that waited might not lose their time, but well employ it, and have a bait laid of some practical, useful Book, and fitted to their capacity, which might catch and take them.[23]

Through communal reading in the hall, visitors, servants and boarders would learn how to be godly and take the practice with them when they

[21] William Hinde, *A Faithfull Remonstrance of the Holy Life and Happy Death, of John Bruen of Bruen Stapleford* (London, 1641), pp. 123–4.
[22] Ibid., p. 128.
[23] Anthony Walker, *Eureka, Eureka. The Virtuous Woman found her Loss Bewailed, and Character Exemplified in a Sermon Preached at Felsted in Essex, April, 30, 1678. At the Funeral of that most Excellent Lady ... Mary, Countess Dowager of Warwick* (London, 1678), p. 85.

moved on. Thus the youthful Christopher Love, on a spiritual journey which took him to Oxford, ended up as a boarder in the household of Dr Rogers. There he participated in family duties with Rogers's own family and a large number of godly women who were sent by their mothers to receive their spiritual education in the household. Communal reading was crucial to their religious development and Love recalled reading and praying in the family every morning and evening, with the whole group remembering what was read, 'then expounding with great plainness'. These godly women, and Love himself, would take this brand of godly household piety with them when they married and set up their own households. Thus family reading was not just an idealized model of household piety but a communal and social practice which had the potential to tap into a more radical religious subculture and to harden the divide between the godly and their enemies.[24]

Reading in the hall was a semi-formal but often quite radical practice. It was not necessarily an everyday, routinized activity but more frequently a part of godly activity on the sabbath. Although it was socially limited to relatively wealthy households, it appears to have been especially common in clerical families and, according to some, in those parts of the country with traditions of self-government and/or at a considerable distance from ecclesiastical authority.[25] But probing how reading was performed in this space, and teasing out some of the intricacies of the reading material, casts further light onto the role that communal reading played in shaping godly identity.

On Sundays, Philip Henry's house became a church, as he rounded up his entire household into family reading and prayer and encouraged any guests to join in. Such reading was performed in the morning before the business of the day started and in the evening 'before the Children and Servants began to be sleepy'.[26] It mimicked the public reading of scriptures in religious assemblies and focused on texts which would add to the day's sermon and reinforce its message. Often, it would involve the

---

[24] BL, MS Sloane 3945 ('The Life of Mr Christopher Love'), fos. 89v–92r. For a useful model of the dynamic between the godly and their enemies, see Peter Lake, '"A Charitable Christian Hatred": The Godly and their Enemies in the 1630s', in Christopher Durston and Jacqueline Eales (eds.), *The Culture of English Puritanism, 1560–1700* (Basingstoke, 1996), pp. 145–83, 301–7. This model was further entrenched by the internships which young godly ministers served in the homes of established clergy. See Tom Webster, *Godly Clergy in Early Stuart England: The Caroline Puritan Movement c. 1620–1643* (Cambridge, 1997), Chapter 1, esp. pp. 24–9.

[25] *The Life of John Rastrick*, pp. 138–9, suggests that such reading was especially common in parts of Yorkshire.

[26] *An Account of the Life and Death of Mr Philip Henry*, p. 51.

repetition of a sermon using notes taken at the time – an indication that hearing, as well as reading, could be an interactive and constructive activity. Countless narratives of the lives of godly individuals recall the repetition of sermons in the family on Sundays. Oliver Heywood's *A Narrative of the Holy Life, and Happy Death of ... Mr. John Angier* highlighted such a model of godly piety by placing a long note entitled 'how the lords day was spent' prominently in the margin of the text. It put strong emphasis upon the repetition of the sermon in the house, after the service, a practice that mirrored its repetition for those who stayed in church to sing Psalms between the morning and afternoon services.[27] And for many, such as Archbishop Tillotson, whose Yorkshire puritan upbringing was fashioned into a more inclusive but still overtly evangel- ical piety at the end of the seventeenth century, it would go hand in hand with communal reading from scripture after public worship. In a sermon 'concerning family-religion', preached in 1684 but published a decade later, he wrote that after public worship on the Lord's Day, 'our Families should be instructed at *Home*, by having the *Scriptures* and other good *Books* read to them'. This, he thought, would be particularly important for servants, since it would be their chief opportunity of 'minding the business of Religion, and thinking seriously of another World'.[28]

Perhaps the nature of this reading can be best explored not through the multiplication of examples but by providing a thicker description of communal reading in the hall of one family. A classic example of such reading is that seen in the diary of Lady Margaret Hoby as it illuminates the piety of her large godly household at Hackness in North Yorkshire at the start of the seventeenth century. There the household hall functioned both as a venue for communal reading on Sundays and as a space in which a wide range of godly reading would be conducted in the evening after supper. On Sundays, rounds of communal reading and sermon repetition would take place in the hall in the time between the morning and afternoon services. These appear to have involved the whole family and to have been given quasi-official status in that they were often led by the household chaplain, Richard Rhodes.[29] This reading was not only drawn from the sermon but would also encompass scriptural passages and

---

[27] [Oliver Heywood], *A Narrative of the Holy Life, and Happy Death of that Reverend, Faithful and Zealous Man of God, and Minister of the Gospel of Jesus Christ, Mr. John Angier* (London, 1683), pp. 60–1.

[28] Tillotson, *Six Sermons*, p. 64.

[29] Joanna Moody (ed.), *The Private Life of an Elizabethan Lady: The Diary of Lady Margaret Hoby, 1599–1605* (Stroud, 1998), p. 10 (example of 26 August 1599).

extracts from semi-canonical godly authors like Perkins.[30] It interacted with prayer, listening and writing and served not only to confirm the godly family in their faith but also to separate the godly from their enemies in the parish environment, notably when only spiritual neighbours and 'good wives' were invited to join in the Hoby family routine.[31]

But such reading extended beyond the routine and outward show of the sabbath. Throughout the week the Hobys held sessions of semi-public communal reading, the practice of which clearly set the godly apart from their neighbours. Lady Hoby's diary illuminates the cyclical reading that was performed in the household hall at night. Just as the day might be punctuated with godly reading, and there are several instances of Richard Rhodes reading to the household before supper from authors like Cartwright, the time after supper was given over to cycles of communal reading.[32] Sermons were clearly repeated in the hall and selected chapters from godly authors were read aloud, by the chaplain, family members, servants and visitors, a little each day before the family retired to their chambers for the night.[33] Returning home after protracted visits among family in Yorkshire, Lady Hoby commented on this reading, reassured at returning to devotional normality. She plunged into a series of domestic, communal spiritual exercises which included the repetition of the 'lecture' in the evening, most likely the previous Sunday's or Wednesday's sermon or a scriptural reading, but also listening to passages of godly books being read aloud by members of the household. A particularly clear instance of such reading occurred in late September 1599, when the family read and listened to passages from Foxe's *Actes and Monuments* for several days, with the reading shared between various members of the family.[34] Such reading cycles were at the heart of advanced domestic devotion, whether they were drawn from John Foxe or Richard Greenham or William Perkins.[35] The style of communal reading strengthened the godly in their faith. This reading also overlapped with the 'publeck exercise', which included several preachers in a series of scriptural readings and discussions, and at which the public face of the godly preaching exercise met with the domestic routine of puritan devotion.[36] This reading was a

---

[30] Ibid., p. 59.
[31] Ibid., p. 107. The hall was a frequent venue for discussion of biblical chapters with Hoby's neighbours; see p. 34.
[32] Ibid., p. 12.   [33] Ibid., p. 35.   [34] Ibid., pp. 22–6.   [35] Ibid., pp. 39–40, 41.
[36] Ibid., pp. 97, 110. The precise nature of the 'publeck exercise' in the Hoby household is unclear. It appears to have drawn on the spirit of the combination lecture translated into a domestic devotional context. For combination lectures, see Patrick Collinson, 'Lectures by Combination: Structures

family activity and was locked into a cycle of godly devotion. Importantly, it both fed on, and gave sustenance to, other forms of godly activity. Communal reading would prompt note-taking and discussion, reflection and diary-writing. It formed part of a routine which involved prayer, singing and writing, as well as reading. Indeed the activities were intertwined and the focus on reading merely serves to confirm the strength of the connection between communal and personal spiritual and textual activities.[37]

As this shows, communal reading in the hall was a crucial strand of godly piety, and its semi-public nature as the outward face of the godly household makes it a critical component of godly identity. Across the long seventeenth century, family reading in this context had a place in both mainstream and more radical spirituality. Thus when Adam Martindale was ejected in 1662 and replaced, he made the effort to hear his successor: 'it was my custom, so long as it would be borne', he wrote, 'to heare my successor constantly, and to recite his sermons; and that evening to repeat his sermons at home to an housefull of parishioners of the devoutest sort, adding a discourse of mine owne, and praying for a blessing upon all'. Here sermon repetition was transformative and more radical, undercutting the authority of the incumbent and suggesting that the power of sermons lay above all in their delivery: 'The people would say', wrote Martindale with some satisfaction, 'that they liked his sermons better in the repetition then in the preaching'.[38] But, as the ground shifted underneath society, such reading was transformed from a broadly licit strand of voluntary religion (albeit a potentially radical one) into a practice potentially tainted with the charge of illegal conventicle. Nevertheless, there is significant overlap between the conventicle and the practice of early Stuart domestic godly piety. Thus while Thomas Jollie, ministering at home to an exclusive godly grouping which he called 'the society', with a purpose-built pulpit and a primitive alarm system, is typically described as a

---

and Characteristics of Church Life in Seventeenth-Century England', *Bulletin of the Institute of Historical Research*, 48 (1975), pp. 182–213.

[37] It should be noted that Ian Green is mistaken in his assumption in *Print and Protestantism in Early Modern England* (Oxford, 2000), p. 531 (n. 131), that the Hoby household was one which involved extensive godly prayer, but no Psalm-singing. Not only is the practice mentioned in the diary (Moody, *The Private Life of an Elizabethan Lady*, p. 38) but, as TNA: PRO, STAC 5/H50/4 (Hoby vs. Eure) makes clear, notably in the statement given by Robert Nettleton, it was the 'usual custom' in the household for the family to come together in the hall and to sing a Psalm before prayers were said.

[38] Richard Parkinson (ed.), *The Life of Adam Martindale, Written by Himself, and now First Printed from the Original Manuscript in the British Museum*, Chetham Society, 1st ser., 4 (Manchester, 1855), p. 173.

conventicle, it drew on an old-fashioned style of family piety.[39] Instances of semi-public reading at home, from the collective reading of printed sermons at the house of Ralph Thoresby in Leeds,[40] to local suspicions regarding Henry Newcome keeping the pulpit cushion at home for family reading,[41] alert us both to the centrality of communal reading to godly identity and to the continuities in that identity, evangelical in style, over the seventeenth century.

THE PARLOUR AND THE KITCHEN

The most important venues for communal reading in the godly household were the kitchen and the parlour. These were noisy, busy and bustling spaces at the heart of everyday life. They were also the most common venues for communal, godly reading. Unlike the more formal and organized reading that would occur in the halls of those who had them, reading in the kitchen and parlour ranged from that done as part of daily devotional duty to more impromptu and indeed extraordinary forms of reading. Examining instances and styles of reading in kitchens and parlours confirms the extent to which reading was interwoven with other activities for the godly and thus emphasizes the depth of godly religious culture: Oliver Heywood's prayers were disrupted by the noise of the women preparing meat in the kitchen of James Holstead in February 1678; families can be seen reading when visitors came to the door; and they could be prompted into devotional reading when freak weather conditions warned them of God's providential interventions in the material world.[42] It is better to think of textual experience as located in a distinctly domestic context – as it was for Alice Thornton, who was pecked in the eye by a chicken while she wrote her diary – than simply in the abstract world of ideas so often

---

[39] Henry Fishwick (ed.), *The Note Book of the Rev. Thomas Jolly, A.D. 1671–1693. Extracts from the Church Book of Altham and Wymondhouses, 1649–1725. And an Account of the Jolly Family of Standish, Gorton, and Altham*, Chetham Society, new ser., 33 (Manchester, 1895), introduction and p. xvii.

[40] See York Minster Archives, Add MS 214 (Diary of Henry Stubbs, 1678).

[41] R. Parkinson (ed.), *The Autobiography of Henry Newcome*, Chetham Society, 26, 27, (2 vols., paginated continuously, Manchester, 1852), p. 144.

[42] In such instances, the parlour could be a forum for contentious reading and fractious discussion. The newly installed (and 'ignorant, idle and malignant') incumbent at Heckington in 1670, wrote John Rastrick, paid the household a visit and 'coming into our parlour saw a Book or two of Mr Baxter's on the Table, and talked on it afterwards, and accused me for reading (as he termed them) unlicensed or unlawfull books.' *The Life of John Rastrick*, p. 65. For Heywood, see Heywood, *Diaries*, vol. I, p. 342.

described by historians of intellectual thought and historians of reading.[43] Although the commonplace that the glance upon the unusual event allows the historian insight into the parts of an alien culture that a glimpse of the normal cannot reach is no longer as convincing as it once was, the sight of unusual scenes of reading at least alerts us to the variety of godly reading and to its potential interaction with other activities. In what follows, godly reading is examined through the lenses both of everyday and extraordinary experiences. This reveals the sociability of communal reading and its interaction with other activities.[44]

Communal reading of scripture and religious literature was a key part of a godly education and, as the circumstances of families with young children no doubt dictated, it was often located in the rooms at the heart of family life. The process of learning to read was a distinctly interactive one in the early modern period, reliant in particular on the adult reading and the child repeating first the sounds of letters and then words and phrases. This can hardly be surprising, but it is important to understand the level of involvement that the family took in this educative social reading and to recognize its overwhelmingly religious character. What is particularly important is that when they reflected upon their education, many recalled the communal reading of godly books as important milestones in their religious development.

Before they progressed to godly books, young readers had to learn the mechanics of reading and this was done with a hornbook, a Bible and an ABC, frequently in the comfort of the household parlour. Although such reading could hardly be doctrinally godly, many reflected that it had bred in them the voracious appetite for reading which later inspired their godliness. Adam Martindale, for example, described this process of learning to read as a key step in the construction of his godly identity. He recalled:

when I was neare six yeares old, one Anne Simpkin, who was one of my sureties at the font, being grown low in the world, but not in goodnesse, out of a reall principle of conscience to performe her promises and engagements for me at my baptisme (as I verily beleeve), bestowed an A B C upon me; a gift in itselfe exceeding small and contemptible, but in respect of the designe and event, worth

---

[43] *The Autobiography of Mrs Alice Thornton, of East Newton, co. York*, Surtees Society, 62 (Durham, 1875 for 1873), pp. 271–3.

[44] Robert Darnton, *The Great Cat Massacre: And Other Episodes in French Cultural History* (New York, 1984), p. 5: 'When we cannot get a proverb, or a joke, or a ritual, or a poem, we know we are on to something. By picking at the document where it is most opaque, we may be able to unravel an alien system of meaning.'

more than its weight in gold. For till that time I was all for childish play, and never thought of learning. But then I was frequently importunate with my mother that had laid it up (thinking I would onelie pull in pieces) to give it into mine owne hands, which being so small a trifle she accordingly did; and I, by the help of my brethren and sisters that could read, and a young man that came to court my sister, had quickly learned it, and the primer also after it. Then of mine owne accord I fell to reading the bible and any other English booke, and such delight I tooke in it, and the praises I got by it from my parents, which preferred my reading before any other in the family, that I thinke I could almost have read a day together without play or meat, if breath and strength would have held out, and thus it continued to the end of the first seven yeares of my life.[45]

The passage stresses not just the religious trajectory launched by the gift, but also the sociable practices at the centre of this educational process: his brothers and sisters, godparents and even one of his sister's admirers all took the time to help him on this path.[46] The gift of a simple ABC was a stepping-stone in the making of the godly Martindale and it prompted special mention at the end of the first chapter of his autobiography: 'What abundance of benefits may arise from a small gift well designed and seconded by God's blessing! A pennie booke accompanied with such advantages was the first occasion of that little learning that I attained to.'[47]

For the young John Rastrick, reading forged godly identity. At the heart of this identity were his relationships with his schoolmaster and his father. Sent to school at the tender age of four, Rastrick was taught to read by his schoolmaster, who instilled in him a routine of godly reading. At the school, Rastrick recalled, there were rounds of morning and evening prayer, with 'a Psalm constantly sung every night before we left School, which one <of> the Schollers read; and when I began to read indifferently <well> my Master put me often to read the Psalm my Self'. The routine gave him a taste for religion which, he reflected, was 'deeply made when I was very young'.[48] Importantly, such reading married well with his

---

[45] Parkinson, *The Life of Adam Martindale*, p. 5.

[46] It is likely that, when the Civil Wars made going to university inadvisable and he was looking for a career, this was a method that Martindale carried on while he was a tutor to the children of one Mr Shevington of Eccles and a schoolmaster in Holland, Wigan. Ibid., p. 29.

[47] Ibid., p. 9. In the post-Reformation, the religious and educative responsibilities of godparents were given extra weight. See Will Coster, *Baptism and Spiritual Kinship in Early Modern England* (Aldershot, 2002).

[48] *The Life of John Rastrick*, p. 31. This clearly drew on long-standing methods of godly education. Pupils in Rotherham, where Rastrick later ministered, spent every Thursday afternoon in the 1630s reading aloud passages from Perkins. See J. A. Newton, 'Puritanism in the Diocese of York (excluding Nottinghamshire) 1603–1640' (unpublished DPhil thesis, University of London, 1955), pp. 288–303. For godly education more generally, see J. Morgan, *Godly Learning: Puritan Attitudes towards Reason, Learning and Education 1540–1640* (Cambridge, 1986).

incipient household piety. He recalled how his 'Father would shew me the
Minister's Texts, and tell me some of the Historys of the Bible when I used
to sit on his Knee, and before I understood what belonged to such things,
or what he meant by them'. Conversation was at the heart of his education:
'I quickly grew very inquisitive after them; and would ask my Father the
meaning of every word and thing that was hard to me, which possibly
might the more prompt him to those endeavours'. It bred, thought Rastrick, clarity of belief: 'I was of a simple nature . . . but very angry with any
that I understood lyed to me. and so, that which I understood to be vice,
I hated and opposed with great eagerness'.[49] Although Rastrick, as a pre-
cocious cross-referencer of biblical texts and psalms, was hardly a typical
child, it is important that his reading was shaped through a continual
conversation with his father, his teacher and the voices of his books.[50]

It is worth pausing over Rastrick's example as his narrative pays such
close attention to the role that youthful reading played in the godly
upbringing. Where many recalled their first intellectual stirrings but
swiftly moved on to their university education, calling and career, Rastrick
detailed the intermediate steps, notably through the reading of devotional
and catechistical works. These books were frequently read in the household parlour and seem more important in the development of the godly
life than Ian Green's description of them as almost theologically neutral
would suggest.[51] We have already seen the importance Rastrick placed on
the roles of Dent's *The plaine mans path-way to heaven* and Dyke's *The
Mystery of Self-Deceiving* in the growth of his spiritual identity. Both books
were also singled out as vital in the emergence of familial piety and
communal reading. It was from them that he extracted prayers 'to say at
nights, when we were in Bed'.[52] When his mother asked him to read to
her from Ovid's *De tristibus*, which he had been reading at the kitchen
table, the young Rastrick 'delayed (turning up and down the book, for a
place fitter for her to hear, than that where I was reading)'. This prompted
his mother 'in a very great passion' to throw him out of the house and to
order him 'to fill the Dung-cart that stood in the yard'. This is a useful
reminder that godly reading was not always a harmonious activity
but could instil hostility, resentment, and manual labour.[53] It is also a
reminder that the godly did not always read godly books. Elizabeth Isham
recalled spending a particularly happy summer as a seventeen-year-old
'for the most part working & hearing one read[;] my cousen being a

---

[49] *The Life of John Rastrick*, pp. 31–2.   [50] Ibid., p. 32.   [51] Green, *The Christian's ABC*.
[52] *The Life of John Rastrick*, p. 33.   [53] Ibid., p. 37.

good reader I loved to hear; the Bookes wherein she read were Ovids Midamorfeces[,] in Sandses travels of the holy land & Gods revenge against Murther[.] so wee profited together working & reading'.[54] Communal godly reading could transcend the godly canon.

Throughout the day the parlour was the forum for rounds of educational reading. Reading could be done there after school, like homework, and might overlap with the making of sermon notes.[55] In households which were not doctrinally godly, but culturally evangelical, this educative process and style of reading was passed on through generations. In Ireland, Alice Thornton's father took in a young boy laid low through illness, who promptly converted from popery when his eyes were opened to the truth 'through all good instructions, and teachings to read, and his catechisme'.[56] Here communal educative reading was contrasted with the collusion of Catholicism which fostered superstition through secrecy. Thus, although social educative reading obviously crossed confessional lines and did not in itself guarantee godliness, it was certainly something that the godly thought essential to their religious culture. And education did not end – it was central to family duties in which social reading was perceived as a key part of the continual education of the godly family. Ralph Josselin certainly thought about it in this way when he read with his 'people' and even chastised himself for neglecting 'reading the word in my family, and personal and particular instructing of my little ones, leaving it to my catechising them and to my wife'.[57] The purpose of this education was to teach the skills necessary to be able to pray and believe properly. Where more radical religious groups valued ecstatic experience above the written word, the godly regarded Bible-reading as the key to faith. Family duty, family prayer, and family religion were all shaped by family reading in the parlour. As such, this reading was at the heart of their religious culture. As if to confirm this, John Bruen set up another desk in his parlour, with an even bigger Bible than that in the hall, for the family to read and hear the word of God.[58]

To understand this reading more deeply, especially as it overlapped with singing, prayer and note-taking in the context of family duties, we

[54] Princeton University Library, MS RTC01 (no. 62) (Elizabeth Isham, 'My Booke of Rememberance'), fo. 20v. George Sandys, *A Relation of a Journey* (London, 1615). John Reynolds, *The Triumph of Gods Revenge, against the Crying and Execrable Sinne of Murther* (London, 1622).
[55] *The Life of John Rastrick*, p. 43.
[56] *The Autobiography of Mrs Alice Thornton*, p. 35.
[57] Alan Macfarlane (ed.), *The Diary of Ralph Josselin, 1616–1683* (Oxford, 1976), p. 410.
[58] Hinde, *A Faithfull Remonstrance of the Holy Life and Happy Death, of John Bruen*, pp. 123–4.

need first to think about what material it included before exploring how the mechanics of the reading further illuminate godly culture. Most common was the use of scripture in leading this fusion of prayer and reading. A particular text would be chosen and read before the family. Henry Newcome, for example, noted, 'Wee had sweet family dutys out of Act xxv'.[59] The biography of Philip Henry, who had an unusually developed interest in turning his house into a church in family worship, even before he became a nonconformist, reveals the extent to which these family duties were structured around scriptural reading. They began with a prayer and then a Psalm was sung. It explained that his

usual way was to sing a whole Psalm throughout, tho' perhaps a long one, and to sing quick ... and that he might do so, usually the Psalm was sung without reading the line betwixt (every one in the Family having a Book); which he preferred much before the common way of singing, where it might conveniently be done, as more agreeable to the Practice of the Primitive Church, and the Reformed Churches abroad ...

Then a portion of scripture would be read, with care taken to read the Bible in order (a practice on which Henry was especially keen). It was then expounded in the family, which Henry thought an excellent means of educating the family in scripture. These expositions often surprised his visitors. He would reduce the text into heads 'not by a Logical Analysis, which often minceth it too small and confounds the Sense with the Terms; but by such a Distribution as the Matter did most easily and unforcedly fall into'. He then made his children write out the expositions, before testing them on the substance of the text once more.[60] Henry Newcome's family exercise was similar in that seven chapters of histories from scripture were chosen and then debated and discussed with his children. Such a practice provided so much 'profit and delight' that the family had soon gone over the whole Bible in the course of their duties.[61]

   Family duty might also include readings that stretched beyond the Bible. Looking back on the year 1652, Henry Newcome recounted how he had 'sometimes at family duties, instead of the chapter read a leaf or two in Mr. Shepherd, and explained it to my family; and it being variety, and as it were change of fare, I found it did relations and servants much

[59] Thomas Heywood (ed.), *The Diary of the Rev. Henry Newcome, from September 30, 1661, to September 29, 1663*, Chetham Society, 1st ser., 18 (Manchester, 1849), p. 132.
[60] *An Account Of The Life and Death Of Mr Philip Henry*, pp. 51–4.
[61] Parkinson, *The Autobiography of Henry Newcome*, p. 143.

good'.[62] Even Philip Henry appears to have understood that a break from the Bible might do his family some good, in that he devoted Thursday evenings to catechizing his children and servants using the *Assemblies Catechism* or the catechism *Concerning the Matter of Prayer* (1674), which was said to have been written by John Collinges, and occasionally 'he examined them in some other useful Book, as Mr Pool's Dialogues against the Papists, the Assemblies Confession of Faith with the Scriptures, or the like'.[63] Occasionally, such reading crossed over from the educational to the overtly moralistic. Ralph Josselin, for example, warned his family of the rod of providence in December 1677 when he read to them 'the judgment of god on John Duncalf of old Swinford in Staffordshire', which he gleaned from a recent pamphlet. Josselin elaborated the printed account, chronicling Duncalf's descent from an honest trade as a wheelwright to a life of 'idleness and intemperence' in which he was in 'want of a morsel of bread'. Things took a turn for the worse when Duncalf stole a woman's Bible and sold it on and promptly denied it, wishing, as Josselin noted, that 'his hands might rott of if he stole it'. Within a fortnight, as Josselin cautioned his family, Duncalf's crime had been revealed and he had got more than he bargained for since not only his hands but also his legs had begun to rot. People came to look at the man with 'one hand so rotten off that it hung onely by the Muscles', his ulcerous flesh eaten by maggots, and his limbs buried piecemeal as they fell off. Such cautionary tales warned of a vengeful and just God; read aloud their warning was salutary. As Josselin wrote, the story of the light-fingered Duncalf served 'to mee and mine to make us more careful of our wayes'.[64] For others, the reading was from more familiar source material, but it was no less vivid. Roger Lowe read from Foxe in a practice that appears to have been half educational and half penitential, since it was partly to atone for his being 'a little mery the other day'.[65]

Such reading confirms the familial nature of this activity and the extent to which it overlapped with prayer. However, the most common form of non-scriptural reading during family duty was from sermons, clearly

---

[62] Ibid., pp. 43–4.   [63] *An Account of the Life and Death of Mr Philip Henry*, p. 56.

[64] Macfarlane, *The Diary of Ralph Josselin*, p. 605. My account is elaborated using Josselin's source: *Digitus Dei. A Faithful Relation and Collection of Seven Wonderful and Remarkable Judgements, Lately Inflicted by God on Several Persons using Execrations and Wicked Wishes to Themselves* (London, 1677), pp. 5–6.

[65] *The Diary of Roger Lowe of Ashton-in-Makerfield, Lancashire. 1663–1678. Including a Record of Burials at Winwick Church 1666–71*, ed. Ian Winstanley (Wigan, 1994), p. 50.

highlighting the intersection between the spoken, the written and the printed word. Sermons, whether printed or heard and hastily noted, were read aloud and repeated as part of family duty. The puritan clergyman Samuel Rogers, for example, repeated a sermon by Stephen Marshall as part of 'dutyes in the family'.[66] Of course, many nonconformists would actually preach at home and attempt to pass this off as part of family duties, rather than illegal conventicle. But many godly households also read printed sermons aloud. Such a practice was perhaps a particularly affected form of godly piety, but its practice seems to have been quite widespread: in the household of Elizabeth Isham, whose sister read to her from the sermons of Dr Preston; between the puritan steward of Northampton Robert Woodford (1606–54) and his wife and family; and also in the houses of more radical Protestants and Quakers, who would recall how they read aloud not only scripture but also sermon books in the family as part of their upbringing.[67] Such practices were in effect sponsored by those authors like Oliver Heywood who collected a large number of copies of their own printed sermons directly from their printer and then distributed them among their own congregations. Heywood's example – for instance detailing to whom he distributed over 150 copies of his *Sure Mercys* in the early months of 1672 – is well known, but we should not assume that it was unique. Indeed, as Arnold Hunt has suggested, the high proportion of surviving copies of printed sermons which contain post-print corrections and additions in the hand of the author is at least suggestive of a similar pattern on a more widespread scale and it also alerts us to how the publication of such material may have been designed for a target audience.[68]

The communal reading of godly sermons, with their many and varied messages, takes us some way from the picture of social reading as patriarchal and conservative. Instead, we are presented with several examples of

[66] Tom Webster and Kenneth Shipps (eds.), *The Diary of Samuel Rogers 1634–1638* (Woodbridge, 2004), p. 65.

[67] Princeton University Library, MS RTC01 (no. 62) (Elizabeth Isham, 'My Booke of Rememberance'), fos. 27v, 31r. For numerous examples of the family reading of printed sermons, see Arnold Hunt, *The Art of Hearing: English Preachers and their Audiences, 1590–1640* (Cambridge, forthcoming), Chapter 4. I am grateful to Dr Hunt for allowing me to read this in advance of publication.

[68] Heywood, *Diaries*, vol. III, pp. 51–3; and see Harold Love, 'Preacher and Publisher: Oliver Heywood and Thomas Parkhurst', *Studies in Bibliography*, 31 (1978), pp. 227–35; Hunt, *The Art of Hearing*, Chapter 4; a similar point about the targeting of Quaker publications is made in Kate Peters, *Print Culture and the Early Quakers* (Cambridge, 2005). The most extensive study of Heywood is now Samuel S. Thomas, 'Individuals and Communities: Religious Life in Restoration England' (unpublished PhD thesis, Washington University, St Louis, 2003).

such reading fermenting domestic crises, more often than not because of the nature of the sociability rather than their theological distinctiveness. John Rastrick's sessions of household reading clearly crossed the line that separated harmonious household piety from transgressive ecstatic activity. Indeed, his reading sessions with two female servants plunged his wife into a melancholy fit and began a spiritual and medical demise that soon ended in her death. Rastrick described how he had led the servants from temptation, notably those presented by the local Anabaptists, and was keen to include them in his family exercises. They proved willing and able in their participation, to the admiration of all the participants but one: Mrs Rastrick. The spiritual affinity which Rastrick struck up with both servants prompted 'Envy and Jealousy' in his wife, who was struck with melancholy and demanded that they be sent away. It was John Rastrick's reading that had caused the decline. As he recalled:

> The true Reason of her distaste of these Maid-Servants was I think … that when I used to read any thing in my Family I usually (but indiscreetly) directed my Self and my Speech to them more than to her[,] looking upon them to be more Capable to understand and reply than my wife was.

His familiarity with the servants during these sessions of spiritual reading was too much for his wife to bear.[69]

Such examples already give some idea as to how collective godly reading in the parlour and kitchen was performed. Although there are of course many examples which are not specific as to the location of reading, there is enough material to elaborate a general model of this less formal and more usual form of godly reading. First and foremost, this was family reading. Although it was not necessarily spontaneous – Henry Newcome, for one, read books about such exercises presumably as a way of tweaking his own family practice[70] – in general this reading was less formal than the scriptural reading in the hall on the sabbath. It would often take place at meal times, whether in one's own home or at that of another godly family.[71] In June 1663, Henry Newcome made a resolution that he would have his children read scripture at mealtimes. The practice evoked the monastic, even though Newcome would be unlikely to have admitted it.[72] Similarly, the father of the future latitudinarian bishop

---

[69] *The Life of John Rastrick*, p. 188.   [70] Heywood, *The Diary of the Rev. Henry Newcome*, p. 29.
[71] Henry Newcome, for example, performed such reading as part of the family duties he led in his visits to other godly households. See Parkinson, *The Autobiography of Henry Newcome*, p. 164.
[72] Heywood, *The Diary of the Rev. Henry Newcome*, p. 194.

Simon Patrick kept up strict Sunday exercises when Psalms would be sung after dinner and the sermon repeated.[73] Among the particularly advanced, different days would be set aside for different forms of this reading. In the household of Philip Henry, on Saturday evenings the children and servants would give an account of the chapters expounded the week before, while on Saturday afternoon the children would read, sing and pray together, particularly from books designed for children. This reading was educational and characteristically interactive. Henry encouraged his children in their collective reading of scripture 'to gather out such Passages as they took most notice of, and thought most considerable, and write them down' and urged them 'to insert in a Paper Book, which each of them had for the Purpose, remarkable *Sayings* and *Stories* which they had met with in reading such other good Books as he put into their Hands'.[74] Although the evidence for how this reading was then performed is less than explicit, certain clues emerge from the ways in which it was described. When reading as part of family duty occurred in the household parlour and was centred around scripture, it was usually noted as being done 'in course'.[75] This confirms both the regularity of the enterprise and its importance as a marker of godly identity and the cyclical nature of the reading. For others, we need to scratch further beneath the surface. Particularly suggestive is the common way of describing such reading. Diarists like Ralph Josselin and Henry Newcome used phrases such as 'wee read' or 'we read in' a particular book. Not only does the 'we' here contrast with readings in other contexts in which 'I read' perhaps stands for more personal styles of reading, but the 'in' is again suggestive of the reading being piecemeal rather than necessarily linear.[76]

Clearly much of this reading was catechetical. It formed a distinct strand of family duty but shared much with the reading discussed above. It was serious and studious. Samuel Clarke contrasted the scholarly speed-reading of the 'ruddy, fat, and corpulent' William Perkins and the equally colourful Banbury preacher William Whately with serious and slow family catechetical reading.[77] Catechisms were the key but not the only texts in this reading. Many of them came with instructions on how they

---

[73] Alexander Taylor (ed.), *The Works Of Symon Patrick, D.D. Sometime Bishop of Ely, Including His Autobiography* (9 vols., Oxford, 1858), vol. IX, p. 410.

[74] *An Account of the Life and Death of Mr Philip Henry*, pp. 57, 61–2.

[75] Heywood, *Diaries*, vol. III, p. 139 and *passim*.

[76] Heywood, *The Diary of the Rev. Henry Newcome*, p. 21 and *passim*; Macfarlane, *The Diary of Ralph Josselin*, p. 423.

[77] Samuel Clarke, *The Marrow of Ecclesiastical History* (3rd edn, London, 1675), pp. 416, 460–1.

were to be used in the family. Thomas Vincent's guide to reading the *Assemblies Catechism* may serve as an example. He instructed that it be read in families at least once but preferably twice each week as a guide to examining children and servants:

The manner of using it in Families must be left to the discretion of the Masters and Governours respectively: though yet we concur with the Author, and think it advisable ... that after a Question in the Catechism is propounded, and an Answer without book return'd by one of the Family, the same person, or some other be call'd upon to read ... the explanation of it, the rest reading along with him, in several books; by which means their thoughts (which are apt to wander) will be the more intent upon what they are about.[78]

Communal reading, whether catechetical or devotional, confirmed the family in their godliness. Interestingly, the texts used to do so extended far beyond the Bible and even included the communal reading of spiritual diaries and memoirs to this end. Thus Nehemiah Wallington read his own 'Record of the Mercies of God' with his son-in-law Jonathan Houghton 'every morning' between November 1647 and January 1648.[79] Such reading obviously confirms the importance of family reading, yet it also sounds a note of caution as to how seemingly individual and personal documents such as diaries have traditionally been read. Their practical importance suggests that family reading was the dominant mode of pious textual activity rather than the necessary custom of the semi-literate and spiritually lacklustre.

The parlour and kitchen were also the venues for a wider range of reading, both in content and in style. It would be foolish to assume that the godly only read godly books, or indeed that they confined themselves solely to works of piety. Instead, the godly might consume a wider range of material provided they did so in a suitable manner, and if they read for a purpose. Still, while visiting Mrs Rose Church in February 1653/4, it certainly shocked Ralph Josselin to see the 'Comedie called Lingua' on the shelves.[80] By contrast, Henry Newcome appears not to have worried about his own reading of Robert Wild's *The Benefice* (1689). This reading

[78] Thomas Vincent, *An Explicatory Catechism, Or, An Explanation Of The Assemblies Shorter Catechism* (London, 1680), sigs. A3v–A4r, A2r–v. There are similar advocations in Richard Alstree, *The Whole Duty of Man* (London, 1684), pp. 118–19.

[79] Guildhall Library, MS 204 (Nehemiah Wallington, 'A Record of the Mercies of God; or, A Thankefull Remembrance'), unpaginated leaf at start of volume. For the importance of such reading, see Cambers, 'Reading, the Godly and Self-Writing'.

[80] Macfarlane, *The Diary of Ralph Josselin*, p. 319. The comedy was Thomas Tomkins, *Lingua: or the Combat of the Tongue* (London, 1607).

was occasionally social – he appears to have taken it out of the library and read it aloud after dinner with Mr Illingworth and Mr Hayhurst – but because he took notes on the book, he approached it as godly reading rather than as a form of recreation.[81] It is, of course, possible that Wild's status as a nonconformist minister – for an angry John Beale he was 'the scarlet staine of Divinity'[82] – made him much more acceptable as a playwright than he might otherwise have been.[83] And likewise, the godly could read in a more relaxed and less overtly pious manner provided that the material itself was appropriate. History seems to have been especially suitable. Thus it was perfectly acceptable for Josselin to read Richard Baker's *Chronicle of the Kings of England* (1643) for his 'recreation' and for Henry Newcome to read the strongly anti-papal speeches of Sir Edward Deering (1598–1644) 'casually'.[84]

Clearly those who read a lot encountered many non-godly and non-religious books. For the clergy, such reading, although not usually a social form of reading, was an essential part of ministerial work. Only in the most extreme puritan households were there regimes in which only religious (and specifically godly) literature was permitted. And such prohibition could have unexpected consequences. John Bruen filled the cultural void that was created by his banning pretty much every form of recreation except pious godly reading and Psalm-singing – which incidentally prompted him to write 'the word Halelu-jah ... in the first leafe of all his bookes' – by inventing a godly game.[85] This game, 'Bruen's Cardes', involved fifty-two thematic sheets of biblical quotations and snippets of godly wisdom from authors such as Babington and Perkins. The themes ranged from sodomy to Satan's monarchy and from the Book of Common Prayer to superstition and the duties of a godly wife. Quite how it was played is not particularly clear and though it would be tempting to think of it as biblical Top Trumps, where quotations from the Geneva Bible or William Perkins would beat all others, it is perhaps more likely that it was a non-competitive memory game whose ends were both spiritual and educational. Certainly it suggests a degree of interaction

---

[81] Heywood, *The Diary of the Rev. Henry Newcome*, pp. 145, 158, 204.

[82] Corpus Christi College, Oxford, MS 332, fo. 22v. See George Southcombe, 'The Responses of Nonconformists to the Restoration in England', (unpublished DPhil thesis, Oxford University, 2005), p. 76.

[83] Heywood read and copied Wild's poetry. See Heywood, *Diaries*, vol. III, p. 58 ff.

[84] Macfarlane, *The Diary of Ralph Josselin*, p. 149; Heywood, *The Diary of the Rev. Henry Newcome*, pp. 84–5. Deering, of course, was a complex figure. See *ODNB*.

[85] Hinde, *A Faithfull Remonstrance of the Holy Life and Happy Death, of John Bruen*, p. 71.

between iconoclastic puritanism and popular culture that might not have been expected; it also reinforces the book-centred nature of this religious culture and the sociability of its book-culture.[86]

The parlour could also be a venue for the shared reading with which the godly would confront more extraordinary threats to their existence. Although they were theoretically distanced from many traditional remedies and doctrinally averse to 'superstition', the godly read and used books to dispel domestic demons. The narratives of cases of demonic possession among the godly, clustered around the late sixteenth and early seventeenth centuries, provide us with remarkable details not only of attitudes towards the Devil, witchcraft and the supernatural but also concerning early modern social relations, the nature of the godly community and – perhaps surprisingly – the practice of reading and book use among advanced Protestants.[87]

The godly family, when faced with a case of possession, would frequently attempt to cure the demoniac through a series of prayers and communal collective readings, from the Bible and other godly books.[88] In part this was to be seen to follow the spirit of the Canons of 1604, which stipulated (if negatively) that the only licit means of casting out devils was to do so through fasting and prayer, once a license from the bishop had

---

[86] BL, MS Harley 6607, 'A Godly Profitable Collection of Divers Sentences out of Holy Scripture And Variety of Matter out of Severall Divine Authors: By that Deare and Faithfull Servant of God John Bruen Who Dyed Wednesday: January the 18th: 1625 Commonly by him Called his Cardes being 52 in Number'. The collection of materials of this kind is also testimony to the continued importance of early Stuart puritan authors long after their deaths, and may be seen in collections of sayings by noted puritans like John Dod and Richard Greenham which were circulated deep into the seventeenth century. See John Dod, 'Dod's Droppings; or, Passadges of Mr Dods', Dr Williams's Library, London, MS 28.2; and the printed broadsheet *Old Mr Dod's Sayings* (London, 1667), which was designed to be pinned up and remained popular (and was frequently reprinted) well into the eighteenth century; John Rylands Library, Manchester, Eng MS 524 ('Theological treatises by Arthur Hildersham'), fos. 1–72, contains the sayings of Richard Greenham. These are reproduced in K. L. Parker and E. J. Carlson (eds.), *'Practical Divinity': The Works and Life of Reverend Richard Greenham* (Aldershot, 1998).

[87] The nature of this reading is rarely commented upon by historians of puritanism, historians of reading or historians of possession. For an attempt to unravel its importance at greater length, and thereby to intertwine the historiographies, see Andrew Cambers, 'Demonic Possession, Literacy and "Superstition" in Early Modern England', *Past and Present*, 202 (2009), pp. 3–35. For a fuller discussion of the Fairfax case, see Andrew Cambers, 'Print, Manuscript and Godly Cultures in the North of England, c. 1600–1650' (unpublished DPhil thesis, University of York, 2003), pp. 190–236.

[88] It is worth noting that the relationship also worked the other way around. There are several instances of religiously suspect books bewitching their readers. See, for example, *Quakers are Inchanters, and Dangerous Seducers. Appearing in their Inchantment of one Mary White at Wickham-skyeth in Suffolk, 1655* (London, 1655), pp. 4–5.

been obtained.[89] It also made sense to read at the possessed because such
reading had a physical effect on demoniacs, frequently causing the demon
within them to try to tear the book or hurl it away. A particularly clear
example of the conflict between the Devil and the godly family was fought
over the possessed body of Alexander Nyndge in Herringswell, Suffolk, in
1574.[90] Nyndge, in the presence of his father, mother and brothers, fell
into a strange and horrific series of fits in which his chest and body
swelled, his eyes glazed over and his back, like that of a contortionist,
bent forwards towards his belly. Edward Nyndge comforted his brother
Alexander with words of scripture and charged the spirit 'by the death and
passion of Jesus Christ' to declare the cause of his torment. He reassured
his terrified brother that the Devil could not harm him if he repented and
prayed for God's forgiveness. But the vexation was severe. Alexander was
taken to the heart of the house and was seated upon a chair, while his
father sent for the neighbours to come and pray for his son. This more
than twenty did, falling to their knees to say the Lord's Prayer together in
the hope of prevailing over the demon. But only in the presence of the
hastily summoned town curate did the spirit give up his name and could
the exorcism begin.

The details of the exorcism show just how reliant the godly could be on
traditional methods of spiritual healing and upon the physical properties
of the sacred book as well as its holy words. The Bible, open at the fourth
chapter of St Matthew's Gospel, was laid upon Alexander, at Christ's
injunction to Satan – 'Thou shalt worship the Lord thy God, and him
only shalt thou serve'.[91] Edward and the curate then told the spirit that he
was an instrument sent to punish the wicked, and laid on Alexander the
eighth chapter of St Luke's Gospel, at the place where Christ cast out
devils,[92] at which the spirit roared 'Baw-wawe, baw-wawe'. Enraged,
the spirit transformed Alexander's body, making it resemble 'the picture
of the Devill in a play, with an horrible roaring voice, sounding
Hell-hound'. While the company prayed for Alexander's deliverance,
Edward sensed that the spirit was tired and asked for the window to be

---

[89] *Constitutions and Canons Ecclesiasticall: Treated upon by the Bishop of London, President of the Convocation for the Province of Canterbury, and the Rest of the Bishops and Clergie of the Said Province* (London, 1604), cap. lxxii.

[90] The story is told in J.W., *A Booke Declaringe the Fearfull Vexasion, of One Alexander Nyndge: Beynge Moste Horriblye Tormented wyth an Evyll Spirit. The xx. Daie of Januarie. In the Yere of our Lorde. 1573. At Lyeringswell in Suffolke* (London, ?1573 [= modern 1574]).

[91] Matthew 4:10.   [92] Luke 8:30–3.

opened. Two minutes later, around eleven o'clock, Alexander's body returned to its true shape.

The spirit was not yet defeated, however, and the fits returned in the night. Around four o'clock, when Alexander had another fit and feared he would go to hell, Edward helped him recover by reminding him to believe in Jesus, telling him to repeat the words 'Speak for me my saviour Jesus', and by taking him the Bible to read until he fell asleep. When he woke at eight o'clock, Alexander cried out for his brother again, as he was taken with another more violent fit which made him spit and swell. He roared until Edward spoke in his left ear, calling him once more to repent and to put his trust in God. But this time Alexander's ear shrivelled and wrinkled, to resemble a walnut. Understandably shocked, Edward swiftly recalled the curate and told him to read from the Bible 'for the losing of the same eare which was so wrinkled together'. Edward continued to repeat sentences in Alexander's right ear and those still assembled called for the spirit to depart in the name of Jesus. Alexander stood up and said the spirit had left him. He was not troubled again.[93]

Nyndge's story is dramatic and highlights the ways that the godly family used the book as a sacred object to ward off evil. It suggests that when the Bible was produced during godly exorcisms, it took effect partly because of its physical properties, like a kind of Protestant sacramental, and partly through its sacred words. Although it might be surprising to those unacquainted with the broader culture of puritanism, it is clear that sacred books had apotropaic and thaumaturgic properties for the godly in England, just as Bob Scribner argued that images of Martin Luther had for Lutherans in post-Reformation Germany.[94]

The practice of families reading to demoniacs sheds much light on the nature of godly identity. Such reading must not be written off as 'superstitious', primitive or indeed magical. Instead, it represented a reasoned

---

[93] *A True and Fearefull Vexation of One Alexander Nyndge: Being Most Horribly Tormented with the Devill, from the 20. Day of January, to the 23. of July. At Lyeringswell in Suffocke: with his Prayer after his Deliverance. Written by his Owne Brother Edward Nyndge Master of Arts, with the Names of the Witnesses that were at his Vexation* (London, 1615) claimed that the troubles continued until 23 July but followed the text of the 1573 pamphlet in stating that he was not troubled after 21 January. The later pamphlet, which declared that the case was 'worthy to be remembered both for example, and learning' (sig. A3r), gave more details on the bodily distress that Alexander suffered, including the words of the prayers said during the possession and exorcism. Only the later pamphlet named Edward as the author. There is no evidence that he wrote the 1573/4 pamphlet, as is assumed by the *STC*. The pamphlet is signed by a J.W., so the authorship of the 1615 pamphlet is at best questionable.

[94] R. W. Scribner, 'Incombustible Luther: The Image of the Reformer in Early Modern Germany', *Past and Present*, 110 (1986), pp. 38–68.

response to the intervention of demons into the godly household. Admittedly such moments were rare and it would be unwise to write the history of a culture outwards starting from moments of strain, but they also offer a three-dimensional picture of the culture of puritanism that cannot be easily dismissed.

Whereas many traditionally believed that the mere presence of the Bible in the household, or even bits of it used as amulets worn on the body, would be an effective preservative, the most acceptable countermeasure against the Devil and witchcraft for the godly was the communal reading of scripture.[95] As Jean Bodin made clear:

> This ... is the way to prevent witchcraft ... each father must instruct his family to pray to God morning and evening, to bless and give thanks to God before and after meals, and to give at least one or two hours one day of the week to have the Bible read by the head of the family in the presence of the whole family.[96]

Several well-documented cases enable us to probe this reading further. The possession of the two daughters of the Yorkshire poet Edward Fairfax in the early 1620s, a case which he wrote up when he failed to secure the prosecutions of those he believed responsible, gives us a particularly vivid description of this reading. Fairfax's daughters, Helen and Elizabeth, were plunged into fits of possession in the household parlour, a room which had the advantage of a sickbed as well as being a communal space.[97] Understandably alarmed at the condition of his daughters, for which he found no remedy or respite either from doctors or from medical books, Fairfax employed the most immediate godly remedy: he and his family read aloud to alleviate, if not entirely cure, the young girls' torments. He recorded in some detail how this reading was performed. First, such reading was almost necessarily oral. When Helen was in a trance and read without speaking, her action was thought to be under the control of the

---

[95] This is not to say that the godly did not also use many traditional practices, such as bibliomancy, although they were condemned by writers such as William Perkins (see William Perkins, *A Discourse of the Damned Art of Witchcraft* (Cambridge, 1608), p. 107). My purpose here is to focus on the communal reading of scripture in such cases. For the layering of traditional and advanced Protestant practices, see Cambers, 'Demonic Possession, Literacy, and "Superstition" in Early Modern England'.

[96] Jean Bodin, *On the Demon-Mania of Witches*, trans. Randy A. Scott (Toronto, 1995), p. 147 (first published as Jean Bodin, *De la Démonomanie des sorciers* (Paris, 1580)).

[97] Edward Fairfax, *Daemonologia: a Discourse on Witchcraft as it was Acted in the Family of Mr. Edward Fairfax, of Fuyston, in the County of York, in the Year 1621*, ed. William Grainge (Harrogate, 1882), pp. 36, 42.

Devil. Only by raising her voice to read aloud would the reading become effective:

Hellen took the Bible and did seem to read, but spake not that was perceived. Signs were made to her to speak up that we might hear her read. She understood the signs and said, 'I do read very high, for now I hear myself, which I did not to-day before'. So she continued reading to herself, but spake not a word, and yet was persuaded that she spake very loud.[98]

Likewise, when Helen read without seeing we are given some insight into how the godly read more generally. Fairfax described how Helen had fallen into a fit of possession while reading the Bible. Alert to the danger, William took over the reading, while Helen followed it with her eyes closed:

At last her eyes were closed, and her brother William read in the book; she did hear, and groping for the candle took it out of the stick and held it to her brother with her hand, following his reading, moving the candle from side to side; yet her eyes were fast closed and she saw not at all.[99]

Such reading might seem confused, but William's action during his sister's torment illuminates for us the detail of communal reading. William 'pointed to the line and words' in the Bible to help Helen recover her senses and read with the full voice required to dispel the demons.[100]

Such reading among the godly was predominately oral and communal. It was a shared experience of religious healing. At times, it appeared ecstatic, such as when the whole Fairfax family joined in the recitation of the Lord's Prayer and the repetition of some Psalms when Helen said she had had a vision of God repeating it during one of her trances. At other times, the communality of the reading appears ritualistic, as the family recited chapter and verse at troublesome familiar spirits. Observing that Psalm 140:8 appeared to alleviate Helen's symptoms, William repeated it 'six or seven times', finally making the familiar spirit, who had heard enough, depart.[101] Such reading was repetitive, indeed it must have sounded like chanting, but it was far from unthinking. On one occasion when both daughters were in trance, the Fairfax children 'made signs for the bible which was given them' and 'Hellen read the 71st Psalm till light failed, and Elizabeth said after her every word', resulting in the departure of the familiar spirit.[102] Shortly afterwards, Helen and Elizabeth read the Psalm together: Helen 'read the 71st Psalm, and the child [Elizabeth] said after her verbatim; which being finished they were both well'.[103] Though

---

[98] Ibid., p. 136.   [99] Ibid., p. 54.   [100] Ibid., p. 65.   [101] Ibid., p. 65.
[102] Ibid., pp. 117–18.   [103] Ibid., p. 118.

Elizabeth was not fully literate (she was just seven years old when the trouble started), she had enough reading ability to participate in this textual healing. Fairfax's account of these tribulations, which he entitled *Daemonologia*, read against the grain, highlights the importance of communal reading in godly culture and provides an unusually detailed picture of how it was performed in the household parlour.

OUT OF DOORS

Although it is rarely discussed by historians of reading, whose eyes are drawn towards the text, the physical context of reading transformed the experience of the reader. As William St Clair explains in his magisterial survey:

> Much reading nowadays is done indoors, sitting on a chair. In the romantic period it was common to read outdoors while walking. We hear of groups of men meeting to read in parks in order to escape the dark and smells of windowless houses. Thomas Carter, a tailor, sat on his heels. To save on the costs of borrowing, the Chambers brothers sat together outside, one holding the book, the other turning over the pages. To minimise on wax candles, which were expensive, and of rushes dipped in animal fat which dripped and stank, many readers read by firelight, stretched on the floor, their hair sizzling with constant singeing, sparks exploding and shadows dancing on the walls. *Frankenstein* by firelight is a different reading experience from *Frankenstein* in a university library.[104]

In the seventeenth century, godly reading also extended beyond the household walls.

At the start of *The Pilgrim's Progress*, John Bunyan provides a well-known description of Christian:

> Now, I saw upon a time, when he was walking in the Fields, that he was (as he was wont) reading in his Book, and greatly distressed in his mind; and as he read, he burst out, as he had done before, crying, *What shall I do to be saved?*"[105]

The image very clearly connects reading, speaking, walking and salvation. But its mere existence is inconvenient – it certainly disrupts any attempt to impose upon reading a progression from private to public as it occurred from private to public spaces. Although the evidence with which to write a history of reading out of doors is thinner than the evidence for that which occurred indoors – and it is complicated both by the proliferation of

[104] William St Clair, *The Reading Nation in the Romantic Period* (Cambridge, 2004), p. 394.
[105] John Bunyan, *The Pilgrim's Progress* (2nd edn, London, 1678), p. 3.

gardening metaphors in the description of the individual spiritual condition and the hugely influential model of Augustine's *Confessions* in which he heard an oracle in the garden calling 'pick up and read, pick up and read'[106] – it must not be ignored. Gardens in particular were key venues for sin in the Bible and they figured prominently as locations for reading in the accounts of sin and salvation in the seventeenth century.

It might be expected that those who read while walking in gardens did so in a particularly individual way.[107] This is as true of post-Reformation Catholics, like Richard Shanne of Methley who took 'much pleasure to walk in woods and to be solitary' while clutching Luis de Granada's *Spiritual Doctrine*, as it was of the godly.[108] Walking was connected with spiritual meditation and many of the godly are described, like John Foxe, as delighting in solitary walking and contemplation.[109] Those who knew William Bradshaw (like Thomas Gataker, who wrote his life) professed that they 'seldome saw him walking abroad without a Book in his hand' and, although he was in many ways a stereotypical godly don, Bradshaw had the unusual talent of reading while he walked: 'and reading usually, if alone, in it, as he walked, though he walked commonly somewhat fast, being therein farthered through the quicknesse of his eyes, and the steadinesse of his hand'.[110] Certainly the connection between reading and walking conjured personal fantasies. The history and geography books Ralph Josselin read in his youth gave him grand ideas about designing 'stately buildings, castles. libraryes: colledges and such like' and he 'walkt with delight to meditate' upon his schemes.[111] When this reading was specifically religious, it appears to have cultivated a distinct style of piety. In his diary, Henry Newcome wrote of 15 June 1663, 'I rose soone after 7. Read Ruth i. Walked out & read in Boyle of Seraphick love.'[112] Although this would appear to be the most affected of reading matter, and summon up an image similar to the Romantic fusion of writing with nature, it was systematic as well as contemplative. Over the

---

[106] St Augustine, *Confessions*, trans. Henry Chadwick (Oxford, 1992), p. 152.

[107] The search for solitude in nature, of course, cut across Reformation divides. See, for example, Trevor Johnson, 'Gardening for God: Carmelite Deserts and the Sacralisation of Natural Space in Counter-Reformation Spain', in Will Coster and Andrew Spicer (eds.), *Sacred Space in Early Modern Europe* (Cambridge, 2005), pp. 193–210.

[108] See Keith Thomas, *Man and the Natural World: Changing Attitudes in England 1500–1800* (Harmondsworth, 1983), p. 215. See also Alexandra Walsham, *The Reformation of the Landscape: Religion, Memory and Legend in Early Modern Britain and Ireland* (Oxford, forthcoming).

[109] Clarke, *The Marrow of Ecclesiastical History*, pp. 416, 460–1.

[110] Samuel Clarke, *The Lives of Thirty-Two English Divines* (London, 1677), p. 59.

[111] Macfarlane, *The Diary of Ralph Josselin*, p. 2.

[112] Heywood (ed.), *The Diary of the Rev. Henry Newcome*, p. 192.

next month Newcome turned to Boyle again and again both during and after his solitary walks.[113]

Clearly the increased popularity of gardens after the Restoration broadened the opportunities for these styles of piety and of reading to be replicated more widely. John Rastrick, though perhaps an unusually melancholic and spiritual twelve-year-old, found comfort in praying in the gardens of his boarding house, only (predictably) to be jeered at by his schoolfellows. Although he fought battles with his mother, who thought he was work-shy, and had to tend his father's cows during the summer of 1665, a book was never far from Rastrick's hand. On the advice of his father, he occasionally took a book with him into the fields. Rastrick endeavoured to read wherever he went and took particular delight in his conversation with God during his morning and evening walks as a student at Cambridge.[114] Indeed, spontaneity was a keynote of Rastrick's reading and his prayer. Granted special access as a teenager to his minister's study, he was fired with a passion to become a minister when he read his first clerical biography: Edward Bagshaw's life of Robert Bolton. Rastrick recalled the effect his reading had:

I was so taken with that little I could get time to read in it, that it mightily excited my endeavours and raised my desires after the Ministry; so that as I went home, there being a hill in a Pasture in my way like an old Mill Hill, I got into the hollow that was in the top of it, and O how zealously and earnestly did I pray to God that he would fit me for his Ministeriall Work.[115]

Although much more restrained in her spiritual life, Anne Clifford might be said to exemplify the garden reader. From the time her 'diaries' began, she recorded getting up early and going to the 'standing' – presumably a sort of gazebo or pavilion – in the garden with her prayer book to seek comfort in God. This spiritual summerhouse offered her a solitary space for reading, prayer and meditation. In it, she relished her morning devotion just as much as she did when praying and reading with her family and servants inside the house.[116] It is possible that Anne learned

---

[113] Ibid., p. 198; Robert Boyle, *Some Motives to the Love of God, better known as Seraphick Love*, in Robert Boyle, *Works*, ed. Michael Hunter and Edward B. Davis (7 vols., London, 1999), vol. I, pp. 51–133. Such reading fits in neatly with the ideal forms of 'seraphick love' as they are outlined by Frances Harris, *Transformations of Love: The Friendship of John Evelyn and Margaret Godolphin* (Oxford, 2002), Chapter 6.

[114] *The Life of John Rastrick*, pp. 36, 40, 50.

[115] Ibid., pp. 42–3. Bagshaw's life of Bolton, E[dward] B[agshaw], 'The Life and Death of the Author', was printed in *The Workes of the Reverend, Truly Pious, and Judiciously Learned Robert Bolton* (London, 1641).

[116] D. J. H. Clifford (ed.), *The Diaries of Lady Anne Clifford* (revised edn, Stroud, 2003), pp. 33, 53.

the variety of places which might be usefully employed for pious reading from her godly mother, Margaret Clifford. For Margaret, godly reading was intimately connected with the landscape and her immediate physical surroundings. She read her Bible while she walked in the woods and placed her book 'in some faire tree' while she meditated on her reading.[117] In a similar way, walking was at the centre of Mary Rich's religiosity and it was while walking in what she called 'the wilderness' that she engaged in meditation. As Anthony Walker explained in her funeral sermon, this meditation 'was her *Master-piece*' and she devoted about two hours to it each day.[118] Although it is tempting to assume that meditation, especially that performed alone, was likely to have been an individualistic activity divorced from the prescription of texts or the pressures of everyday life – the very use of the term 'wilderness' conjures up modern notions of solitude in ways which were probably alien to seventeenth-century ears – Mary Rich's diaries suggest otherwise. The meditation she performed while walking could be implicitly textual, as she mulled over a biblical text or a recent sermon while she walked. But it could also be overtly so. On occasion, for example, she noted that she read while she walked, in particular from some letters by a Mr Rutherford which appear to have been bespoke items of spiritual direction and which she obviously saw as especially appropriate texts to be read while walking in the wilderness.[119] Perhaps this was a particularly affected form of aristocratic godly piety. But we should not forget either that such walking and meditation came directly after her early morning (closet) reading and the two were obviously connected. Rich used her walks as occasions on which to meditate on issues raised in her godly reading and the two activities shared a single purpose in opening up her heart to the Lord.[120]

But reading in gardens or while walking was not always or necessarily individual. When he stumbled across 'a shepheard and his little boy reading, far from any houses or sight of people, the Bible to him' during a visit to Ashtead Downs in Surrey in 1667, it conjured up for Samuel Pepys an image of almost perfect religious sociability: it was, he wrote,

---

[117] See Harold Love, *Scribal Publication in Seventeenth-Century England* (Oxford, 1993), p. 197.
[118] Walker, *Eureka, Eureka*, p. 61.
[119] BL, Additional MSS 27351–5 (Diaries of Mary Rich, Countess of Warwick, 5 vols., 1666–77), vol. I, fos. 11v, 14v, 16r, 22r and *passim*.
[120] Ibid., vol. II, fo. 8v, for an explicit connection between the two activities.

'the most pleasant and innocent sight that ever I saw in my life'.[121] But such outdoor communal reading also occurred in more explicitly godly contexts. When he was not reading and praying inside, and not smashing images, John Bruen was always ready to read. For the purposes of worshipping God, he had not only the rooms of his home but also 'his Gardens, Orchards, Arbors, Groves, Woods and Fields, Walkes and Shades, where he did delight to speak and commune with his best friend'.[122] As his biographer recalled, 'he did usually carry about him some part of the Bible, or his Sermon Note booke, if he went abroad into the field to meditate'. When he had been journeying to sermons, he would repeat his notes to those who travelled with him, whether on foot or in his carriage.[123] Likewise, William Gouge took with him a little book with the heads of every chapter in the Bible wherever he went.[124] For Anne Clifford, walking could be a bookish activity. Her diary entry for 16 March 1617 reads, 'This day I spent walking in the park with Judith, carrying my Bible with me, thinking on my present fortunes & what troubles I have passed through.'[125] In contrast, Margaret Hoby's walks around the garden would be taken up either with meditation or with wholesome conversation. Although she occasionally noted being read to from Perkins by her 'women' while she worked in the granary, in general Hoby would return from her meditative walks and immediately write notes upon them, or in the margins of her Bible or Testament.[126] There are many examples of those who, although not bold enough to read while walking, would do so on their return, the meditative process of their walking feeding into the devotion required for spiritual reading. Thus 'When he was in the Countrey', the puritan figurehead Arthur Hildersham 'used to walk alone every morning near on an hour' and when he returned, he would read a single chapter of a book with some intensity, making observations in the margin and cross-references in his commonplace book.[127] Such reading, when combined with industriousness, appealed to nonconformists too.

[121] *The Diary of Samuel Pepys*, ed. R. C. Latham and W. Matthews (11 vols., London, 1970–83), vol. VIII, p. 338 (14 July 1667). That the shepherd had once been a household servant also suggests the connection between domestic piety and that reading practised out of doors.
[122] Hinde, *A Faithfull Remonstrance of the Holy Life and Happy Death, of John Bruen*, p. 156.
[123] Ibid., pp. 142, 102.   [124] Clarke, *The Lives of Thirty-Two English Divines*, p. 236.
[125] Clifford, *The Diaries of Lady Anne Clifford*, p. 54.
[126] Moody, *The Private Life of an Elizabethan Lady*, pp. 27, 51.
[127] Clarke, *The Lives of Thirty-Two English Divines*, pp. 121–2.

Anne Dawson, the early eighteenth-century Rochdale nonconformist diarist, described her upbringing as including sessions of such reading. In July 1722, she wrote in her diary:

This day my Father read to us most of the day as we sat out at work[.] I thought it pleasant the book was to assist us in preparing for the plague by way of Dialogue, Lord help me to get ready for death and then I may say welcome even Pestilence.[128]

Hardly a defining aspect of puritan culture, reading out of doors nevertheless seems to have been something that many of the godly did. It also tended to reinforce what to their enemies was a suspicious biblio-centric fundamentalism. Perhaps they could recall those early Protestants for whom certain features of the landscape provided not only spaces for reading books in the earth that God had created but also places in which to conceal the Word from enemies of the truth, with trees in particular being common hiding places for illegal books and outlawed meetings.[129] The stereotypical puritan was described with a Bible under the arm, perhaps gadding to a sermon or a conventicle. William Weston, a Jesuit with an eye for detail and a nose for a good story that would damage his adversaries, described the scene at a godly exercise. Thousands of ordinary Protestants, wrote Weston, 'their horses and pack animals burdened with a multitude of Bibles', gathered to hear sermons 'on a large level stretch of ground' within the precincts of Wisbech prison:

Each of them had his own Bible, and sedulously turned the pages and looked up the texts cited by the preachers, discussing the passages among themselves to see whether they had quoted them to the point, and accurately, and in harmony with their tenets. Also they would start arguing among themselves about the meaning of passages from the Scriptures – men, women, boys, girls, rustics, labourers and idiots – and more often than not, it was said, it ended in violence and fisticuffs.[130]

For Weston, this was a seditious meeting on a par with a witches' sabbat, and it was entirely predictable that his account of unrestrained Bible-reading would end in disorder. The bookishness of the godly extended beyond institutions and buildings, and outdoors it could clearly be both individual and communal, depending again on context rather than on

---

[128] BL, Add MS, 71626 ('The Diary of Anne (Dawson) Evans'), fo. 38v.
[129] *Actes and Monuments* (1583), p. 815.
[130] William Weston, *The Autobiography of an Elizabethan*, trans. Philip Caraman (London, 1955), p. 164.

Figure 2. John Bunyan, *The life and death of Mr. Badman* (London, 1696), p. 106.
© The British Library Board. Shelfmark 4414.aaa.15.

levels of literacy. As the illustration in Bunyan's *The life and death of Mr. Badman* (1696) (Figure 2) shows, communal reading out of doors did not only smack of an illegal conventicle but was also part of the self-representation of the godly.

CONCLUSION

Where the previous chapter examined those spaces within the household which we might have expected to provide ample evidence of individual, private and silent reading and found a significant amount of collective reading and piety, by focusing on the more clearly social spaces of the household this chapter has delineated some of the contours of communal reading among the godly. Naturally, not all godly reading was communal and oral and we have seen those who cultivated individual styles of piety by reading alone, for instance in their gardens, but communal reading has been shown repeatedly to have been a central strand of godly piety.

This reading, as we have seen, was far from static or mundane. Instead, by reading their diaries and memoirs against the grain, we have seen how individuals could read in different ways in part depending on the physical and social contexts in which they were set. And godly reading stretched beyond the idealized, ordered, patriarchal scene of a father reading the Bible to his nuclear family. Instead, although it would be wrong to play down the importance of the Bible to godly families, we have seen how they drew spiritual succour from a broader godly canon of literature, a canon that retained its currency over the seventeenth century. And this reading formed part of a wider godly culture that must not be contrasted too sharply with more 'popular' forms of culture. Godly reading was about style as well as content and we have seen some of the historiographical consequences of unpicking the nature of godly reading practices. In particular, a close focus on forms of communal reading has added weight to the argument that puritanism was a culture which engendered radicalism as well as conformity. Reading reveals a spectrum of puritan activity, from reading in the family (although when 'family' is understood culturally and the practices unpicked this reading is not without radicalism) to reading in the conventicle or when confronted with demoniacs. In fact, analysing reading in such apparently unusual contexts tends to show that we should place the culture of the conventicle and the spectacle of demonic possession much closer to the mainstream of puritan culture. And, throughout, communal reading had a key part to play in this culture. The complexities of godly reading and godly readers have been evident throughout this chapter and they will be developed further when we expand our analysis beyond the confines of the household in subsequent chapters.

CHAPTER 4

Reading the library

INTRODUCTION

The previous chapters have explored spaces of reading within the household as places of cultural transaction. This chapter examines the reading of the godly in spaces specifically designed for reading – libraries. From small collections of cheap books in English, prized as tokens of England's elect status in the aftermath of the Reformation, to the larger parish collections designed to instruct parishioners in England and its colonies in the eighteenth century, the library was of prime importance in the fashioning of godly identity.

Defining what we mean by 'library' is not entirely straightforward, as the word has several meanings which are used with some elasticity.[1] A library is a building (or room) which houses a collection of books, a room set apart for reading, and the collection of books themselves. Such elasticity poses some questions pertinent to this book, notably the point at which a collection of books becomes a library. In the early modern period, it is enough to say that the library was either a relatively large personal collection of books, or a building or institution in which books – but not just books – were to be housed and read. John Rastrick's brief recollection of a visit to Manchester at the very end of the seventeenth century gives us an insight into what struck contemporaries about libraries. Rastrick wrote:

We dined at the Town called Chappel in the Frith, and got that night to Manchester. What pleased us best there was the Library a place of easie access at the due hours and there I spent some time. The Books are many and all chained. There I saw the Skin (stuffed) of an American Snake (I think a Rattle

---

[1] See Roger Chartier, *The Order of Books: Readers, Authors, and Libraries in Europe between the Fourteenth and Eighteenth Centuries*, trans. Lydia G. Cochrane (Cambridge, 1994), Chapter 3, esp. the helpful discussion on pp. 69–70.

Snake) of a vast length I think about 14 or 16 foot. A pair of large Globes in an Apartment by themselves, (locked up.) and a handsome Barometer.[2]

Libraries were places of knowledge and cultural exchange. They were places to read and to talk and to discuss. While behaviour in a modern library is likely to be defined by a series of negative commandments – no talking, no mobile phone, no food or drink, no writing in books, etc. – the atmosphere in an early modern library was more creative. The library was a bustling space where meetings and discussions could take place, and where reading was one activity among many. Strikingly, many of the readers were likely to be stood at sloping desks which adjoined the bookshelves, rather than ensconced in an individual desk. And they might be in the library to look at coins and artefacts and scientific instruments as well as to read in the narrow sense. Such a convergence of intellectual and social pursuits makes the library an especially important place in which to examine the relationship between reading and the formation of godly identity.

Since the mid-nineteenth century, there has been a vast amount of scholarly research into early modern libraries and their contents, particularly by bibliographers.[3] Much of this work has been concerned with cataloguing and reconstructing the contents of individual libraries.[4] Another strand in bibliography explores the organization of early modern libraries, frequently taking its lead from key texts like Gabriel Naudé's *Advis pour dresser une bibliothèque*.[5] And there have been some recent attempts to pull together the strands of such work, notably the huge collaborative editions *Histoire des bibliothèques françaises* and *The Cambridge History of Libraries in Britain and Ireland*.[6]

---

[2] *The Life of John Rastrick*, p. 141. The presence of the snake indicates that this was Humphrey Chetham's Library.

[3] For two general works, see Edward Edwards, *Memoirs of Libraries* (2 vols., London, 1859), Sears Jayne, *Library Catalogues of the English Renaissance* (2nd edn, Winchester, 1989). Particularly valuable, among many others, are James Carley (ed.), *The Libraries of King Henry VIII* (London, 2000); Jennifer Summit, *Memory's Library: Medieval Books in Early Modern England* (Chicago, 2008); and William H. Sherman, *Renaissance Libraries* (forthcoming).

[4] See esp. R. J. Fehrenbach and E. S. Leedham-Green (eds.), *Private Libraries in Renaissance England* (Binghamton, NY, 1992–).

[5] Gabriel Naudé, *Advis pour dresser une bibliothèque* (Paris, 1627) (English translation, John Evelyn, *Instructions Concerning Erecting of a Library* (London, 1661)). For a good example of the broader intellectual history into which such works can be placed, see Paul Nelles, 'The Library as an Instrument of Discovery: Gabriel Naudé and the Uses of History', in Donald R. Kelley (ed.), *History and the Disciplines: The Reclassification of Knowledge in Early Modern Europe* (Rochester, NY, 1997), pp. 41–57.

[6] André Vernet, Claude Jolly, Dominique Varry and Martine Poulain (eds.), *Histoire des bibliothèques françaises* (4 vols., Paris, 1988–92); Peter Hoare (ed.), *The Cambridge History of Libraries in Britain and Ireland* (3 vols., Cambridge, 2006).

For all this valuable work, such studies do not get us very close to the heart of the matter when it comes to exploring how people read. For this, we must look to those who have taken up the mantle of Lisa Jardine and Anthony Grafton's seminal article on reading for action and explored libraries as sites of exchange and uncovered something of the reading which went on there. There is strikingly less on this subject than there is on the contents of the libraries, little that pushes the boundaries of this subject after Bill Sherman's *John Dee: The Politics of Reading and Writing in the English Renaissance.*[7] This is particularly unfortunate for studies of reading because working outwards from catalogues is often unreliable, tending towards an irenicism that is particularly misleading in studies of religious cultures. An extreme example of the absurdity such an approach could potentially provide might be found in Sion College library, established as the intellectual hub of an institution dedicated to fostering the interests of hotter Protestant clergy. Through donation and confiscation, this collection contained both the canon of radical Protestant theology and the library of the Jesuit community which operated out of Holbeck in Nottinghamshire, which was seized in 1679.[8] Although puritans and Catholics read the books of their opponents, working outwards from a library list would in this case be likely to produce absurd results. Likewise, work that focuses on the moment of establishment of a library, or the wishes of its founder, is sure to run into trouble. The character of a library was defined by its use and its users.

Instead, we need to be alert to the use of these libraries in context and in particular to the overlap between the library as a site of cultural exchange and the intersections and mutual dependence of speech, manuscript and print which D. F. McKenzie rightly identified as being at the heart of an understanding of the history of communication in the seventeenth century.[9] Such fluid boundaries are attested to by John

---

[7] Lisa Jardine and Anthony Grafton, '"Studied for Action": How Gabriel Harvey Read his Livy', *Past and Present*, 129 (1990), pp. 30–78; Anthony Grafton, *Commerce with the Classics: Ancient Books and Renaissance Readers* (Ann Arbor, MI, 1997); William H. Sherman, *John Dee: The Politics of Reading and Writing in the English Renaissance* (Amherst, MA, 1995). There is, of course, rather more on the library as a focus for cultural exchange in work on the Enlightenment, some of which makes some useful observations about the later seventeenth century. See, for example, Justin Champion, *Republican Learning: John Toland and the Crisis of Christian Culture, 1696–1722* (Manchester, 2003), pp. 25–44; and Jonathan I. Israel, *Radical Enlightenment: Philosophy and the Making of Modernity 1650–1750* (Oxford, 2001), 119–41.

[8] See Hendrik Dijkgraaf, *The Library of a Jesuit Community at Holbeck, Nottinghamshire (1679)* (Nijmegen and Cambridge, 2003).

[9] D. F. McKenzie, 'Speech–Manuscript–Print', in D. Oliphant and R. Bradford (eds.), *New Directions in Textual Studies* (Austin, TX, 1990), pp. 86–109 (reprinted in D. F. McKenzie, *Making Meaning: 'Printers of the Mind' and Other Essays*, ed. Peter D. McDonald and Michael F. Suarez, SJ (Amherst, MA, 2002), pp. 237–58).

Favour, the godly vicar of Halifax, who compiled his *Antiquitie Triumph-ing over Noveltie* (1619) with considerable help from Archbishop Tobie Matthew's 'plentifully furnished' library. Who better to dedicate his book to, wrote Favour in a moment of uncharacteristic deference, than Matthew, 'who hath not onely read all the *Ancient Fathers* with a dilligent eye, but hath also noted them with a judicious pen (as mine owne eyes are witnesses, and God reward you for such my libertie) and made continuall use of them in his Sermons'.[10] Favour was aware of the intersections between printed books, manuscript notes and the spoken word and between the library as a place for the exchange of knowledge and the defence of the Reformation in the north of England.

Favour's comments, however formulaic, also alert us to the importance of the library in the godly imagination. It is a commonplace that commentators associated the emergence of Protestantism with the development of printing. For John Foxe, as we have seen, 'the excellent arte or science of printing' was a bomb which exploded the myths of popish superstition and tore open the truth of the gospel to the people of the world: 'the penne of Luther', when transformed into print, 'set the triple crown so awry on the popes head, that it is like never to be set streight agayne'.[11] And such an association persisted into the seventeenth century (and beyond). So Nehemiah Wallington, perhaps more sensitive than most to the legacies of the Reformation, collected a list of 'Judgments of God upon those that will destroy good Bookes'.[12] Libraries figured especially strongly in the godly imagination, and formed a crucial part of their religious and cultural identity. Sometimes the association was meta-phorical. The godly Essex rector Richard Crakanthorpe (1568–1624), for example, described his puritan mentor John Rainolds (1549–1607) as 'a walking library of all learning and all knowledge'.[13] At other times, the association was between real libraries and budding godly identity. John Rastrick remembered how catching sight of his minister's library ignited his own desire to become a clergyman. Like a cowboy without his horse, the godly minister without his books was intellectually impotent and spiritually deadened. During the Civil War, ministers defended their libraries as markers of their religious identity. Plundered and pillaged, the fate of libraries mirrored the sufferings of the clergy. Time and again,

[10] John Favour, *Antiquitie Triumphing over Noveltie* (London, 1619), sigs. A2v, A3r–v.
[11] *Actes and Monuments* (1583), p. 708.
[12] BL, Sloane MS 1457 (Nehemiah Wallington, 'A Memoriall of Gods Judgments upon Sabbath Breakers, Drunkerds and Other Vile Livers'), fol. 73r.
[13] Richard Crakanthorpe, *Defensio ecclesiae Anglicanae* (London, 1625), p. 494.

those who survived the revolution bemoaned the fate of themselves and their books. Publishing a Fast Sermon in 1644, the presbyterian preacher John Shawe grumbled about the times 'when my poor library and I are so far asunder' and equated the plundering of his library with the 'quarrelling times, wherein men turn Plow-shares into swords'.[14] Likewise, nonconformists after the Restoration routinely had their libraries confiscated as part of persecution and went to elaborate lengths to avoid being deprived of the books which played such a central role in their ministry. Oliver Heywood, for instance, on being warned of an impending raid, remarked in his diary that he 'removed in the night my bookes ... and dispersed them into severall houses'.[15]

Of course, there was a danger of venerating the library and treating it with a mystical awe. When the nonconformist minister Thomas Goodwin (1600–80) lost half of his library – valued at more than one thousand pounds – in the Great Fire of 1666, it was, he wrote, 'a rebuke of Providence, for having loved his library too much'.[16] But the records we have attest to how important the library was to the godly. Thomas Jollie's will, for example, was bound into an octavo book in which he kept a catalogue of the books of the dissenting meeting's library.[17] The godly would seek out libraries when they travelled abroad and praise them as underpinning the culture of Protestantism. A world without libraries was too much to bear. John Rastrick even wrote a poem in which he considered the fate of the Bodleian Library in the everlasting fire of the apocalypse.[18]

Libraries were intellectual centres in which godly religiosity was shaped and honed. Over the course of the seventeenth century, they also became one of the key arenas in which orthodoxy was contested. As such, they were vital places in the making of godly identity. This chapter will focus

---

[14] John Shawe, *Two Clean Birds: Or, The Cleansing of the Leper* (York, 1644), sig. B1r.

[15] Heywood, *Diaries*, vol. II, pp. 248–9. I am grateful to Sam Thomas for this reference.

[16] Cited in David L. Ferch, '"Good Books Are a Very Great Mercy to the World": Persecution, Private Libraries, and the Printed Word in the Early Development of the Dissenting Academies, 1663–1730', *Journal of Library History*, 21 (1986), p. 350.

[17] This library was essentially his own personal collection but was circulated and appeared to function as a quasi-institutional collection. See Henry Fishwick (ed.), *The Note Book of the Rev. Thomas Jolly, A.D. 1671–1693. Extracts from the Church Book of Altham and Wymondhouses, 1649–1725. And an Account of the Jolly Family of Standish, Gorton, and Altham*. Chetham Society, new ser., 33 (Manchester, 1895), p. 152.

[18] See John Rastrick, 'The Dissolution', reproduced in Andrew Cambers, '"But Where Shall My Soul Repose?" Nonconformity, Science and the Geography of the Afterlife, c. 1660–1720', in Peter Clarke and Tony Claydon (eds.), *The Church, the Afterlife and the Fate of the Soul*, Studies in Church History, 45 (Woodbridge, 2009), pp. 276–8.

on those libraries which were associated most with the formation of religious identity – the personal library, the parish library, the town library, and those connected with institutions: schools, universities and colleges. Frequently, those libraries under discussion will not be easily categorized as *simply* personal or institutional, for example, and they might cross over two or more categories. This is particularly the case with those libraries which we track over the long seventeenth century – some started out as personal collections and we can trace their journey from personal to parish to town libraries. Although the material for library usage is spread more thinly than we might wish, there is enough to make some generalizations about how people read in libraries in seventeenth-century England. What follows uses this evidence to explore how the godly read in libraries and asks how far this reading contrasted with the self-consciously devotional reading of the household, as well as probing how far the library was the means through which the broader godly canon was disseminated. It also examines how such libraries became signs of godly identity – for, as libraries were bequeathed, sold and exchanged, they were prized, like the lives and diaries examined in the previous chapters, as markers of religious identity as well as repositories of useful information. Indeed, it was not only in libraries that godly identity was shaped; it has often been through the same libraries that our knowledge of puritanism has survived.[19]

PERSONAL LIBRARIES AND THE GODLY COMMUNITY

An individual's collection of books might be transformed into a library for the religious community when their owner allowed access to a large collection of books which remained in the home or when their books were transferred to institutions. The transition from personal to institutional library often came through bequest. In such bequests, as well as in those between individuals, we can see the importance the godly placed on their libraries in fashioning their religious identity. Many of these bequests had elaborate provisions intimately connected with the maintenance of

---

[19] For useful remarks on libraries as centres of intellectual exchange, see F. J. Levy, 'How Information Spread among the Gentry, 1550–1640', *Journal of British Studies*, 21 (1982), pp. 11–34, esp. p. 25; Dr Williams's Library both shows the overlap between puritanism and nonconformity and is itself partially responsible for providing continuing access to materials relating to the godly. A similar point can be made about the Cottonian Library, for which see Colin Tite, *The Early Records of Sir Robert Cotton's Library: Formation, Cataloguing, Use* (London, 2003); and Kevin Sharpe, *Sir Robert Cotton, 1586–1631: History and Politics in Early Modern England* (Oxford, 1979).

godliness, through hardening familial ties and entrenching the godly in the established church. These connections come through clearly in those who left sizeable, but not enormous, collections to family members. The will of the godly Essex rector Richard Crakanthorpe, which he drew up three months before his death in November 1624, may serve as an example. Like so many testators, Crakanthorpe bequeathed single volumes to named individuals, cementing godly alliances and passing down relics of the faith. More unusually, he stipulated in some detail what should happen to his library after his death:

> Touching my library and bookes hereafter not perticulerly bequeathed I give them all to my sonne John so soone as hee shall have taken the degree of Batchelor of Arts in either Universitie Oxford or Cambridge. And if hee shall not have taken that degree before his age of twentie six yeares complete: Then I give all the said Bookes to my daughter dorothie and her husband if shee bee att that time married to a minister for which bookes they shall pay to my said sonne John the whole somme of fourescore pounds att his age of twentie seaven yeares compleate

If this did not happen, the library would be left to his other two daughters in turn upon the same conditions. But if none of his children fulfilled his requirements, he willed that the library, whose value he estimated at two hundred and thirty pounds, should be offered to Michael Honywood for one hundred and forty pounds. Crakanthorpe clearly thought that Honywood, who was by then a fellow of Christ's College, Cambridge, and had helped him write his *Logicae libri quinque* (1622), would be a safe pair of godly hands for his godly books. He was not to know that he would only be half right and that Honywood would indeed be a trusty bibliophile but would side with Anglican royalism during England's troubles. Honywood remained within the Church of England, living in exile in Utrecht between 1643 and 1660, becoming friends with the future archbishop of Canterbury William Sancroft and apparently allowing the exiled Anglican clergy in the Netherlands the full use of his extensive library in the preparation of their polemic. At the Restoration, Honywood became dean of Lincoln, funded the building of the cathedral library from Sir Christopher Wren's design, and placed his books there for the defence of the Anglican establishment.

Like many other godly ministers, Crakanthorpe had a series of 'paper bookes', which probably included things like sermon notes and skeletons, accounts and perhaps even material designed to be circulated in manuscript. However, although few ministers mention them explicitly in their wills and most bequeathed them as a job lot, Crakanthorpe made provision for these books, noting:

For my paper bookes as also for the preserveing of them together that they bee not lost or dispersed I have left private Instructions written with mine owne hand and adjoyneing to the catalogue of my Bookes which I desire my executor and all whome it may concerne to see duely observed.

Crakanthorpe's example sheds some light on how the godly saw their libraries, in particular their desire for them to be kept whole and to function as repositories for the maintenance of the godly clergy. It also illuminates how books could be used to cement godly dynasties and, of course, how the intentions of testators did not always turn out as expected.[20]

Libraries were clearly useful gifts for budding clergy but it is note-worthy how many left their children, or relatives, books on condition that they keep the faith. Robert Middleton, the vicar of Cuckfield in Sussex, for example, left nearly seven hundred books to the son of his deceased friend Simon Patrick, bishop of Ely, on condition that the young student give up the legal career on which he was intent and become a clergyman.[21] Although we will discuss those collections designed for public use in later sections, it is also noteworthy how many godly and nonconformist clergy bequeathed their libraries for the use of a wider range of clergy and laity. The moderate puritan clergyman Thomas Pierson, for example, beside bequests of single volumes of works of practical divinity to family members, gave his personal library of more than 450 books to be used by fourteen named local ministers in their parishes. Twenty-four of these books survive in More parish library in Shropshire, comprising staples of continental Reformation history and theology, alongside works of prac-tical puritan divinity.[22] Likewise, John Rastrick's will sheds light on how the godly style of religiosity spanned church divides in the late seventeenth and early eighteenth centuries. In his will, Rastrick bequeathed his books, manuscripts, mathematical instruments, telescopes, double barometer, portrait (painted by Daniel de Koninck, an artist of some standing who had moved to England in 1690), and everything else in the shelves and cases of his study and parlour to his son William. The bequest was 'upon condition that he continue a minister and preacher of the Gospell whether in a Conforming or nonConforming capacity'. If his son did not continue

---

[20] London Metropolitan Archives, DL/C/362/Richard Crakanthorpe/1625/April, M/F X19/16, fols. 2r–3v. For Honywood, see *ODNB*, s.v. 'Honywood, Michael (1596–1681)'; and Naomi Linnell, 'Michael Honywood and Lincoln Cathedral Library', *The Library*, 6th ser., 5 (1983), pp. 126–39.

[21] See D. R. Woolf, *Reading History in Early Modern England* (Cambridge, 2000), p. 158.

[22] See TNA: PRO PROB 11/164, fo. 358r–v; Conal Condren, 'More Parish Library, Salop', *Library History*, 7 (1987), pp. 141–62; and Jacqueline Eales, 'Thomas Pierson and the Transmission of the Moderate Puritan Tradition', *Midland History*, 20 (1995), pp. 73–102.

in the profession, or leave Rastrick a scholarly grandson, he bequeathed the collection first to any conformist or nonconformist minister that any of his daughters should marry and if this did not prevail then it was his wish that

my said Library shall not be auctioned out or Sold to any Booksellers but be disposed of to raise a publick Library for the use of the Dissenting Ministers in the City of Norwich ... to be managed at the Discretion of the said Dissenting ministers in Conjunction with an Equall number of the City Clergy whom they the Dissenting ministers shall chuse.[23]

Such bequests reveal a continuity in evangelical identity over the long seventeenth century that does not sit easily with received notions of church divides. Indeed, it is noteworthy that the only named donor of money, rather than individual books, to Lincoln cathedral library throughout the seventeenth and eighteenth centuries was the very same John Rastrick, whose gift of fifty shillings towards books for the library which were to be chosen by the dean and chapter came in 1707, despite the fact that he had left the Church of England acrimoniously twenty years previously.[24] Others made similar bequests. Joseph Robinson, the ejected minister of Cottingham, Yorkshire, bequeathed all his books that were not in English to his 'loving friend Thomas Revell, Curate of Hemmingbrough'.[25]

The same continuities are also occasionally evident in those godly libraries which were purchased wholesale, usually after their owner's death. Such purchases were doubly beneficial to canny godly book buyers since not only would they get a collection of books with which they would sympathize and which might further their family piety but they were also likely to get it at a knockdown price. During a visit to Wormingford in Essex to see Lady Waldegrave in February 1646, Ralph Josselin had the good fortune to purchase the library of Mr Thomas Pilgrim, the appropriately named vicar of Wormingford. Pilgrim had suffered a seizure in 1644, when he 'fell downe dead in his pulpitt ... he dyed not outright but

---

[23] Norfolk Record Office, Norwich, Will Register, Kirke, 82–4 (will of John Rastrick of King's Lynn, 1727); *The Life of John Rastrick*, p. 205.

[24] Lincoln Cathedral Library, Lincoln MSS 256, p. 10: '1707 Mem. that Mr Rastrick formerly Vicar of Kirton in Holland having some years ago subscribed fifty shillings for the use of the Library hath paid the said fifty shill. which is to be laid out in such books as the Dean and Chapter think fit'. Cited in Naomi Linnell, 'The Catalogues of Lincoln Cathedral Library', *Library History*, 7 (1985), p. 6.

[25] See Samuel S. Thomas, 'Individuals and Communities: Religious Life in Restoration England' (unpublished PhD thesis, Washington University, 2003), p. 264.

their was expected no great hopes of his life', and he died shortly afterwards. Josselin bought his library for sixteen pounds and eighteen shillings and was doubly pleased that, despite transporting the collection back to Earls Colne on a rainy February afternoon, 'the books had no hurt'.[26] For others, the purchase of whole libraries appears to have been less like picking over the intellectual carcasses of deceased brethren and more like an acceptable charitable means of supporting clerical widows deprived of income or support. Archbishop Tobie Matthew, for instance, reportedly purchased the libraries of deceased clerics more as a way of supporting their widows than of bolstering his already considerable personal collection of books.[27]

Particularly among nonconformists after the Restoration, the library could function as a hub for godly sociability and a location for communal reading. The library of Samuel Jeake of Rye (1623–90) provides a fascinating insight into the nature of the godly library in the seventeenth century. Jeake was first a lawyer, then town clerk, and after the Restoration the leader of the nonconformist congregation in Rye. He built up a remarkable library of more than two thousand items and kept a catalogue of its contents.[28] The contents of the library shed some light on how nonconformists understood their religious culture. Jeake assembled a wide-ranging collection which included works of literature, law, science and magic. Strikingly, he collected both the radical pamphlets of the Civil War era (including a collection of pamphlets bound under the name of Hendrik Niclaes) and the canon of seventeenth-century puritan practical divinity, including works by Perkins, Ames, Bolton and Baxter.[29] Though caution should be exercised when working outwards from library catalogues, in particular because Jeake appears to have built up his collection in part through the purchase of smaller libraries, the collection at least appears to suggest both the continuity of puritanism over the seventeenth century and the interwoven nature of puritanism and radicalism. Jeake's notebooks attest to how he used his library in the compilation of his sermons, but it is also possible that, since Jeake was the leader of the

---

[26] See Alan Macfarlane (ed.), *The Diary of Ralph Josselin, 1616–1683* (Oxford, 1976), pp. 18, 55.

[27] See *ODNB*, s.v. 'Matthew, Tobie (1544?–1628)'.

[28] See Michael Hunter, Giles Mandelbrote, Richard Ovenden and Nigel Smith (eds.), *A Radical's Books: The Library Catalogue of Samuel Jeake of Rye, 1623–90* (London, 1999).

[29] Ibid., p. xlvii. That such collections should be treated with caution when trying to extrapolate towards religious identity need only be seen in the example of Richard Bancroft, who labelled his collection of puritan and Martinist pamphlets as 'Libri Puritani' but had no sympathy at all with them.

nonconformists in Rye who on occasion met in his house, the library functioned as the hub of the religious community there.[30]

The lending of books formed part of godly sociability in the seventeenth century. We can see this particularly clearly in the case of the early dissenting academies, which relied on books to meet their educational and religious objectives but which were also denied institutional libraries until 1730.[31] Before then, they relied on the private libraries of puritan divines which were often circulated to good effect, and, as Daniel Defoe remarked of the Newington Green academy, those academies without recourse to the use of a large private collection were hamstrung in their evangelical endeavour.[32] Dissenting tutors often kept large collections which could be used by their students. The ejected minister Theophilus Gale amassed a large collection of books which might have been used by his students at Newington Green academy, although his bequest of his library of one thousand books to Harvard on his death in 1679 cut short its influence on the academy.[33] John Woodhouse, the presbyterian minister who established an important dissenting academy at Sheriffhales, Shropshire, kept a library for the use of his students which was based on the works of early Stuart puritanism.[34] James Forbes put his theology collection to good use in training students at his Gloucester academy and on his death in 1712 bequeathed his library, which comprised 1,300 printed books and three hundred pamphlets, as well as numerous manuscripts, in trust for the use of dissenting ministers in the county. Interestingly, he

left his books upon Trust to permit the Dissenting Protestant Ministers who should succeed the said James Forbes and live in the said city to use the same and at their discretion to lend one book at a time to any of the Protestant Dissenting

---

[30] For further commentary on Jeake, see Giles Mandelbrote, 'Personal Owners of Books', in G. Mandelbrote and K. A. Manley (eds.), *The Cambridge History of Libraries in Britain and Ireland. Volume II 1640–1850* (Cambridge, 2006), pp. 182–3.

[31] Many of the libraries of the dissenting academies have been preserved but are remarkably little-studied. See, for example, the relatively thin coverage in Herbert McLachlan, *English Education under the Test Acts: Being the History of the Non-conformist Academies, 1662–1820*, University of Manchester Publications no. 213, Historical series no. 59 (Manchester, 1931). The forthcoming collaborative *A History of the Dissenting Academies in the British Isles, 1660–1860* promises to shed new light on these collections and their use.

[32] See H. Morley (ed.), *The Earlier Life and the Chief Earlier Works of Daniel Defoe* (London, 1889), p. 16.

[33] See *ODNB*, s.v. 'Gale, Theophilus'.

[34] See Ferch, 'Good Books are a Very Great Mercy to the World'; for the use of Woodhouse's library in the academy's curriculum, see Joshua Toulmin, *An Historical View of the State of the Protestant Dissenters in England* (London, 1814), pp. 225–30, 559–67.

Ministers in the County of Gloucester or to any of the Protestant Dissenting Congregation in the said City so [long] as they return it within a month.[35]

Such collections, as Ian Green has argued, became 'virtual circulating libraries for ministers, tutors and students'.[36] Although, as we have seen in the case of Michael Honywood, they could also be employed by Anglicans, the godly made particularly good use of the circulating library. In part, this was a product of circumstance but it was also because the circulating, borrowing and lending of books meshed well with their ethos of godly sociability and the devotional style that accompanied it. Oliver Heywood's diaries and papers offer a particularly good insight into the ways in which the personal library could become quasi-institutional through its use. Heywood allowed his library to be used by the students of Frankland's academy at Rathmell and donated them copies of his own printed works. In his notebooks he recorded those books he loaned out to individuals, striking through the name of the borrower on the book's safe return. Inevitably, not all were returned, and Heywood waited in vain for James Oates of Norwood Green in Halifax, who was one of his most dedicated followers, to return his copy of Christopher Love's *The Penitent Pardoned* (London, 1657).[37] Heywood's most extensive of these lists (which is not included in the printed edition) includes the details of almost one hundred book loans and allows us further insight into the practice. Again, it shows just one reader who failed to return a book – ironically, Samuel Smith, a member of Heywood's society, failed to return Henry Newcome's *The Sinner's Hope* (1660). More importantly, not only does the list show Heywood repeatedly lending books to the same men and women, it also reveals the extent to which the character of the books uncovers how far the post-Restoration nonconformist mindset remained firmly rooted in the early Stuart puritan past: the most frequently borrowed volumes included Samuel Clarke's *Martyrology* and Thomas Beard's *Theatre of Gods Judgements*.[38]

---

[35] A. G. Matthews, *Calamy Revised: Being a Revision of Edmund Calamy's Account of the Ministers and Others Ejected and Silenced, 1660–2* (Oxford, 1934), p. 205; on Forbes, see *ODNB*, s.v. 'Forbes, James'; A. T. S. James, 'The Forbes Library Southgate Chapel, Gloucester', *Transactions of the Congregational Historical Society*, 10 (1927–9), pp. 100–4; P. Heyworth, *James Forbes, Nonconformist: His Library* (Toronto, 1968).

[36] See Ian Green, 'Libraries for School Education and Personal Devotion', in Mandelbrote and Manley, *The Cambridge History of Libraries in Britain and Ireland. Volume II*, p. 53.

[37] Heywood, *Diaries*, vol. II, p. 184; vol. III, p. 65: BL, Additional MS 45965 ('Diary of the Rev. Oliver Heywood, March 1665/6–November 1673'), fos. 122–3.

[38] See BL, Additional MS 45965 ('Diary of the Rev. Oliver Heywood, March 1665/6–November 1673'), fos. 122v–123v. Samuel Smith was a member of Heywood's society, and lived in Farsley township in Calverley parish. He hosted two sermons in 1670, and Heywood stayed for the night after one of them. I owe this reference to Sam Thomas.

The authorities were clearly aware of the dangers of the religious and intellectual networks which the dissenters forged through the book and went to great efforts to seize those books which might have circulated and substituted for a dissenting ministry. It was in this context in 1664 that Heywood made a careful list of the titles and prices of the 265 books which had been taken from him 'for preaching the gospel'. The list is steeped in the literature of the Reformation and the English Calvinist tradition, and includes the works of Thomas Beard, William Perkins, Richard Rogers, William Prynne, John Dod, Samuel Clarke, Edmund Calamy, Henry Newcome and Richard Baxter.[39] Heywood created a ministry not only through the preached word but also through the printed book and he distributed many copies of his printed books free of charge among his wider congregation. The books circulated among the godly, much as the books dubbed 'domme preachers' did in the English Catholic community.[40]

The library of the journalist and frustrated historian of puritanism Roger Morrice both reflected and to some extent shaped his godly, Whig identity at the end of the seventeenth century. Morrice, who was amazingly well informed about the politics of the years 1677 to 1691, clearly got much of his information by keeping his ears open and being in constant contact with his informers. But his library, thrice catalogued in the 1680s and 1690s, also has much to tell us. It was, as Mark Goldie has written, 'the working library of a chronicler of contemporary affairs and historian of English Puritanism'.[41] The library complemented Morrice's (probable) work as a supplier of newsletters to a group of presbyterian–Whig politicians. It is unlike almost any other library catalogue of the period in that, despite containing perhaps 1,700 books and pamphlets, it focuses almost exclusively on works in English and more than half of its contents were published after 1670. Alongside the printed controversies of the period in which Morrice lived and worked, the collection was especially strong in the works of Elizabethan puritanism and early Stuart Calvinism. These stretched from the work of John Field, Thomas Cartwright and Walter Travers through to an impressive collection of the works produced by

[39] Heywood, *Diaries*, vol. II, pp. 123–7.
[40] For Heywood's distribution of his books, see ibid., vol. II, pp. 211–15; vol. III, pp. 51–7, 66–73, 75–6; Alexandra Walsham, '"Domme Preachers"? Post-Reformation English Catholicism and the Culture of Print', *Past and Present*, 168 (2000), pp. 72–123.
[41] Mark Goldie et al. (eds.), *The Entring Book of Roger Morrice 1677–1691* (6 vols., Woodbridge, 2007), vol. I, pp. 81, 79–86 (for Goldie's commentary on Morrice's library), and 352–93 (for the catalogue).

puritan clandestine presses in the Netherlands, and the works of early Stuart puritan devotional literature, from Arthur Dent's *The plaine mans path-way to heaven* (1601) and Lewis Bayly's *Practice of Piety* (1612) through to the bestsellers of Samuel Clarke and Richard Baxter. Such a collection is of considerable interest for it reveals not only a library with which Morrice worked and through which he hoped to write his long-planned but never realized history of puritanism, but also a collection which informed his own (and perhaps a wider) godly identity. The identity of the godly in the later seventeenth century was not divorced from the radicalism of their Elizabethan forebears but forged through it and informed by it. Like Jeake's library, Morrice's collection reminds us of the importance of casting our gaze over the long seventeenth century and not being blinded by the logic of the neat historiographical divides which did not matter to those who lived through this era.

The final way in which we might think about personal libraries and their relation to communal puritanism is through their dispersal. Even in their fragmentation, godly books had the power to strengthen social ties and forge collective piety. Godly social ties could make the dispersal of a library a pious event. In his will of 1689, Richard Baxter stipulated that Matthew Sylvester and Roger Morrice distribute his library to 'such young students as the said Mr. Silvester and Mr. Morrice shall nominate'. Thomas Parkhurst, the bookseller who was the crucial lynchpin in presbyterian networks, sent parcels of Baxter's books to nineteen individuals across England and Wales early in 1693. Such a gift clearly inspired awe in the recipients, many of whom carried the torch of nonconformity into the eighteenth century, as Baxter clearly intended.[42] Such dispersal was the safest option to that end before the establishment of Daniel Williams's library in 1729 and the flourishing of those attached to the dissenting academies after 1730.

Indeed, the connections between the godly and a novel method of disposing of libraries – the book auction – are revealing. The earliest English printed book auction catalogue was that of Lazarus Seaman's library in 1676.[43] It was announced in the final notice in the *London Gazette* on 19 October 1676 as an event worthy of curiosity:

[42] Ibid., vol. I, pp. 339–41; Dr Williams's Library, Morrice MS M, no. 12 and Morrice MS X. For the volumes which were dispersed, see Geoffrey F. Nuttall, 'A Transcript of Richard Baxter's Library Catalogue', *Journal of Ecclesiastical History*, 2 (1951), pp. 207–21; 3 (1952), pp. 74–100.

[43] *Catalogus variorum & insignium librorum instructissimæ bibliothecæ clarissimi doctissimiq[ue] viri Lazari Seaman, S.T.D. Quorum auctio habebitur Londini in ædibus defuncti in area & viculo Warwicensi, Octobris ultimo. Cura Gulielmi Cooper bibliopolæ* (London, 1676).

These are to give Notice, That the Sale of Dr *Seaman's* Library, by Auction, or who bids most, will begin in the Doctor's House in *Warwick lane* Court, on Tuesday, the last of *October*, and so continue from day to day, till they be all sold, according to the order of the Catalogue.[44]

This innovation was apparently inspired by the contact English presbyterian ministers had with the Dutch book trade, where such catalogues had been used since 1599.[45] The auctioneer Edward Millington credited the nonconformist Joseph Hill with this development, noting in a letter of June 1677 the 'great Service done to Learning and Learned men in your first advising and effectually setting on foot that admirable and Universally approved way of selling Librarys by Auction amongst us'.[46] The innovation, which was likely to have been born in part out of the lack of suitable institutions for dissenters to leave their libraries to, is important and had the added effect of establishing further links among the godly. It is striking how many of the early printed library auction catalogues were those of dissenters. As well as Lazarus Seaman, they included Thomas Manton, Thomas Watson, Thomas Vincent, Stephen Charnock, Owen Stockton, John Owen, Thomas Lye, William Cooper, Thomas Jacombe and Samuel Annesley.[47] The titles of the auction catalogues, many of which were

---

[44] *London Gazette*, no. 1140 (19 October 1676).

[45] On book auctions, see A. N. L. Munby and L. Coral, *British Book Sale Catalogues 1676–1800* (London, 1977); Robin Myers, M. Harris and Giles Mandelbrote (eds.), *Under the Hammer: Book Auctions since the Seventeenth Century* (London, 2001).

[46] Matthews, *Calamy Revised*, p. 265. It might be significant that one of Millington's first book auctions was that of the library of the Dutch Calvinist minister Gijsbert Voet (1589–1676) in November 1678. See *ODNB*, s.v. 'Millington, Edward.'

[47] See *Catalogus variorum & insignium librorum instructissimæ bibliothecæ clarissimi doctissimiq; Viri Thomæ Manton, S.T.D.* (London, 1678) (Thomas Manton); *Bibliotheca Charnockiana, sive, Catalogus librorum selectissimae bibliothecae clarissimi, doctissimiq; viri domini Steph. Charnock, S.T.B. nuperrime defuncti* (London, 1680) (Stephen Charnock); *Catalogus variorum librorum instructissimae bibliothecae doctissimi viri D. Thomae Watson, A.M. Scholae Suttonianae apud Charter-House, Londini nuperrime archididaschali* (London, 1680) (Thomas Watson); *Catalogus librorum in bibliothecis selectissimis doctissimorum virorum viz., D. Georgii Lawsoni, Salopiensis, D. Georgii Fawleri, Londinensis, D. Oweni Stockdoni, Colcestriensis, D. Thomæ Brooks, Londinensis* (London, 1681) (Owen Stockton); *Catalogus variorum librorum bibliothecae selectissimae Rev. Doct. Viri D. Tho. Lye B.D. nuperrime Londinensis, defuncti cui accessit bibliotheca Anglica non minus elegans & copiosa, M. Tho. Jennings civis Londinensis ingeniosissimi* (London, 1684) (Thomas Lye); *Bibliotheca Oweniana, sive, Catalogus librorum plurimis facultatibus insignium, instructissimæ bibliothecæ Rev. Doct. Vir. D. Joan Oweni* (London, 1684) (John Owen) – catalogues distributed in London, Oxford and Cambridge. *Bibliotheca Jacombiana, sive, Catalogus variorum librorum plurimis facultatibus insignium instructissimae bibliothecae Rev. Doct. Thomae Jacomb, S.T.D. ...: quorum auctio habebitur Londini in aedibus Nigri Cygni ex adverso australis porticus ecclesiae Cathed. Paulin. in Caemiterio D. Paul* (London, 1687) (Thomas Jacombe); *Catalogue of Library March 18 1697* (London, 1697) (Wing A3226: Samuel Annesley); *Catalogus variorum librorum ex bibliothecis selectissimis doctissimorum virorum, viz. R.D. Johan. Bradford, D.D., R.D. Gulielmi Cooperi, A.M. londinensium* (London, 1686) (William Cooper); *Catalogus variorum librorum in selectissimus*

distributed gratis by booksellers like Parkhurst, reveal that attention was drawn not only towards the contents of the books, which were usually organized by format and subject, but also towards their godly owner. Thomas Jacombe's status as a prominent nonconformist minister ensured that the catalogue of his library, when it was auctioned in 1687, was entitled *Bibliotheca Jacombiana*. Some of these nonconformist preachers clearly had a measure of celebrity, as we can see in further titles like *Bibliotheca Charnockiana* and *Bibliotheca Oweniana*. Clearly, this was not confined simply to clergy, and the library of Arthur Annesley, first Earl of Anglesey, went on sale as *Bibliotheca Anglesiana*. But it is striking how the libraries of those like Arthur Annesley and Lazarus Seaman, which were in some ways open to readers, were themselves sold on. As Annabel Patterson and Martin Dzelzainis have demonstrated, the interleaved copy of *Bibliotheca Anglesiana* at Lambeth Palace Library shows that the authorities were well aware that the recirculation of some of the radical books in such a well-known and well-used library was itself imbued with potential religious and political significance – Sir Roger L'Estrange appears to have withdrawn from the sale works by the likes of Harrington, Hobbes, Milton, Prynne and Baxter.[48] The purge of works from the sale was effective but the printed catalogue meant that readers were aware of these gaps. Roger Morrice, for example, drily recorded those volumes withdrawn from the sale, although he could not resist remarking that the very copy of Milton's *Eikonoklastes* in French translation, which had originally been included in the inventory, in fact bore the inscription 'Ex dono Rogeri Le Strang Armigeri'.[49] The sale of libraries clearly had the potential to unite the godly even when particularly sought-after radical books were removed, as well as recirculating the books that comprised their religious and cultural identity. That they were part of the dynamic culture of puritanism which encompassed a range of media and modes of communication is, of course, also apparent in the very locations where they were held. The libraries were sold and the auctions held at sites of sociable reading and conversation: the areas around St Paul's, at coffee houses, and in bookshops.

bibliothecis doctissimorum virorum; viz. D. Hen. Stubb nupperrime Londdinensis D. Dillinghami de Oundle Northamptoniensis D. Thomæ Vincent Londinensis D. Cautoni Westmonasterieusis (London, 1680) (Thomas Vincent).

[48] Lambeth Palace Library, shelfmark Z999; see Annabel Patterson and Martin Dzelzainis, 'Marvell and the Earl of Anglesey: A Chapter in the History of Reading', *Historical Journal*, 44 (2001), p. 712. Roger Morrice provides the fullest account of the censorship. See Goldie et al., *The Entring Book of Roger Morrice*, vol. III, pp. 279, 306, 309.

[49] Goldie et al., *The Entring Book of Roger Morrice*, vol. III, p. 306.

It might well be the case that the book auction – a one-off occasion which was presumably difficult to regulate (with the exceptions of high-profile auctions like that of Annesley's library) – was as likely a place to purchase a more radical godly volume as a bookshop. Indeed in 'The Compleat Auctioner' (Figure 3), a remarkable satirical engraving by Sutton Nicholls, dating from around 1700, the auctioneer was the sales-man for a remarkable range of literature. Although, as Brian Cowan has noted, the purpose of the engraving was clearly to satirize 'the pretensions to learning harbored by both the auctioneers and their many customers' who, as the verse at the foot of the engraving remarks, were attempting to purchase 'wit', the titles of the volumes, inscribed on the bottom edges of each book, at least suggest a connection between radicalism – sexual, religious, political – and the book auction. Among the titles clearly visible in the detail (Figure 4) are not only works like Peter Heylyn's ubiquitous *Cosmographie*, but also works of religious radicalism such as those of Lodowicke Muggleton, books which had been censored like Richard Head's *The English Rogue* (1665), the Earl of Rochester's poems, and clandestine works of pornography like the 'Play of Sodom'. Although it is impossible to be certain to which books the engraving alluded, it is interesting that titles like *Fam. of Love* might have referred to works of the mystical sect or conversely to works of satire against Familists, like Thomas Middleton's *The Family of Love* (1607).[50]

THE PARISH LIBRARY

The Clarendon Code, burgeoning Anglicanism and political suspicion limited the licit public venues for godly sociability and communal reading in the years after the Restoration. Such activities were at best questionable and at worst smacked of the illegal conventicle. It was as if government policy was based on Thomas Hobbes's theory that one of the key causes of the revolution had been 'the Reading of the books of Policy, and histories of the antient Greeks, and Romans'.[51] This suspicion meant that the godly had difficulty gaining access to parish libraries after the Restoration, in stark contrast to the freedom they had enjoyed before the Civil Wars. Indeed, the godly had been enthusiastic innovators in the creation and use of parish libraries in the late sixteenth and early seventeenth centuries,

---

[50] See Brian Cowan, *The Social Life of Coffee: The Emergence of the British Coffeehouse* (New Haven, CT, 2005), pp. 141–2.

[51] Thomas Hobbes, *Leviathan*, ed. Richard Tuck (Cambridge, 1991), p. 225.

Figure 3. Sutton Nicholls, 'The Compleat Auctioner' (ca. 1700), BM Sat., no. 1415.
© Trustees of the British Museum.

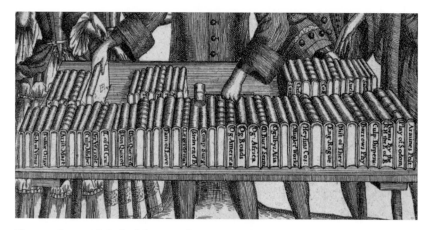

Figure 4. Sutton Nicholls, 'The Compleat Auctioner' (ca. 1700), BM Sat., no. 1415, detail.
© Trustees of the British Museum.

as the education of clergy and laity alike formed part of their desire for further religious reform. Although there are examples of parish libraries before the sixteenth century, and there was of course a long tradition of monastic libraries, the parish library was essentially a post-Reformation innovation.[52] Before then, what some call parish libraries were in effect personal (and usually small) collections of books, with little by way of the formal institutional arrangements in place to make them libraries in any meaningful sense. In contrast, post-Reformation parish libraries were frequently conceived of as part and parcel of the drive for further reformation and were often included in the religious, moral and educative programmes of reformations of manners in the period.[53]

Although twelve 'libraries' were founded before 1500 and a further nine between 1500 and 1573, the true beginnings of the post-Reformation parish library started with the library at St Martin's, Leicester, in 1586, perhaps under the benevolent eye of the puritan earl, Henry Hastings,

[52] For a useful overview see Teresa Webber, 'Monastic and Cathedral Book Collections in the Late Eleventh and Twelfth Centuries'; David N. Bell, 'The Libraries of Religious Houses in the Late Middle Ages'; and Peter J. Lucas, 'Borrowing and Reference: Access to Libraries in the Late Middle Ages', all in E. Leedham-Green and T. Webber (eds.), *The Cambridge History of Libraries in Britain and Ireland. Volume 1 To 1640* (Cambridge, 2006), pp. 109–25, 126–51, 242–64.

[53] See T. C. Curtis and W. A. Speck, 'The Societies for the Reformation of Manners: A Case Study in the Theory and Practice of Moral Reform', *Literature and History*, 3 (1976), pp. 45–64; and, for a broader overview, Martin Ingram, 'Reformation of Manners in Early Modern England', in Paul Griffiths, Adam Fox, and Steve Hindle (eds.), *The Experience of Authority in Early Modern England* (Basingstoke, 1996), pp. 47–88.

who donated 'many books' 'for the help and benefit of Ministers and Scholars'.[54] Including the library at Leicester, to whose later history we will return, thirty-six libraries were founded before 1640. Perhaps surprisingly, eleven more were established between 1645 and 1659, including five funded by Humphrey Chetham. Thereafter, the history of the parish library was more of an Anglican affair: a further fifty-two libraries were established between 1661 and 1695, including the multiple libraries established by the will of Barnabas Oley, before the explosion in the provision of parochial libraries, especially outside large towns and cities, which came between 1695 and 1720. In particular through the efforts of Thomas Bray, 196 libraries were established between 1695 and 1720.[55]

There has, of course, been considerable bibliographic work on these post-Reformation parish libraries, from individual studies of single collections to the indispensable surveys of Neil Ker and Michael Perkin.[56] Inevitably the greater part of this research has focused on the later seventeenth century, and especially upon the efforts of Thomas Bray and the subsequent Act for the better Preservation of Parochial Libraries in ... England of 1709.[57] Such a focus tends to obscure the associations that many parish libraries had with puritanism in the earlier seventeenth century and create a mythology that the establishment of all such libraries was somehow inevitably part of an Anglican agenda. In addition, there has been relatively little work on how parish libraries were used, especially on a more general level.[58] This section tries to resolve this neglect by thinking about how the parish library was first a site of both reading and cultural exchange for the godly in the early seventeenth century and later a key component in the establishment of Anglican orthodoxy. Parish libraries are rarely mentioned in work on early Stuart puritanism but the tension

---

[54] See Michael Perkin (ed.), *A Directory of the Parochial Libraries of the Church of England and the Church in Wales* (London, 2004), p. 265; John Nichols, *The History and Antiquities of the Countie of Leicester* (London, 1795–1815), vol. I, part ii, p. 505.

[55] These figures, which exclude desk libraries, are based on the list in Perkin, *A Directory of the Parochial Libraries of the Church of England*, pp. 59–82.

[56] N. R. Ker (ed.), *The Parochial Libraries of the Church of England* (London, 1959); Perkin, *A Directory of the Parochial Libraries of the Church of England*.

[57] See, for example, W. M. Jacob, 'Provision of Books for Poor Clergy Parochial Libraries in the British Isles and the North American Colonies, 1680–1720', in R. N. Swanson (ed.), *The Church and the Book*, Studies in Church History, 38 (Woodbridge, 2004), pp. 257–67; W. M. Jacob, 'Libraries for the Parish: Individual Donors and Charitable Societies', in Mandelbrote and Manley, *The Cambridge History of Libraries in Britain and Ireland. Volume II*, pp. 65–82.

[58] Graham Best, 'Books and Readers in Certain Eighteenth-Century Parish Libraries' (unpublished PhD thesis, Loughborough University, 1985). An exceptionally useful recent survey is Arnold Hunt, 'Clerical and Parish Libraries', in Leedham-Green and Webber, *The Cambridge History of Libraries in Britain and Ireland. Volume I*, pp. 400–19.

between the contents of these libraries (which were in many ways unsurprising) and the ways in which they were used (which were potentially more radical and divisive) mirrors the debates over the nature of puritanism between Patrick Collinson and Peter Lake.

By focusing on individual libraries in a more general context, we can see the true nature of the godly involvement in the establishment of parish libraries. This involvement not only formed part of the drive to supply clergy with adequate material and educational resources but was also designed to spread a particular style of religiosity. Although there were libraries established by moderate religious figures, like the clergyman and social reformer Francis Trigge who bequeathed books to the value of one hundred pounds to establish a library at Grantham in 1598 for the use of 'the cleargie & others aswell being inhabitantes in or near Grantham', several notable early post-Reformation parish libraries were undeniably of a godly nature.[59] They include those founded at Leicester in 1586, at Bury St Edmunds in 1595, at Ipswich in 1599 and at Halifax in 1628. Some idea of the puritan character of an early library can be seen in the contents of the library established at Repton, Derbyshire, before 1622, when one William Bladone sent a parcel of fourteen books to the vicar, which could be loaned out to the parishioners. These books included several puritan bestsellers: *The workes of ... Gervase Babington* (London, 1615); Edward Elton's *An exposition of the Epistle of St Paule to the Colossians* (London, 1615); William Perkins's *An exposition of the Symbole or Creede of the Apostles* (Cambridge, 1595); John Dod and Robert Cleaver's *A plaine and familiar exposition of the Ten commandements* (London, 1604); all three parts of John Brinsley's *The True Watch* (London 1606, 1607, 1622); Arthur Dent's *The plaine mans path-way to heaven* (London, 1601); and two copies of Foxe's *Actes and Monuments* (London, 1563). Although modest in size, the puritan character of the collection is unmistakable. Interestingly, the churchwardens' accounts of 1622 also record the arrangements made for the circulation of the library. They record that the minister or any of the churchwardens had the authority to lend any of the books 'to any of the parish of Repton, for the space of one, 2, or 3 moneths' provided that the borrower subscribed his name. In addition, if any reader was guilty of 'foully bruising, tearinge, defacinge, or embezelling', then they were required to 'make good' the damage.[60]

[59] See Perkin, *A Directory of the Parochial Libraries of the Church of England*, p. 217.

[60] See Robert Bigsby, *Historical and Topographical Description of Repton, in the County of Derby* (London, 1854), pp. 147–8; and Perkin, *A Directory of the Parochial Libraries of the Church of England*, p. 329. I have given the date and place of publication for the first edition of each work.

Some other parish libraries seem to have taken on board the comments of the thirteenth-century archbishop of Canterbury Stephen Langton, who argued that the sixth commandment – you shall not kill – should be extended to include books: 'not to lend books is a type of homicide'.[61] Although it clearly functioned as both a parish library and a personal one, books from the large collection of Anthony Higgin, dean of Ripon, now at the Brotherton Library in Leeds, appear to have been circulated among local clergy.[62] Arnold Hunt has shown how the Derbyshire minister William Hall kept a record of book loans – including books by Alexander Cooke and Thomas Brightman – on the flyleaves of his sermon notebooks. The notes reveal, Hunt argues, 'the existence of a network of local clergy and gentry who were able to borrow new works of theology and religious controversy almost as soon as they were published'.[63] Indeed, Hunt lists several examples of libraries which had at least embryonic lending arrangements, including the tiny library of just six books established in 1635 at Measham, Leicestershire, by the clergyman John Jackson, with each book being lent quarterly to families through the parish.[64] Even the celebrated parish library established by Sir John Kederminster at Langley Marish, Buckinghamshire, in the early seventeenth century, which was housed in an ornate panelled room, and which might seem to evoke notes of private scholarly reading and individual piety, was explicitly established not only for the use of the clergy at Langley Marish but also for the use of 'all other ministers and preachers of God's Word that would resort thither'.[65]

Although records of lending arrangements for parish libraries in the early seventeenth century are far from widely available, it is significant that many of those that do survive relate to godly parishes. Indeed, extending the range of material to those libraries in which we have some idea of the nature of the use of the parish library, it is evident that not only did such use reflect a godly ideal of an educated ministry but it also helped to shape godly learning and sociability among both clergy and laity. Most

---

[61] Cited in Lucas, 'Borrowing and Reference', p. 246.

[62] See J. E. Mortimer, 'The Library Catalogue of Anthony Higgin, Dean of Ripon (1608–1624)', *Proceedings of the Leeds Philosophical and Literary Society, Literary and Historical Section*, 10 (1962), pp. 1–75; J. Barnard and M. Bell, 'The Early Seventeenth-Century York Book Trade and John Foster's Inventory of 1616', *Proceedings of Leeds Philosophical and Literary Society, Literary and Historical Section*, 24(2) (1994), pp. 42–3.

[63] Trinity College, Dublin, MS 709, vols. I–II; Hunt, 'Clerical and Parish Libraries', p. 409.

[64] See Hunt, 'Clerical and Parish Libraries', p. 418, citing *Maggs Bros Ltd, Catalogue 1350: STC and Wing Books Printed in England 1500–1700 from the Library of James Stevens-Cox (1910–1997)* (London, 2003), pp. 32–3.

[65] See J. Harris, 'A Rare and Precious Room: The Kederminster Library, Langley', *Country Life* (1977), pp. 1576–9; Jane Francis, 'The Kederminster Library: An Account of Its Origins and a Reconstruction of Its Contents', *Records of Buckinghamshire*, 36 (1996), pp. 62–85.

notable, and most closely integrated into the puritan movement, was the parish library established by the preacher Miles Mosse at Bury St Edmunds in 1595. An inventory of the library, taken just four years later, reveals that it had swelled to two hundred volumes. The bookplates in the surviving volumes, which are now in Cambridge University Library, show how a range of local clergy and laity donated books in support of this collection. Although there were lay donations to the library and some suggestion that local people might have had access to the books, the Bury St Edmunds library was, as John Craig has argued, 'primarily a clerical collection'. Indeed, given the number of donations from members of the town's combination lecture, including Nicholas Bownde, Robert Price of Dedham and Laurence Chaderton, it is probable that the library was designed and used as an extension of these meetings of godly clergy.[66] As such the collective piety and charity of the laity fed into these collections, which were used in the furtherance of puritan sermons.[67]

The parish library could clearly be integrated into a wider vision of godliness and at times it appears to have formed part of the reformation of manners which was characteristic of many puritan towns. When Robert Clay succeeded John Favour as vicar of Halifax in 1624, he proceeded to dig out the charnel house to create a space for a parish library and to consolidate his predecessor's ministerial work.[68] This library, which was modest in size, also attracted donations from local men, and was perhaps linked to the Halifax preaching exercise.[69] Oliver Heywood praised the

[66] On the Bury library see John Craig, *Reformation, Politics and Polemics: The Growth of Protestantism in East Anglian Market Towns, 1500–1610* (Aldershot, 2001), pp. 116–21, 205–19; J. S. Craig, 'The Bury Stirs Revisited: An Analysis of the Townsmen', *Proceedings of the Suffolk Institute of Archaeology and History*, 37 (1991), pp. 208–24.

[67] The essential work on combination lectures is Patrick Collinson, 'Lectures by Combination: Structures and Characteristics of Church Life in Seventeenth-Century England', *Bulletin of the Institute of Historical Research*, 48 (1975), pp. 182–213. For the Bury exercise, see Craig, *Reformation, Politics and Polemics*; and Patrick Collinson, John Craig and Brett Usher (eds.), *Conferences and Combination Lectures in the Elizabethan Church: Dedham and Bury St Edmunds 1582–1590* (Woodbridge, 2003).

[68] The Churchwardens accounts for 1626 record that four shillings was paid 'for dressing both Revestry and carrying out the bones' and four shillings and sixpence 'for making of two great graves for laying the bones in which came out of the Revestry.' See T. W. Hanson, 'Halifax Parish Church Library', *Transactions of the Halifax Antiquarian Society* (1951), p. 37.

[69] On the Halifax exercise, which was in fact held at a variety of locations, including Halifax, Farnley, Bradford, Pudsey, Leeds, Sheffield and Rowley, see the notes taken by Elkanah Wales in BL, Additional MS 4933 A and B ('Notes from Sermons Preached in the West Riding, circa 1609–1661); and more generally Andrew Cambers, 'Print, Manuscript, and Godly Cultures in the North of England, c. 1600–1650' (unpublished DPhil thesis, University of York, 2003), pp. 129–32; for Halifax more generally, see William and Sarah Sheils, 'Textiles and Reform: Halifax and Its Hinterland', in Patrick Collinson and John Craig (eds.), *The Reformation in English Towns, 1500–1640* (Basingstoke, 1998), pp. 130–43.

exercise for the survival of Elizabethan radicalism and suggested that the combination lectures attracted a 'multitude of hearers' that included laity as well as clergy.[70] It seems that the parish library was an attempt to provide continuity to the intense phase of a reformation of manners that John Favour had brought to Halifax in the preceding decades.[71]

Although far from all parish libraries in the early seventeenth century were godly in character, it is striking how many were designed to foster such a form of religious culture. This situation was not revived after the Restoration. From the middle of the seventeenth century onwards, there was a corresponding drive to use the parish library as a means with which to secure the domination of Anglican orthodoxy over Catholicism and nonconformity alike. In the midst of this metamorphosis, parish libraries were transformed as institutions. They remained centres of cultural exchange and of social reading, but access to the libraries and conditions for reading in them was restricted. From their godly, reforming origins, parish libraries became pillars of the establishment, perceived as keystones in the defence of the building of 'Anglicanism' against the combined threat of low-church piety, dissent and Catholicism.

This change is not evident in those libraries established or provided for in the 1650s, such as the five chained parish libraries which were founded in Lancashire by the bequest of Humphrey Chetham at Bolton, Gorton, Turton, Manchester and Walmesley. The books purchased for these parish libraries, which were installed in magnificent presses bearing the inscription 'The gift of Humphrey Chetham Esquire 1655', were drawn straight from the well of early seventeenth-century puritan piety. It was Chetham's desire that they be furnished with 'godly English books ... most proper for the edification of the common people, to be ... chained upon desks or to be fixed to the pillars or in other convenient places' of the churches and chapels he specified.[72]

But the change is certainly evident in those libraries established after the Restoration, in terms both of their content and of the conditions stipulated for using the collections. The library established by John Newte (1656–1716) at Tiverton in Devon, for example, sheds light not only on the importance of the parish library in the creation of orthodoxy but also

---

[70] Heywood, *Diaries*, vol. IV, p. 16.
[71] For detail on Favour and Halifax, see Chapter 5 below.
[72] See Perkin, *A Directory of the Parochial Libraries of the Church of England*, p. 280.

upon the cementing of religious identities and allegiance over the seventeenth century. Like many other towns, by the late seventeenth century Tiverton had become a hotly contested religious environment. Its divisions had their roots both in an unusual ecclesiastical arrangement, whereby the town was divided into four portions – three held by rectors and one by King's College, Cambridge – and in the legacies of Civil War divisions between staunch royalists and independents. Late seventeenth-century Tiverton was a town divided, principally between the Tory high-church Newte (whose father had also been a rector of the Tidcombe portion, sequestered in 1650, but holding onto his place for several years and returning at the Restoration and remaining there until his death in 1678) and a significant dissenting population, which included Baptist and presbyterian congregations. Such tensions were available for all to see, especially after the head of a dissenting minister who had been executed for his involvement in Monmouth's Rebellion was displayed upon the market cross in 1685.[73]

These divisions can also be seen in the provision of libraries. There were significant bequests to sustain the presbyterian minister at Tiverton, and John Moore (d. 1730) recorded in his diary from 1705 to 1721 the systematic collection of books in preparation for the opening of the Tiverton Academy (1721–9). These included works of theology, philosophy, history and medicine, and demonstrate once more how personal collections of books might be assembled in anticipation of founding institutional libraries.[74] There were also significant bequests to the Anglican church and orthodox education. In addition, the Newtes themselves were particularly generous benefactors (and John Newte, who held two wealthy livings in plurality and was a chaplain to Charles II, could certainly afford to be): Richard bequeathed money for a fellowship for a pupil from Blundell's School to Balliol College, Oxford; John bequeathed a sum of forty pounds as an investment, one pound and ten shillings of which was to be used each year to buy devotional books for poor families; and John also bequeathed the same amount to support a school at Cove and to instruct poor children to read, write and say the church catechism; and established an exhibition to Balliol.[75]

---

[73] See Martin Dunsford, *Historical Memoirs of the Town and Parish of Tiverton in the County of Devon Collected from the Best Authorities, with Notes and Observations* (Exeter, 1790).

[74] See McLachlan, *English Education under the Test Acts*, p. 14.

[75] For Richard Newte's will, see TNA: PRO PROB 11/357, sig. 101; for John Newte's will, see TNA: PRO PROB 11/551, fos. 294v–296v.

John Newte's will also reveals how important libraries were in his vision of the maintenance of religious orthodoxy. He bequeathed his library, which included his father's books, to the parish, to be kept in a room over the vestry. Remarkably, the library remains almost complete and in place in the parish church as it was in 1716. Newte's bequest numbered 332 volumes whose contents ranged from the works of the Church Fathers, through to those of Elizabethan and early Stuart divines and theologians, and was particularly strong in later Stuart Anglican theology. It included works of history and works of science, and a few volumes by those with whom neither Newte would have shared common ground, such as Catholics and nonconformists. In general, however, the contents of the library mirrored the character of its compiler and its donation reflects the image of religious orthodoxy he wished to survive him in Tiverton. The strength of the collection in works virulently pitched against dissenters and Quakers is striking, as are its holdings in avant-garde conformity (Andrewes, Hooker) and staunch royalism (including *The History and Troubles and Tryal of William Laud*, to which was added a long note in support of Laud; the *Trial of Regicides* (1660); Peter Heylyn's *Aerius Redivivus* (1670); and the works of John Walker, Jeremy Taylor and Edward Stillingfleet). The most remarkable aspect of the collection, however, and perhaps the most revealing of the collective memory Newte surely aimed to impress on future readers of the parish library, was the collection of more than three hundred tracts and pamphlets covering 'news' events from 1603 to 1709 which were bound into sixteen volumes.[76] The contents of this part of the library preserved the realities of the religious and social meltdown which arose from political sedition during the Civil War. In particular, those pamphlets collected by John Newte in the 1680s warn very clearly of the dangers Newte saw not only in popery but also in the machinations of dissenters and those of the Church of England willing to engage with them. The same sentiment is clear in a volume of trial pamphlets, detailing the religious as well as political conspiracies alive during the exclusion crisis.[77] A similar situation can

[76] Several of the volumes of pamphlets, not included in the count, are now missing. They would most likely have contained scores of pamphlets.

[77] See Anne Welsford, 'Mr Newte's Library in St Peter's Church, Tiverton', *Devonshire Association for the Advancement of Science, Literature, and Art. Report and Transactions*, 106 (1974), pp. 17–31, and 107 (1975), pp. 11–20. I am grateful to Alex Walsham for providing me with a copy of the manuscript catalogue of the library. Although Newte's will noted that the library was designed for the rectors and curates of Tiverton, as well as for the local school, it is also possible that he envisaged a lay readership.

be seen in the library established by Andrew Cranston, vicar of Reigate, Surrey, between 1697 and 1708. This was designed as 'a publick library for the use and perusall of the freeholders, vicar and inhabitants' of Reigate, as well as neighbouring gentlemen and clergy. This library, which was quickly augmented through donation, contained a range of material, but the holdings in anti-Quaker pamphlets are particularly noteworthy, and, like the pamphlets in Tiverton, suggest that the parish library was one of the means used to fashion Anglican orthodoxy in the early eighteenth century in response to the threats of local opposition.[78] Indeed, the topical nature of much material in parish libraries is only very sketchily known, but those libraries like Crediton, which contained over two thousand pamphlets, would certainly repay further study in the context of the ways in which their founders and donors attempted to forge religious orthodoxy in the years after the Restoration.

One effort at establishing religious orthodoxy through the parish library is well known: Thomas Bray's almost single-handed mission to establish parish libraries in England and its colonies. Prior to this, Barnabas Oley attempted to furnish poorer livings with small libraries through a bequest of 1685. His gift was relatively modest – sixteen volumes to each of ten parishes in the diocese of Carlisle – but its character is suggestive of the change from the parish library's status as a fulcrum of godly piety to its position as a bastion of Anglicanism. Oley's libraries, which were purchased for the parishes in 1687, included George Herbert's *Country Parson*, Izaak Walton's *Lives* and the works of Joseph Mede and Lancelot Andrewes.[79] Probably because of their size, those collections started by Oley did not last long. Those established by Thomas Bray, on the other hand, were both more numerous and more enduring. Bray's realization that more remote parishes were woefully inadequate when it came to books came in part through his experience in the colonies. His first published plea for establishing parish libraries was printed in 1696 and referred to America; his second, printed in 1697, referred both to colonies and to the homeland.[80] Bray's proposals, most famously

---

[78] On Reigate, see Perkin, *A Directory of the Parochial Libraries of the Church of England*, pp. 326–9; and Mary C. Spinks, 'The Cranston Library: An Eighteenth Century Parish Library at Reigate, Surrey' (unpublished postgraduate diploma in librarianship, University of Sheffield, 1966).

[79] On Oley, see Perkin, *A Directory of the Parochial Libraries of the Church of England*, pp. 34–5.

[80] Thomas Bray, *Proposals for the Encouragement and Promoting of Religion and Learning in the Foreign Plantations* (London, 1696); Thomas Bray, *An Essay towards Promoting all Necessary and Useful Knowledge … both at Home and Abroad* (London, 1697); Thomas Bray, *Bibliotheca Parochialis* (London, 1697).

elaborated in his *Bibliotheca Parochialis*, are well known, as are the ways these activities were sustained through the Society for Promoting Christian Knowledge. Libraries on the Bray model were each dispatched in a travelling cupboard to fifty-one locations between 1710 and 1712 and many more followed in later years.

The contents of these libraries, as well as the seventeen libraries on the Isle of Man to which Bishop Wilson gave forty volumes each in 1699, repay some consideration. The libraries on the Isle of Man contained, in addition to Bibles and practical liturgical books, works by William Allen, Hugh Blair, Thomas Bray, George Herbert, Edward Harley and Richard Sherlock, and William Wake's discourse on swearing.[81] Michael Perkin has tabulated the holdings of many of the Bray libraries and compared them with those of Oley and Wilson.[82] The contents are revealing, as they show how many of the Bray libraries received an almost identical core of books and how these books were rigidly orthodox. They included works like Thomas Bennet's *A Confutation of Popery* (3rd edn, 1706) and *A Confutation of Quakerism* (2nd edn, 1709), a series of Anglican sermons and catechisms, Gilbert Burnet's *The Abridgement of the History of the Reformation* (4th edn, 1705), George Herbert's *A Priest to the Temple* (1671), works providing comfort at the deathbed, and works against the challenge of deism. What is immediately obvious, despite the latitude of some of these authors, is the disappearance of the key texts of early Stuart godly piety and the preponderance of English works of practical Anglican worship.

Although the early Bray libraries were established as parochial libraries and not as lending libraries as Bray had originally intended (although many of the mid-eighteenth-century Bray libraries did function as lending libraries), we should not assume that early seventeenth-century godly libraries were well used, while later seventeenth-century Anglican libraries gathered dust. Instead, there is some evidence of the books of these libraries being borrowed, circulated and read. The library at Reigate, for example, contains a register of loans, from the early eighteenth century, which reveals that around 40 per cent of its eighteenth-century borrowers were women. Parish libraries became sites of sociability for Anglican clergy and there is evidence of informal societies for buying books for the clergy. At Wisbech a library was established in a chamber over the church porch shortly after the Restoration. The library was soon neglected, but in 1712

---

[81] James P. Ferguson, *The Parochial Libraries of Bishop Wilson* (Douglas, Isle of Man, 1975).
[82] Perkin, *A Directory of the Parochial Libraries of the Church of England*, pp. 444–52.

'some of the Neighbouring Clergy and Gentlemen, considering the advantage of Parochial Libraries, formed themselves into a Club or Society; and agreed annually to contribute Twenty Shillings each to buy Books; hoping that others would take this opportunity to forward such a Publick Good'.[83] At Doncaster, a group of clergy met monthly to read and exchange information – in this case the sociability of the clergy became an early book club.[84] And there was certainly excitement in some quarters that the projected Bray libraries were going to be lending libraries. As Abraham de la Pryme, the curate of Holy Trinity, Hull, wrote enthusiastically in his diary in 1697, 'There is a project come out of a lending library in every deanery. I subscribed 5s towards the first trial of it.'[85] In some cases, large donations may even have been made to parish libraries to fight the rise of low-churchmanship. In Halifax, for example, after a quarrel between Simon Sterne, the son of Archbishop Richard Sterne and resident of Halifax, and Edmund Hough, the friend of Henry Newcome, over the installation of a lecturer, resulted in the installation of a low-church candidate, Francis Parratt, Simon Sterne's ultra-orthodox library, based in part upon the Laudian collection he had acquired from his uncle William Sterne, was given to the parish by his son Richard Sterne. Although there is no evidence of its use in the dispute, it is at least possible that the library might have been used as a weapon in the fight between proponents of high- and low-church models.[86] In any case, it is clear that although the parish library remained a site of cultural exchange for Anglicans in the later seventeenth century, it was neither quite so crucial to the practice of piety nor a site of godly reading. The godly were effectively excluded from the parish library by the end of the seventeenth century, their social reading transferred to the libraries of dissenting academies, to private collections and to the libraries of other institutions.

[83] R. M. Massie, *A Catalogue of Books in the Library at Wisbech in the Isle of Ely* (Wisbech, 1718), sigs. A2r–v.

[84] W. M. Jacob, 'Libraries for the Parish: Individual Donors and Charitable Societies', in Mandelbrote and Manley, *The Cambridge History of Libraries in Britain and Ireland. Volume II*, pp. 68–9; K. A. Manley, 'The SPCK and English Book Clubs before 1720', *Bodleian Library Record*, 13 (1989), pp. 231–43.

[85] See C. Jackson (ed.), *Diary of Abraham de la Pryme*, Surtees Society, 54 (Durham, 1869), p. 133.

[86] On the quarrel, see Samuel S. Thomas, 'Individuals and Communities: Religious Life in Restoration England', Chapter 8; for the donation, see Hanson, 'Halifax Parish Church Library', p. 44; on the contents of William Sterne's library, see Andrew Cambers, 'Pastoral Laudianism? Religious Politics in the 1630s: A Leicestershire Rector's Annotations', *Midland History*, 27 (2002), pp. 38–51.

TOWN LIBRARIES AND PUBLIC LIBRARIES

Further venues for godly reading, which frequently intersected with or grew out of parish libraries, were town and public libraries. Town or borough public libraries developed later and more slowly than parish and school libraries but they nevertheless occupied an important place in the development of godly identity since they provided a location for godly reading and cultural exchange. Recognizably public town libraries were a development of the early seventeenth century. There were establishments at Norwich in 1608, at Bristol in 1615, at Leicester in 1632 and at Wisbech in 1654. Others soon became public libraries: Samuel Harsnett's library at Colchester had been designed for the use of local clergy but was placed under the control of the town bailiffs; and the parochial library at King's Lynn, established by gifts of money to the mayor and burgesses in 1631, was in effect a public lending library under municipal control.

While there was obviously encouragement from different religious and political quarters – and Harsnett's library in particular might have been meant to further anti-puritanism among local preachers and was held in such low esteem by the godly during the Interregnum that the books were mortgaged in 1654 – there was a significant level of godly involvement in many of these foundations. The parish library at Leicester, for example, which had received donations from key godly magnates like Henry Huntingdon in the 1590s, was placed in the care of the town corporation and moved to the guildhall in 1632, through the energies of the godly preacher John Angell and the bishop John Williams. It became a public library.[87] The famous godly preacher Samuel Ward was largely responsible for the establishment of the town library at Ipswich in 1614, transforming a small parish library intended for the use of the town preachers into a more substantial collection housed in Christ's Hospital. The collection, which was chiefly theological, over time came to include a wider range of historical, scientific and philosophical works. Some of the

---

[87] See Perkin, *A Directory of the Parochial Libraries of the Church of England*, p. 265; John Angell's 1632 catalogue of 876 manuscripts and printed books is now lost but is described in Nichols, *The History and Antiquities of the Countie of Leicester*, vol. I, pp. 505–10. Williams seems to have focused on helping to bring in funds to establish the library, and encouraged donors to pay for stalls for the books. His correspondence reveals that he was responsible for gaining the support of the Earl of Huntingdon before work began and that Elias Travers DD (d. 1641), the godly rector of Thurcaston, Leicestershire, who was educated at Emmanuel College, Cambridge, was also involved in its establishment. See B. H. Beedham, *Notices of Archbishop Williams* (London, 1869), p. 45.

gifts to the library are noteworthy in their preservation of the memory of Ipswich's radical past. In 1725, the Ipswich cleric William Matthews donated to the library six volumes containing 158 sermons preached before Parliament in the 1640s, which had been assembled and heavily annotated by the puritan iconoclast William Dowsing.[88] Sometimes, more unusual forms of evidence can also testify to the involvement the godly had with their town libraries. An eighteenth-century annotator of John Favour's *Antiquitie Triumphing over Noveltie*, for example, noted that the town library of Southampton still contained 'an ancient table' with an inscription of 1612 celebrating that

John Favour Doctor of the Lawes and Vicar of Halifax born at Southampton in the parish of holy wode the xxith of Januarie 1556 ... bestowed this Bible that it may be chayned to a deske in the Councell Chamber of the Audit house for the edification of them who shall read therein ...[89]

There are important examples of town libraries which played a significant role in the establishment and maintenance of godly civic and religious identity in the years before the Civil War. Perhaps unsurprisingly, we can see this especially well in celebrated godly towns like Dorchester. Perhaps significantly, Dorchester had no parish library to speak of in the early seventeenth century, merely a cleric's desk library of just a few volumes, and it would lack a parish library until the Bray trustees sent them a collection of sixty-seven volumes in 1710.[90] Instead, puritan Dorchester had a town library, which was housed in a room over the free school (this position showing once more the overlap and interplay between different types of library). David Underdown describes the library as being 'stuffed' with puritan books, many of which had been donated by prominent Dorchester puritans. An inventory of the library's contents taken in 1631 confirms its character. It contained many of the staples of Reformation theology, including the works of Calvin, Zwingli and Melanchthon (but, perhaps importantly, no Luther); the works of puritan divines like William Perkins and Richard Greenham; numerous refutations of Catholic authors; and also more 'popular' puritan works

---

[88] See Perkin, *A Directory of the Parochial Libraries of the Church of England*, p. 250; J. Blatchly, *The Town Library of Ipswich* (Woodbridge, 1989); and Woolf, *Reading History in Early Modern England*, p. 194. For analysis, see John Morrill, 'William Dowsing, the Bureaucratic Puritan', in John Morrill, Paul Slack and Daniel R. Woolf (eds.), *Public Duty and Private Conscience in Seventeenth-Century England* (Oxford, 1992), pp. 173–203.

[89] John Favour, *Antiquitie Triumphing over Noveltie* (London, 1619), HEHL, call no. 37962.

[90] See Perkin, *A Directory of the Parochial Libraries of the Church of England*, p. 197.

like Thomas Beard's *Theatre of Gods Judgements* and Foxe's *Actes and Monuments*.[91] Along with the work of the godly preacher John White, the library solidified the godly identity of Dorchester and its books were both used within its walls and borrowed by its godly users, like the diarist William Whiteway.[92] Indeed, it is suggestive that the inventories of the private libraries of two wealthy townsmen, Denis Bond and William Whiteway, reveal collections of a very similar character. Bond's collection included works by Calvin, Beza, Perkins and Greenham; the Heidelberg Catechism; and Thomas Brightman's *A Revelation of the Apocalyps* (1611). Whiteway's contained similar material, even if it is usually better known for his outstanding collection of works of recent history.[93]

During the Civil War many libraries originally designed for use in other institutions, such as universities and cathedrals, became in essence public libraries. Parliamentary forces took Winchester Cathedral library in the 1640s and placed it in Winchester College 'for public use'.[94] The commander of parliamentary forces in the north, Ferdinando Lord Fairfax (1584–1648), took care to secure York Minster Library while besieging York in 1644. He prevented the sacking of the library, gave orders to save the archives of the chapter and archbishopric and instructed the corporation of York to pay the salary of the library keeper. The library clearly operated as a public library in these years – in the 1650s it was styled as 'the publique librarie in Yorke Minster' – and Fairfax donated 443 items from his personal library, which included smaller collections of others like Sir John Hotham, to the library sometime between 1644 and his death in 1648.[95] And Ferdinando's famous son Thomas performed a similar service by guarding the Bodleian from the ravages of war after the surrender of Oxford in 1646.[96]

---

[91] C. H. Mayo (ed.), *The Municipal Records of the Borough of Dorchester, Dorset* (Exeter, 1908), pp. 581–3.

[92] See David Underdown, *Fire from Heaven: Life in an English Town in the Seventeenth Century* (London, 1992), p. 55.

[93] For the Dorchester town library, see ibid., pp. 46–8, 54–5; for the inventory of Bond's books, see Dorset History Centre, D 413/22/1, p. 17; for the inventory of Whiteway's books, see BL, Egerton MS 784 (The Diary of Mr William Whiteway, of Dorchester), fos. 114v–18.

[94] See Green, 'Libraries for School Education and Personal Devotion', p. 54.

[95] See Bernard Barr, 'The Minster Library', in G. E. Aylmer and R. Cant (eds.), *A History of York Minster* (Oxford, 1977), pp. 487–539; for its status as a public library, see C. B. L. Barr and David Selwyn, 'Major Ecclesiastical Libraries: From Reformation to Civil War', in Leedham-Green and Webber, *The Cambridge History of Libraries in Britain and Ireland. Volume I*, p. 396.

[96] For Thomas Fairfax's guard of the Bodleian, see the description in John Aubrey, *Brief Lives*, ed. Richard Barber (Woodbridge, 1982), p. 112; on Thomas Fairfax, see Andrew Hopper, *'Black Tom': Sir Thomas Fairfax and the English Revolution* (Manchester, 2007).

The importance the godly placed upon good libraries can also be seen in the petitions to establish a university in the north of England in 1641. The petitions, which clearly set out the need for a third university in the north of England which would counter the supposed Catholic character of the northern counties, placed considerable emphasis on the value of a library. While the petition for Manchester stressed its location, the subsequent petition for a university at York trumped it by calling attention to its established library and press.[97]

The godly found particular comfort in public libraries, which although thin on the ground, performed a similar function in facilitating their religious sociability after the Restoration to that performed by many of the parish libraries earlier in the century. Chetham's library in Manchester in particular became an important venue both for dissenters and for evangelicals within the Church of England. Although John Rastrick was pleased by the library's regular opening hours and its chained books, as we have already seen, his eye was caught by the exoticism of the stuffed snake, the room for globes and the fine barometer. Others used the library for godly reading and conversation. Henry Newcome's diary demonstrates in remarkable detail how Chetham's library was at the heart of his godly spirituality. He read there, met with fellow nonconformists and discussed important issues. The diary is peppered with references to his reading in near daily visits to Chetham's library. Much of the reading was to keep up with fresh material for the composition of his sermons but it also informed him of wider events and issues and provided a forum in which to meet with and talk to fellow dissenters.[98] In 1670, John Worthington, the Master of Jesus College, Cambridge, even described Chetham's library as more useful than those at Cambridge. It was, he wrote, 'a very fair library of books (where I might pursue my studies) better than any college library in Cambridge'.[99] Public libraries and town libraries were key venues for shaping the faith.

[97] The petitions can be followed through the correspondence between Henry Fairfax and his brother Ferdinando. See G. W. Johnson, *The Fairfax Correspondence: Memoirs of the Reign of Charles the First* (2 vols., London, 1848), vol. II, pp. 271–80.

[98] See Thomas Heywood (ed.), *The Diary of the Rev. Henry Newcome, from September 30, 1661, to September 29, 1663*, Chetham Society, 1st ser., 18 (Manchester, 1849), *passim*. Later, Chetham's library also functioned as a quasi-institutional library for the Manchester Academy.

[99] R. C. Christie (ed.), *The Diary and Correspondence of Dr John Worthington*, Chetham Society, 1st ser., 114 (Manchester, 1886), p. 326.

GODLY SCHOOL AND COLLEGE LIBRARIES

Further libraries full of potential for godly reading were found in schools and colleges. The young were clearly important to godly designs to train up new generations of suitable clergy and acceptable laity. Catching them early was seen as a means of instilling godly piety and communal reading in souls that might otherwise be lost. Thus Richard Rhodes, the puritan who had been chaplain to the Hoby family, was brought before the church courts at York for holding conventicles with schoolchildren from Beverley in his house in the 1630s, where sermons were repeated and notes taken on tablets.[100] In the many puritan-influenced schools, godly piety was an intrinsic part of education, even if there are relatively few records to compare with those of the grammar school at Rotherham in the 1630s, where pupils spent each Thursday afternoon reading aloud passages from books by William Perkins.[101] Certainly the godly contributed much to the provision of schools and their libraries, as is amply documented in John Morgan's *Godly Learning*,[102] and seen in schools like the grammar school at Leeds, to which the Earl of Huntingdon sent books in 1589. Such schools could be important to the wider religious community, and in Bradford the appointment of a new headmaster in 1635 spilled over into open conflict between Archbishop Richard Neile and the local godly, when Neile forced in his own nominee and cited those who opposed him to appear before the High Commission.[103] But more often than not the records are more ambiguous. The 1607 schoolmaster's oath for Wakefield Grammar School, for example, began with a promise to 'in harte abhor all Popish Superstition and renounce all forraine jurisdiction of the Church of Rome and the now Pope', and despite its apparently godly character, the books given to the school were resolutely traditional (and practical), including commentaries upon Terence and Juvenal, Bibles and books of grammar.[104] Likewise, the statutes for Wigan's Free Grammar School

---

[100] See R. A. Marchant, *The Puritans and the Church Courts in the Diocese of York 1560–1642* (London, 1960), pp. 271–2.

[101] For Rotherham, see J. A. Newton, 'Puritanism in the Diocese of York (excluding Nottinghamshire) 1603–1640' (unpublished DPhil thesis, University of London, 1955), pp. 288–303.

[102] J. Morgan, *Godly Learning: Puritan Attitudes towards Reason, Learning and Education 1540–1640* (Cambridge, 1986).

[103] See Marchant, *The Puritans and the Church Courts*, pp. 112–13. The opposition may also have been motivated by an aversion to outside influence in such matters, as well as hostility to Neile's religious policy.

[104] BL, MS Lansdowne 973 ('Collections for a History of the Grammar School at Wakefield' etc.), fols. 15r, 20v.

stipulated that a chapter of the Bible be read each morning and a Psalm read before the pupils went home in the evening, and (more suggestively, since it intersected with the puritan desire for self-examination) that each pupil give an account of how they had spent the Sabbath when they returned to school on Monday morning – which would apparently be of 'singular use' in training the pupils 'in the knowledge of the oracles of God' – but the books mentioned in the statutes are drawn from the likes of Tully, Caesar, Sallust, Livy, Ovid, Horace, Terence and Socrates, with only a more general reference made to books of 'the Protestant religion'. In addition, the statutes seem much more concerned about keeping the books in the library than in allowing other potential readers access to them, and they make a point of outlawing scholars who 'write in, scratch on, or deface with pen or otherwise, any of the said books', while making sure that once a week 'the dust shall be beated and putt of the said books'.[105] The godly gave books to school libraries, but they also took them from them. Henry Newcome did both. He congratulated himself on a visit to the (nonconformist) charity school at Poulton, when he left them 'many good books for poor families, a matter to be rejoiced in',[106] and, when he visited the school founded by the recently deceased Mr Hiet in April 1663, he selected books from the library for the use of Mrs Hiet: he chose works by Perkins, Sibs, Bolton, Love, Watson and Foxe, but left other English books that were 'above her capacity'.[107]

In many smaller and poorer schools, the library and even the school-books were likely to have been provided by the schoolmasters and thus unless they are mentioned in other sources – Ralph Josselin's diary, for example, suggests that he used his own books for teaching at the school in Earls Colne – they leave no mark upon the historical record. Instead, those schools for which any kind of useful information can be gathered are those with large, established, often purpose-built and clearly atypical libraries. Even these might have intersected with other types of library or served a dual function. As we have already seen, the town library in Dorchester was positioned in a room above the free school and John Newte willed that his library at Tiverton be used both by clergy and by Chilcot's School. It also needs to be remembered that school

---

[105] The statutes (1664) are reproduced in Nicholas Carlisle, *A Concise Description of the Endowed Grammar Schools in England and Wales* (2 vols., London, 1818), vol. I, pp. 725–31.
[106] See R. Parkinson (ed.), *The Autobiography of Henry Newcome*, Chetham Society, 26, 27 (2 vols., paginated continuously, Manchester, 1852), p. 274.
[107] See Heywood, *The Diary of the Rev. Henry Newcome*, p. 175.

libraries in this period were probably designed more for the use of the schoolmasters than for the pupils directly.

For all this, and even if we lack information on the reading that went on in school libraries, it is suggestive that some school libraries appear to have functioned as quasi-public collections. The library of Guildford Royal Grammar School – established in 1586 and containing a theological core of sixty-four items (including works by Zwingli, Bullinger and Calvin) donated by John Parkhurst, bishop of Norwich, and other godly works by donation (a copy of Foxe's *Actes and Monuments* in 1578, more Calvin in 1597) – 'seems to have been open to the public'.[108] There appears to have been a similar situation in the library of Shrewsbury School, which had been built by the long-standing headmaster John Meighen – he served between 1583 and 1635 – and by 1634 contained 704 books, which were chained and arranged by subject. It has been suggested that the library became 'a sort of local centre of learning, not merely for the school, but for general use, and perhaps especially for the local clergy, for whose benefit the vast theological and patristic tomes were thought to be needed'.[109] Rather unusually, this godly school library fused seemingly high and low, puritan and educational literature, as can be neatly seen in the copy of one of Erasmus's works in the library into which was bound *A mirrour for murtherers or a caveat for disobedient children* (1633), one of the puritan pamphlets surrounding Enoch ap Evan's murder of his mother and brother in July 1633, a case which prompted a series of ideologically charged publications.[110] Clearly there is far from enough information to be certain, but it is at least possible that the libraries established at schools of a godly persuasion could provide a venue for reading for those within and without the school walls.

When we turn to the libraries of the colleges in Oxford and Cambridge, we see collections that evolved over the seventeenth century. Much work has been done on the changes that occurred within such libraries, in particular the important developments in the furnishings and

[108] William Barber, 'School Libraries (c. 1540 to 1640)', in Leedham-Green and Webber, *The Cambridge History of Libraries in Britain and Ireland. Volume I*, pp. 444–5.
[109] See J. B. Oldham, 'Shrewsbury School Library', *The Library*, 6th ser., 14 (1959), pp. 81–99, p. 82.
[110] Ibid., p. 96. On Enoch ap Evan, see Peter Lake, 'Puritanism, Arminianism and a Shropshire Axe-Murder' *Midland History*, 15 (1990), pp. 37–64; Peter Lake, 'Deeds against Nature: Cheap Print, Protestantism and Murder in Early Seventeenth-Century England', in Kevin Sharpe and Peter Lake (eds.), *Culture and Politics in Early Stuart England* (Basingstoke, 1994), pp. 257–83; Peter Lake with Michael Questier, *The Antichrist's Lewd Hat: Protestants, Papists and Players in Post-Reformation England* (New Haven, CT, 2002), pp. 6–12.

structures such as the gradual shift from desk libraries to stall libraries.[111] Before thinking about any reading that went on in these libraries, there are some familiar problems to consider. Like school libraries, college libraries (at least at the start of the seventeenth century) tended to be for the use of fellows rather than of students. They were not always coherent single collections and for much of the period other places in colleges would have housed books and sometimes in large numbers. John Bateman's study in mid-sixteenth-century Gonville and Caius College, Cambridge, housed five hundred books, while most of Andrew Perne's massive collection was kept in the master's lodge at Peterhouse, Cambridge.[112] Nevertheless, over the century college libraries were gradually brought together into one physical space. They became better stocked with books and, presumably to the relief of their users, they began to be swept and dusted on a regular basis.[113]

Few college libraries can, as collections of books, be described as godly. Clearly those attached to puritan institutions, like Emmanuel College, Cambridge, have the best claim, but even there it was possible to get hold of a wider range of reading material. Emmanuel's library, established in 1584, had an unchained library of five hundred volumes by 1600.[114] Famous collections like that of Matthew Parker at Corpus Christi College, Cambridge, seem not to have been venues for godly reading. There is in fact very little information on how students read in college libraries. John Rastrick's spiritual autobiography provides as good a guide as any as to how such collections were used and how much of the godly reading at colleges actually happened outside the library. Rastrick went up to Trinity College, Cambridge, in 1667. He mentions the college library just once, but interestingly this was to note that the first time he read Samuel Clarke's *Lives* it was from a copy which his chamber-fellow had borrowed from that library. Rastrick soon bought his own copy. It seems that godly reading at university involved collective reading in tutors' rooms and books that students bought for their own personal use. Commenting upon the company of his fellow students – 'their Society was generally

[111] See, for example, N. R. Ker, 'Oxford College Libraries in the Sixteenth Century', *Bodleian Library Record*, 6 (1959), pp. 459–515.

[112] See Elisabeth Leedham-Green and David McKitterick, 'Ownership: Private and Public Libraries', in John Barnard and D. F. McKenzie (eds.), *The Cambridge History of the Book in Britain* (7 vols., Cambridge, 1999–), vol. IV, *1557–1695* (2002), pp. 323–5.

[113] See Clare Sargent, 'The Early Modern Library (to c. 1640)', in Leedham-Green and Webber, *The Cambridge History of Libraries in Britain and Ireland. Volume 1*, p. 64.

[114] Ibid., p. 59; Sargent Bush and Carl J. Ramussen, *The Library of Emmanuel College, Cambridge, 1584–1637* (Cambridge, 1986).

worse than none' – Rastrick recalled how his reading set him apart from his contemporaries:

I was ever the object of their Scorn and derision: If I did but read a Greek chapter at Prayer times, or repeat my Sermon notes on a Lord's Day at night, in our Tutor's Chamber ... my very tone was enough for them to laugh at and jeer me for afterwards.

For them, 'Comedies and Playbooks were in greater Reputation ... than Divinity Books'. Rastrick's account was clearly coloured by his disdain for the lack of piety of his high-church contemporaries, but it is interesting how often he recalled buying his own books to read at university. He bought works of practical divinity like Robert Bolton's works and his tutor advised him on what titles he should buy to continue his studies while away from Cambridge.[115] The implication was that Cambridge and its libraries were no better as venues for godly reading than his rural family home. If this sounds like the rant of a bitter old man (and it probably was), others confirm that the usual lot of students in the seventeenth century was to buy their own books. A manuscript in Chetham's library lists those books a seventeenth-century student should buy to read while studying to be a cleric – interestingly, the volumes of practical divinity are of a godly bent and included works by Perkins, Hildersham, Sibbes, Preston, Goodwin, Byfield, Gataker and Reinolds.[116] Likewise, Alice Thornton's mother, Lady Wandesford, bought her son John a list of books he needed before he went off to Dr Widdrington at Christ's College, Cambridge.[117]

Perhaps the most important college library for godly reading was located outside the universities. Sion College, which had been established by Thomas White, rector of St Dunstan in the West, as a meeting place for London clergy, became something of a godly community centre in which the library functioned as a key venue for intellectual, social and cultural exchange. Although not part of the original foundation, the library was added in 1630 through the energies of John Simson, White's executor and the rector of St Olave's, Hart Street. Many gave money at the library's inception for the purchase of books, but others gave books and manuscripts, including George Walker, the puritan rector of St John the

---

[115] *The Life of John Rastrick*, pp. 51, 58, 46, 59.
[116] Chetham's Library, MS A.2.21 ('A Catalogue of Books for a Young Divine to Make Use of Given by Dr Conaut to a Friend, upon his Request').
[117] *The Autobiography of Mrs Alice Thornton, of East Newton, co. York*, Surtees Society, 62 (Durham, 1875 for 1873), p. 105.

Evangelist; the renegade bookseller Michael Sparke; and the puritan divine Walter Travers, who bequeathed at least 150 books.[118] Bequests are recorded in a benefactors' register, a magnificent parchment book adorned with silver bosses and clasps donated by Simson, dating from 1629, which is now in Lambeth Palace library, and which records the support that the library attracted from the wider godly community.[119] During the Civil War the library expanded, not least because it housed the Library of St Paul's Cathedral from 1647 (there were even plans for it to buy Archbishop Ussher's library). A printed catalogue was published under the title of *Catalogus universalis librorum omnium in Bibliotheca Collegii Sionii apud Londinenses* in 1650, alerting potential readers to the library's growing contents and, like the printed catalogues of the Bodleian library, helping existing readers negotiate the holdings.[120] Around one-third of the books were destroyed by the Great Fire in 1666, when the ashes of the capital's literary stocks were (according to John Evelyn) dispersed as far as Windsor. Nevertheless, like a phoenix, Sion College library emerged from the ashes. Donors included London's laity as well as clergy like William Sancroft, Edward Stillingfleet and Simon Patrick, and the library took on that seized from the Jesuits at Holbeck in 1679. By 1712, it contained 10,000 volumes and in 1720 Strype recorded proposals that it might grow further, through becoming in effect a copyright library whereby every author would 'give a Book of whatsoever he shall publish' and every bookseller provide 'one Copy of every of the Books they Print', and that every London minister donate a book.[121]

Although many of the books were stored off-site before 1670, the arrangements for and evidence of the library's use testify to the importance of the library as a site of cultural exchange for the godly. The core of the readership was that of the London clergy, who had the privilege of borrowing books for their own use and for their friends. But the readership stretched further. Each member of the college could introduce other

---

[118] See Barr and Selwyn, 'Major Ecclesiastical Libraries', p. 393.
[119] Lambeth Palace Library, Sion College MS, ARC L40.2/E.64 ('Sion College: Register of Benefactors').
[120] T. James, *Catalogus librorum bibliothecae publicae quam vir ornatissimus Thomas Bodleius nuper instituit* (Oxford, 1605).
[121] John Strype, *A Survey of the Cities of London and Westminster ... By John Stow* (2 vols., London, 1720), vol. I, pp. 147–8 (original mispaginated as pp. 155–6). For further detail on the library, see E. H. Pearce, *Sion College and Library* (Cambridge, 1913); Edward Edwards, *Memoirs of Libraries* (2 vols., London, 1859), vol. II, p. 86; William Reading, *The History of the Ancient and Present State of Sion College ... and of the Library there* (London, 1724); Richard Palmer, 'In the Steps of Sir Thomas Bodley: The Libraries of Lambeth Palace and Sion College in the Seventeenth Century', *Lambeth Palace Library Annual Review* (2006), pp. 53–67.

readers to the library, so that the library became a semi-public lending library for godly clergy and reasonably well-connected laity. The library itself was open at regular hours, from 8 a.m. until noon and from 2 p.m. until 5 p.m.[122] A register of external students who used the library includes the names of 765 students by 1666, including students of Oxford and Cambridge, but also students from Europe and America, many of whom were preparing for life in the church and who were offered accommodation by the college. The students were from within and without the Church of England and in the later seventeenth century, when many other libraries were effectively off-limits, Sion College remained a centre for godly reading.[123] Although it was something of a one-off, Sion College library reveals some of the connections between the college's design as a place of intellectual and cultural exchange for clergy and its use as a place in which to enhance such exchange through sociability and godly reading.[124]

CONCLUSION

Libraries were important venues for the godly in the seventeenth century, both as sites for reading and for wider intellectual, religious, and cultural exchange. Indeed, as we have seen in the previous chapters, the sociability of godly identity was heavily intertwined with the communal nature of the practice of reading and this is no less true of libraries than of the domestic spaces we have already explored. Not only were libraries areas in which to read and share ideas, but as spaces and as collections of books they often came to symbolize godly identity. To this end, they were prized as markers of godliness as they were passed down through generations and between godly friends, a form of transmission which once again highlights the importance of the continuities in evangelical identity over the long seventeenth century. Clearly, there is not always as much information on the reading that went on in libraries as we would like, and we need to ensure that attention is not taken away from the library as a centre for reading by a bibliographic myopia which insists that the most important thing about the collections is the books that they contained, rather than their actual use. And it can be tricky to decide exactly how to describe a

---

[122] Patterson and Dzelzainis, 'Marvell and the Earl of Anglesey', p. 723.

[123] See Lambeth Palace Library, Sion College MS, ARC L40.2/E29 ('Sion College: Student Admissions to the Library, 1632–1693').

[124] Admittedly, the statutes of the library placed limits on this sociability, stipulating that readers 'should behave quietly and modestly, not disturbing others by walking about or chatting, but getting on with their studies in silence'. See Palmer, 'In the Steps of Sir Thomas Bodley', p. 64.

collection, as collections could cross between individuals and institutions. For all this, the evidence discussed in this chapter has revealed how important libraries could be to godly communities and how the reading connected with them could be distinctly social and extend far beyond the walls of the library, through the lending and recirculation of books to individuals and families. Many parish libraries contained distinctively godly collections and were frequently incorporated into a broader religious culture. Likewise, after the Restoration the parish library appears to have been used to shape religious orthodoxy and social memory, and in particular it seems to have played an important role in the promulgation of what Diarmaid MacCulloch called 'the myth of the English Reformation'.[125] Nevertheless, the library was clearly a site for godly sociability and communal identity. Although there is an urgent need for further research, in particular into the usage of parish and more public collections, libraries clearly could function as venues for godly reading. Their status as centres of religious and cultural exchange and sociability enhanced their importance in the fashioning of godly identity.

---

[125] Diarmaid MacCulloch, 'The Myth of the English Reformation', *Journal of British Studies*, 30 (1991), pp. 1–19.

CHAPTER 5

Reading in the parish and the town

INTRODUCTION

To present godly reading as operating solely or even primarily in the domestic arena, however elastically considered, would be fundamentally misleading. Not least, it would both underestimate the range of types, contexts and styles of godly reading and suggest that any potential radicalism in their communal religious reading was to some extent circumscribed by its place within the confines of the early modern household. In part, the examination of libraries in the previous chapter has suggested how far reading as a sign of godly identity as well as a communal social practice was visible in more public spaces. But a consideration of reading in some of the more distinctly public spaces of the early modern parish and the explicitly public spaces of the town extends this analysis and confirms just how important reading was both to godly identity and to the ways in which the godly were perceived from outside.

Any such consideration of reading in the urban environment clearly calls for an engagement with the frequently deployed paradigm of the 'public sphere'. Whether carrying its considerable (yet often overlooked) ideological baggage – it might be thought of as a cloak for latter-day Marxists – or used in a non- or a not-especially-Habermasian sense as a way of characterizing the new and open world of printed propaganda and news, particularly as it emerged in the middle of the seventeenth century, the concept of a public sphere has been much used by early modern historians in recent years.[1]

[1] Jürgen Habermas, *The Structural Transformation of the Public Sphere: An Inquiry into a Category of Bourgeois Society*, trans. Thomas Burger with the assistance of Frederick Lawrence (Cambridge, 1989). There is a vast literature on Habermas's model and an increasing amount of work on early modern England in recent years engaged to some extent with his theory. For a helpful starting point, see Peter Lake and Steven Pincus, 'Rethinking the Public Sphere in Early Modern England', *Journal of British Studies*, 45 (2006), pp. 270–92; and the essays in Peter Lake and Steven Pincus (eds.), *The Politics of the Public Sphere in Early Modern England* (Manchester, 2007). Studies of the eighteenth century adopted Habermasian models well in advance of those focused on the sixteenth and seventeenth centuries.

While I have no intention to wade into the debate on its applicability to the culture of seventeenth-century England, there is no denying its usefulness in describing some of the changes in the nature of printed material and in particular in the gear change in the volume of printed news in the early 1640s.[2] The notion of the public sphere has (in combination, of course, with other historiographical impulses) helped to focus attention on the audiences for printed propaganda and privileged spaces of reading in this transformation of public political discourse. Even if its focus on secular politics and a relatively smooth transition to a culture of politeness now seems old-fashioned and out of keeping with what we know about the mid-seventeenth century and later, the 'public sphere' remains a useful way of thinking about the wider political context in which some forms of reading in the parish and town took place.

This chapter examines a variety of spaces connected with the parish and the town, from reading within the parish church and at the pulpit to reading in the quintessentially Habermasian venue of the coffee house and in the booksellers' shops which were at the heart of the early modern book trade. Although these are far from the only urban spaces in which reading took place – a comprehensive sweep would be tedious and repetitive – the chapter offers an insight into some different styles of reading than have previously been encountered. In particular, it shows the connections between social practices and moral imperatives, like the reformation of manners. To do so, it utilizes a more capacious definition of 'reading' and a wider range of source materials: not just books and manuscripts but also verse libels, transcripts of parish registers and even instances of writing on church benches and the like. Of course, such reading intersected with and was informed by the more domestic forms and styles of reading we have already encountered. But it was also in some senses distinct in being

---

[2] For the explosion of printed material between 1640 and 1642 as a key revolutionary impulse, see David Cressy, *England on Edge: Crisis and Revolution, 1640–1642* (Oxford, 2006); for its transformative role – in the creation of democratic culture – see David Zaret, *Origins of Democratic Culture: Printing, Petitions, and the Public Sphere in Early-Modern England* (Princeton, NJ, 2000). I should make it clear that I am in no way attempting to deny the insights of revisionist works which have taken issue with the applicability of Habermas's model to early modern England, in particular for its oversight of the continued importance of manuscript transmission, the sermon, and non-written forms of communication and expression. See Lake and Pincus, 'Rethinking the Public Sphere in Early Modern England'; and, among others, Peter Lake and Michael Questier, 'Puritans, Papists, and the "Public Sphere" in Early Modern England: The Edmund Campion Affair in Context', *Journal of Modern History*, 72 (2000), pp. 587–627; and Tony Claydon, 'The Sermon, the "Public Sphere" and the Political Culture of Late Seventeenth-Century England', in Lori Anne Ferrell and Peter McCullough (eds.), *The English Sermon Revised: Religion, Literature and History, 1600–1750* (Manchester, 2001), pp. 208–34.

shaped not only by the spaces and the contexts in which it was performed but also by the very publicity of the events – reading in public, in short, prompted in the godly an urge to display their collective spirituality through their styles of piety and their relationship with the book.

READING IN CHURCH

Within the parish, there were many potential sites for godly reading as well as other forms of religious and non-religious textual engagement. Given the portability of the book and the lack of a need for specialist equipment to read, practically every place could be a venue for godly reading, from the parish church itself to the churchyard and the vicarage. Exploring some of these spaces of godly reading and focusing on how it was performed provides further insight into the place of reading in godly religious culture. Churches themselves were social as well as sacred spaces where a range of tasks and practices were undertaken – services, rituals and prayers, but also social gatherings and business transactions. They were multi-purpose buildings and as such they provided several spaces for books and reading and writing, from the church door to benches marked 'For the Poor', to the parish chest, to Bibles set out for people to read from in the body of the church.[3] And scriptural passages and homilies would be read from the pulpit to the congregation during services.

Reading within the church, in particular social reading combined with the exposition of the scriptures, became an important issue in the early days of the Reformation and as such was a form of reading subjected to novel legislation. In many ways such reading – when thought of in broad terms – remained contentious throughout the period, as can be seen in the controversy over the Laudian drive to 'beautify' churches by including (among other things) tablets with the ten commandments on the walls of the chancel. Social reading in churches became the target of state action in the early days of the Reformation, in part because after the translation of the Bible into the vernacular, collective reading and exposition swiftly became a marker of evangelical religious identity. The importance of such Bible-reading to early evangelicals was cautiously welcomed immediately after the Reformation since the translation of the Bible brought significant advantages in the battle with Rome but it also brought with it a series of

---

[3] On the parish church as a multi-dimensional arena, see N. J. G. Pounds, *A History of the English Parish: The Culture of Religion from Augustine to Victoria* (Cambridge, 2000).

distinctly unwelcome social consequences. The Tudor state had not appropriated the church and its lands only to let the people read for themselves that it was to be the meek who would inherit the earth. They feared that Bible-reading unchecked by the bounds of social hierarchy would result in revolution, and thus set about restricting reading by controlling who did it and how it was done.

The authorities sought such power over the readership of the Bible in several key ways. Before the Reformation, such reading had simply been outlawed: Tyndale's work had been banned in 1526, although whether prohibition stimulates or restricts readership is debatable. After the Reformation, the state sanctioned Bible translations. The Matthew's Bible of 1537, produced at a time of evangelical ascendancy, attempted to control how it was read, in particular through its marginal notes.[4] Something of a compromise brought about through evangelical lobbying, this edition was soon replaced by the distinctly official Great Bible of 1539, with its famous Holbein frontispiece where Henry VIII literally distributed the word of God – first to Cromwell and Cranmer, who in turn passed it to clergy and laity who then rejoiced by proclaiming 'Vivat Rex' and 'God save the Kinge'. Around this time there appears to have been some confidence that Bible-reading in churches might uphold the social order and that certainly seems to have been the intention of the 1538 Injunctions which ordered that English Bibles be set up in parish churches, 'in some convenient place … whereas your parishioners may most commodiously resort to the same, and read it'. And it seems that those who welcomed reform did engage in such practices, with public Bible-reading in English quickly becoming, in the words of Eamon Duffy, 'a badge of support' for the evangelicals.[5] One of the most frequently cited examples of such reading is that of William Maldon, who later reflected on the time in his youth when evangelical collective reading in church came into conflict with the conservative impulses of his father. He reflected that immediately after the 1538 Injunctions, a group of 'dyveres poore men' from Chelmsford in Essex joined together to buy an English New Testament and 'on Sundays dyd set redinge in lower ende of the churche, and many wolde flocke about them to hear theyr redinge'. Maldon himself went among them 'to here their redyng of that glad and sweet tydyngs of the gospell', at least until

---

[4] For an interpretation, see Evelyn B. Tribble, *Margins and Marginality: The Printed Page in Early Modern England* (Charlottesville, VA, 1993), pp. 20–3.

[5] Eamon Duffy, *The Stripping of the Altars: Traditional Religion in England c. 1400–c. 1580* (New Haven, CT, 1992), p. 420.

his father objected and had him read Latin Matins with him instead.[6] Such practices apparently went on elsewhere. Many people took advantage of the Bibles that had been set up at St Paul's at the end of the 1530s, 'especially when they could get any that had an audible voyce to read unto them'. This was not without its dangers, as one John Potter who 'became very expert' in such reading found out – he was rebuked by Bishop Bonner for expounding as well as reading and sent to Newgate.[7]

Although such cultural transformations were not easily erased or modified, the fluctuations of religious policy under Henry VIII meant that the official line moved from encouraging such reading to attempting to restrict it by law. With the ascendancy of conservatives, Bible-reading was severely restricted by the appearance of the King's Book in 1543. This book of official standards in religion saw the authorities attempt to halt the growth in lay Bible-reading. It lamented the inclination in 'some of our people's hearts' towards a 'sinister understanding of scripture, presumption, arrogancy, carnal liberty, and contention' and separated those who needed to read scriptures from those for whom it was 'not so necessary'.[8] While this reads like an intransigent rant, in fact it carried more than usual force because the injunctions of the King's Book were upheld by a new law, the Act for the Advancement of True Religion (1543). This legislation, in its final form, restricted the reading of the Bible along social lines, declaring that it should be read by 'no women or artificiers, prentices, journeymen, serving men of the degrees of yeomen or under, husbandmen, nor labourers'. Although there was a provision to allow women of the nobility and the gentry to read the scriptures in private, the Act effectively prevented the vast majority of the population from reading the scriptures lawfully. And it defined very clearly the line where even licit Bible-reading, by the right people in private places, transgressed into illegal exposition. The last clause of the Act declared that no one should 'take upon him openly to dispute or argue, to debate or discuss or expound Holy Scripture or any part thereof ... upon the pains of one month's imprisonment'.[9] It also required that all

---

[6] See John Gough Nichols (ed.), *Narratives of the Days of the Reformation: Chiefly from the Manuscripts of John Foxe the Martyrologist*, Camden Society, old ser., 77 (1859), p. 349. The experience prompted Maldon to learn to read for himself, after which he swiftly clubbed up with his father's apprentice to buy an English New Testament, which they hid in the straw of their bed and read when it was safe.

[7] *Actes and Monuments* (1583), pp. 1200, 1206.

[8] *A Necessary Doctrine and Erudition for any Christen Man* (London, 1543), pp. 3, 6.

[9] 34 & 35 Henry VIII, cap. 1. On the Act, see Stanford Lehmberg, *The Later Parliaments of Henry VIII, 1536–1547* (Cambridge, 1977), pp. 186–8.

annotations – presumably including readers' manuscript marginalia as well as printed notes – in previous editions of the English Bible be removed. Predictably, the legislation angered evangelicals, like the preacher Michael Dunn who decried those who 'went about to pluck Christ's words and the Holy Ghost's from the people',[10] although the effectiveness of the law is somewhat debatable. The singularity of the example of the Gloucestershire shepherd Robert Williams who traded in his Bible for a copy of a book by Polydore Vergil 'when the Testament was abrogated, that shepherds might not read it', is perhaps notable for its lack of companions.[11]

The Edwardian regime, in many ways radical, encouraged Bible-reading in churches but retained something of the previous regime's desire to keep it contained by social boundaries. They did this by ordering parishes to purchase Erasmus's *Paraphrases* to be kept in churches alongside their English Bibles as well as through the *Homilies* of 1547, which both encouraged the reading of the Bible – Cranmer's first was entitled 'A Fruitfull Exhortation to the Readyng and Knowledge of Holy Scripture' and it encouraged the reading of scripture, if still with necessary humility – but since the homily was designed to be read out to congregations, this also set such reading within a hierarchical framework.[12] This was certainly recognized by some evangelicals since many of those who objected to the homilies did so on the grounds that a preacher reading from a printed text could not be moved by the spirit. Homilies thus on the one hand encouraged reading but on the other also established orthodoxy. This desire for orthodoxy continued through successive regimes. Under Mary, it meant that lay Bible-reading was not possible; under Elizabeth, it was not desirable.[13] And in any case the focus of such styles of reading now

---

[10] J. S. Brewer et al. (ed.), *Letters and Papers, Foreign and Domestic, of the Reign of Henry VIII* (23 vols., London, 1862–1932), vol. XVIII, ii, no. 546, cited in Felicity Heal, *Reformation in Britain and Ireland* (Oxford, 2003), p. 270.

[11] On Williams, see Christopher Haigh, *English Reformations: Religion, Politics, and Society under the Tudors* (Oxford, 1993), p. 161.

[12] These homilies proclaimed that scriptures 'ought to be much in our hands, in our eyes, in our ears, in our mouths, but most of all in our hearts ... For that thing, which by continual use of reading of Holy Scripture, and diligently searching of the same, is deeply printed and graven in the heart, at length turneth almost into nature'. On Erasmus's *Paraphrases*, see John Craig, 'Forming a Protestant Consciousness? Erasmus' *Paraphrases* in English Parishes, 1547–1666', in Hilmar Pabel and Mark Vessey (eds.), *Holy Scripture Speaks: Studies in the Production and Reception of Erasmus' Paraphrases on the New Testament* (Toronto, 2002), pp. 313–58.

[13] Where the proponents of the Reformation encouraged Bible-reading, the impetus of the counter-Reformation was to restrict such reading. At the Council of Trent in 1546, there was a ban on the interpretation of holy scripture. In 1564, the Tridentine Index decreed that anyone who desired to read the Bible in the vernacular needed to obtain permission from a bishop. In the Index of 1596, reading the Bible in the vernacular was outlawed.

had a novel forum in the guise of the prophesyings and preaching exercises where Bible-reading and exposition were more clearly linked with advanced Protestant identity. In some ways that very desire for orthodoxy was also apparent in the size and form of subsequent editions of the Bible. Although the book itself was portable, the Geneva Bible's (1560) marginal instructions were designed to guide readers and limit interpretation (admittedly in a more radical way than previously). Likewise, the very size of the massive Bishops' Bible (1568) made it a book laden with institutional authority.[14]

This meant that by the end of the sixteenth century, although public reading in churches might still be seen to have been a facet of godly culture, the association of authority and such reading (and its control) had largely shifted godly reading into the more domestic and clandestine arena of the conventicle.[15] Although there remained a tension between the godly imperative to read the scriptures and their desire for only particular forms of reading in church (their hostility towards reading set forms of prayer from the pulpit was constant), there was, by the seventeenth century, a shift in the forms of godly reading that took place within the church. To examine this reading, we need not only to take a broad view on what counted as 'reading' but also to widen the net of the sources which might be read, to take in more institutional books (which are usually referred to as 'sources' rather than 'books') such as parish registers as well as more ephemeral matter.

READING IN THE PULPIT

Many satirical descriptions of godly clergy imagined them as vigorous readers, who expounded their texts from the pulpit. Indeed, in an early seventeenth-century Star Chamber case, a Yorkshire Catholic was accused of mocking a Protestant cleric by breaking into the parish church on a Saturday night, setting up a wooden effigy of a preacher, adorned with a

---

[14] The marginal glosses on the Geneva Bible were certainly more radical than they had been before this point and this became the favoured edition of the godly in the later sixteenth century. But that radicalism should not conceal the fact that this printed marginalia was explicitly designed to restrict and control the reader. On this function of printed marginalia, see the comments of William W. E. Slights, *Managing Readers: Printed Marginalia in English Renaissance Books* (Ann Arbor, MI, 2001).

[15] This was hardly a total shift and neither were the two arenas entirely distinct. Households like that of John Bruen appear to have designed their domestic piety in a fashion which imitated that of the parish church and collective reading was absolutely vital to their spiritual existence. Of course, in imitating church practices, the godly also opened themselves up to the accusation of semi-separatist behaviour.

surplice and with books in front of it, before setting it alight.[16] Certainly the public nature of the space and the platform of the pulpit made for some distinctly public forms of reading, many of which intersected with the emergent news culture. A particularly intriguing example of the kinds of reading which might be engaged in within the church and the wider importance of such reading through its connection with preaching exercises and manuscript transmission comes from the parish of Halifax in the West Riding of Yorkshire. We have already seen some of the efforts to establish a godly parish library in Halifax in the early seventeenth century and drawn upon the writings of Oliver Heywood's extensive descriptions of his ministry there in the latter half of that century. But in many ways the groundwork for religious radicalism in Halifax which was later expressed in support of Heywood and was evident in its radical weavers in the eighteenth century was done by John Favour. Favour was born in Southampton and educated at Winchester and New College, Oxford, before taking up the post of vicar of Halifax in 1593. Remaining there until his death in 1624, Favour struggled to impose a godly regime on his congregation, probably seeing himself as a pilgrim in an unholy land. He described his routine in his *Antiquitie Triumphing Over Noveltie*:

notwithstanding I had many impediments, well knowne unto the places of my residence: as preaching every Sabbath day, lecturing every day in the week, exercising justice in the commonwealth, practising of physicke and chirurgerie in the great penury and necessity thereof in the country where I live, and only for God's sake.[17]

Preaching was at the core of this effort and Favour was instrumental in the establishment of the godly preaching exercises in Halifax and other locations in the West Riding early in the seventeenth century which

---

[16] TNA: PRO, STAC 8/19/10, fo. 22. The bookishness of godly laity was frequently mocked in equally inventive ways. One verse satire, entitled 'Off a Puritane', entwined godly bookishness with alleged sexual hypocrisy by depicting a puritan couple having sex on the Bible. In it, 'a puritanicall ladd' named Mathias – the characters were given Dutch names to highlight their religious radicalism – met with a young woman and 'laid his bible under her breeche,/ and merilie hee kist her'. As a prop, this Bible did not quite do the trick: as the woman exclaimed, 'my Buttocckes they lie to lowe: I wisht / appocrypha were in itt!' See John S. Farmer (ed.), *National Ballad and Song: Merry Songs and Ballads, Prior to the Year 1800* (5 vols., [London], 1897), Vol. I, p. 73, cited in W. P. Holden, *Anti-Puritan Satire, 1572–1642* (New Haven, CT, 1954), pp. 58–9.

[17] John Favour, *Antiquitie Triumphing over Noveltie* (London, 1619), epistle to the reader. For religion in sixteenth-century Halifax, see William and Sarah Sheils, 'Textiles and Reform: Halifax and Its Hinterland', in Patrick Collinson and John Craig (eds.), *The Reformation in English Towns, 1500–1640* (Basingstoke, 1998), pp. 130–43. For a somewhat later period, see M. E. Francois, 'The Social and Economic Development of Halifax, 1558–1640', *Proceedings of the Leeds Philosophical and Literary Society: Literary and Historical Section*, 11 (1964–6), pp. 217–80.

continued perhaps until the outbreak of the Civil War.[18] The purpose of these exercises, which took place on the last Wednesday of each month and which were documented in minuscule detail by their secretary Elkanah Wales, the puritan preacher and long-standing curate of Pudsey, was primarily to educate local clergy and consolidate social links between them but there is also evidence of involvement from enthusiastic laypeople.[19] Indeed, it was said of Elkanah Wales that 'multitudes travelled several miles to profit by a minister whom his own people heard with indifference or scarcely heard at all'.[20] Likewise, Oliver Heywood later recalled that there was a 'multitude of hearers' at the Halifax exercise, and noted that Favour

was a great friend to the Non-Conformists, maintained two famous men as lecturers at Halifax, whom he shrouded under his authority and interest with the bishop, namely, Mr Boys, banished out of Kent for his Non-Conformity . . . and Mr Barlow, that writ upon Timothy, a choice man, who had been shrouded under Dr Favour.[21]

These, and other famous godly preachers – including Thomas Shepard and Alexander Cooke – came to Halifax to participate in this programme of evangelization.

But perhaps the most revealing picture of Favour's efforts in Halifax is seen through an unlikely source, the parish register. Starting a new book on his arrival at Halifax, Favour went beyond the official purpose of the register – to record baptisms, marriages, and burials – to chronicle judgements on the vices and virtues of his parishioners.[22] In so doing, Favour recorded the spiritual plight of his parishioners and showed a parish where the godly and their enemies lived starkly different lives. Among the enemies of the godly were a string of drunkards for whom Favour had little time, except to point out that their behaviour was evidence of their probable damnation. The deaths of drinkers and adulterers were recorded with no suggestion of forgiveness. In January 1596, on the death

---

[18] J. A. Newton, 'Puritanism in the Diocese of York (excluding Nottinghamshire) 1603–1640' (unpublished DPhil thesis, University of London, 1955), pp. 220–36.

[19] BL, Additional MS 4933 A and B ('Notes from Sermons Preached in the West Riding, circa 1609–1661). That these volumes formed part of Ralph Thoresby's papers demonstrates some of the continuity between his religious identity and that of his predecessors.

[20] See T. D. Whitaker, *Loidis and Elmete* (Leeds, 1816), p. 94.

[21] See Heywood, *Diaries*, vol. IV, p. 16.

[22] Sections of the register have been printed in W. J. Walker (ed.), *Chapters on the Early Registers of Halifax Parish Church, from the Local Archaeological Collection of the Late E. J. Walker* (Halifax, 1885), pp. 1–130. For an alternative analysis, using the same source, see A. L Rowse, *The England of Elizabeth* (2003 edn, ed. Christopher Haigh; originally published London, 1950), pp. 482–4.

of William King of Skircote, Favour wrote, 'This William Kinge was a swearer, drinker, and a most filthy adulterer, amonge others hee kept longe one Dorothy Brigg a wydowe, in whose house and hand hee was stricken with sudden deathe: his last words were oaths and curses.' Other drunkards fell off their horses and broke their necks.[23] In some cases, Favour inserted into the register short providential narratives of the lives of these sinners. In 1609, for example, he wrote,

John Parkinson and Giles Coweheard were common drunkards, who mistakinge the preacher that denounced God's judgement against wilfull obstinat sinners, swore greevouse othes that they came to the church to bee blessed, and not to be cursed, and therefore would never come to the church agayne. This they blasphemed the 5th February, and both fell presently sicke, and never came to the church but to bee buryed.[24]

A man who profaned the sabbath died a miserable death in the snow; another drunkard and blasphemer hanged himself at his house.[25] Favour recorded the death of a 'child who no man knewe', a suffocation in a coal pit, a drowning, and the death of Anne Ingham, who 'knewe no father to her child, but being an idiot was forced by a stranger in the field'. Sexual sins drew his condemnation. Sara Fearnesyde was a blind woman who 'had five bastards' and was 'a most damnable wicked queane'.[26] If the details of God's judgements against the ungodly seem extensive, the records of particularly virtuous parishioners are somewhat thinner. Still, Favour made sure to record the charity of those who gave money to support the church and the steadfastness of those who had led exemplary lives. Robert Hemmingway bequeathed sixty pounds for pious uses, while others left money for the education of the young.[27] Very occasionally, Favour commented upon the remarkable qualities of some of his godly parishioners: James Robinson, for example, was 'a very religiouse, zealouse honest old man, not able to read, yet very ready in the scriptures, with prompt use and application as I have never heard without learning'.[28]

The depth of such social detail, with all it suggests about the relative success of a puritan imposition of a reformation of manners in Yorkshire, is impressive but remains one-dimensional when we think of it as a document – merely an official transcript of what happened. But Favour's comments on his parishioners went beyond simple record keeping and as such they allow some room for speculation as to how such apparently

---

[23] Walker, *Chapters on the Early Registers of Halifax Parish Church*, pp. 11, 13.
[24] Ibid., p. 49.   [25] Ibid., pp. 90, 13.   [26] Ibid., pp. 19, 24, 63, 30, 25.
[27] Ibid., pp. 46, 88.   [28] Ibid., p. 90.

administrative 'documents' might have been used in practice. Although it was described by its editor as a parish register, Favour's book was a bishop's transcript – that is, the parchment book in which the parish kept a copy of the records it sent to the bishop of the baptisms, marriages and burials in the parish.[29] Favour began such a transcript in a new parchment book in December 1598 and it is likely that his comments were not sent to his bishop but confined to the copy. What is striking about the commentary is not only the way it reads as a narrative of God's providences as they were visited upon the people of Halifax but also the orality inherent in such descriptions. It seems probable that some parishioners would have been allowed access to this record – such transcripts were, after all, public documents – but the element of performance in the judgements also makes it possible that Favour read such statements aloud at the burials of his parishioners or even that, using the pulpit as a forum for news, he read such judgements to those that came to his church as a guide to their behaviour, letting them know the ultimate rewards of lives of vice and virtue. This is clear in many of the entries, particularly those warning of the dangers of moral transgressions. It is not difficult to hear Favour in his register, telling his congregation, many of whom would not have known the goings on in the more remote corners of the parish, that 'John Pillinge, a most wicked and incorrigible drunkard, died miserably in want'. These were cautionary tales which let people know how to behave, for instance in the judgement of Giles Cowheard and John Parkinson, who died shortly after expounding 'that they came to the church to bee blessed, and not to bee cursed'.[30] If it was read aloud in this way, the book bears some comparison with the way Christopher Trachay used the parish accounts at Morebath in Devon in the early sixteenth century, as well as how the long-serving conservative vicar of Heydon in Essex Thomas Sheppard used his parish register to record the 'beneficial good deeds' of his flock and even how Edmund Bunny used his tithe book in Bolton Percy in Yorkshire.[31]

---

[29] Bishops' Transcripts were copies of the parish register. Parishes had been required to keep registers since 1538 but, with less than universal compliance, in 1598 the clergy were once again instructed to keep registers and permitted to keep a copy in a parchment book for the sake of preservation. After 1598, the clergy were required to send their registers to the bishop each Easter, so they needed to keep a copy. See G. R. Elton, *The Sources of History: Studies in the Uses of Historical Evidence. England 1200–1640* (London, 1969), pp. 111–12.

[30] Walker, *Chapters on the Early Registers of Halifax Parish Church*, p. 49.

[31] For Morebath, see Eamon Duffy, *The Voices of Morebath: Reformation and Rebellion in an English Village* (New Haven, CT, 2001). For Sheppard, see Patrick Collinson, 'Shepherds, Sheepdogs, and Hirelings: The Pastoral Ministry in Post-Reformation England', in W. J. Sheils and

In fact, one further piece of evidence tends to confirm that Favour used the register in this way. In his 'An Extract of the Passages of my Life, or The Book of All my Writing Books', in which (among other things) he went over all his other writings, Nehemiah Wallington referred to passages he had written in a notebook entitled 'Examples of God's Wrath upon Those that have broke His Commandments', which was compiled in 1645 and bound together with Thomas Beard's *The Thunderbolt of Gods Wrath* (1618) and John Vicars's *A Looking-Glasse for Malignants* (1643) but which no longer survives.[32] Among the points he extracted from his own book were those on 'Punishments upon the breakers of the Seventh Commandement', among which were six full pages of

Examples of Gods Iudgments in Halifax parish upon Sundry Adulterers and profaine parsons in the vicaridge of Hallifax Since January the first 1598 as they were left in writting by that Reverent Docter Favor the Late Rector there (in the Rigistor Bookes).

The reference is frustratingly brief, although Wallington also alludes to his further use of the Halifax material in these pages of his book and mentions one

Edward Hurse of Hallifax a secret Adultarer after he had gotten a bastard vpon notice thereof into the world he fell distracted and in his madnes Cutt his throat and have himselfe nine stabs in the belly whereof he died: He was buried May 2. 1599.[33]

D. Wood (eds.), *The Ministry: Clerical and Lay*, Studies in Church History, 26 (Oxford, 1989), p. 212. For Bunny, see W. J. Sheils, '"The Right of the Church": The Clergy, Tithe, and the Courts at York, 1540–1640', in W. J. Sheils and D. Wood (eds.), *The Church and Wealth*, Studies in Church History, 24 (Oxford, 1987), pp. 231–55. For parish registers as spaces for autobiographical writing, see now Adam Smyth, *Autobiography in Early Modern England* (Cambridge, 2010), Chapter 4.

[32] Folger MS V.a.436 (Nehemiah Wallington, 'An Extract of the Passages of my Life, or The Book of All my Writing Books'); Paul S. Seaver, *Wallington's World: A Puritan Artisan in Seventeenth-Century London* (London, 1985), p. 202, judges 'Mr Vicker's Looking Glass' to be John Vicars, *A Prospective Glasse to Looke into Heaven* (London, 1618), but it is much more likely in this context (and at this date) to have been John Vicars, *A Looking-Glasse for Malignants: or, Gods Hand against God-Haters. Containing a Most Terrible yet True Relation of the Many Most Fearefull Personall Examples (in these Present Times, Since the Yeere, 1640.) of Gods Most Evident and Immediate Wrath against our Malevolent Malignants* (London, 1643) or his *The Looking-Glasse for Malignants, Enlarged. Or, The Second Part of Gods Hand against God-Haters* (London, 1645). Seaver also apparently mistakes *The Thunderbolt of Gods Wrath* as Wallington's own subtitle rather than the much more probable abridgement of Thomas Beard's *Theatre of Gods Judgements* (London, 1597) which appeared as Edmund Rudierd, *The Thunderbolt of Gods Wrath against Hard-Hearted and Stiffe-Necked Sinne[r]s, or An Abridgement of the Theater of Gods Fearefull Judgements Executed Upon Notorious Sinners* (London, 1618).

[33] See Folger MS V.a.436 (Nehemiah Wallington, 'An Extract of the Passages of my Life, or The Book of All my Writing Books'), fo. 150.

In some ways, Wallington's readership prompts a series of questions – had he seen the Halifax register himself? Or did Favour use the registers to circulate his judgements on his parishioners among the godly in manuscript? Had Favour perhaps printed such an account which is now lost? Or did someone else use the register to compile such a record? We do not know. But in all of these cases, what is clear is that a seemingly straightforward administrative document like a register was in fact an important part of godly reading, with the initial judgements of Favour, perhaps via the pulpit, eventually being spread to a wider audience.[34]

In fact, when we think about forms of public reading beyond the printed book it opens up a much more dynamic picture of puritanism. The godly read and used and circulated manuscripts in particular ways which stretched from the use of manuscripts in the regulation of internal godly disputes as a means of restricting publicity (and limiting diversity and outright separatism among themselves) to looser and less restricted circulation among the religious community.[35] In Halifax, the manuscript catechisms of John Boyes, the town preacher who had been banished from Kent and who was sheltered by Favour, circulated among the godly. 'Mr Boyes Principles wherein he catechized the poor people at Halifax' and 'Mr Boyes catechism to the congregation at Halifax' appear to have been cherished as tokens of religious identity by the godly and were painstakingly written out by local parishioners.[36] The godly also prized collections of sermon notes – the practice described by the Cranbrook schoolmaster Thomas Good as 'pens walking at sermons'[37] – and circulated them, sharing them in the religious community and rereading them in the family, just as the Hoby family used the notes they took of Stephen Egerton's godly sermons. Such notes were circulated in the religious community, along with the spiritual diaries and autobiographies of the

---

[34] A point made in Alexandra Walsham, *Providence in Early Modern England* (Oxford, 1999), p. 66, which also refers to other ministers (such as the Cheshire vicar Edward Burghall) preparing such accounts which were subsequently printed.

[35] On this, see Peter Lake and David R. Como, '"Orthodoxy" and Its Discontents: Dispute Settlement and the Production of "Consensus" in the London (Puritan) "Underground"', *Journal of British Studies*, 39 (2000), pp. 34–70.

[36] BL, Additional MS 4928 ('Mr. Boyes Principles wherin he Catechised the Poore People at Hallifax', and 'The Christians Horne Booke or A.B.C.'). A copy of the manuscript came into the hands of Oliver Heywood. See Walker, *Chapters on the Early Registers of Halifax Parish Church*, p. 36.

[37] See Patrick Collinson, 'Cranbrook and the Fletchers: Popular and Unpopular Religion in the Kentish Weald', in P. N. Brooks (ed.), *Reformation Principle and Practice: Essays in Honour of Arthur Geoffrey Dickens* (London, 1980), p. 192.

godly. They were prized artefacts of godly identity which were read and cherished over the generations, showing once more the transition of puritanism into dissent.[38] The interfaces between speech, manuscript and print are particularly clear in such instances. The sayings of John Dod (1550–1645), for example – which were memorably entitled Dod's Droppings – were collected, copied, circulated, printed and even pasted onto the walls of godly householders long after those with first-hand memories of this godly figurehead had died.[39]

But godly clergy also read and circulated manuscripts as part of a more public religious practice. Since each instance of such reading is unique, it makes sense to proceed here on the basis of a single example where the reading and circulation of manuscripts is best understood in the context of local religious practice and politics, in this case in early seventeenth-century Leeds. In this large parish, where the outlying chapels had fallen into disuse and the minister had around five thousands souls in his care, puritanism was imposed on the congregation by a small group of local gentry who, aided by the Earl of Huntingdon, purchased the right of presentation to the living in 1588 and swiftly installed the godly Robert Cooke.[40] Soon he had cultivated a loyal following and it was not long before some of the parishioners were asking for funeral sermons, which were at this stage novel and overtly public displays of godly religiosity.[41] After Cooke's death in 1615, his brother Alexander, a first-rate preacher and polemicist who in 1605 had been deprived from his living at Louth for his refusal to wear the surplice, and had since served his brother as an

---

[38] Andrew Cambers, 'Reading, the Godly, and Self-Writing in England, circa 1580–1720', *Journal of British Studies*, 46 (2007), pp. 796–825.

[39] Beinecke Library, Yale University, Osborn MS b.236 ('Dods Droppings a Few of them as at Severall Times they have been Gathered from his Mouth', 1617); other copies at Dr Williams's Library, London, MS 28.2; and at Jesus College, Cambridge. See Arnold Hunt, 'The Lord's Supper in Early Modern England', *Past and Present*, 161 (1998), pp. 39–83. Some of these fed into a printed broadsheet of 1667 entitled *Old Mr Dod's Sayings*, which was very popular and went through many editions. On one account, this could still be seen in the mid-eighteenth century, pasted onto the walls of cottages. See Adam Fox, *Oral and Literate Culture in England, 1500–1700* (Oxford, 2000), p. 149. A book containing copies of the letters and papers of John Rastrick and his family, compiled in the mid-eighteenth century, includes two pages of Dod's sayings. See Lincolnshire Archives, MS 2 Cragg 4/7, fos. 61r–v.

[40] See Claire Cross, *The Puritan Earl: The Life of Henry Hastings, Third Earl of Huntingdon, 1536–1595* (London, 1966), pp. 256–7; and Claire Cross, *Magistrates and Ministers: Religion in Hull and Leeds from the Reformation to the Civil War*, Borthwick Papers, 67 (York, 1985), pp. 18–19. On Robert Cooke, see *ODNB*.

[41] On the request, see Cross, *Magistrates and Ministers*, p. 19.

unofficial curate, was collated to the vicarage by Archbishop Matthew (the only instance in which Matthew appointed a vicar who refused to wear the surplice).[42] Cooke became something of an icon to the godly, who long remembered the power of his preaching and his character, his hatred of popery and his revulsion towards sinners.[43] In the case of the possession of the Fairfax children, Cooke made an appearance in one of their visions, clutching a white parchment book and then reading prayers in order to dispel the devil.[44] The surviving notes of Cooke's sermons confirm his zealotry as well as pointing towards some of the difficulties he had in evangelizing his parishioners – particularly in a rant about 'our bastard-getters that will not come to penance' – and the stark divisions between the godly and their enemies in the north of England.[45] Likewise his publications such as *Pope Joane* brought him notoriety, even if they also brought him into conflict with opponents, one of whom (John Walker) wrote an anti-puritan tract which attacked the preacher and the preaching

---

[42] The legal wrangling is complicated. A Leeds partnership bought the advowson to the parish around 1588. In 1615, on the death of Cooke, the purchasers refused to convey the advowson to the feoffees the parish proposed to nominate and tried to sell the right of presentation. This resulted in the choice of rival candidates, where at the request of (some of) the parishioners, Matthew presented Alexander Cooke, while the purchasers, led by Robert Brickhead, put forward Richard Middleton, chaplain to Charles, Prince of Wales. The parishioners lodged a bill of complaint in chancery (3 November 1615) and won, though Robert Brickhead contested the decision with a case of *quare impedit* in 1618. Interestingly, the chancery decree appointed 'five eminent divines ... as assistants to the said assignees and patrons upon the next vacancy of the vicarage'. They were all puritans: Favour of Halifax, Lister of Wakefield, Moore of Guisley, Pullen of Ripley and Stock of Kirkheaton. *Quare impedit*, in English law, is a form of action by which the right of presentation to a benefice is tried. It is so called from the words of the writ formerly in use, which directed the sheriff to command the person disturbing the possession to permit the plaintiff to present a fit person, or to show cause 'why he hinders' the plaintiff in his right.

[43] See, for instance, Ralph Thoresby, *Vicaria Leodiensis* (London, 1724), pp. 71–9. Elkanah Wales preached a sermon on his character at the Leeds exercise shortly after Cooke's death, notes of which Ralph Thoresby made on the endpapers of his copy of Alexander Cooke, *Pope Joane* (London, 1625). York Minster Library, shelfmark Y/CMA 115.9 COO.

[44] See William Grainge (ed.), *Daemonologia: A Discourse on Witchcraft, as it was Acted in the Family of Mr Edward Fairfax, of Fuyston, in the County of York, in the Year 1621: Along with the only Two Eclogues of the same author Known to be in Existence* (Harrogate, 1882), pp. 39–40. For such reading as a means of dispossession and its place in godly culture, see Andrew Cambers, 'Demonic Possession, Literacy and "Superstition" in Early Modern England', *Past and Present*, 202 (2009), pp. 3–35.

[45] A list of sermons preached by Cooke may have included those in BL, Egerton MS 2877 (Commonplace Book of Gilbert Freville of co. Durham, 1591–1625), which includes eleven sermons preached by a 'Mr Cooke' on Luke and Revelation, preached in London c.1606. For Cooke's sermons at Halifax, see BL, Additional MS 4933 A and B ('Notes from Sermons Preached in the West Riding, circa 1609–1661). This paragraph is based on Ralph Thoresby's notes in Alexander Cooke, *Pope Joane* (London, 1625). York Minster Library, shelfmark Y/CMA 115.9 COO.

exercises and encouraged the puritans to go 'to Virginia, or some other place where Christ was never heard before'.[46]

Cooke's puritanism, in particular its radical edge, can be seen in his public reading as it formed part of his godly programme, which in turn provoked legal action against him. The case of John Metcalf and Thomas Jackson against Cooke and a group of Leeds puritans came before Star Chamber on 11 June 1622.[47] Metcalf and Jackson accused Cooke of being 'a sectary or a puritane' who had abused his position as vicar of Leeds in resisting the laws, rites and ceremonies of the Church of England, ignoring the instructions on burial in the Book of Common Prayer in favour of the 'unseemly dragging of the dead corps ... into their graves' while 'leavinge others unburied'. The complaint listed Cooke's macabre deeds, including his refusal to say prayers or read scriptures at the burial of one Robert Benson in 1618 and leaving his grief-stricken father 'to carrie his owne childe to the grave and then and there to interre and bury him himself'; not allowing the body of Elizabeth Mawer to be brought into the church, but leaving it in the church porch before dragging her by the legs to her grave and throwing her into it uncovered; and dragging the body of John Broadley to a grave in the dead of night and burying him 'then and there, without reading anie prayers appointed to be saide at the buriall'.[48] They argued that Cooke turned his enemies away from communion and called those that knelt for it papists, and that he nevertheless administered it to those who stood or sat. In the pulpit, they said, he used 'unseemly and unreverent' words and named and shamed his opponents as 'Atheists, whoremongers and other ... foul and odious names'. In his heterodox sermons, he railed against the celebration of Christmas in winter, the naming of Good Friday, and the use of rings in marriage. On occasion, he allowed widows to give their daughters away in marriage. He was accused of the 'furious and abrupt' breaking of prayers on Sundays, telling the congregation to depart, while entreating only those who shared his views

---

[46] John Walker, *The English Pharise, or Religious Ape* (n.p., 1616), p. 84. Cooke's publications were *The Abatement of Popish Braggs, Pretending Scripture to be theirs. Retorted by the Hand of Alexander Cooke* (London, 1625); *Pope Joane. A Dialogue Betweene a Protestant and a Papist* (London, 1610); *The Weather-Cocke of Romes Religion: with her Severall Changes. Or: The World Turn'd Topsie-Turvie by Papists* (London, 1625); *Worke for a Masse-Priest (London, 1617); More Worke for a Masse-Priest* (London, 1621); *Yet more Worke for a Masse-Priest* (London, 1622); *Worke, More Worke, and a Little More Work for a Masse-Priest Reviewed and Augmented by the Authour* (London, 1628); *Saint Austins Religion Wherein is Manifestly Proued out of the Works of that Learned Father, that he Dissented from Popery, and Agreed with the Religion of the Protestants in all the Maine Points of Faith and Doctrine* (London, 1624).

[47] TNA: PRO, STAC 8/215/6 (*Metcalf and Jackson v. Cooke et. al.*).   [48] Ibid., m. 3.

to go to the 'vicarage to heare prayers and sermons or this defendants preaching thereupon in the yeard on the backside of his howse'.[49] He was also accused of disrupting the local rushbearing ceremonies in 1619 and 1620, in contravention of the Book of Sports. Cooke, it was alleged, deliberately preached against the Book of Sports – he claimed that the King's warrant 'could never save theire soules from hell fyre' – and did his best to disrupt these festivities by preaching the whole day, locking the church doors against the revellers, calling them 'rogues, rascalls, whores and whoremasters', carrying pistols and a dagger and even beating a man with an iron bar and striking a woman to the ground: she was so badly beaten and bruised that she could not stand up or move her arms and 'for the space of ten dayes after shee spitt nothing but bloud'.[50]

Although Cooke denied most of these accusations as 'mere fictions' conjured up by the complainants' 'owne braynes', and although it is perfectly conceivable that he was innocent of all the charges, one of the accusations (true or not) casts more light upon the place of public reading in godly culture.[51] Cooke was accused of composing a set of verse libels, reading them from the pulpit and spreading them through Leeds, and of being responsible for their repetition in York, Kingston upon Hull, Wakefield, Halifax and elsewhere. Metcalf and Jackson claimed that Cooke and his confederates did 'make, frame, devise and write divers scandalous and infamous and libellous writings' against those who did not share their 'factious opinions', with the dual aim of destroying their 'creditts and reputacons' and attempting to 'scandalize the present government and conformitie of the Church and religion established' with their 'puritan ... and precise opinions'.[52] The libel read:

> Old Converus with poysoned dart
> A doe to shoot belowe her heart
> As God was wont with every Trull,
> In hope to gett a newe Towne bull,
> A spayede in whyne to run the ringe,
> That nere was hit but by a king
> That word recall I must anon
> Or else doe wrong to civill John,
> Whose still to shoote that harmlesse deere
> Was such that downe shee fell for feare

---

[49] Ibid., m. 2.   [50] Ibid., m. 2.

[51] Cooke refused to answer the charges which related to ecclesiastical matters, arguing that they were solely for bishops or ecclesiastical commissioners to decide. Ibid., m. 2.

[52] Their story is told in ibid., m. 3.

And then the wood man made a squier,
A creaturre worse were came in hell fier.
This bellowing bull hath all his life,
Sought to defloure both maid and wife,
His owne maie sigh and sobb in bedd,
Hee whoaringe annother steade,
The contriving of his vile deeds
And for his syinnes my heart yet bleeds,
This calfe of late occasion tooke
To quarrell with our learned Cooke,
A man whose life and learning doth appeare
In towne and cittie both to the most pure
Though impure tongues against him Raile,
In wicked songe but all in vaine
Jehovah keepes him from them wakeing
And a sleep his manners vile and beastlie life,
His sonne detests though want of wife,
Force him sometimes against the streame
To travell upp to hilary Towne;
He is chiefest of all our saplinge crewe
A sect I think the devill did spewe
Amongst them all I doe knowe none
But cunning cheating knaves each one
Whoe make a prey on clothiers poore;
Gehenna gapes for them therefore,
With brazen fan they met our knight
When to this towne hee came to right
What had bin wronge and soee undone
By meanes of him ande another John
All holie men doth knowe this beast
Of heaven and hell to make a feast
This towne this cruell Tiger
Seekes to overthrowe by cursed tricks
High waies the poore and all must bleede,
On them by toll dish hee wil feede,
The backe house hee hath raised to hell
His soule to the devill I think hee will sell
The knave is brought from beggars state;
To equalize the best in the gate;
Yet doth oppresse his neighbours poore
By setting stalls before their dore,
For amerciament, hee spares not one
Old Henry is next when hee is gon.[53]

---

[53] Ibid., m. 3.

John Metcalf recognized himself as the target of the libel and was furious: he knew that others would also read calf for bull. Metcalf, who had had the audacity 'To quarrell with our learned Cooke', was portrayed as an adulterer hewn from a sect spewed up by the Devil: he was dishonest, he oppressed his neighbours, and he was going to hell. Metcalf claimed that Cooke and his confederates were guilty of 'divulging and publishing' this libel in 'publique assemblies' to the ruin of the complainants' names, reputations and credit. He accused Cooke of reciting it privately at his conventicles, telling his friends 'wee have not only fornicators and adulterers amongst us, but also a knowne towne bull'. He claimed that Cooke climbed into the pulpit and slandered him and his associates, sometimes naming them and at other times using the allusion provided by the libel, calling them 'irreligious atheists, whoremasters, drunkards, epicures, infidells, abbey lubbers, and other odious names not fitt to be uttered by anie true professor of the gospell'.[54]

Remarkably, Metcalf and Jackson accused Cooke of using the public reading of libels in the exercise of ecclesiastical justice, through an arrangement struck with one Richardson in the consistory court at York. They claimed that Cooke oppressed his subjects by bringing 'a multitude of vaine and frivolous suits' for small sums of money. Since he had become vicar, he had cited around two hundred people a year 'to extract and get money ... and ... to wreake his malice and revenge against such his parishioners as ... dislike his factious and distempered humour ... and are not of his sect and faction'. Cooke made his parishioners 'take copies of severall libells put into the said court by him and the said Procter'.[55] He was accused of making John Metcalf appear and take a copy of his libel for not paying his Easter dues. The complainants alleged that, from the pulpit, Cooke had called those parishioners who did not hold his views 'buggerers and murderers', decrying those who foolishly thought that the giving of money to the poor only at Christmas would save their souls from the Devil. He had accused one George Yeadon of 'buggery and that hee had gotten a cowe with calfe', which prompted his confederates to bar

---

[54] Cooke denied that he had composed the libels or used their words in his sermons and denied naming Metcalf, but admitted preaching against whoremongers and bullerers. This was, he argued, against 'divers of the said parish theire loose and disordered course of life and of their insolent and shameles bouldnes to attempt and drawe women to that shamfull horrible sinne'.

[55] The lawyer was Thomas Procter, from Newhall-with-Clifton, near Otley. He was a barrister-at-law and died in December 1646. Edward Fairfax described his visit, regarding the possession of his daughters, to 'Mr Procter ... a lawyer who lives three miles from me'. Grainge, *Daemonologia*, p. 56. It is instructive that Fairfax visited Procter with his brother-in-law, Martin Laycock, one of Cooke's 'confederates.'

Yeadon, his friends and his servants from the communion and to force
them from the church, despite the fact that they were in charity and well
prepared for communion.[56] Cooke was accused, in short, of forms of
godly reading which contrasted starkly with those we have seen up to this
point. Such reading was public and unashamedly divisive and it drew
upon a cultural repertoire more often confined to descriptions of 'popular
culture'.

Although the charges brought against Cooke are remarkable, there are
other examples of godly and clerical involvement in the writing, reading
and distribution of libels which reinforce this picture of public godly
reading as at least potentially radical. As Alastair Bellany has shown, a libel
was attached to the hearse of the late Archbishop Whitgift – a satirical
attack on anti-puritan policies in a space usually reserved for congratu-
latory verse. It was written (or at least copied) by the Northamptonshire
puritan Lewis Pickering, who then felt the full force of the law.[57] There
are also several other cases which also show how the godly used the libel
not only as a form of satirical verse but also as a means of intervention in
religious policy – enough at least to show that this was another of the ways
in which the godly used aspects of traditional popular culture to further
their own ends.[58] Such interventions had of course been on display in the
Marprelate controversy, where puritan and downright anticlerical texts,
although produced in the most clandestine of circumstances, circulated
widely and provided ample opportunities for less-than-typical forms of
godly reading. As we will see, the name of Marprelate had an enduring
legacy, resurfacing in the early 1640s as a pseudonym which still
possessed – through its links with the past – a cultural value and ideological
positioning which was obvious to its readers.[59] In some cases, however,

---

[56] TNA: PRO, STAC 8/215/6, m. 3.
[57] Alastair Bellany, 'A Poem on the Archbishop's Hearse: Puritanism, Libel, and Sedition after the
      Hampton Court Conference', *Journal of British Studies*, 34 (1995), pp. 137–64.
[58] See, among others, Adam Fox, 'Ballads, Libels and Popular Ridicule in Jacobean England', *Past
      and Present*, 145 (1994), pp. 47–83; Alastair Bellany, '"Raylinge Rymes and Vaunting Verse":
      Libellous Politics in Early Stuart England, 1603–1628', in Kevin Sharpe and Peter Lake (eds.),
      Culture and Politics in Early Stuart England (Basingstoke, 1994), pp. 285–310; Thomas Cogswell,
      'Underground Verse and the Transformation of Early Stuart Political Culture', *Huntington Library
      Quarterly*, 60 (1998), pp. 303–26; Alastair Bellany, 'Libels in Action: Ritual, Subversion and the
      English Literary Underground, 1603–42', in Tim Harris (ed.), *The Politics of the Excluded,
      c.1500–1850* (Basingstoke, 2001), pp. 99–124; Andrew McRae, *Literature, Satire, and the Early
      Stuart State* (Cambridge, 2004); Andrew McRae (ed.), *"Railing Rhymes": Politics and Poetry in
      Early Stuart England*, themed issue of *Huntington Library Quarterly*, 69 (2006).
[59] The original Marprelate tracts are STC 17453–9. Much of the literature on Marprelate is of dubious
      quality, but essential are Patrick Collinson, 'Ecclesiastical Vitriol: Religious Satire in the 1590s and
      the Invention of Puritanism', in John Guy (ed.), *The Reign of Elizabeth I: Court and Culture in the*

we can trace the public reading as well as the writing of puritan libels and speculate on their importance to godly identity. Many of these, such as 'The poormans joy and the gentlemans plague', a libel which was circulated in Lincolnshire in 1607, used the parish church as a means of dissemination and public reading.[60] In another case, a libel against Dr Henry Hickman and the ecclesiastical officers of the diocese of Peterborough which which was made and circulated in September 1607 to coincide with Archbishop Bancroft's metropolitical visitation, can be traced as its impact spread throughout Northamptonshire and beyond.[61] A series of individuals were accused of publishing this libel on the sabbath in All Saints Church, Northampton, as well as in the street, in inns and alehouses and in the shops of blacksmiths, saddlers and other tradesmen. Their evidence shows how a libel passed into the public domain. Edmond Wheatley, a husbandman, claimed that on 22 September 1607, 'he found the libell in the church of All Hallowes in Northampton', and he delivered it to Alexander Hall, a yeoman, to read, and that Hall explained to him what the libel said. That afternoon, Wheatley showed it to his brother who read it aloud before two others in the church. And, since

---

Last Decade (Cambridge, 1995), pp. 150–70; Leland H. Carlson, *Martin Marprelate, Gentleman: Master Job Throckmorton Laid Open in his Colors* (San Marino, CA, 1981); J. S. Benger, 'The Authority of Writer and Text in Radical Protestant Literature 1540 to 1593 with Particular Reference to the Marprelate Tracts' (unpublished DPhil thesis, Oxford University, 1989); and Laurence Black, 'Pamphlet Wars: The Marprelate Tracts and "Martinism"', 1588–1688' (unpublished PhD thesis, University of Toronto, 1996). In the early 1640s, a number of the original Marprelate pamphlets were re-published – STC 6805.3 and Wing R741, H1205, and C1987 – while other clandestine publications used the Marprelate name as a pseudonym which possessed a clear religious and political ideology: George Walker, *A Sermon Preached in London by a Faithfull Minister of Christ. And Perfected by him: and Now Set Forth to the Publike View of all, for the Justification of the Truth, and Clearing the Innocencie of his Long Suffering for it.* (London, printed by Margery Mar-Prelate, 1641); *Questions to be Disputed in Counsell of the Lords Spirituall after their Returne from their Visitation* (printed at London: by Pasquin, Deputy to Margery Marprelate, 1641); *The Lawfulnesse of our Expedition into England Manifested* (printed, first in Scotland, by Robert Bryson, and now reprinted in England, by Margery Mar-Prelat, 1640); *Our Demands of the English Lords Manifested, being at Rippon Octob. 8. 1640* (n.p.; printed, by Margery Mar-Prelat, 1640); *Vox Borealis, or the Northern Discoverie: by Way of Dialogue between Jamie and Willie* (Amidst the Babylonians: printed, by Margery Mar-Prelat, 1641). For a conclusive demonstration that Richard Overton was behind the 'Cloppenburg Press' on which four of these were printed, see David R. Como, 'Secret Printing, the Crisis of 1640, and the Origins of Civil War Radicalism', *Past and Present*, 196 (2007), pp. 37–82.

[60] Fox, *Oral and Literate Culture in England*, p. 333, n. 66; John Walter, '"The Poormans Joy and the Gentlemans Plague": A Lincolnshire Libel and the Politics of Sedition in Early Modern England', *Past and Present*, 203 (2009), pp. 29–67.

[61] See TNA: PRO STAC 8/205/19 and 8/205/20 (*Lambe* v. *Lowe, Oliver, Decons et al.*) and HEHL, MS EL 5965, which records the 'confessions' of the accused and those relating to another libel of 1607. Hickman LLD was Vicar General to the Diocese of Peterborough, MP for Northampton 1601 and Master in Chancery 1602–16.

he dined 'at one Elliots' in Northampton that day he also showed it to one of Elliot's kinsmen who read it before several others. He then lent it to one Thomas Hopkins, a gentleman, who read it in his family and to some others before passing it on to a saddler called Richard Trewman who read it with others at his shop. By this stage, the libel was hot property and Thomas Burton was said to have offered 'an angell for a coppie of it', while a local butcher promised to send a copy to friends in Cambridgeshire. The libel was spread quickly in particular through public forms of reading in public places such as the parish church – a copy left in the church was read by the joiner Samuel Chester to some of his associates. The Star Chamber case dwelt on the fact that the libels were left in the church and 'read often and openly' throughout Northampton and elsewhere and that they were 'copied forth & lent to others to the great spreading and divulging' of the libel. It also noted that the same defendants had been involved in the circulation of another particularly notorious libel 'against the knightes and justices' of Northamptonshire which was written earlier that summer and spread in numerous copies. The latter libel was also circulated in puritan circles, from the puritan physician John Cotta to Sir William Tate, who used his home at Delapré Abbey as a centre for the local godly.[62] As these examples show, the reading and distribution of libels by the godly as a form of intervention in local politics was clearly a further important facet of their religious culture, albeit one which might be overlooked with an overly narrow definition of either the book or of reading.

Indeed, it is worth remembering that the godly culture of the book encompassed not only textual uses of the book but also more physical and symbolic dimensions which took on added significance when they occurred in public spaces. Prominent among such symbolic uses was the gift of Bibles to those who were too poor to afford them.[63] Many of the godly recorded their distribution of Bibles and godly books, along with other reading equipment, and the pride of place such acts of generosity was given in their biographies and autobiographies is testimony to how the

---

[62] The libels can be found in TNA: PRO, STAC 8/205/19 (*Lambe* v. *Lowe, Oliver, Decons et al.*) and 8/205/20 (*Lambe* v. *Lowe, Oliver, Decons et al.*). There is a brief discussion in Fox, *Oral and Literate Culture in England*, pp. 332–3; and contextual information in W. J. Sheils, *The Puritans in the Diocese of Peterborough 1558–1610* (Northampton, 1979). A different version of the libel against the Justices exists in the Brotherton Library, Leeds, MS Lt q 17 ('Satire on Justices of the Peace for Northamptonshire, c. 1605–06'). It comprises three stitched leaves in narrow folio format and was clearly intended for circulation.

[63] On books as gifts, see Natalie Zemon Davis, 'Beyond the Market: Books as Gifts in Sixteenth-Century France', *Transactions of the Royal Historical Society*, 5th ser., 33 (1983), pp. 69–88; and Jason Scott-Warren, *Sir John Harrington and the Book as Gift* (Oxford, 2001).

godly themselves saw such acts of textual generosity as an intrinsic part of living a good life. Examples abound. So, as well as clothing the naked and feeding the hungry, the popular puritan preacher Samuel Fairclough

> gave away as many *Bibles, Catechisms* and *good Books* ... When the sight of Old people was decayed, he would furnish them with Bibles of a larger Print; and he gave an incredible number of spectacles away (for their help) always speaking of the Invention of them by *Metius*, with expressions of *love* and *praise* unto God, for his great *goodness* to the Souls of men thereby.[64]

And of course such gifts would then provide each family with the means of practising communal and social Bible-reading among themselves. Likewise, Herbert Palmer distributed Bibles to the poor that could read, and John Bruen gave Bibles, catechisms and other good books to poor souls.[65] Such instances stretched across the long seventeenth century. Roger Morrice recorded as evidence that Mr Robert Mayott of Oxford was 'a very holy man' the fact that he 'gave the greatest part of his Estate (which was about two or three hundred a yeare) whilst living to charitable uses, particularly in giving of Bibles and other bookes to poore sober people'.[66] Where the godly tended to give their libraries to particular family members or close clerical colleagues (and martyrs tossed their Bibles to bystanders in the hope of preserving their faith), the money they laid out for the purchase of Bibles was more often to promote godliness in the places they grew up. So Roger Morrice himself, who died in January 1702, used his own will to arrange for the distribution of Bibles at new year to young children who went to school at Meerbrook Chapel in Leek Frith in Staffordshire and who were already able to read and write. He also gave Bibles away in other Staffordshire parishes.[67]

Countless godly wills record the setting aside of money for the purchase of Bibles and godly books to be distributed usually among children and the poor, although it is interesting how many stipulate that those who received them did so on condition that they were already able to read. Occasionally, there are more illuminating instances of such distribution. Oliver Heywood, as we have already seen, distributed copies of books which he

---

[64] See Samuel Clarke, *The Lives of Sundry Eminent Persons in this Latter Age* (London, 1683), p. 180.
[65] See Samuel Clarke, *The Lives of Thirty-Two English Divines Famous in their Generations for Learning and Piety, and most of them Sufferers in the Cause of Christ etc.* (London, 1677), p. 188; William Hinde, *A Faithfull Remonstrance of the Holy Life and Happy Death, of John Bruen of Bruen Stapleford* (London, 1641), p. 184.
[66] Mark Goldie et al. (eds.), *The Entring Book of Roger Morrice 1677–1691* (6 vols., Woodbridge, 2007), vol. II, p. 473.
[67] Ibid., vol. I, p. 329.

had written among his faithful followers in Halifax and its surroundings. Likewise, Richard Baxter gave to the poor many of the copies he received of his own books from his publishers, as well as attempting a wider-than-usual distribution of Bibles among his parishioners in Kidderminster by giving a Bible to 'every family that was poor, and had not a Bible' – he gave away a total of eight hundred copies.[68] Such godly initiatives set a pattern of evangelical generosity which would be taken up a level by the SPCK in the eighteenth century. But perhaps the most remarkable instance of the distribution of Bibles was the Bible lottery established by Robert Wild in his native St Ives, Cambridgeshire. Wild was a godly cleric who, despite a brief venture into creeping royalist panegyric, was turned out in 1662 and lived out his days as an apparently commercially successful nonconformist poet. By the terms of his will, which was framed in 1677 and amended the following year, Wild established a Bible-dicing charity. The interest earned on the sum of fifty pounds was to be used to buy Bibles which were to be distributed in an unusual way. Twelve children – six boys and six girls – who were at least twelve years old and 'able to read in the Bible', were to be selected each year to compete for six well-bound English Bibles on the Tuesday after Whitsunday. A saucer with three dice was placed on the communion table and each pair of children would compete for a Bible with those gaining the highest score receiving the sacred book. Wild encouraged those who lost out to return the next year and asked those who received Bibles never to sell them. The trustees used Wild's money wisely, investing it in land – the area they purchased is now called Bible Close – and using the rents to purchase Bibles; thus the charity endured. But it was transformed over the centuries, including prayer books as well as Bibles after 1868 and allowing Catholic and Methodist children to enter in the twentieth century. Wild's example shows not only the enduring legacy of the gift of Bibles among the godly but also how such initiatives might intersect with popular culture and survive in a distinctly Anglican context.[69]

READING IN THE COFFEE HOUSE

No discussion of reading in public spaces would be complete without considering the coffee house – perhaps the key venue in the paradigm of the 'public sphere', a place in which news was discussed and from which

[68] David Cressy, *Literacy and the Social Order: Reading and Writing in Tudor and Stuart England* (Cambridge, 1980), p. 50. On Baxter's distribution of copies of his own books, see below, n. 162.
[69] See David R. Viles, *The Revd. Dr Robert Wilde 1615–1679: Poet, Preacher, Provider of Bibles by Dicing in His Native St Ives* (Hemingford Grey, 2003).

'public opinion' emerged.[70] Coffee houses were novel commercial venues, which operated independently of traditional centres of authority like the church and the court, where not only was an apparently civilized (i.e. non-alcoholic) beverage consumed, but news, newspapers and other printed material was read and discussed. Even if many commentators have exaggerated the novelty of these places and their distinction from the much more ubiquitous alehouse, and others have exaggerated the 'politeness' or 'civility' of their customers, there is no doubting the popularity of the coffee house – by the end of the century there were more than five hundred in London alone.[71]

Coffee houses were places of reading and conversation and the reading material on offer was absolutely crucial to their success. This reading was also critical to how coffee houses were viewed by contemporaries and how they have been evaluated by historians. Famously, apparently alarmed at the coffee house as a venue for the spread of false news and rumour, Charles II attempted to close coffee houses through a proclamation of December 1675. That this failed is often used to support a distinctly Whiggish view of the irrepressible rise of English liberty, but even when we reject such an opinion of the function of coffee houses,[72] there is much to learn from them, in particular – for our purposes – in evaluating the types of reading that went on there and the links to the oppositional, nonconformist, and Whig politics which the government so feared.[73]

Whether graphically or textually, coffee houses were rarely depicted without books and readers. In graphic form, books played a central role

[70] Habermas, *The Structural Transformation of the Public Sphere*, esp. pp. 32–3.

[71] For an excellent survey of the rise of the coffee house, see Brian Cowan, *The Social Life of Coffee: The Emergence of the British Coffeehouse* (New Haven, CT, 2005). For corrections of some of the misconceptions surrounding coffee houses, see Brian Cowan, 'The Rise of the Coffeehouse Reconsidered', *Historical Journal*, 47 (2004), pp. 21–46; Phil Withington, 'Public Discourse, Corporate Citizenship, and State Formation in Early Modern England', *American Historical Review*, 112 (2007), pp. 1016–38; and Mark Knights, *Representation and Misrepresentation in Later Stuart Britain: Partisanship and Political Culture* (Oxford, 2004), pp. 248–52.

[72] For a survey of the historiography surrounding the coffee house and its place in larger narratives, see Cowan, 'The Rise of the Coffeehouse Reconsidered'.

[73] For a recent analysis of coffee house libraries which has a slightly later chronological focus, see Markman Ellis, 'Coffee-House Libraries in Mid Eighteenth-Century London', *The Library*, 7th ser., 10 (2009), pp. 3–40. Ellis demonstrates (p. 13) that at least thirty coffee houses had some sort of book collection in the mid-eighteenth century and that most of these were clustered around the Inns of Court, the Royal Exchange and the Strand and Charing Cross.

Figure 5. 'Interior of a London Coffee-house' (c.1700); British Museum, Department of Prints and Drawings, No. 1931,0613.2. © Trustees of the British Museum.

in the social life of the coffee house, for instance in apparently highly ordered and presumably idealistic depictions such as that of the interior of a coffee house around 1700 (Figure 5) where the customers clutched reading material, engaged in thoughtful conversations and examined the pictures and the printed materials which adorned the walls.[74] Likewise, in rowdier scenes which run counter to notions of coffee houses as bastions of civility, such as the famous engraving of the coffee house mob in Edward Ward's *Vulgus Britannicus* (1710) (Figure 6), the coffee house is still depicted primarily as a place of reading and conversation.

Similarly, when it was mentioned in other media, the textual character of the coffee house was remarkably consistent. Thus in the comic play *Tarugo's Wiles: or, The Coffee-House* (1668), the master of the coffee house

---

[74] In fact, as Brian Cowan has shown, the material on the walls is rather less august than we might imagine, since it was written by Grub Street hacks. See Cowan, *Social Life of Coffee*, pp. 225–8.

Figure 6. Edward Ward, *The Fourth Part of Vulgus Britannicus: or, the British Hudibras. In Two Cantos: On the Coffee-House Mob, or Debates Pro, and Con, on the Times. A Character of several Sorts of Whigs, and False Brethren, that are Enemies to the Church. On the Paper-War betwixt High and Low-Church. The Loyal Englishman's Prayer for the Queen and Church* (London, 1710), frontispiece. © Trustees of the British Museum.

exemplifies the social reading central to the public spaces of polite Restoration society. He brings a gazette to the table and, at the exhortation 'Pray let one read for all', the paper is read aloud in company and interrupted by the listeners' comments and questions. Although this was a theatrical device, it also sent up a novel form of sociability in ways that audiences would presumably recognize.[75]

Although it would be difficult to find examples of devotional godly reading in coffee houses, many of them offered a venue for radical anti-governmental reading by Whigs and nonconformists.[76] There were dissenting keepers of coffee houses like John Thomas, who ran a house on Aldersgate Street, and most famously Peter Kidd, the master of Amsterdam Coffee house, a place most closely associated with Whig opposition. This held true in the provinces too, whether for coffee houses or inns. The inhabitants of Northampton, for example, could choose between the Swan Inn, which was associated with Whigs, and the Goat Inn, associated with Tories.[77] Among York's merchants, the nonconformist William Wombwell opened a coffee house in 1667. Coffee houses in particular were places of dissent and reading. It was, for example, from one Pearce's coffee house that a group of Devonshire Baptists were plotting to topple the government and restore republicanism in 1682: as part of that plot, they used the coffee house as a venue for reading a series of seditious pamphlets.[78] Indeed, the (feared) associations between sober religious radicals and the coffee house were apparent from as early as the late 1660s, when a manuscript report entitled 'The state of the nonconformists in England soon after the Restoration' testified that radical religious groups – explicitly 'Independents and Anabaptists with some of the fiercer Presbyterians' – were 'great Frequenters of Coffeehouses'. And it was there that they tried 'to disperse ... scandalous Verses'.[79] As Adrian Johns has noted, the 'coffeehouse was easily the Restoration's most notorious center for conspiracy and communal reading'.[80]

---

[75] Sir Thomas St Serfe, *Tarugo's Wiles: or, The Coffee-House. A Comedy. As it was Acted at his Highness's, the Duke of York's Theater* (London, 1668), p. 24; cited in Harold Love, *Scribal Publication in Seventeenth-Century England* (Oxford, 1993), p. 206.

[76] Although there were coffee houses of Catholic and Anglican persuasions, Steven Pincus, "'Coffee Politicians does Create": Coffeehouses and Restoration Political Culture', *Journal of Modern History*, 67 (1995), pp. 807–34, argues that their overall character can be deduced from the fact that much of the venom in the drive to regulate them came from Anglican royalists. Markman Ellis's copy-specific analysis of the titles which were available at particular coffee houses confirms the prevalence of items that can be classified as news and politics (and the absence of sermons and works of devotion). See Ellis, 'Coffee-House Libraries in Mid Eighteenth-Century London', p. 29.

[77] See Fox, *Oral and Literate Culture in England*, pp. 375–6.

[78] See ibid., pp. 403–4.

[79] BL, MS Stowe 185, fos. 175r–v. Cited in Love, *Scribal Publication in Seventeenth-Century England*, p. 205.

[80] Adrian Johns, *The Nature of the Book: Print and Knowledge in the Making* (Chicago, IL, 1998), p. 112.

They were places of sociability, where books were borrowed and exchanged, and printed material read aloud.

The ability to read in coffee houses was in part determined by their location. Edmund Curll's short-lived 'Literatory', the notorious club for reading and conversation, was next door to Will's Coffee house.[81] The proximity of coffee houses and booksellers – both of which functioned as places of reading and conversation – is well known. There were coffee-houses right at the centre of London's bookselling area, with the Chapter Coffee house in Paternoster Row, for example, providing refreshment and an important place of business and social exchange for those in the book trade: it later played host to trade meetings.[82] Coffee houses, with their relatively open spaces and large tables, provided suitable venues for the sale of second-hand libraries by auction and they were certainly places where, from the late 1660s onwards, the *Term Catalogues* were distrib-uted.[83] On occasion, bookshops and coffee houses shared a frontage – most shops were divided in this way – Daniel Pakeman, for example, the bookseller who published Harrington's *Oceanea*, is known to have shared his building with a coffee house.[84]

Inside, coffee houses were crammed with chairs and tables, on which reading material was spread out. Although this was most often printed news, coffee houses were frequently much more than simply places to read a newspaper. As Harold Love has shown, they were venues of scribal publication, where written verses and libels might be read.[85] They could be used as mailing addresses and were obvious places of advertising. Sometimes, they provided a venue for social reading of a different form. A group of young Oxford scholars gave books so that a library could be set up at Short's Coffee house in the late 1660s, for example, and they donated poems and plays. There are even some suggestions that books could be borrowed and purchased from coffee houses.[86] Pepys bought a book in a coffee house in the Exchange and in January 1694/5 Houghton's *Collection for the Improvement of Husbandry and Trade* made notice that 'Walsal the coffee man against Cree Church in Leadenhall Street keeps a library in his coffee room for his customers to read. He also buys and sells

---

[81] Ibid., p. 124.

[82] See James Raven, *The Business of Books: Booksellers and the English Book Trade 1450–1850* (New Haven, CT, 2007), pp. 109–10, 128–9.

[83] Ibid., p. 110.   [84] Johns, *The Nature of the Book*, p. 111.

[85] Love, *Scribal Publication in Seventeenth-Century England*, pp. 203–7.

[86] Cowan, *The Social Life of Coffee*, p. 108. Cf. Ellis, 'Coffee-House Libraries in Mid Eighteenth-Century London', p. 32.

books'.[87] The volume of reading material available at some coffee houses necessitated a rudimentary form of organization, with the items being numbered and arranged by format.[88] Certainly the supply of news to coffee houses was a commercial enterprise – Giles Hancock made as much as £150 per year by supplying coffee houses with news – and for the customers it appears that newspapers and the opportunities to discuss and debate current affairs were at least as important as the coffee.[89]

Remarkably, despite the relative scarcity of evidence illuminating the styles of reading that were practised in the coffeehouse, there is near-universal agreement that these were spaces for social, communal reading and that the sociability of the space helped to define the types of reading that went in them.[90] This is interesting, because in many ways it runs counter to ideas about the emergence of modern society – in which private reading takes an important place and communal reading is usually seen as either backward or fanatical – but it is a hallmark of the historiography on the coffee house and vital in its connection with emergent civility and the public sphere.

Other such commercial spaces could also be used for communal social reading even if they lacked the strength of the connection between print and the coffee house. Much was once made about the alehouse as a venue for religious dissent, usually by way of early sixteenth-century Cambridge, but such a role would have been through song, gossip and conversation more than through reading – there are relatively few records of godly reading in the alehouse in the seventeenth century and much puritan vitriol against the excessive drinking, dancing and debauchery which went on there. In contrast, there are, as we have seen, notable instances of the godly both reading and spreading libels in and through other places of commerce. Likewise, it is probable that Nehemiah Wallington read while he worked. Certainly the opponents of the godly sometimes made the

---

[87] John Houghton, *A Collection for the Improvement of Husbandry and Trade*, vol. 6, no. 129, 18 January 1694/5. Cited in Knights, *Representation and Misrepresentation*, p. 250; R. C. Latham and W. Matthews (eds.), *The Diary of Samuel Pepys* (11 vols., London, 1970–83), vol. IV, p. 162 (28 May 1663). Pepys heard much news at coffee houses but did not record reading newspapers there.

[88] See Ellis, 'Coffee-House Libraries in Mid Eighteenth-Century London'.

[89] See Fox, *Oral and Literate Culture In England*, p. 378. Several newspapers were intrinsically linked with the coffee house, such as the *Athenian Mercury*. See Helen Berry, 'An Early Coffee House Periodical and Its Readers: The *Athenian Mercury*, 1691–1697', *London Journal*, 25 (2000), pp. 14–33; and Helen Berry, *Gender, Society and Print Culture in Late-Stuart England: The Cultural World of the* Athenian Mercury (Aldershot, 2003).

[90] The sociability of such reading is more often asserted than analysed but see the excellent section in Ellis, 'Coffee-House Libraries in Mid Eighteenth-Century London', pp. 31–4.

connection between their reading and places of work. A Catholic bulletin of 1624 included mention of one such case:

The sad fate of a certain Puritan which lately occurred ought to be noticed in this report, rather than left unrecorded, and it may well rebuke the rashness of heretics in handling the sacred pages. An aged cobbler, an assiduous reader of Holy Writ, which, according to the foolish vanity of such men, he was in the habit of himself interpreting, stood him in public estimation as a man of great skill, and even as one divinely taught. It was his custom when mending shoes to have an English Bible open before him, so that he might employ himself during work either in reading, or in meditating upon what he had read. At length when he had stuffed himself with various inconsistent errors, and daily imbibed new dogmas, and could find nothing but hopeless confusion, he was driven to desperation, and resolved to commit self-murder. After several attempts, all of which were frustrated, he at last hanged himself in the parish church itself by a bell-rope. This sad event was published far and wide; the people flocked to see the sight; the church was declared polluted, the royal seal affixed, which was only removed at a great cost, and the place purified by the pseudo-bishop with I know not what ceremonies.[91]

READING IN BOOKSHOPS

One such commercial space in which there was plenty of reading was the bookshop. From permanent shops to more temporary stalls, booksellers provided another public, or at least semi-public, venue for reading. At the heart of the book trade, booksellers performed a variety of services for their customers and operated as a crucial hub in godly networks. As we will see, they sometimes offered venues for sociable godly reading.

To talk of booksellers and bookshops is, of course, to use language which was relatively unfamiliar to the period, at least in the earlier seventeenth century. And even when they were used, terms like 'bookseller' and 'printer' were particularly elastic and could be applied to a very wide range of activities.[92] Adrian Johns, in his survey of print culture, adopts a framework structured by 'domains', which include the printing house, the bookshop, the city square and the coffee house. These, Johns argues, were 'dynamic localities defined by physical environment, work,

[91] Henry Foley, *Records of the English Province of the Society of Jesus: Historic Facts Illustrative of the Labours and Sufferings of its Members in the Sixteenth and Seventeenth Centuries* (7 vols., London, 1877–82), vol. VII, part ii, p. 1105.
[92] On terminology, see especially Raven, *The Business of Books*, p. 4.

and sociability'.[93] Even if such an approach tends to divorce the locations of the print trade from the practice of reading, this makes some sense, not least because focusing on the person rather than the location would be much more problematic. 'Bookseller' was not a recognized occupation and contemporaries would have used the term 'stationer', replete as that term was with meanings either as members of the Stationers' Company or as a shorthand occupational term which belied an aspiration to associate with the Stationers with a capital S.

There were, of course, many other places to buy books and many people other than booksellers to buy them from. Books were left in wills and prized as gifts; they might be bought from grocers and sold at auction, although auctions frequently occurred at bookshops and coffee houses. There were many occasional sellers of books, a parallel network of chapmen and pedlars as well as the 'hawkers' and 'mercury women' who were more closely linked to the heart of the London book trade.[94] And books continued to be sold at fairs, the most famous of which, Stourbridge Fair, had a row of booksellers throughout our period.[95] But despite these and other locations, a focus on booksellers is quite appropriate. Over the seventeenth century, booksellers came to predominate in the Stationers' Company and in the book trade as a whole. It was booksellers who effectively 'published' books and their names and addresses came to be advertised on the title pages of books. And the physical spaces of bookshops offered potential for reading and religious sociability.

A focus on bookshops, like that on coffee houses – which were frequently adjacent to the bookshops and sometimes the lease for a shop might be divided between these two interlinked commercial and social hubs, which were centres of news culture and close to the heart of the body of early modern communications – also allows us to engage with the now extensive historiography of the places at the core of the 'public sphere' and the ways in which the uses of these spaces helped to transform the nature of early modern communications. As centres of social reading, such places perhaps played a part in the shifting settings in which a new kind of public opinion was formed, particularly after the Restoration. However, to invoke the terminology of the 'public sphere' is here meant

---

[93] Johns, *The Nature of the Book*, p. 59.
[94] On occasional sellers of books, see Raven, *The Business of Books*, p. 85.
[95] See Raven, *The Business of Books*, p. 60; [Thomas Corbett], *Bibliotheca Sturbitchiana, &c. A Catalogue of Curious Books, Selected out of Several Libraries and Parcels Bought at Sturbitch-Fair ... with an Uncommon Collection Belonging to the Late Famous Mr. Winstanley of Littlebury* (London, 1722).

mainly as a relatively helpful way in which to describe the new and markedly different world of print, communications and, to a certain extent, reading which emerged after the 1640s, rather than to further a Habermasian notion of the development of society. Indeed, the very notion of godly reading in such places runs against the grain of Habermas's theory that it was in such spaces that a more secular public politics was developed.

At least until recently, with the publication of James Raven's sweep of the trade, there has been a lack of understanding of the general substance of what booksellers actually did, despite considerable work on individual booksellers. As Raven makes clear, however, it is only when we understand what booksellers did, how they operated and the spaces and circumstances in which they worked that we can really appreciate a general picture of the importance of the trade more broadly. In fact, although much of the work on booksellers is of use, it is hampered by a tendency, which of course derives from the source materials, to list a bookseller's stock. Not only are there many problems with inventories – booksellers' inventories listed unsold stock, in addition to the more familiar problems with such records – but the analysis of titles, in the wrong hands, has led to some clumsy and bad history. In particular, such stock lists have been used as a warning against associating particular booksellers with a particular cause. Booksellers, much like the printers described by Ian Green and others, were, we are told, motivated more by cash than by any convictions. But such assumptions, especially that profit and principles are almost opposite forces, rest on some shaky foundations. In particular, there seems to be a trend towards a position that a godly bookseller must *only* sell godly books to be described as such and that the sale of other books undermines any such credentials. As we will see, this is an unnecessarily gloomy assessment, and one which derives from thinking about what a bookshop sold without considering how a bookshop was actually used. As James Raven notes on this neglected aspect of the historiography of the book trade: 'By gleaning more information about how people used the developing bookshops and how these shops operated, we start to learn more about reading practices and how ideas circulated and were discussed.'[96]

As some excellent recent work has cautiously concluded, it is worth taking the allegiance of booksellers seriously, thinking about booksellers

---

[96] Raven, *The Business of Books*, p. 6, which also refers to Kevin Sharpe, *Reading Revolutions: The Politics of Reading in Early Modern England* (New Haven, CT, 2000), pp. 45–6.

who fought in the Civil War, who funded radical religious and political movements, and about the place they occupied in such cultures.[97] Of course, it is certainly not the case that the only radical or principled booksellers were godly Protestants, for there were many Catholic booksellers, booksellers who saw their role as upholding Anglican Toryism after the Restoration, and even perhaps Laudian booksellers in the 1630s. What does seem to be the case, however, is that many booksellers were particularly associated with the puritan cause (especially by their enemies), an association which is hardly surprising given the privileged place which reading occupied within both the practice of puritanism and the mythology which grew up around it.[98] If at times printers and booksellers had competing interests, we need only look to the career of John Day (1522–84) to see how ideology, office and the pursuit of personal wealth were far from necessarily contradictory. Day rose to fame under Edward VI and was briefly imprisoned under Mary. Under Elizabeth, he built his commercial reputation from the ownership of patents, notably for printing the *Psalms* and the *ABC with the Little Catechisme*, but he is best known to early modern scholars as the publisher of four editions of Foxe's *Actes and Monuments*. He was close to the centre of the Protestant establishment, notably through his links with William Cecil, and he rose to become master of the Stationers' Company in 1580. Indeed, both the portrait of Day of 1562 and the brass family memorial to him at Little Bradley Church in Suffolk depict a strongly Protestant, perhaps godly, cultural identity. In the portrait, the first of an English bookseller, Day sports a long tapered beard redolent of evangelical reformers and perhaps cast in the image of John Calvin. In the brass, he knelt opposite his wife in prayer, with book before him and surrounded by his children.[99] Despite commercial imperatives and a spell printing under Mary, Day's career as a bookseller and printer, which betray both his connections to the Stranger communities of London and the influence he brought to bear on religious policy through his work, shows how important religion could be to the trade.

[97] A particularly good example is Ann Hughes, *Gangraena and the Struggle for the English Revolution* (Oxford, 2004), esp. pp. 145–50. Also Raven, *The Business of Books*. For the religious sympathies of booksellers as attested by the Civil War allegiances of those who fought for Parliament, see Johns, *The Nature of the Book*, p. 148.

[98] See, among others, Peter McCullough, 'Print, Publication, and Religious Politics in Caroline England', *Historical Journal*, 51 (2008), pp. 285–313; and Jason McElligott, *Royalism, Print and Censorship in Revolutionary England* (Woodbridge, 2007).

[99] These images are described in Raven, *The Business of Books*, p. 41. On Day's career, see Elizabeth Evenden, *Patents, Pictures and Patronage: John Day and the Tudor Book Trade* (Aldershot, 2008).

This section examines godly connections in the book trade and explores bookshops as spaces for sociable godly reading. Although the source material is not always extensive – this was a shadowy world – there is reason to suppose that booksellers were vital to the culture of puritanism and its dissemination and that the physical spaces of their shops offered an important outlet for a range of godly activities, including reading. Such reading practices provide an interesting comparison with other public spaces, especially because bookshops were at once domestic and semi-public commercial spaces.

Anyone wanting to buy a book from a bookseller, rather than an occasional seller who by definition sold books when it suited the vendor rather than the consumer, had to know where to go to find them. Outside London this was, perhaps, not particularly difficult. Although there was marked growth over the period, even at the beginning of the seventeenth century most provincial centres had at least one bookshop. These would be well known, with some located next to the churches and cathedrals whose clergy were regular customers; others were simply part of a shop which sold other things, notably grocers'.[100] Some of these shops, like the Foster bookshop in York, were considerable operations, but many more were smaller makeshift outlets.[101] That smaller urban centres had fewer bookshops, often just one, meant that a bookseller ran considerable risks in supplying illicit books. But some clearly did, and sometimes in support of the puritan cause. Thomas Smith, a Manchester stationer, was an active proponent of puritanism in the 1630s.[102] He was charged with attending conventicles and known as 'a hot zealot or a strict nonconformist', and he used his shop to sell to the Manchester godly 'divers Scottish and other schismatical books, containing in them ... bitter invectives and railings against the government and discipline of the Church of England'.[103] Peter

---

[100] See, for example, P. C. G. Isaac, *An Inventory of Books Sold by a Seventeenth-Century Penrith Grocer* (*History of the Book Trade in the North*, 53 (1989)). Benson was a Quaker.

[101] The Foster inventory reveals how the shop supplied a wide range of godly clergy, like Alexander Cooke, but the (unsold) stock of the shop in 1616 reveals no obvious religious allegiance of either seller or customers and there is little suggestion that the shop itself served as a site of godly identity. See J. Barnard and M. Bell, 'The Early Seventeenth-Century York Book Trade and John Foster's Inventory of 1616', *Proceedings of Leeds Philosophical and Literary Society, Literary and Historical Section*, 24(2) (1994), pp. 17–132.

[102] See the charges brought against Smith in 1638. Cheshire Record Office, Consistory Court papers, EDC 5, 1638.

[103] Cheshire Record Office, Consistory Court papers, EDC 5, 1638. The charges are related in R. C. Richardson, *Puritanism in North-West England: A Regional Study of the Diocese of Chester to 1642* (Manchester, 1972), p. 10. Thomas Smith also effectively published some of the works by the Manchester puritan Richard Hollingworth.

Ince, the only stationer in Chester, was clearly the man suspected by John Bridgeman, the bishop of Chester, of supplying illicit books in 1637, a charge made worse by the fact that four citizens of Chester entertained William Prynne warmly when he stopped in Chester on his way from being mutilated in London to being incarcerated in Caernarvon. 'We have no other stationer in the city', fumed Bridgeman, 'yet no Puritanicall bookes [appear] but our citizens get them as soon as any'. Ince was fortunate (in the bishop's opinion) that 'he be so cunning as it will hardly be discovered', because by the time the shop was searched, 'all the birds were flown'.[104] Interestingly, Ince, whose son was a preacher, had previously visited Prynne when he was being held in the Tower.[105] Our knowledge of such connections is relatively slight, but this does not mean that they did not exist. In the 1650s, the Kendal ironmonger George Taylor was an important conduit in the sale and distribution of Quaker books and pamphlets.[106]

For all this, it is the London booktrade which really allows us an insight into the connections between booksellers and godly culture. Few provincial booksellers were as brazen as those mentioned above and the lack of choice of destination for a customer meant that successful booksellers had to sell a wide range of material and that as such their shops were unlikely to function openly as centres of godly identity. The singularity of provincial booksellers, who have been over-represented in the historiography of bookselling, makes it difficult to assess them and their importance in the round.[107]

London, on the other hand, as the centre of Britain's book trade, offers much richer pickings since there were enough booksellers for particular shops and particular sellers to be known for their role in the sustenance of particular causes. Among crowded streets and dark alleyways, there were as many as 188 bookshops in London by 1700.[108] The majority of booksellers were concentrated in key areas of the city, close to the centres

---

[104] See John Barnard and Maureen Bell, 'The English Provinces', in John Barnard and D. F. McKenzie (eds.), *The Cambridge History of the Book in Britain* (7 vols., Cambridge, 1999–), vol. IV, *1557–1695*, p. 679, citing R. Stewart-Brown, 'The Stationers, Booksellers and Printers of Chester to about 1800', *Transactions of the Historic Society of Lancashire and Cheshire*, 83 (1932), p. 131.

[105] Richardson, *Puritanism in North-West England*, p. 182.

[106] See Kate Peters, *Print Culture and the Early Quakers* (Cambridge, 2005), p. 64. Connections with the London book trade were largely carried out through Giles Calvert, for whom see below.

[107] On the curious overrepresentation of the provinces, especially in the eighteenth and nineteenth centuries, see Raven, *The Business of Books*, pp. 376–7.

[108] Johns, *The Nature of the Book*, p. 66.

of ecclesiastical and legal authority: first and foremost in St Paul's Churchyard, where the Stationers' Company was located, and in the adjacent streets to the north such as Paternoster Row and the adjoining area known as Little Britain, but also in the streets leading to the west, along Fleet Street and the Strand, as well as in the area south of St Paul's, in the alleyways down to the Thames and along to the east and London Bridge, which was the only way to cross the river by road throughout our period. Excepting more specialized and isolated areas for booksellers such as in the stalls at Westminster Hall, the centre of the trade was remarkably compact.[109]

Success in the book trade was not necessarily determined by the extent of one's shop frontage or the occupancy of a particular location, for shops moved fairly regularly and were held by lease. Instead, a good location was largely determined by proximity to other sellers. Indeed, it becomes apparent that there were particular zones within this area which attracted particular specialisms, be they legal works, books for the clergy, or (on a much smaller scale) radical books. As Adrian Johns helpfully speculates: 'contemporaries knew well the differences and similarities between such zones'.[110] Such zones were of particular importance in difficult times, when the purchase of puritan literature was obviously more dangerous, such as at the end of the sixteenth century, in the 1630s and again after the Restoration. Although the north side of St Paul's Churchyard was, according to Macky's *Journey through England*, the place to go for 'divinity and classics', other parts of the Churchyard were home to booksellers who sold more illicit works.[111] As we have already seen in the satirical engraving *The Compleat Auctioner*, some bookstalls might sell politically radical books alongside pornography. Accepting that this was indeed a satire and not designed as a particularly accurate representation of the book trade, it is still suggestive that the engraving mocked the east end of St Paul's Churchyard as a location for the sale of illicit books. It was here and at his bookseller's in the Strand, for instance, that Samuel Pepys browsed for hours on end and bought some of his pornography.[112] That St Paul's Churchyard was an area in which it was possible to buy illicit

---

[109] The best overviews of the locations of London's book trade are Raven, *The Business of Books*, Chapter 6; and Johns, *The Nature of the Book*, Chapter 2. Paternoster Row took its name from the types of books of religious instruction that were sold there. See John Strype, *A Survey of the Cities of London and Westminster . . . By John Stow* (2 vols., London, 1720), vol. I, p. 174.

[110] Johns, *The Nature of the Book*, p. 66.   [111] Cited in Raven, *The Business of Books*, p. 157.

[112] Latham and Matthews, *The Diary of Samuel Pepys*, vol. IX, pp. 57–8 (8 February 1668).

puritan literature can be confirmed by the two judges at Prynne's Star Chamber trial who wanted his punishment carried out in St Paul's Churchyard, and also by the proposal in the 1680s – with the aim of countering the types of reading more common there – to place a religious library aimed at young gentlemen in the yard.[113] The conjunction of radical literature and pornography is certainly an intriguing one and it was clearly replicated in the other areas which sold books for the puritan underground.

There were, of course, areas of professional specialisms, with shops near the Inns of Court catering, for example, to law students, and the book-shops of Little Britain, in particular that of Christopher Bateman, being the centre of the second-hand booktrade, which was vastly increased over the seventeenth century and included the sale by auction of entire libraries in what were clearly cultural events that provided entertainment (as well as books) to seventeenth-century Londoners.[114] A crude general pattern to these zones emerges. The further north one went from St Paul's, the seedier the fringes of the book trade became. Smithfield, Bartholomew Close and Aldersgate Street were 'areas of dubious character'. It was here that 'lurked nonconformist conventicles, currency counterfeiters, repub-lican plotters, and illicit printers alike'.[115] Located on the fringes of the centre of the book trade, Moorfields was a notorious area which housed many brothels – it was the site of the Bawdy House riots of 1668 – but it was also home to numerous bookstalls and illicit printers, notably printers of Quaker pamphlets and, as David Como's recent detective work has taught us, it was almost certainly home to the so-called Cloppenberg Press (of which Richard Overton was the principal steward) from which dis-tinctly radical pamphlets rolled in the early 1640s.[116] Moorfields was a

---

[113] Johns, *The Nature of the Book*, p. 67.

[114] In addition to the auction of libraries discussed in Chapter 4 above, the rise in the second-hand trade was certainly viewed with some suspicion by the authorities. In 1628, thirty-nine second-hand booksellers were required to provide the archbishop of Canterbury with catalogues of the books they sold; he was presumably concerned about the recirculation of illicit/puritan books. See *Calendar of State Papers Domestic*, CXVII, 9 (13 September 1628), and Raven, *The Business of Books*, p. 52. And there might be good reason for such suspicion. In Dublin, an eagle-eyed customer at a bookstall who was also a correspondent of the earl of Arran spotted a copy of Robert Ferguson's *The Third Part of No Protestant Plot* (London, 1682) which bore manuscript annotations by Sir John Davys. See Raymond Gillespie, *Reading Ireland: Print, Reading and Social Change in Early Modern Ireland* (Manchester, 2005), p. 89.

[115] Johns, *The Nature of the Book*, p. 73. For detail, see J. S. T. Hetet, 'A Literary Underground in Restoration England: Printers and Dissenters in the Context of Constraints, 1660–1689' (unpublished PhD thesis, University of Cambridge, 1987).

[116] Como, 'Secret Printing, the Crisis of 1640, and the Origins of Civil War Radicalism', pp. 37–82.

seedy area where customers of all types might indulge in forbidden pleasures and the conjunction of its trades alerts us that those in search of underground godly literature would have to hunt for it in distinctly ungodly places.

Of course, the specific identity of these zones can be vastly overstated and there was considerable overlap between them. In addition, die-hard enemies might be situated right next to each other, as for example were the high-church Rivingtons and the nonconformist Griffiths in the late eighteenth century. Fortunately, for those who sought clandestine books, the streets of London were full of signs which might allude to the identity of booksellers, as they did to those of other trades, often in subtle or meaningful ways. At least 250 signs were used by London booksellers before 1641, a number that includes a host of varied symbols such as fourteen different Bibles, seven crowns, four mermaids, and even a grasshopper.[117] These signs were perhaps more important than the physical location of the shops, for when booksellers moved they took their signs with them. And they had resonance. The General Baptist bookseller Francis Smith, who had been a youthful separatist and associate of Giles Calvert and who was licensed as a preacher in 1671, was known simply as Elephant Smith because the sign of his shop, first at Temple Bar and then on Cornhill, was the Elephant and Castle. Obviously, it would be wrong to make too much of the imagery of signs – of course, the most radical and illegal works did not advertise the printer or bookseller on their title pages and those shops like that of Thomas Simmonds at the Bull and Mouth, which was a centre for London Quakers, had no obvious imagery – but some of them, as well as operating as a shorthand for places in which to conduct godly business safely and to engage fruitfully in religious sociability, used images on their signs which alluded to the type of books that might be found there. Thomas Parkhurst, the principal presbyterian publisher, had a shop at the Bible and Three Crowns in Cheapside between 1670 and 1711. More suggestively, some signs carried religious and political associations with which their customers might identify. The radical bookseller Langley Curtis, for example, hung outside his shop in Goat Court on Ludgate Hill 'the Sign of Sir *Edmundbury Godfrey*' in the 1680s.[118] Even false imprints and satirical signs provide a window onto the kind of association which might be made between printers and booksellers, the places in which they operated and the signs

[117] Raven, *The Business of Books*, p. 56.   [118] Johns, *The Nature of the Book*, p. 108.

they hung outside their doors. In 1645, Richard Overton, writing under the loaded pseudonym 'Martin Mar-Preist, son to old Martin the Metrapolitane', styled his *The araignement of Mr. Persecvtion: presented to the consideration of the House of Commons, and to all the common people of England* as being published in 'Europe: printed by Martin Claw Clergie ... and are to be should [*sic*] at his shop in Toleration Street, at the Signe of the Subjects Liberty, right opposite to Persecuting Court'.[119]

Looking further inside bookshops gives more of an insight into the kinds of reading that took place there. Very few records survive which tell us how booksellers displayed their books in windows, although we do know that John Wilkins's *The Discovery of a World in the Moone* (1638) was given pride of place in Michael Sparke's window, an association which gave its anonymous author a clear connection with a man Adrian Johns has described as 'the most incendiary Puritan bookseller in London'.[120] Although there are very few contemporary pictures of seventeenth-century bookshops to guide us, the physical layout of the shop provides us with the best initial clues as to the kind of reading which might take place. Bookshops were more than retail outlets. They were houses in which the bookseller and his family lived and they consequently comprised a range of spaces from the public to the more private. Such arrangements meant that there were usually inner or upper rooms where more illicit books might be sold and private business conducted. Of course, this could open a proprietor up to allegations, if the private spaces within were deemed suspicious. Christopher Barker, for example, claimed that John Wolfe (the pirate printer and, significantly, his business rival) 'gathered diverse Conventicles in his house'.[121] That upper rooms were also frequently let out to paying guests and that booksellers often acted as bankers for their customers and provided mailing addresses for those who were staying in London temporarily only added to the suspicion with which the activities of the bookshop were viewed. Of the more open and public space of the shops themselves, there was a gradual change in design over the seventeenth century, from relatively cramped spaces stuffed with books and with little frontage onto the street, to larger premises which had spaces for browsing, display and conversation. The change in the physical layout went hand in hand with a change in the way that space was

[119] Ibid., pp. 73–4.
[120] Ibid., p. 52. Title pages might be displayed in windows for passers-by to see.
[121] Ibid., pp. 120, 122. Johns (p. 94) also makes much of the language (domestic and religious) in which print houses and bookshops were described. On Wolfe, see Harry R. Hoppe, 'John Wolfe, Printer and Publisher, 1579–1601', *The Library*, 4th ser., 14 (1933), pp. 241–88.

used. Bookshops 'became a focus for news and information exchange', serving their customers as 'a cultural frontier between street and home'.[122]

Many recent commentators have placed considerable stress upon the bookshop as a site of social interaction, conversation and intellectual exchange.[123] But deeper questions need to be asked: what evidence is there of reading in the seventeenth-century bookshop? What styles of reading might occur in such locations? And what part, if any, did such reading play in the maintenance of godly religious culture? The evidence is scattered and fragmentary and overwhelmingly textual, but at times it is also revealing. A range of examples reveals an equally diverse range of examples of reading styles. We see that authors sometimes went to a bookshop in order to check their proofs and, more familiarly, that one of the privileges expected by those who worked at a bookshop was the freedom to read there.[124] But most of the information on instances of reading in bookshops surrounds the relatively novel practice of browsing. The usual suspects, notably Samuel Pepys, with his almost Rankean desire to record the minutiae of his daily cultural life, confirm that they read books whilst stood in the bookshop, often for several hours at a time.[125] Although this was likely to have been much more common and accepted in London, there are examples of browser–readers from provincial shops. John Ward, for example, the vicar of Stratford upon Avon who was sympathetic to nonconformists, frequently recorded browsing and reading in bookshops in his extensive notebooks.[126] In Restoration Manchester, Henry Newcome stopped on his way home from the burgeoning English Library (Chetham's Library) at Ralph Shelmerdine's bookshop and his diary records how he read for a while 'of a booke of the *morninge*

---

[122] Raven, *The Business of Books*, p. 113; Johns, *The Nature of the Book*, p. 120. Johns's description evokes the bookshop as a 'third place', for which see Ray Oldenburg, *The Great Good Place: Cafés, Coffee Shops, Community Centers, Beauty Parlors, General Stores, Bars, Hangouts and How They Get You Through the Day* (New York, 1989).

[123] For bold statements, see Johns, *The Nature of the Book*, p. 40 (where bookshops were places which encouraged 'novel interactions'), and p. 120 (where the home and shop of the bookseller 'doubled as sites for conversation'); and D. R. Woolf, *Reading History in Early Modern England* (Cambridge, 2000), esp. p. 263 ('Booksellers' premises were social spaces that . . . had a place in the creation of a "public sphere" of English intellectual life').

[124] Johns, *The Nature of the Book*, pp. 103, 115.

[125] Samuel Pepys notes that he spent several hours reading single books at the booksellers in January 1661, reading Fuller's *The history of the worthies of England*. See Latham and Matthews, *The Diary of Samuel Pepys*, vol. II, p. 21 (22 January 1661). For other instances, see vol. IV, pp. 410–11 (10 December 1663).

[126] Folger MS V.a. 284–99. For commentary, see Woolf, *Reading History in Early Modern England*, pp. 108–13.

exercise at Cripplegate' there.[127] At another time he noted, 'I read in the Stationer's Shop in a new booke of Duke of Holstein ambassador's travells.'[128] Although we might expect that the practice of borrowing books from a bookseller for a limited time – as is seen in the diary of Robert Hooke – might have been limited to the metropolis, Newcome's diary confirms that it might well have been more widespread. He recorded borrowing a book by Mr Ball from Ralph Shelmerdine and using it in preparation to take the sacrament.[129]

At any rate, browsing certainly appears to have been a common enough activity in the bookseller's shop. Henry Vaughan, the Grantham minister imprisoned for his nonconformity, whom Edmund Calamy explained 'often exposed himself to great danger by being over zealous' in the testing times of 1659–60, found a bookshop a convenient refuge:

> As he was reading in a bookseller's shop in London, with his back towards the door, a pursuivant came in and told the bookseller, that he and three more had spent four days in searching for one *Vaughan*, who the Lord's-day before preached a seditious sermon against the government ... but said they could not find him.

Presumably Vaughan's heart beat faster at the encounter, but it alerts us to how booksellers might be asked to supply information and also how browsing was enough of a common experience for his seeker not to think it suspicious.[130]

Reading in bookshops was certainly not limited to individual and silent browsing and there are some examples of conversations in bookshops prompting godly reading. Among the remarkable instances in the life and legacy of John Flavel, who had been ejected from his living in Dartmouth and whose effigy was burnt in the streets there in 1685, were not only the

---

[127] See Thomas Heywood (ed.), *The Diary of the Rev. Henry Newcome, from September 30, 1661, to September 29, 1663*, Chetham Society, 1st ser., 18 (Manchester, 1849), p. 29. This was *The Morning-Exercise at Cripple-Gate* (London, 1661).

[128] Heywood, *The Diary of the Rev. Henry Newcome*, p. 103.

[129] Hooke's borrowing of books directly out of his stationer's warehouse is recorded in his diary and has formed the basis of some bold claims as to the prevalence of this practice. Adrian Johns, for example, notes 'people could often stay and read within the premises before choosing whether to buy'. Johns, *The Nature of the Book*, pp. 98, 117. See also, for Pepys's reading of Fuller's *The Church History of Britain* in St Paul's Churchyard, Latham and Matthews, *The Diary of Samuel Pepys*, vol. I, pp. 56–7 (15 February 1659/60). For Newcome, see Heywood, *The Diary of the Rev. Henry Newcome*, p. 120. It is, of course, possible both that Newcome borrowed from the bookseller's personal library rather than his stock and that his was a special arrangement as a no-doubt prized customer given his role in setting up and furnishing the English Library at Manchester.

[130] See Samuel Palmer (ed.), *The Nonconformist's Memorial* (3 vols., London, 1802 edn), vol. II, p. 417.

ways his 'conversation and prayers' converted to the faith a young man who was bent on suicide but also a remarkable providential instance of a book effecting conversion in ways only rarely found in the historical record. A bookshop conversation brought about a surprising effect upon the wider population:

A profane person coming into a bookseller's shop to inquire for a play-book, the bookseller recommended to him Mr *Flavel's* Treatise *On Keeping the Heart*, as likely to do him more good. After having grossly abused the author and ridiculed the book, he was prevailed upon to promise that he would read it. He accordingly did so; and about a month after, came and thanked the bookseller for putting it into his hand; telling him, it had saved his soul; and bought a hundred copies of it to give away.'[131]

Likewise, the ever-informative John Rastrick helps to shed light on how the conversations in bookshops might feed into the creation of religious identity. Rastrick recalled a providential moment of spiritual epiphany:

being in a Booksellers Shop in Cambridg with my Chamberfellow there lay one of Mr Baxter's books in binding which me lightly and transiently looking at (for I cannot remember which it was) says my Chamberfellow 'twill be time enough to buy such books as those when we have taken our Degrees. But I thought with my Self (and I think said to him) I wod never buy such Books as those of a man's never educated in the University what could be got by them? &c. with such like under valuing thoughts. (for something I had heard of him and his Books; his Call and that of Crucyfying the world, I remember we had in the house where I boarded at Sleeford, which those in the house much valued, but I little minded.) But soon after … my Chamberfellow … buying his Reasons of the Christian Religion, hugely commended it to me for the Learning of it, and philosophy in it &c. and told me he proceeded in the method of Des Cartes (which our Tutor then read to us) from things more known to things less known in nature, beginning at Cogito, ergo sum.[132]

Looking back on this scene from his old age, Rastrick thought it crucial to the direction his religious identity took in adulthood. The conversation with his chamberfellow in the bookshop in Cambridge in 1670 sparked his lifelong love for the works of Richard Baxter.

Conversations in bookshops were often heated and discussions of the merits of religious books often got out of hand there. Oliver Heywood noted that one Mr Wood, the vicar of Sandal, 'expressed himself with such scorn and rage' in John Richardson's bookshop in Wakefield 'against the Assemblys Catechism, saying we should be called in question for

---

[131] Ibid., vol. II, p. 21.   [132] *The Life of John Rastrick*, pp. 64–5.

selling such stuff, using horrid opprobrious language as ever was against the vilest pamphlet'.[133] Such mentions of reading in bookshops provide tantalizing snippets of godly readerly praxis, but they are frustratingly brief. Instead, the clearest facet of godly culture which emerges from this and related evidence is the ways in which booksellers and the physical locations of their shops were crucial people and places in the creation and maintenance of godly religious culture.[134]

Print was, of course, one of the key means of communication in the Elizabethan puritan movement and the printer–bookseller Robert Waldegrave (c.1554–1604) exploited the medium in spreading the message. He was twice imprisoned in the early 1580s and went on to print Marprelate tracts on an itinerant basis, before fleeing to Scotland to take refuge as the King's Printer.[135] By the early seventeenth century, booksellers played a vital role in keeping puritanism alive, by reselling old books, peddling Calvinist practical divinity and, as Ian Green has shown, taking an active role in marketing new works which reused the names of famous Elizabethan puritan authors.[136] In this environment, it was people like Philemon Stephens and Christopher Meredith, who shared a shop at the Golden Lion in St Paul's Churchyard throughout the 1630s and published a string of works by key godly authors, who helped to sustain puritanism. In troubled times, their shop 'was a known meeting place for the godly'.[137]

But we have much more information as to the cultural impact of booksellers and bookshops after the interlinked explosions of religious

[133] Heywood, *Diaries*, vol. II, p. 223.
[134] Of course, I am certainly not arguing that all booksellers, or indeed the majority of them, had sympathies with puritanism, rather that certain booksellers – whether for ideological reasons or to turn a profit or both – played an active and important role in the fashioning of godly culture. For examples of Laudian printer–booksellers, see Peter McCullough, 'Print, Publication, and Religious Politics in Caroline England', p. 301; George Thomason, of course, was a Presbyterian stationer who held meetings with Stuart agents in his shop; see Johns, *The Nature of the Book*, p. 125. For examples of Catholic booksellers, see Johns, *The Nature of the Book*. The Half-Moon bookshop in St Paul's Churchyard was a high-church tory hangout which was an important site in the notorious quarrel between Richard Bently and Charles Boyle at the end of the seventeenth century. Of course, many booksellers did not display an obvious religious prejudice and many of those that did would still stock works with a range of religious positions. The point is that particular booksellers acted as focal points of godly religious sociability.
[135] For Marprelate, see above, n. 59. On Waldegrave, see *ODNB*.
[136] See Ian Green, *Print and Protestantism in Early Modern England* (Oxford, 2000), pp. 479–87.
[137] Jacqueline Eales, 'A Road to Revolution: The Continuity of Puritanism, 1559–1642', in Christopher Durston and Jacqueline Eales (eds.), *The Culture of English Puritanism, 1560–1700* (Basingstoke, 1996), p. 199. This also notes that one of Stephens's apprentices (Humphrey Blunden) kept up a correspondence with Richard Baxter in the 1630s. See *Reliquiæ Baxterianæ: or, Mr. Richard Baxter's Narrative of the Most Memorable Passages of his Life and Times*, ed. Matthew Sylvester (London, 1696), part i, p. 11.

radicalism and printed publications in the early 1640s. Booksellers were key figures in the fusion of religious zeal and printed polemic. Chief among them were men like Michael Sparke, who published puritan and anti-Arminian works before and during the Civil War and had particularly strong links with William Prynne. Sparke's ideology was clear to see. In his will he insisted that the mourners at his funeral be given copies of his own *Crumms of Comfort* (1652), the second part to his bestselling devotional treatise *Groanes of the Spirit*, instead of the traditional offerings of 'biskett or plums'; that fifty apprentices receive a copy of Lewis Bayly's *Practise of Piety*, and that the poor of Virginia and Bermuda be given copies of Thomas Warmstry's *A Hand-Kirchife for Loyall Mourners*.[138] Other booksellers were well known for their religious radicalism. In *Gangraena*, Thomas Edwards portrayed booksellers as sowers of radical dissent. He bemoaned Richard Overton as 'an Independent Book-seller and a member of Master John Goodwin's Church' and lambasted him for selling 'all kinds of unlicensed books that make any ways for the Sects, and against Presbyterians' which were 'sold at his shop'.[139]

Probably the most illuminating example of the ways in which booksellers acted as a centre for radical religious identity can be seen in the person and shop of Giles Calvert. Lawrence Clarkson's stylized spiritual autobiography of 1660, *The Lost Sheep Found*, is frequently employed as a key source in the history of the Ranters but since its subject moved almost seamlessly from the Church of England to pre-Civil War puritanism, through presbyterianism, to become a Baptist, Seeker, Digger and Muggletonian, it also tells us something about the shared culture of religious radicalism that could lead from puritanism to the world of the Ranters and later to the followers of the 'prophet' John Reeve. And in

---

[138] See Leona Rostenberg, *Literary, Political, Scientific, Religious and Legal Publishing, Printing, and Bookselling in England, 1551–1700: Twelve Studies* (2 vols., New York, 1965), vol. I., pp. 164, 202. Edward Pearse's *The Great Concern*, a godly devotional treatise on the need to be prepared for death, which was frequently reprinted after its first publication in 1671 and which found ready audiences on both sides of the Atlantic, had inscribed on its title page (in some editions at least), 'Recommended as proper to be given at FUNERALS', with a supplementary preface ('A proposition for the more profitable improvement of burials by giving of books') urging that mourners at funerals be given the work in multiple copies. Although this was obviously a marketing strategy, and the works recommended straddled conformist and nonconformist authors, as is argued by Green, *Print and Protestantism in Early Modern England*, pp. 367–8, there is certainly a case for interpreting this kind of distribution as part of the culture of puritanism, as is argued in Matthew P. Brown, *The Pilgrim and the Bee: Reading Rituals and Book Culture in Early New England* (Philadelphia, PA, 2007), p. 158, where it is cited in a section on books as godly funeral tokens.

[139] Thomas Edwards, *Gangraena* (3 parts, London, 1646), part II, p. 9; part III, pp. 148–52.

this spiritual journey the bookshop played a pivotal role.[140] Taking a room in a house in Smithfield with an old friend, Clarkson heard about 'a people called *My one flesh*' and that the person who could direct him to them was none other than Giles Calvert. Since the group was markedly radical, Calvert was understandably cautious when Clarkson arrived unannounced at his shop to seek out this underground anti-nomian group. 'He was', as Clarkson admitted, 'afraid I came to betray them', but in part through testing his language – a striking example of validating affinity through vocabulary – Calvert saw that Clarkson was genuine and gave him a letter of reference which authenticated him in the eyes of the sect.[141]

As Christopher Hill put it, 'The printer Giles Calvert's shop perhaps came nearest to uniting the radicals in spite of themselves'.[142] From his shop at the sign of the Black Spread Eagle on Ludgate Hill, close to St Paul's – a shop which had quite a narrow frontage but a series of upper rooms and bedrooms – Calvert offered a range of services which illumin-ate how the bookseller might be at the centre of networks of religious identity.[143] His shop was the first port of call for a range of radicals. Although it is hard to imagine that the prophet TheaurauJohn Tany was not well known to neighbours for miles around, he noted on the title page of *Theauraujohn High Priest to the Jewes* that he lived at Eltham in Kent and that more specific directions would be given to interested parties by Giles Calvert.[144] Booksellers were well placed to give such directions in

---

[140] The progress of Clarkson's religiosity and its positioning is much debated, but it is worth noting that his initial move towards radicalism came from a strand of religiosity at the fringes of puritanism in the form of the sermons of Tobias Crispe. See Lawrence Clarkson, 'The Lost Sheep Found', in John Bunyan, *Grace Abounding with other Spiritual Autobiographies*, ed. John Stachniewski with Anita Pacheco (Oxford, 1988), p. 178. On Clarkson's spiritual metamorphoses, see David R. Como, *Blown by the Spirit: Puritanism and the Emergence of an Antinomian Underground in Pre-Civil-War England* (Stanford, CA, 2004), p. 446; and Jonathan Scott, *England's Troubles: Seventeenth-Century English Political Instability in European Context* (Cambridge, 2000), p. 241.

[141] Lawrence Clarkson, 'The Lost Sheep Found', pp. 184–5.

[142] Christopher Hill, *The World Turned Upside Down: Radical Ideas during the English Revolution* (London, 1972), p. 373.

[143] According to Ariel Hessayon, *'Gold Tried in the Fire': The Prophet TheaurauJohn Tany and the English Revolution* (Aldershot, 2007), p. 192, 'Calvert's premises consisted of a cellar (used for storing coal, waste printed paper and other lumber), a shop with street frontage (measuring twelve feet in breadth and ten feet four inches in depth), four rooms above the shop (kitchen-cum-dining room, bedroom, master bedroom, garret), and a little yard behind the property where the privie and the stairs leading up into the house were located.'

[144] TheaurauJohn Tany, *Theauraujohn High Priest to the Jewes, his Disputive Challenge to the Universities of Oxford and Cambridge, and the whole Hirach. of Roms Clargical Priests* ([London], 1652), p. 1.

part because of their location near St Paul's meant they were at the centre of London's traffic network, close to the river and the major coaching inns like the Goose and Gridiron.[145] Likewise, travelling Quakers in particular sought out Calvert's shop as their first point of refuge in the capital. Quakers sent mail to Calvert's shop safe in the knowledge that he would pass it on to its intended recipient.[146] They used his shop as a meeting place, and if they were stuck for money they could even turn to Calvert for financial assistance. There are several examples of Calvert effectively giving out loans by advancing batches of books to impecunious Quakers who would sell their wares in the provinces before paying Calvert for his stock. Such arrangements no doubt assisted Calvert's business by ensuring a ready market and distribution network for the Quaker works he printed, but they also aided the Quaker cause and Calvert was an important supplier of Quaker material to regional book distributors.[147] Although Calvert himself was apparently not a Quaker, he had an important role in the formation of Quaker identity and this, as well as other activities, put him under suspicion by the authorities. At times, he was under surveillance and he was spotted at an important meeting of Quakers in Leicestershire in 1655.[148] In particular, his role as publisher and bookseller ensured his notoriety. Calvert printed works without license and his shop was raided in February 1655. A list of some of the authors whose works bore Calvert's name throughout the 1640s and 1650s is a clear indication of the focus of the energies of radicalism that might be channelled through a bookseller.[149] They include William Carter, Richard Bernard, Joseph Caryl, John Saltmarsh, Henry Burton, Edward Bowles, William Dell, Edward Fisher, Thomas Tookey, William Walwyn, Mary Cary, Thomas Collier, Hugh Peters, William Sedgwick, Gerrard Winstanley, Abiezer Coppe, Hendrik Niclaes, Thomas Tany, Christopher Atkinson, George Fox, John Webster, James Naylor, Jakob Böhme, Samuel Hartlib, John Pordage, Richard Farnworth, John Lilburne, Martha Simmonds (his sister) and Edward Burrough. Clearly this was not an ideological 'group', but that should not detract from what is a

---

[145] See Raven, *The Business of Books*, p. 104 for coaching inns.
[146] Peters, *Print Culture and the Early Quakers*, p. 59.   [147] Ibid., esp. p. 59.   [148] Ibid., p. 58.
[149] Indeed, the role of the bookseller–publisher in creating as well as dispersing radicalism has been underestimated. Kate Peters's detailed analysis of the title pages of Quaker works, where she argues that the use of typography (in particular the placing of the word Quakers in large font and capital letters) helped to add coherence to Quakerism as a thing, might be extended to include the role that the typesetters as well as the authors had in this process. Ibid., Chapter 4.

remarkable roll-call of mid-century religious radicalism.[150] This was not lost on contemporaries. In *Gangraena*, Thomas Edwards lambasted Calvert as 'a Sectary and a Book-seller' for his role in selling and dispersing *The last warning to all the inhabitants of London* (1646), alongside the other 'sectaries' like Richard Overton and Samuel Fulcher. He also suggested that Calvert used his shop to help to shelter radical preachers like 'Floid', a twenty-year-old radical preacher who 'did lie at master Calverts the Bookseller at Ludgate Hill'.[151] Richard Baxter likened those who sold the radical literature which brought Christianity into disrepute and made every pulpit 'Satans Oracle' to apothecaries who sold 'an open shop of poysons' – chief among them, he continued, was Giles Calvert, who sold particularly 'foul-poysons'.[152] And in 1654 Thomas Hall railed against 'what stuffe still comes from Lame Giles Calver[t]s shop', which he described as 'that forge of the Devil, from whence so many blashphemous, lying, scandalous Pamphlets, for many yeers past, have spread over the land, to the great dishonour of the Nation, in the sight of the Nations round about us, and to the provocation of Gods wrath against us'.[153]

Imprisonment after the Restoration, as well as advancing years, effectively brought to an end Calvert's publishing career, but we can trace its further impact in the work of his family and his associates. As we have already seen, Calvert's sister Martha, who was a Quaker author, married Thomas Simmonds, who became the key Quaker publisher in London and worked out of the Bull and Mouth, the principal Quaker meeting house in London.[154] Elizabeth Calvert, Giles Calvert's widow, managed to continue to support nonconformist publications despite being imprisoned several times after her husband's death, and she appears to have maintained connections with former radicals and Quakers until her death.[155] Likewise, Calvert's close associates John Streater and the Baptist bookseller Francis Smith continued to promote their causes, and Calvert's

---

[150] This list is compiled with the information on the English Short Title Catalogue (http://estc.bl.uk) and may not be definitive. Calvert was a Quaker specialist and in the early 1650s he was the main Quaker publisher, responsible for more than half of all Quaker publications between 1653 and 1656. Thereafter, Thomas Simmonds, Calvert's brother-in-law who had the advantage of actually being a Quaker, became the major Quaker publisher. See Peters, *Print Culture and the Early Quakers*.

[151] Edwards, *Gangraena*, part II, p. 9; part III, p. 62.

[152] Richard Baxter, *The Worcester-Shire Petition ... Defended* (London, 1653), p. 39.

[153] Thomas Hall, *Vindiciae Literarum, the Schools Guarded* (London, 1654), p. 215.

[154] Peters, *Print Culture and the Early Quakers*, p. 51.

[155] See Maureen Bell, 'Elizabeth Calvert and the "Confederates"', *Publishing History*, 32 (1992), pp. 5–49; Maureen Bell, '"Her Usual Practices": The Later Career of Elizabeth Calvert, 1664–75', *Publishing History*, 35 (1994), pp. 5–64.

former apprentices, like Richard Moon, who set up shop as a bookseller in Bristol and was a prominent Quaker there, confirm that the influence of Calvert was long-lived.[156]

Although there are few examples so unambiguous as that of Giles Calvert, bookshops continued to act as centres of religious activity and identity after the Restoration. While there were Tory and Anglican booksellers, as well as Whig and nonconformist booksellers, together with those of no obvious persuasion, it is nevertheless clear in assessing godly culture that nonconformists made use of booksellers and that booksellers traded off their associations with particular types of author. The connections between religious identity and those in the book trade were perhaps clearest among Quakers, who stipulated that only Friends should be allowed to print and distribute Quaker writings. But bookshops also remained centres for nonconformists. The Whig intelligencer Roger Morrice, for example, appears to have used Robert Gibbs's shop at the Golden Ball in Chancery Lane as a meeting place.[157] But such examples of diarists and letter writers recording religious exchanges at bookshops are necessarily haphazard and we need not sift endless spiritual diaries to find evidence of bookshops being central to religious networks. Instead, the evidence of books themselves and the activities of booksellers is revealing. Presbyterian ministers in particular used specific booksellers to market their works and some of these sellers clearly specialized in such volumes, often to the exclusion of almost all else. These included those such as Brabazon Aylmer, Thomas Parkhurst and John Dunton who published presbyterian books with lists of related works advertised at the end, thereby cementing a more exclusive kind of religious textual identity. The activities of Parkhurst offer some evidence of how strong such networks remained. Parkhurst operated at the Bible and Three Crowns at the lower end of Cheapside, close to the Mercers' Chapel, between 1670 and 1711 and, excepting a very few Anglican authors, his authors were overwhelmingly dissenting ministers.[158] Their books were sold in his shop, where religious networks were also consolidated by other means. Daniel Williams, for example, left a tract concerning the antinomian controversy at Parkhurst's shop in the mid-1690s in the hope that his customers would

[156] See Jonathan Barry, 'The Press and the Politics of Culture in Bristol, 1660–1775', in Jeremy Black and Jeremy Gregory (eds), *Culture, Politics and Society in Britain 1660–1800* (Manchester, 1991), pp. 49–81.
[157] See Goldie et al., *The Entring Book of Roger Morrice*, vol. I, p. 67.
[158] Ibid., vol. I, Appendix 37, lists the dissenting ministers who were published by Robert Gibbs, Brabazon Aylmer, John Darby, Thomas Parkhurst and John Dunton.

add their names to it.[159] But just as important is the information that has survived of Parkhurst's ties with the authors he published, especially Oliver Heywood. As Heywood's extensive notebooks show, his arrangement with Parkhurst was to pay for a number of copies of his own book before they had been printed and accept more in lieu of payment after publication, with the purpose of distributing the copies to members of his congregation in the Halifax area, and the result that print acted as an integral part of his ministry. The deal was obviously lucrative for Parkhurst and since it was arranged before publication it was also relatively risk-free. It helps to explain the comment of John Dunton, Parkhurst's former apprentice, that his master was 'the most eminent Presbyterian bookseller in the Three Kingdoms . . . He has met with very strange success, for I have known him sell off a whole impression before the book has been almost heard of in London'.[160]

Harold Love, who examined the relationship between Parkhurst and Heywood, suggested that such arrangements might have been common among other ejected clergy and some fragmentary evidence bears out his suggestion. Henry Newcome, recording that Parkhurst printed one of his sermons with great speed – he received printed copies within two months of sending his manuscript – also noted that while he was in London, Parkhurst gave him 'a dozen of Mr Caley's books' which he distributed among his friends on his return to Manchester.[161] Defending himself in a letter of 1678 against an accusation that he took excessive rates from his publisher, Richard Baxter gave an insight into what he called 'the art of booksellers', where he described how he usually took the fifteenth book (which he gave away) rather than any capital from the first edition and would only make money out of subsequent impressions. When he had become more savvy as to the ways of the book trade, Baxter demanded each fifteenth book for himself and his friends and eighteen pence more

---

[159] Ibid., vol. I, p. 67.

[160] See John Dunton, *The Life and Errors of John Dunton Late Citizen of London; Written by Himself in Solitude* (London, 1705), p. 281. For Parkhurst and Heywood, see Harold Love, 'Preacher and Publisher: Oliver Heywood and Thomas Parkhurst', *Studies in Bibliography*, 31 (1978), pp. 227–35. Of the extensive documentation surrounding their relationship, the most revealing passages are in Heywood, *Diaries*, vol. II., p. 213; vol. III, pp. 229, 335–6. Heywood paid for a large number of bound copies of his books up front but also received more (probably without charge) back from Parkhurst after successful publication. Heywood's distribution of some of these books is detailed in ibid., vol. III, pp. 51–7, 66–73, 75–6. On the occasions when he received hundreds of copies, his arrangements for distributing them were more elaborate and appear to have involved collaboration with a bookseller in Halifax.

[161] See R. Parkinson (ed.), *The Autobiography of Henry Newcome*, Chetham Society, 26, 27 (2 vols., paged continuously, Manchester, 1852), pp. 257, 263.

for every ream of the other fourteen – and he gave the money to the poor. Like Heywood, he sometimes paid for the printing of a book himself and sometimes he bought out the stocks of his books from the bookseller.[162] Similar was an arrangement between Adam Martindale and his printer. Revising a manuscript he had composed in answer to Mr Smith's *The Patriarchal Sabbath*, which had originally been requested by Mr Moxon, a bookseller of Manchester, Martindale sent the manuscript to Moxon who passed it on to Philip Burton of Warrington, who had an arrangement with a London bookseller operating out of the Poultry. The deal struck was that Martindale would take 150 copies, Moxon a hundred, and Burton fifty.[163]

Although any definition of puritanism is exceptionally complex after the Restoration and any connections between the religious cultures of presbyterians, radical separatists and Quakers can only loosely be described as godly, booksellers continued to craft themselves as guardians of religious and political cultures. In this, family connections were paramount. John Dunton, who cut his teeth while apprenticed to Parkhurst, married the daughter of Samuel Annesley and published for Annesley, Sylvester and Baxter. Henry Overton, the radical bookseller, was the son of Valentine Overton, the Warwickshire orthodox puritan minister. Overton's sister married the godly biographer Samuel Clarke.[164] Some traded off these long-standing connections. Jacob Tonson (1656–1736), for example, made much of his connections with the puritan past through his grandfather, the bookseller Matthew Walbancke. Clearly, it makes little sense to style Tonson a puritan himself, but such an ancestry was an important dimension in the fashioning of his own Whig identity, an identity which was shaped not only by his family connections but through his publishing of Milton and founding of the Kit-Cat Club.[165] Other connections extended into the future. The eighteenth-century bookseller Samuel Chandler was the son of Henry Chandler, who had been a dissenting minister in Bath. He in turn also became a dissenting minister and a bookseller in London, and the next owner of his shop was a

---

[162] See William Orme, *The Life and Times of the Rev. Richard Baxter: with a Critical Examination of his Writings* (2 vols., London, 1830), vol. II, pp. 321–3.

[163] See Richard Parkinson (ed.), *The Life of Adam Martindale, Written by Himself, and now First Printed from the Original Manuscript in the British Museum*, Chetham Society, 1st ser., 4 (Manchester, 1855), p. 231. In fact, the London bookseller did not pass on any copies because he claimed that Burton owed him money.

[164] See Hughes, *Gangraena*, p. 146, which argues that this shows that we should not attribute too much coherence to the ideological connections between families, authors and booksellers.

[165] See Raven, *The Business of Books*, p. 119.

Mr J. Gray, who was first a dissenting and then a conforming minister.[166] Of course, much of the evidence presented above is hostile and therefore tends to portray bookshops as sites of religious subversion and radicalism, and also to overstate the coherence of religious radicals, particularly after the Restoration. But as long as we remain aware of this and do not, for instance, fall into the trap of equating presbyterians with more radical nonconformists, we can still see that there was potential for a range of styles of radical reading in bookshops.

CONCLUSION

Following on from our discussion of reading in the domestic arena and in libraries, this chapter has explored the importance of collective reading in a series of more overtly public spaces in the early modern urban landscape: in the church, pulpit and parish; in coffee houses and in bookshops. The picture presented in these spaces – where the godly could not set themselves apart, but necessarily rubbed shoulders with a range of their religious and cultural 'enemies' – is of collective reading as absolutely critical to the ways in which they practised their religiosity and the ways they represented their faith in the public arena. Although we have seen how many instances of collective reading in public spaces drew on modes of reading and piety we have already encountered in the domestic arena, it has become clear that such reading was associated with radicalism and that it helped to sustain puritanism in the longer term. Interestingly, where collective reading in the domestic arena ran counter to many received understandings about private spaces and private reading, the focus on collective reading in public spaces fits much more easily with current trends in early modern historiography, in which ideas were printed, discussed, debated, negotiated and shaped in the spaces of the public sphere.[167] Even if the latter is usually formulated from a more secular standpoint, this disjuncture underscores a tension between two of the master narratives underpinning the transition from early modern to modern society: on the one hand, social reading in places like coffee houses, where print and conversation combined in the creation of political allegiance as well as cultural categories like civility, is seen as a key component of the drive towards modernity; on the other, social reading

---

[166] See John Nichols, *Literary Anecdotes of the Eighteenth Century* (9 vols., London, 1812–15), vol. V, pp. 304–5.
[167] See, for instance, Knights, *Representation and Misrepresentation in Later Stuart Britain*.

in the more private spaces of the household is seen as 'backward', since private reading is associated with puritanism and 'rational' behaviour. At the same time, the chapter has underlined the importance of thinking about reading beyond the book and of employing a more capacious definition of what constituted reading. This has brought further attention to the interaction and mutual reinforcement of speech, manuscript and print in the culture of puritanism, a concern which will be apparent once more in the following chapter.

CHAPTER 6

Reading in prison

INTRODUCTION

By tackling a further space of godly reading – the prison – this chapter extends our discussion of the place of reading in shaping and perpetuating godly religious identity. The experience of imprisonment and the potential for subsequent execution and martyrdom played a well-recognized role in the shaping of religious identity: it dovetailed both with the idea of religious separation and with the concept of the true church as one which was persecuted by its opponents. Martyrdom was hardly distinctive to the godly – it was vital to other Protestants and to Catholics and it was of course influential beyond Christianity too.[1] But it was certainly one of the most important cultural tools with which the godly fashioned their identity in the seventeenth century and it was the cornerstone of the most influential of godly books – John Foxe's *Actes and Monuments*. In Foxe's book, prisons were spaces of reading and the construction of godly identity and such reading helped to shape models of godly religiosity, which were then preserved in godly books. Of course, it would be possible to examine other spaces of godly reading – in particular spaces of the representation of godly reading, like the theatre – but the choice of prisons helps to unravel how, despite the continued importance of communal reading and collective piety, the godly came to be represented as the archetypes of both individual piety and solitary reading.

'NO BOOKS, NO PAPER, NO PENNE, NO INKE, OR CONVENIENT PLACE FOR STUDY'

Despite the fact that relatively few people were incarcerated in the filth and gloom of an early modern prison in the course of their lives, such

---

[1] Brad S. Gregory, *Salvation at Stake: Christian Martyrdom in Early Modern Europe* (Cambridge, MA, 1999).

places loomed large in the early modern imagination. The subject of conversation, confessional debate and salacious and providential pamphlets, prisons were, in the words of their most astute recent commentators, 'public and private places' and 'liminal spaces; ostensibly the ultimate locus of public, state power, they were also, like so much of the royal bureaucracy, run for the private profit and in the private interest of those contracted to administer them'.[2]

These conjunctions and contradictions offer considerable advantages to the historian, particularly when combined with the dual fact that prisons were at or near the centre of early modern news networks and that, as locations, they figured prominently in the key text of godly culture, John Foxe's *Actes and Monuments*.[3] Foxe's work is of considerable significance here since not only does it provide numerous examples of Marian Protestants finding ingenious ways to continue reading as part of their religious practice within prison walls, but it also offered a model of religiosity that served as the blueprint for an ideal of godly devotion throughout the period. The prison was the perfect place in which to continue reading, for it showed that even in the most dire of circumstances, members of the true church – that is, the church under the cross – would persist in their godly reading. And through Foxe's work the model he constructed of the godly martyrs reading in prisons was exported to early modern households, where it became the paradigm of early modern godly spirituality.

The sources for prison reading are inevitably problematic, since those who recorded religious reading in prisons did so either to complain about the extent of the religious freedom given to prisoners who should have been treated as enemies of the state or, conversely, to show how prisoners themselves maintained their faith despite unjustified religious persecution and the removal of their religious liberty. In neither instance should such records be read with anything other than a healthy dose of scepticism, since it was in the interests of prisoners (and their biographers) to show that they were steadfast in their faith, while it was in the interest of those who favoured harsher prison conditions, and in particular a more rigorous regime of confinement, to plead with the authorities that conditions were so lax that (particularly Catholic) prisoners were able to use the books that

---

[2] Peter Lake with Michael Questier, *The Antichrist's Lewd Hat: Protestants, Papists, and Players in Post-Reformation England* (New Haven, CT, 2002), p. 187.

[3] For prisons and news networks, see Joad Raymond, *Pamphlets and Pamphleteering in Early Modern Britain* (Cambridge, 2003).

were the props of their faith. That said, such problems permeated most of the biographies, autobiographies, letters and other printed and manuscript works that have been considered throughout this book and, when read carefully, and often against the grain, they offer further insight into practices of reading and early modern spirituality. Furthermore, in some ways prison reading and writing has left more material traces than that reading which occurred in the freedom of the home because there is a significant amount of surviving early modern prison graffiti, which prisoners etched into cell walls and floors in the torment (or boredom) of their confinement. Other prisoners, in particular those of a high enough social status to be housed in a prison with windows rather than simple iron bars, might use rings to etch the panes of glass behind which their voices were otherwise trapped: Elizabeth I was reported to have made a testimony of her innocence by scratching the windows of her cell at Woodstock with a diamond ring, while Lady Jane Grey wrote verses in the Tower of London 'with a pin'.[4] Juliet Fleming, who has written a remarkable book on the subject of early modern graffiti, describes the walls of prisons as a kind of vast and untapped 'archive of verse'.[5] Although this kind of material is problematic as well as full of potential, it seems foolish to harbour prejudice against such writing because it is not on paper or parchment and was thus not what nineteenth-century historians deemed 'evidence'. For Foxe's martyrs, the graffiti written on prison walls was an opportunity for polemic against the tyranny of the Catholic state. Thus the evangelical painter Edward Freese, who was imprisoned for painting sentences of scripture on cloths in Henrician Colchester, 'would ever be writing on the walles with chauke or a coale', even noting on his cell wall that 'Doct. Dodipall would make me beleve that the Moone were made of grene cheese'.[6] Similarly, we should not discount the possibility of prison reading and writing on the body in the form of the tattoo. Despite the injunction of Leviticus 19:28 – 'You shall not make any cuttings in your flesh for the dead, nor print any marks upon you' – and the association many made of the tattoo with native Americans, ancient Britons and thus non-Christian practices, there is evidence of

[4] John Foxe, *Actes and Monuments of these Latter and Perillous Dayes* (London, 1563), p. 922 (Jane Grey), p. 1730 (original mispaginated as p. 1714) (Elizabeth).
[5] Juliet Fleming, *Graffiti and the Writing Arts of Early Modern England* (London, 2001), p. 56. See also Ruth Ahnert, 'Writing in the Tower of London during the Reformation, ca. 1530–1558', in William H. Sherman and William J. Sheils (eds.), *Prison Writings in Early Modern England*, themed issue of *Huntington Library Quarterly*, 72 (2009), pp. 168–92.
[6] *Actes and Monuments* (1583), p. 1027.

religious tattooing among early modern Britons, some of whom branded themselves with the mark of Jesus, crosses or other symbols. Such writing, as it had been for their medieval predecessors, was not necessarily incompatible with Christianity.[7] Of course, not all such forms of writing were equally licit – and some of them flirted with the occult and the demonic – but when thinking about reading in prisons, we should keep our eyes open to a full range of source materials.

A more significant obstacle is the distance between the kind of place we tend to *assume* that prisons were – that is, the harsh, ordered and relatively impenetrable building blocks of a Foucauldian state apparatus – and the evidence we have of the organization, management, ownership, order and chaos of the operations of early modern prisons in practice. Although a burgeoning historiography has begun to tease out the differences between these two images with some success, a few observations might be made before we proceed to instances of prison reading.[8] First and foremost, early modern prisons were private institutions run for profit. That the prisoners themselves paid for their own food and lodging had significant financial advantages for the state but it also had numerous downsides. Simply put, it meant that prisons, far from being impenetrable fortresses of unbending state power, were in fact only as secure as their keepers. With those prisoners who were obviously a threat to the body politic, such as murderers and felons, the dual interests of the state and the prison were happily intertwined, but when it came to those incarcerated for political or religious crimes, the conjunction of interests had the potential to unravel. Prisons could be run by people sympathetic to a particular cause, indeed they might have been especially likely to have been run by sympathizers, and even unsympathetic gaolers seem to have been fairly easily persuaded by prisoners with private means and deep pockets. Thus there are numerous

---

[7] On tattooing, see Fleming, *Graffiti and the Writing Arts of Early Modern England*, Chapter 3. Such evidence is, of course, usually textual (or graphic), as authors and draughtsmen wrote or drew what they saw. See, for example, Fynes Moryson, *An Itinerary* (London, 1617), part i, pp. 233–4. For the potential of writing upon the body to reveal layers of meaning about early modern culture that might otherwise remain hidden, see Simon Schaffer, '"On Seeing Me Write": Inscription Devices in the South Seas', *Representations*, 97 (2007), pp. 90–122; Geraldine Barnes, 'Curiosity, Wonder, and William Dampier's Painted Prince', *Journal for Early Modern Cultural Studies*, 6 (2006), pp. 31–50; and Jennifer Allen Rosecrans, 'Wearing the Universe: Symbolic Markings in Early Modern England', in Jane Caplan (ed.), *Written on the Body: The Tattoo in European and American History* (London, 2000), pp. 46–60, 264–7.

[8] Compare, for instance, Michel Foucault, *Discipline and Punish: The Birth of the Prison*, trans. Alan Sheridan (London, 1977); and James A. Sharpe, '"Last Dying Speeches": Religion, Ideology and Public Execution in Seventeenth-Century England', *Past and Present*, 107 (1985), pp. 144–67; with Lake, *The Antichrist's Lewd Hat*.

examples of Marian prisons run by Protestant sympathizers and some Elizabethan prisons were in part staffed by Catholics and served as centres of Catholicism. In October 1588, Catholic prisoners were hearing Mass in the most secure state penitentiary – the Tower of London. They even had keys to rooms so they had freedom of movement within prisons. In the late 1590s, Winchester gaol was being run by Hampshire recusants, who allowed priests in and out. It was, 'stuffed with altars, vestments, candles, and liturgical and polemical books'.[9] As a sign of the laxity of prison management and their permeability, it is worth noting that there are records of prisoners being given the keys to the outside world and being allowed out on condition that they return.[10]

The structures by which prisons operated also made them difficult to police. Prisoners were expected to have visitors and only in very rare circumstances would they be denied (since they brought them food and money). Visitors might bring books or bribe the gaolers to let them do so. Such conditions meant that reading in prison was neither licit nor impossible and they also made prisons semi-public venues, neither fully open nor completely sealed, which operated at or close to centres of early modern communications networks. Prisons were, in the characteristic formulation of Lake and Questier, 'the moral and spiritual nerve centre of the church under the cross'.[11]

Prisons were almost universally described as places where the regulations were as lax as the conditions were filthy.[12] These conditions varied between individual prisons, rather than between parts of the country. There were badly managed prisons notorious for being both insalubrious and lenient and others, like the Tower of London and that at Wisbech in Cambridgeshire, which were at least in theory high-security prisons for dangerous prisoners. No obvious pattern emerges, although it does seem likely that London prisons, which were often located close to printshops and booksellers in the seedier parts of the town, were rather closer to centres of communication than some of their provincial counterparts, which might in theory be able to shut down contact with the outside world more successfully.[13]

---

[9] Lake, *The Antichrist's Lewd Hat*, p. 196.　　[10] Ibid., p. 195.　　[11] Ibid., p. 293.

[12] Ibid., p. 194.

[13] Of course, it is certainly not the case that the authorities and personnel of the state were happy with the conditions of their prisons. While dean of Durham, Tobie Matthew wrote to the Earl of Huntingdon in 1592 expressing his fury at the freedom given to Waterson the seminary priest to say masses at the prison in Newcastle and assuring Huntingdon that 'the gaoler Musgrave wolde be accordingly handled, for examples sake'. HEHL, MS HA 9211 (letter of Tobie Matthew to the Earl of Huntingdon, 23 November 1592).

Reports of prison life are, of course, almost all factional, political and polemical, whether they are drawn from the correspondence of the worthy or the printed pamphlet literature of the scurrilous. There were no sociologists of the early modern prison system. But even when we have scraped away the layers of scum built up by pamphlet exchanges and piles of polemic, it is still clear that prisons were horrible and dirty and corrupt and bungling. The main interest of prison-keepers, however important security may or may not have been to that interest, was profit. This is stressed in what literature there is about early modern prisons and it is only recently that work has started to tease out the importance of the prison to debates about early modern religion and politics. Peter Lake and Michael Questier, for example, have highlighted the multitude of debates which revolved in and around prisons and prison life, in particular through their readings of murder pamphlets and their contexts. They have very successfully shown how prisons functioned as sites of ideological and confessional conflict in this period.[14] Lake and Questier have used such materials in particular to unravel debates about Catholicism and the early modern state but it is also worth remembering that one of the significant ironies of imprisonment in early modern England is that a relatively short period of persecution and imprisonment of English Prot-estants, in particular during Mary's reign, had a disproportionate effect culturally. There remained an association between Protestantism and persecution as others suffered at the hands of overbearing state powers on the Continent and, especially, as godly people read about the impris-onment of their spiritual forebears in Foxe's *Actes and Monuments*. In short, after 1558 the state imprisoned Catholics for their beliefs (even if they claimed that it was not for their beliefs that they were imprisoned but for their actions) and yet prisons and imprisonment remained ingrained in the English Protestant (especially godly) imagination. Prisons were vital to godly identity. Stories of imprisonment and persecution were spread through oral tradition as well as through Foxe, and tales of martyrdom and religious constancy remained strong. Indeed, the test of how strong it was can be seen in how easily the trope was latched onto by Protestant dissenters after the Restoration. Then it became one of the defining

---

[14] Lake, *The Antichrist's Lewd Hat*, esp. Chapters 6 and 7. Lynn Robson has recently described the murder pamphlet as a Protestant form of print, concerned with sin and justification. See Lynn Robson, '"No Nine Days Wonder" Embedded Protestant Narratives in Early Modern Prose Murder Pamphlets 1573–1700' (unpublished PhD thesis, University of Warwick, 2003); and her '"Now Farewell to the Lawe, too Long Have I Been in thy Subjection": Early Modern Murder, Calvinism and Female Spiritual Authority', *Literature and Theology*, 22 (2008), pp. 295–312.

characteristics of their own religious identity, and something that set the godly nonconformist apart from the Anglican.[15]

An analysis of godly reading in early modern prisons extends our understanding both of prison life and of the nature and meaning of the practice of early modern reading (and writing). Certain familiar themes emerge – the overlap of reading and writing, the conjunction of reading and prayer, and the complex interplay of individual and communal reading, for example – but so too do others which were more or less peculiar to prisons. Of course, I am not suggesting that it was only the godly who read in prisons or that prison reading was inherently godly, merely that prisons offer an excellent vantage point from which to observe godly reading and in particular to examine some of the peculiarities of such reading and its place in godly culture more generally. Depending on the circumstances, for the conditions and provisions of prisons and prisoners varied both between and within institutions, prisons could be locations for a range of types of godly – and other – reading.[16]

Given its significance in the crafting of a model of prison piety, it seems sensible to start with Foxe's *Actes and Monuments* and the story of Thomas Bilney which offers a snapshot of the prisoner as reader and the complexities of this neglected subject which was nevertheless crucial in godly self-perception. Thomas Bilney is, of course, remembered as a martyr, executed in 1531 for beliefs which he refused to renounce and which made him the archetypal early Protestant martyr. In most accounts of his resolution and his demise, reading understandably plays only a very minor role, at least compared to the strength of his faith and his constancy in the face of persecution. Yet his reading was also at the heart of what it meant to be godly in prison – and again it intersects with, and perhaps is the axis around which revolve, a series of other religious activities, such as prayer, conversation and meditation. Bilney's

---

[15] If debates about English Catholics and their imprisonment seem to have little to do with incarcerated Protestants and their spirituality, it is worth remembering that comparisons between Catholicism and puritanism make sense and are worth making in part because, as John Bossy taught us, the English Catholic community is best considered 'a branch of the English nonconforming tradition'. See John Bossy, *The English Catholic Community 1570–1850* (London, 1975), p. 7.

[16] On prison writing, see Sherman and Sheils, *Prison Writings in Early Modern England*. For an innovative case study of the prison as a site for reading, writing and experimental science, see Deborah E. Harkness, *The Jewel House: Elizabethan London and the Scientific Revolution* (New Haven, CT, 2007), Chapter 5 (Clement Draper's Prison Notebooks: Reading, Writing, and Doing Science), pp. 181–210.

Figure 7. The imprisoned Thomas Bilney proving the fire with his finger, from John Foxe, *Actes and Monuments* (London, 1563), p. 482. By permission of the Huntington Library, San Marino, California.

reading highlights the social experience which was at the heart of his suffering. He is famously depicted in the *Book of Martyrs* holding his finger in the fire (Figure 7).

Although the woodcut is well known, it is often forgotten that Bilney's holding of his finger in the flame was not simply a test of the strength of faith against the pain of the body: it was also a textual event. While Bilney 'prooved the fire' by placing a finger of his right hand in the flame of a candle, with a finger of his left hand he was following a passage in the book which lay open on the table in front of him. The trial of his faith was sustained by his godly reading, as he quoted Isaiah 43 ('When thou walkest in the fire, it shall not burne thee, and the flame shall not kindle upon thee, for I am the Lord the God, the holy one of Israell') while holding his finger to the flame. Foxe noted that this performance was done while he was 'sitting with his ... friendes in godly talke' and that these friends took comfort from Bilney's strength of faith, afterwards writing down his words in their 'Tables' and 'theyr bookes' for their comfort.[17] Bilney's strength was drawn from and sustained by his reading of the sacred book. His reading not only intersected with his trials and tribulations, it was also transformed into the textual mementoes carried by his friends, which in turn they read to sustain their faith before they were printed in the pages of the *Book of Martyrs*, where they were read as an example of perseverance by the godly as a whole.

One of the main reasons why prisons are important in descriptions of godly reading is because they highlight the dichotomy between the authorities, who tried to prevent reading, and the truly religious, who went to extraordinary lengths to continue the reading that formed part of their religious practice. As numerous accounts testify, among the first thing that the prison authorities did when admitting prisoners was to confiscate books. As T. P. Connor has observed, 'deprivation of books formed part of routine harassment by bullying gaolers'.[18] Although it is not true that there was a blanket ban on prisoners keeping books with them, it is certainly true that the authorities tried to exercise caution in this respect. Prisoners were often denied books and writing materials. This might be for a number of reasons. Peter Smart's books were taken from him by the deputy marshall of King's Bench Prison because of a debt, although Smart complained that this was a pretence.[19] Most common, however, was the deprivation of books which supported illegal religious and political activities. Such deprivation was used on occasion by Foxe as the reason why information about certain martyrs was slight. There were few extant letters of Robert Farrar, he noted, because 'his imprisonment was so strait, that at no time it was permitted to hym to write'.[20] John Bradford refused to debate with his captors in part because he had been kept 'in prison long without bookes and al necessaries for study'.[21] The treatment of Catholics mirrored that of Foxe's Protestant martyrs. The manuscript life-story of Francis Tregian, for example, noted that Cuthbert Mayne, the first seminary priest to fall victim to the Elizabethan regime, 'was laid in a most loathsome and lousy dongeon, scarce able at high

[17] *Actes and Monuments* (1583), p. 1012.
[18] T. P. Connor, 'Malignant Reading: John Squier's Newgate Prison Library, 1642–46', *The Library*, 7th ser., 7 (2006), p. 162.
[19] *Fourth Report of the Royal Commission on Historical Manuscripts* (2 vols., London, 1874), vol. I, p. 84.
[20] *Actes and Monuments* (1583), p. 1555.   [21] Ibid., p. 1615.

noon to see his hands or legs, so laden with iron, deprived of the use of writing and bereaved of the comfort of reading'.[22] Tregian himself was imprisoned and deprived of pen and ink, but he managed to compose English verses and prayers 'written with a pin and the snuff of a candle'.[23]

Sometimes, gaolers would allow prisoners books when they trusted them a bit more. Although Daniel Featley complained of the 'unfurnishing me of all Books, and helps of mine owne Notes and Collections (lately taken from me)', he was later allowed to use three of his books at any one time.[24] Mostly, however, what books prisoners got their hands on were smuggled in by visitors and sympathizers. In fact, it is remarkable how many prisoners got their hands not only on books but also on paper and writing materials too; the tools which would enable them, among other things, to communicate with the outside world, continue a written ministry and tell their side of their story. Such communication shows how books were used for more than reading. On the day before she was executed, Lady Jane Grey wrote a letter to her sister on the blank endpaper of her Greek New Testament, in effect freely sending a message out of prison.[25] Only slowly did the authorities come to realize that their failure to confiscate books enabled clandestine forms of communication. When the bishop's agents took away William Stillington's Bible, they 'founde certaine notes in it, whereof was geven out that they touched on matters of staite, and that he should be hanged'.[26] Those who had been addicted to reading outside prison were frequently unwilling to give up such a sign of their godliness inside. In Scotland, Adam Wallace, who had previously carried his English Bible with him 'wherever he went', was sent to prison and took with him 'certaine bookes to read & comfort his spirit'. His captor, Sir Hugh Terry, whom Foxe described as 'an impe of Sathan', swiftly took his books away and left him 'desolat ... of al consolation'.[27] Yet for all Foxe expressed his outrage at the confiscation

[22] John Morris (ed.), *The Troubles of Our Catholic Forefathers Related by Themselves* (3 vols., London, 1872–7), vol. I, p. 67.

[23] Ibid., vol. I, p. 125.

[24] Daniel Featley, *The Dippers Dipt* (1646). See Connor, 'Malignant Reading', p. 162. Hugo Grotius's captors brought him large numbers of books while he was imprisoned in Loevestein Castle between 1619 and 1621. Their willingness eventually provided Grotius with a means of escape – he climbed into an empty chest and his captors, assuming that the chest was fully of heavy books, unwittingly carried him to freedom. See Sherman and Sheils, 'Preface', in Sherman and Sheils, *Prison Writings in Early Modern England*, p. 130.

[25] *Actes and Monuments* (1583), p. 1422.

[26] BL, Add MS 34250 (William Richmont, 'A Trewe Storie of the Catholicke prisoners in Yorke Castle'), fol. 20r.

[27] *Actes and Monuments* (1583), p. 1273.

of books from prisoners, he presents an image of very leaky prisons indeed. What is remarkable is that gaolers were not more vigilant in searching out, confiscating and destroying not only writing materials but also the books in which secret messages and letters of comfort and consolation might be smuggled in and which helped to solidify religious resolve.

Certainly, prisoners and their visitors went to considerable lengths to get books into prisons and, once there, these books were not always easy to sniff out. Occasionally, prison wardens colluded in the devotional reading of the inmates. Samuel Clarke recounted the imprisonment of Edwin Sandys under Mary. Such was the faith of Sandys, who was kept with John Bradford, that his gaoler was soon converted from popery and bringing along a service book on Sundays when the others went to Mass so that they could celebrate the sacrament.[28] More often, books were smuggled in. Robert Glover, for example, was confined to a small, dark dungeon and deprived of daylight and company. He was deprived of paper, pen and ink. Yet even in these strict conditions, Glover apparently 'stole in' his 'new Testament in Latine, & a praier booke', although what use they were in near total darkness is not clear.[29] One Edward Benet was asked by a prisoner in Newgate to 'bring him a new testament, He procuring one of M. Coverdals translation, wrapt it in a hand kerchiefe, saying to George the keeper whiche asked hym what he had, that it was a piece of poudred biefe'.[30] If this seems unlikely, it should be remembered that prisoners had to fend for themselves and relied on food brought in for them. It also allowed opportunities for smuggling in writing materials, with John Philpot, for example, receiving dried ink and a knife inside a roasted pig.[31]

Even when they were subjected to bodily searches, some managed to conceal their writings about them. When it came to John Hooper, Foxe noted how he was able to write his account of his internment whilst in the Fleet prison, even though his manservant was strip-searched for incriminating correspondence.[32] Likewise, John Philpot was searched by a keeper for 'pen, inkhorne, girdle and knife',[33] but before this was done, he went to the privy and 'cast away many a sweet letter', since the authorities

[28] Samuel Clarke, *The Lives of Thirty-Two English Divines Famous in their Generations for Learning and Piety, and most of them Sufferers in the Cause of Christ etc.* (London, 1677), p. 8.
[29] *Actes and Monuments* (1583), p. 1712.
[30] Ibid., p. 2075.
[31] Thomas S. Freeman, 'Publish and Perish: The Scribal Culture of the Marian Martyrs', in Julia Crick and Alexandra Walsham (eds.), *The Uses of Script and Print, 1300–1700* (Cambridge, 2004), p. 243.
[32] *Actes and Monuments* (1583), p. 1506.   [33] Ibid., p. 1813.

might use the letters to track down fellow brethren and apprehend them. Philpot also had a highly original way of disguising his textual remains, shifting his copy of his examination under his codpiece.[34] As Foxe wrote, Philpot's writings were

mervaylously [p]reserved from the sight and hands of hys enemies: who by all maner meanes sought not onely to stop hym from al writing, but also to spoyle and deprive him of that which he had written. For the which cause he was manye tymes stripped and searched in the prison of his keeper: but yet so happily these his writinges were conveyed and hid in places about him or els hys keepers eies so blinded that notwithstanding all this malicious purpose of the Bishops, they are yet remayning and come to light.[35]

Indeed, in stark contrast to the white light of the modern prison, or even the imagined openness proposed in Jeremy Bentham's *Panopticon*, the darkness and gloom of the early modern prison allowed numerous places in which to conceal books, pens and papers.[36] John Philpot hid some of his letters down the side of his bed and threw them out of the window before his cell was searched.[37] John Rogers left his account of his examinations hidden in a dark corner under the stairs. Even when Rogers was denied visitors – presumably in part to stop him handing over any writings he had composed in prison – luck was on his side. After his death, his wife and son went to the prison 'to seeke his bookes and writings' and, just as they were about to give up, his son spotted a 'blacke thing ... lying in a blind corner under a payre of stayres'. Providence, it had transpired, had found a means of protecting the truth as it was preserved in Rogers's writings.[38]

The most common books to find their way into prisons appear to have been Bibles and prayer books. Of course, Catholic prisoners were more likely to smuggle in a Psalter and Protestants an English Testament, but those in search of religious solace wanted and needed these practical books with which to pursue their religious practice. Thus Agnes Bongeor, a martyr, had a Psalter in prison with her,[39] while in 1588, Lord Burghley was informed that Catholic prisoners in Newgate had 'popish books' in their cells.[40] In some cases, books could be sent into prison cells to try to convert the prisoner back to the true religion. Thus Laurence Saunders's

---

[34] Ibid., p. 1814.   [35] Ibid., p. 1830.
[36] On Jeremy Bentham's *Panopticon* (1787), see the comments in Foucault, *Discipline and Punish*, pp. 195–228.
[37] *Actes and Monuments* (1583), p. 1814.   [38] Ibid., p. 1492.   [39] Ibid., p. 2020.
[40] Lake, *The Antichrist's Lewd Hat*, p. 203.

brother sent him a copy of the Meditations of St Bernard, asking him if it was really abhorrent to true religion.[41] The chancellor of Ely, John Fuller, gave the would-be martyrs William Wolsey and Robert Pygot a book of sermons written by Dr Watson to affect their conversion. Wolsey certainly did not fall for what Foxe portrayed as an underhand trick. Instead, he read the book and 'raced with a pen' all the passages he disagreed with. There were evidently a fair few of these since Fuller declared Wolsey 'an obstinate hereticke' and expressed his outrage at his acts of textual vandalism, saying he 'hath quite marred my booke'.[42] Certainly Foxe dwelt on the book as a tool of re-conversion as a dirty trick, noting how prisoners were brought printed copies of Cranmer's recantation in an effort to break their resolve.[43]

But prisons and individual prisoners sometimes possessed collections of books larger than a handful of devotional volumes, be they those of Catholics or Protestants. Some prisoners were able to purchase current titles while behind bars.[44] Others accumulated significant collections. Francis Tregian the younger was able to keep his library while imprisoned in the Fleet Prison, where he died in 1619.[45] Stephen Vallenger, who had been imprisoned for printing Catholic literature, had a personal library of more than a hundred volumes in the Fleet in the late sixteenth century.[46] Many of the volumes which were written in early modern prisons would have been impossible without recourse to books. Perhaps the most remarkable surviving collection is that of John Squier, the Anglican royalist who was imprisoned in Newgate from 1642 to 1646, which was later given to Eton College as part of the collection of Edward Waddington, bishop of Chichester (c.1670–1732). John Squier's library contains 150 items dated between 1642 and 1646, sixty percent of which were signed and dated. The 'vigorous marginalia' on these books reveal his 'vehement engagement with contemporary controversies'.[47] Squier was the vicar of St Leonard's, Shoreditch, and no puritan, but the sheer size of the collection he built up while in prison is suggestive of the range of reading which might be possible while in prison and illustrative of how

---

[41] *Actes and Monuments* (1583), p. 1502.   [42] Ibid., p. 1715.   [43] Ibid., p. 2075.
[44] Raymond, *Pamphlets and Pamphleteering*, p. 37.
[45] See *The Oeconomy of the Fleete*, ed. Augustus Jessop, Camden Society, new ser., 25 (London, 1879), p. 141.
[46] See Anthony Petti, 'Stephen Vallenger (1541–1591)', *Recusant History*, 6 (1962), p. 257. For further examples of prisoners with large collections of books, see Molly Murray, 'Measured Sentences: Forming Literature in the Early Modern Prison', in Sherman and Sheils, *Prison Writings in Early Modern England*, pp. 152, 156.
[47] Connor, 'Malignant Reading', p. 154.

imprisonment did not necessarily mean that one would be cut off from the news. Indeed, while in prison, Squier used his library to write a manuscript tirade against Christopher Davenport's *Deus Natura Gratia* (Lyon, 1634) and to compose another work entitled 'An English Rhapsodie'.[48]

In the imagination, and given the books and light with which to read, the prison cell is a place for reading which is solitary and silent, and almost penitential. This is the world of Thomas More's *Dialogue of Comfort* and the isolated prison cells which housed Bunyan and Milton. Certainly, the idea of prison reading and writing conjured up images of isolation and inner truth, where the book was a tool of revelation, a source which brought light from the literal darkness of the prison to illuminate the spiritual gloom of the outside world. Thus, when John Dod's parishioners suggested that he had placed 'informers and spies' among them because he knew their sins so well, Dod answered that it was simply the word of God that led him 'and that if he was shut up in a dark Vault, where none could come at him, yet allow him but a Bible and a Candle' then he would still be able to preach as he did.[49] And for some, prison reading really was an isolated experience which was recorded only through their tortured writing of painful prayers.[50] Yet such reading frequently intersected with writing, prayer and spiritual contemplation. When he was imprisoned, Thomas More took with him an inexpensive printed Book of Hours which had been manufactured in Paris for English readers. Attached to it – presumably so More might have a complete set of the Psalms while in prison – was a Latin Psalter, and remarkably the composite volume survives. More annotated the volume, using its pages to write a manuscript prayer, as well as making notes relating to spiritual tribulations. To read the Psalms in prison was to affect a particular mode of devotion. This reading was *individual,* in that More read alone, but, as Eamon Duffy has observed, this does not quite mean that his spiritual experience within the prison was *individualistic.* More's marginal notes point to a continued concern for the welfare of the wider spiritual community.[51]

There are a few more extended examples of more individualistic piety and reading, usually drawn from those less saintly than More, whose

[48] Ibid., p. 169.　　[49] Clarke, *The Lives of Thirty-Two English Divines,* p. 173.

[50] On this, see John Stachniewski, *The Persecutory Imagination: English Puritanism and the Literature of Religious Despair* (Oxford, 1991).

[51] Eamon Duffy, *Marking the Hours: English People and Their Prayers, 1240–1570* (New Haven, CT, 2006), pp. 107–18.

thoughts in prison focused principally on the process of their own personal redemption. Such is the case in the chequered life and painful end of John Atherton, the bishop of Waterford and Lismore who was executed in 1640 on charges of sodomy. Even a figure like Atherton could adopt a godly mode of prison piety and reading, despite his Laudian credentials and his role as – in Alan Ford's words – 'Wentworth's personal pit bull terrier', with the responsibility for branding the Irish Church with the Laudian stamp.[52] Perhaps there was never a less likely godly reader but Atherton's life was changed as well as curtailed by his conviction for sodomy. His story was pieced together by Nicholas Bernard, Archbishop Ussher's former chaplain, in an intriguing pamphlet of 1641 – *The Penitent death of a woefull sinner* – a work which placed Atherton's life-story within the framework of a conversion narrative. In this work, it is interesting how far Atherton's prison reading, in both form and content, was a key component of a newly discovered (and frankly hardly believable) godly religiosity. In Bernard's telling, and it is worth stressing that this was a piece of propaganda and damage limitation, which only through somewhat surprising reprinting managed to act as a sort of fire extinguisher to snuff out (some of) his subject's misdemeanours, Atherton saw the errors of his Arminian ways in the weeks before his death and was transformed in prison into a godly reader. He read of the importance of not going back on his faith and was provided with the helpful story of Francis Spira, presumably in the form of Nathaniel Bacon's *The Fearfull Estate of Francis Spira* which was first published in 1638 and which had both 'gripped the Puritan imagination' and acted as a model which others used to comprehend their own religious despair and to frame their own works of spiritual experience.[53]

Atherton clearly read the Bible in prison but he also read more widely. Reading about the troubles of sinners who were penitent in prison helped him escape, or at least to come to terms with, his own sinful state. This process was simultaneously one of affirmation and negation. He had to repent his own ungodly reading and behaviour, lamenting of his 'reading

---

[52] Alan Ford, *James Ussher: Theology, History, and Politics in Early-Modern Ireland and England* (Oxford, 2007), p. 242.

[53] Nicholas Bernard, *The Penitent Death of a Woefull Sinner. Or, The Penitent Death of John Atherton Executed at Dublin the 5. of December 1640. With Some Annotations upon Severall Passages in it* (Dublin, 1641), pp. 8–9. For the citation, see Stachniewski, *Persecutory Imagination*, p. 38; and for a brilliant reading of the cultural impact of the Spira story, see Michael MacDonald, '"The Fearful Estate of Francis Spira": Narrative, Identity and Emotion in Early Modern England', *Journal of British Studies*, 31 (1992), pp. 32–61. For an account of Bernard's narrative, see Peter Marshall, *Mother Leakey and the Bishop: A Ghost Story* (Oxford, 2007), Chapter 5.

of naughty books, [of which he named some, and wished they were burned] viewing of immodest pictures, frequenting of Playes, Drunkennesse, &c'.[54] With such purgation made, he also read puritan books in prison. Bernard continued,

> It is scarce to be beleeved in this little space, how much he had read in some practicall books of our late Divines, [the being not acquainted with whom before, he much bewailed] in speciall that of Doctor Prestons of Gods all-sufficiency, and Bishop Downhams of the Covenant of Grace, [which had been call'd in] did him much good, his conversing with Mr. Fox his book of Martyrs, in viewing the manner of some godly mens deaths, did much animate him against his owne.[55]

The individual reading of godly authors – Downham, Foxe and Preston – helped to transform the lowly sinner. Atherton went on to read the Psalms before his execution (and at his execution, where he asked the people to say a series of Psalms with him[56]), and assimilated the words of godly forebears as his execution loomed. A friend related to him the story of Robert Glover from Foxe.[57] And on seeing him on the morning of his execution, he used the martyr's words 'Oh, he is come! he is come!'[58] Clearly, Bernard was at the very least an active editor, since when he could not bend Atherton's words to make his connections with godly martyrs visible, he shoved in a marginal note, for instance in drawing a comparison between Atherton's desire to read the service book on the morning of his execution and the comfort Rowland Taylor gained by reading the service book throughout his imprisonment.[59] Indeed, Atherton's individual reading intersected with his writing out of his own sins. It was by writing out a relation of his sins shortly before his execution in 1640 that Atherton was able 'at once, as in a glasse, [to] view the face of his soule'. After penning a rough draft of these sins – it must have been quite lengthy – 'he went over them againe with marginall aggravation' and their force was heightened.[60] He wrote letters to his wife and children the night before his execution,[61] and disposed of the books he had with him in prison as tokens to his friends,[62] along with his gloves, girdles and some pious devotions which were inscribed with the name of the intended recipient. Reading was now at the centre of Atherton's imagination, alongside prayer and penitential tears, as he pictured himself at the day of Judgment 'reading before men and angels'.[63] Bernard's account, whatever the truth in it, shows just how prevalent the godly telling of a pious

---

[54] Bernard, *The Penitent Death of a Woefull Sinner*, p. 14.   [55] Ibid., p. 17.   [56] Ibid., pp. 28–9.
[57] Ibid., p. 20.   [58] Ibid., p. 20.   [59] Ibid., p. 21.   [60] Ibid., p. 3.   [61] Ibid., p. 17.
[62] Ibid., p. 22.   [63] Ibid., p. 4.

end had become by the middle of the seventeenth century and how close reading was to the centre of that culture (regardless of the affiliation of the sinner). Indeed, part of the success of Bernard's retelling of Atherton's story can be seen in the cases in which his pamphlet was subsequently handed out to prisoners convicted of heinous crimes – a Welshman who murdered his own mother in 1672, a Shropshire minister executed for infanticide in 1679 – in the hope that they would repent as Atherton was purported to have done.[64]

But reading in prison was not always an individual or an interior practice. Prisons were, for one thing, places where people could learn to read, usually with the help of religiously inclined cellmates or visitors. The Marian martyr Derrick Carver, though not young, entered prison illiterate but 'he could before his death read perfectly'.[65] Prisoners could help others read. Joan West, who came to be a Protestant through hearing sermons but who could not read and yet burned with ambition to read the scriptures, always carried her book with her so that others might read it to her. To this end, she befriended a septuagenarian prisoner in Derby called John Hurt, who was incarcerated for debt, and he 'did for his exercise dayly read unto her some one chapter of the new Testament'.[66] And, of course, Margaret Clitherow famously learned to read in prison, a place which was, for her, as John Mush put it, 'a most happy and profitable school'.[67] Clitherow was a fast learner and was soon gaining spiritual comfort from reading the Rheims New Testament, Thomas à Kempis, Perin's Exercises, and other books.[68]

More experienced readers also read orally and collectively in prison as part of their religious practice in the long hours of confinement. In this their reading often overlapped with prayer and spiritual conversation. Indeed, prisons seemed to conduct the electricity of religious heterodoxy

---

[64] See Marshall, *Mother Leakey and the Bishop*, pp. 152–3. Bernard's pamphlet caused further controversy when it was reprinted in 1710 by Edmund Curll as *The Case of John Atherton* (London, 1710); for which see Marshall, *Mother Leakey and the Bishop*, Chapter 6. For its place in Curll's publishing ventures, see Paul Baines and Pat Rogers, *Edmund Curll, Bookseller* (Oxford, 2007), p. 35.

[65] *Actes and Monuments* (1583), p. 1682. Since Carver was Flemish, it is also possible to read Foxe's account as suggesting that he learned to read English in prison, but the sense of the text appears to suggest that he learned the skills of literacy there. Carver had been arrested in 1554 for holding conventicles at his house.

[66] Ibid., p. 1952.

[67] Peter Lake and Michael Questier, 'Margaret Clitherow, Catholic Nonconformity, Martyrology and the Politics of Religious Change in Elizabethan England', *Past and Present*, 185 (2004), p. 46.

[68] Morris, *The Troubles of Our Catholic Forefathers*, vol. II, p. 393.

Figure 8. 'A Picture describing the maner and place of them which were in bondes for the testimony of the truth, conferring together among themselves', in John Foxe, *Actes and Monuments* (London, 1563), p. 1260. By permission of the Huntington Library, San Marino, California.

and provide forums for (admittedly limited) social exchange. Thus, when Rowland Taylor was sent to prison in King's Bench, he quickly came across John Bradford and they 'lauded God, and continued in prayer, reading, & exhorting one the other'.[69] Robert Smith was imprisoned in Newgate along with other prisoners and they 'had godly conference with themselves, with dayly praying, and publick reading, which they to theyr great comforte used in that home together'. This gave them comfort and it intersected with the letters Smith wrote to friends outside prison.[70] The illustration in Foxe's *Book of Martyrs* (see Figure 8) perfectly captures how prayer and spiritual reading combined and how they were social, collective practices. Smith appears to lead the group, perhaps articulating his spiritual point from the book in front of him. Of the others, one appears in deep meditation and perhaps sorrow, another has his hands clasped

[69] *Actes and Monuments* (1583), p. 1521.   [70] Ibid., p. 1695.

together in the archetypal picture of individual prayer (although in this case his prayer is obviously aided by the oral reading of Smith). On the bottom right (although the image was clearly printed the wrong way around) a man sits and listens but has access to a book, in which his finger is placed, presumably marking a passage, while another listened with the book fully open in front of him. Clearly, there was no tension between reading and such spiritual exhortation. The two figures in the top right of the picture peered over the shoulder of the reader in front of them, their eyes switching back and forth between Smith as the reader leading the prayers and the book of the man in front of them. The image conjured is one with no distinction between read and extempore prayers. Indeed, the centrality of the book in the picture of spiritual edification appears to enhance the godliness of their prayer.[71]

Communality was clearly forced upon prisoners, as they shared cells and beds, but it is interesting how the collective aspects of religious practice are stressed in accounts of prison life. Rowland Taylor, whom we know annotated his Bible, was described by Foxe: 'Being in prison, Doctour Taylour spent all hys tyme in prayer, reading the holy Scriptures, and writing, and preaching, and exhorting the prisoners and such as resorted to him, to repentance and ammendment of life'.[72] Indeed, the problem for the authorities was that by arresting religious dissidents, prisons were soon transformed into seminaries. As Foxe put it:

almost all the prisons in England were become right Christian schooles & Churches, so that there was no greater comfort for Christian harts, then to come to the prisons, to beholde their vertuous conversation, and to heare their prayers, preachings, most godly exhortations, and consolations.[73]

Of course, that prisoners were forced together could have benefits for the authorities. It was a key part of the policy against Catholics, putting together opposing factions (essentially Jesuits and their opponents) and hoping thereby to dissolve any cohesion that the Catholic community might develop. But at the same time, the sociability allowed in prisons could strengthen piety. Some Catholic-dominated prisons took on the character of the cloister, with set times for prayer, reading and study.[74]

---

[71] There is a brief account of this picture and of that of Bilney in Evelyn B. Tribble, 'Godly Reading: John Foxe's *Actes and Monuments* (1583)', in Sabrina Alcorn Baron (ed.), *The Reader Revealed* (Washington, DC, 2001), pp. 38–43.

[72] *Actes and Monuments* (1583), p. 1521. On Taylor as annotator, see John S. Craig, 'The Marginalia of Dr Rowland Taylor', *Historical Research*, 64 (1991), pp. 411–20.

[73] *Actes and Monuments* (1583), p. 1521.   [74] Lake, *The Antichrist's Lewd Hat*, p. 200.

There are even some reports of cases of Catholic parents sending their children into prisons so that they might receive a Catholic education and training.[75] There is need for caution here, as prisons were often represented as sites of sociability and as commonwealths in satirical portraits like William Fennor's comic pamphlet *The Comptors Common-Wealth* (1617). But certainly they were also places of aggressive evangelism where visitors as well as prisoners would engage in collective reading and spirituality.

Indeed, many of the artefacts used to construct the prison as a place of interior piety and solitary individualism are rather more complex when examined critically. This is particularly the case when we consider prison writings as things that were read and circulated. Thus the spiritual journal composed by Thomas Swadlin, the curate of St Botolph's, Aldgate, who was imprisoned in Newgate in the 1640s, was written while he was confined with John Squier and Thomas Soam, the vicar of Staines.[76] Likewise, a closer examination of letters and epistolary networks heightens the sense of collectivity among religious prisoners. These prison writings were also read in prisons and circulated among prisoners. Foxe's *Book of Martyrs* offers a key case study of how letters operated in the godly community and why they mattered. Foxe's martyrs often went to great lengths to get their hands on the materials with which to write letters and showed ingenuity in writing, reading, hiding and distributing letters in prison. Ralph Atherton, for example, must have had a strong constitution if we are to judge by the length of the letter he wrote with his own blood in prison.[77] He was also accused of writing instructions on slips of paper and on boards with chalk asking for books to be smuggled in to him in prison.[78] The scale of the martyrs' prison writing was remarkable. John Bradford was a prolific prison writer who wrote 'so many' letters 'that they are able to fill a booke'.[79] He could write to other prisoners like Laurence Saunders,[80] and his overall output was staggering.

---

[75] Ibid., p. 205.
[76] See Connor, 'Malignant Reading', p. 160. For Swadlin's journal, see Bodleian Library, MS Rawlinson D.1289. For the circulation and reading of such journals, see Andrew Cambers, 'Reading, the Godly, and Self-Writing in England, circa 1580–1720', *Journal of British Studies*, 46 (2007), pp. 796–825.
[77] *Actes and Monuments* (1583), p. 2017.   [78] Ibid., p. 2018.   [79] Ibid., p. 1624.
[80] Ibid., p. 1633.

Such letters sometimes reveal many more instances of godly reading. Although Bradford's writing was apparently secret, it betrays a significant freedom in his ability to read and write. His letter to Sir Thomas Hall, for example, revealed that he had sent him a Latin Testament.[81] Another to Elizabeth Fane came with the promise of a book in the post.[82] To Sir Thomas Hall, he wrote, 'I have sent to you other bookes which I pray you read, I have written your name in them.'[83] Bradford even sent Traves three pairs of spectacles along with a pile of books in which he had written Traves's name.[84] Clearly, the extent of this kind of activity necessitated the existence of illicit book carriers among the godly. The scale of letter writing, as well as the copying of manuscripts – a task performed by poorer prisoners as a way of earning money[85] – was almost industrial.

Prisons were the hubs in an effective network of manuscript distribution. But these letters also performed a more public and arguably more important purpose. As Tom Freeman has argued, they show that it was through the written word, as opposed to the printed word, that imprisoned Protestants were able to maintain relations with their lay following, control local congregations, and communicate with each other.[86] Through their letters, prisoners conducted a significant pastoral ministry in the outside world – according to Foxe, Laurence Saunders's prison letters were 'diversly dispersed and sent abroad to divers of the faythfull congregation of Christ'.[87] Such letters encouraged steadfastness in faith, but importantly for Protestants incarcerated under Mary they did not breed radicalism. Indeed, just like the use of manuscript circulation in the London puritan underground under James I, manuscript was the means with which to stifle dissent among the fringes of one's own group – in this case with Freewillers and Nicodemites – without granting easy polemical opportunities to one's natural opponents.[88] At the same time, these clandestine letters could perform a range of spiritual tasks, from setting out a manifesto of beliefs to providing spiritual support for family, friends and fellow believers and laying down the rules by which followers should live. Through letters, prisoners were able to communicate with each

---

[81] Ibid., p. 1660.   [82] Ibid., p. 1642.   [83] Ibid., p. 1660.   [84] Ibid., p. 1662.

[85] For a series of examples, see Freeman, 'Publish and Perish', p. 241.

[86] Ibid., pp. 235–6.   [87] *Actes and Monuments* (1583), p. 1502.

[88] On this, see Thomas Freeman, 'Dissenters from a Dissenting Church: The Challenge of the Freewillers, 1550–1558', in Peter Marshall and Alec Ryrie (eds.), *The Beginnings of English Protestantism* (Cambridge, 2002), pp. 129–56; Peter Lake and David R. Como, '"Orthodoxy" and Its Discontents: Dispute Settlement and the Production of "Consensus" in the London (Puritan) "Underground"', *Journal of British Studies*, 39 (2000), pp. 34–70.

other and ensure a united front. One such letter was entitled, 'To the
brethren remaining in captivitie of the flesh, and dispearsed abroad in
sundry prisons'.[89]

The books and letters of the Marian martyrs were circulated in the
outside world and read communally. They seemed to confirm that
suffering, in the form of imprisonment, was a central part of Protestant
religious self-identity. This is particularly the case when we consider what
happened to such letters on the one hand as they were transformed into
printed volumes, such as Henry Bull's collection of the letters of the
martyrs and Foxe's great compendium,[90] and on the other as they were
held onto and treasured by family members and religious sympathizers.
And the letters themselves reveal the spiritual significance of post-mortem
gifts of books. Gifts of books and writings from religious prisoners gained
added spiritual significance. Weeping, Rowland Taylor 'gave to his wife a
booke of the Church service, set out by Kyng Edward, which in the time
of his imprisonment he daylye used'. And he gave his son a Latin book
with the sayings of the old martyrs, at the end of which he had written his
own will and testament.[91] They were treasured personal mementoes but
also documents of communal faith, and many were read aloud among
communities in search of spiritual support.

As should be clear, it was not simply the cultured world of the salon or
the humdrum world of the household which might be venues for sociable
reading but also the semi-public world of the prison. This survived well
beyond the seventeenth century. Although eighteenth-century sociable
reading was often described – and fictionalized – as a genteel enterprise,
whether situated within the walls of the household or those of the gentleman's club, there are many examples drawn from a wider social spectrum.
Although they clearly had social hierarchies of their own, prisons offered a
potential venue for sociable religious reading which criss-crossed normal
social patterns of class interaction. Such patterns of reading in prison were
not confined to early Protestants; they re-emerged after the Restoration
and became a crucial part of the identity of radicals. Reflecting upon a
stretch in prison in the 1820s, the radical bookseller James Watson
recalled, 'The evenings I usually spent with another fellow prisoner',
'For three or four hours after dark we read to each other'.[92] This might

---

[89] *Actes and Monuments* (1583), p. 1726.
[90] Henry Bull (ed.), *Certain most Godly, Fruitful and Comfortable Letters of such True Saintes and Holy Martyres* (London, 1564).
[91] *Actes and Monuments* (1583), p. 1524.
[92] See William St Clair, *The Reading Nation in the Romantic Period* (Cambridge, 2004), p. 395.

not be godly reading, but the continuation of collective reading by radicals in prisons persisted in the imagination.

In part, this association was fed by the more public set-pieces of reading associated with prisons, which include occasions on which prisoners were read to to effect conversion, the times when prisoners managed to stage public readings to those outside their walls, and in particular the final hours of a prisoner's life when he (or she) was taken back into the outside world to be executed. The book played a part in the staged religious debates which were held in gaols. Despite the fact that many books were clearly smuggled into prisons, Protestants could use the lack of books as a reason not to dispute with Catholic opponents when they saw no advantage in it. John Bradford and some of his fellow prisoners refused a disputation in part because they had been incarcerated for '8. or 9. moneths, where we have had no bookes, no paper, no penne, no inke, or convenient place for study'.[93] But denying prisoners the books they would need in such disputations did not necessarily work. In the disputation against him, Edmund Campion was allowed only to refer to a Bible, whereas his opponents had access to whatever books they wanted, but it was still far from clear who actually 'won' the debate.[94] At York Castle, the Catholic prisoners who were preached at by a series of puritan preachers, including John Favour, Edmund Bunny, Alexander Cooke, the apostate Thomas Bell and Richard Crakanthorpe, faced the dual hindrance of having books taken away from them and used against them. Books were taken away from prisoners while the preachers used them in their armoury against Catholicism as bulwarks of the Protestant truth. Thus in the staged debates at the King's Manor, Robert Cooke stood 'at a table [with] divers bookes before him' to refute Catholic doctrine. Later he opened a volume of Bellarmine to dispute the existence of Purgatory.[95] The physical book carried a symbolic and cultural value in such debates in addition to the authority provided by its contents.

All this is not to say that the traffic of such public readings moved steadily in one direction. Instead, prisoners often exploited opportunities to spread their faith through public reading. Prisoners read and preached to those beyond their cell walls, often attracting large audiences. Samuel

---

[93] *Actes and Monuments* (1583), p. 1470.   [94] Lake, *The Antichrist's Lewd Hat*, p. 258.

[95] BL, Add MS 34250 (William Richmont, 'A Trewe Storie of the Catholicke prisoners in Yorke Castle'), fols. 22v–23r.

Eaton held conventicles for up to seventy people in Newgate.[96] John Lilburne used his imprisonment as a way of extending his fame. In Newgate, wrote William Prynne, Lilburne stood 'with the Statutes before him reading and interpreting the law to the crowds that came to visit him'.[97] Such reading also overlapped with preaching and many godly prisoners, such as Christopher Love, both preached and read from behind bars, instructing their followers who came to hear them.[98] Such examples might be multiplied for the turbulent middle of the seventeenth century, when prisons were particularly overcrowded and a polarized society meant that gaolers were perhaps more likely than usual to bend the rules or allow greater personal freedom. But they were not confined to this period. Again, Foxe provides a number of similar instances. At Lancaster, George Marsh and his cellmate Thomas Warbarton spent each day kneeling, praying and reading. They were allowed to read and pray with the English litany twice each day 'both before noone and after, with other praiers moe, & also read every day certain chapters of the Bible, commonly towards night'. In fact, they read 'all these thinges with so high & loude a voyce, that the people without in the streetes' could hear them read and would often in the evening sit down under their windows at night and listen to the godly reading.[99] Certainly such lenient treatment was not tolerated at higher levels – in this case it drew a severe rebuke from the bishop of Chester – but it was hard to secure compliance without the support of wardens.

While the authorities had a modicum of control regarding behaviour in prisons, they had less when it came to the ultimate sanction against religious dissidents – execution. On such occasions, the state used reading and performance to symbolize justice, power, and their religious authority. The executed would be encouraged to confess, and to make a penitent speech before their execution, as well as to read the Lord's Prayer or Ten Commandments in an affirmation that the authority which put them to death was sanctioned by God and the law. Executions are often thought of as performances but they were also texts: these occasions were permeated by writing and print, with tickets being printed and pamphlets produced which detailed the crime and the criminal's sticky end. Occasionally, the state made a public text out of the convicted, burning their books along

[96] Connor, 'Malignant Reading', p. 162.
[97] William Prynne, *The Lyar Confounded* (London, 1645), p. 22.
[98] BL, Sloane MS 3945 ('The Life of Mr Christopher Love'), fo. 100v.
[99] *Actes and Monuments* (1583), p. 1565.

with them, or, as in the case of Edmund Campion, mocking them – in a stark inversion (and sick joke) of Campion's membership of the Society of Jesus, he had the words 'Campion the Seditious Jesuit' stuck to his hat.[100] Such, of course, was the theory, but, as Peter Lake and Michael Questier have made abundantly clear in a series of essays, such occasions also flirted with distortion both in the manipulation of the captive audience at the last dying speech and in the transformation of the whole event in print afterwards. Just as that other grand textual set piece, the book-burning, had a tendency to backfire in the faces of those who had arranged them, so spectacular executions were often hijacked by the criminal making a last stand.[101]

Their transportation to the place of execution offered an opportunity for godly reading as a demonstration of faith. For some, simply carrying a book under one's arm was a sign of religious identity. In a rare depiction within Foxe's *Book of Martyrs*, two of the twenty-two Christians apprehended in and around Colchester and taken to London carried books with them (Figure 9).[102]

Reading was amongst the things that martyrs would do on their way to the stake as a visual sign that their faith had not been defeated. Alongside singing Psalms, or just humming their tunes, and, of course, saying prayers and quoting scripture, reading from a Bible, or from a Protestant prayer book, carried symbolic capital since such public reading in the face of adversity might negate opponents who claimed that their faith had wavered or had been defeated. George Eales, for example, was bound to a

---

[100] Lake, *The Antichrist's Lewd Hat*, 243.

[101] See Peter Lake, 'Popular Form, Puritan Content? Two Puritan Appropriations of the Murder Pamphlet from Mid-Seventeenth-Century London', in Anthony Fletcher and Peter Roberts (eds.), *Religion, Culture and Society in Early Modern Britain: Essays in Honour of Patrick Collinson* (Cambridge, 1994), pp. 313–34; Peter Lake, 'Deeds against Nature: Cheap Print, Protestantism and Murder in Early Seventeenth-Century England', in Kevin Sharpe and Peter Lake (eds.), *Culture and Politics in Early Stuart England* (London, 1994), pp. 257–83, 361–7; Peter Lake and Michael Questier, 'Agency, Appropriation and Rhetoric under the Gallows: Puritans, Romanists and the State in Early Modern England', *Past and Present*, 153 (1996), pp. 64–107; Peter Lake and Michael Questier, 'Puritans, Papists, and the "Public Sphere" in Early Modern England: The Edmund Campion Affair in Context', *Journal of Modern History*, 72 (2000), pp. 587–627; Peter Lake, '"A Charitable Christian Hatred": The Godly and Their Enemies in the 1630s', in Christopher Durston and Jacqueline Eales (eds.), *The Culture of English Puritanism, 1560–1700* (Basingstoke, 1996), pp. 145–83, 301–7; Lake, *The Antichrist's Lewd Hat*. On book-burnings, see David Cressy, 'Book Burning in Tudor and Stuart England', *Sixteenth Century Journal*, 36 (2005), pp. 359–74; and Cyndia Susan Clegg, 'Burning Books as Propaganda in Jacobean England', in Andrew Hadfield (ed.), *Literature and Censorship in Renaissance England* (Basingstoke, 2001), pp. 165–86.

[102] *Actes and Monuments* (1583), pp. 1972–3. They had been ordered to bring their illegal books with them.

Figure 9. 'The Picture of xxii. godly and faythfull Christians, apprehended about Colchester, prisoned together in one band, and so with three leaders at the most, brought up to London', in John Foxe, *Actes and Monuments* (1583), p. 1973. By permission of the Huntington Library, San Marino, California.

hurdle and carried behind a sled, yet managed to hold onto a 'Psalme booke, of the whiche he read very devoutly all the way with a loud voyce'.[103] Martyrs were keen to display their religiosity through reading when they were brought to the place of execution. John Tooly was led to the gallows at Charing Cross, and although he was 'standing upon the Carte' he 'readde a certayne prayer in a printed booke, and two other prayers written in two severall papers'.[104] Once he had finished reading them, he gave the book to an officer who stood by 'and wylled hym to deliver it to one Haukes, saying that it was hys Booke'[105] – this was Thomas Hawkes, another martyr – and one of the papers to Robert Bromley. Incarceration and the prospect of execution seem not to have deterred the godly from reading and circulating their books and papers. Instead, they ratcheted up the importance of demonstrating their faith through reading and being seen to be reading.

[103] Ibid., p. 2010.   [104] Ibid., p. 1583.   [105] Ibid., p. 1584.

Such reading continued to the execution itself and indicated, often comically, how the intentions of the authorities were frequently subverted, even if they ultimately achieved their bloody goal. In the reign of Henry VIII, the London merchant Thomas Sommers was condemned for owning Lutheran books. His punishment 'was that he should ride from the tower into Cheapside carying a new booke in his hand and be hanged with bookes round about him'. Neatly sidestepping the instructions of the bishop's officers, who wanted to attach the books to his clothes with strings, Sommers instead had them strung together and wore them over his neck. When instructed to throw them into the fire, however, Sommers threw them over the fire and they were snapped up by a lucky bystander.[106] Likewise Derrick Carver, awaiting burning in a barrel in Lewes, was thrown a book to be burnt with him. Carver, however, threw it back to the people in an attempt to spread the word and spare the book from the fire.[107] Although some were thwarted in their efforts to pass on their books, such as John Noyes who was denied his last request that his wife and children be given his psalter,[108] others managed to continue reading right up until the very end. In so doing, whether by singing Psalms or reading from a book, they were actively transforming the scaffold into a text. To be sure, such events were not confined to godly Protestants, and Anne Dillon has written about the importance of the scaffold as text and image in English Catholic culture, exploring the printed image of martyrdom in Richard Verstegan's work. Indeed, many of the images of Catholic martyrdoms are actually closely aligned to notions of godly book-based religiosity, as the persecutors read at devout Catholic martyrs. For instance, an image which shows imprisoned priests being taken on a hurdle to the gallows also shows in vivid detail a Protestant minister reading from a book at the priest (see Figure 10).

Such images were copied and modified, reappearing in Giovanni Battista de Cavalleriis's *Ecclesiae Anglicanae Trophaea* (Rome, [1584]), a book of engravings which itself transmuted the martyr murals of the English College at Rome into print. These images furthered the

---

[106] Ibid., p. 1207. There are, of course, examples of people being burnt along with their books and of books taking a symbolic place in their punishment. In 1530, for example, four booksellers were punished by their sitting backwards on horses and riding through London, with their coats 'pinned thick' with copies of Tyndale's *New Testament* and other heretical books as well as with placards detailing the nature of their crimes. See Susan Brigden, *London and the Reformation* (Oxford, 1989), p. 183.

[107] *Actes and Monuments* (1583), p. 1682. [108] Ibid., p. 2022.

Figure 10. William Allen, *Historia del Glorioso Martirio* (Macerata, 1583), Plate 5.
© The British Library Board. Shelfmark 4705.a.8.

association of the Protestant authorities with the book, as volumes were again thrust in the faces of pained prisoners (see Figure 11).[109]

Through a combination of media and modes of communication, the image of the prisoner comforted by reading the book was spread far and wide and it gained currency as a mode of devotion, both among Catholics and Protestants. The models of printed books were particularly influential, whether drawn from Bull's *Certain most Godly, Fruitful and Comfortable Letters* (London, 1564) or Foxe's *Actes and Monuments*. Such works show that prison reading and writing had a lasting impact in sustaining godly culture which continued long after the turbulence of the middle of the sixteenth century, as successive generations of godly readers were sustained in their faith by reading the prison writings of the Marian martyrs. Nehemiah Wallington's volume of 'Coppies of profitable and Comfortable Letters' began with a series of letters extracted from Foxe's martyrology, including those by Saunders, Hooper, Haukes, Bradford,

---

[109] See Anne Dillon, *The Construction of Martyrdom in the English Catholic Community, 1535–1603* (Aldershot, 2002), p. 219.

Figure 11. Giovanni Battista de Cavalleriis, *Ecclesiae Anglicanae Trophaea*
(Rome, [1584]), Plate 32. © The British Library Board.
Shelfmark 551.e.35.

Robert Smith, Robert Glover, John Careless, John Rough and Cuthbert
Symson. These letters of Marian martyrs acted as a necessary preface
to the letters of the godly from the seventeenth century, which in turn
benefited from their adhesion to this pious tradition.[110] Ever one to
provide clues as to books he read, Wallington notes that he returned to
this volume, which he had composed in the 1630s, early in the 1650s and
again before he died. As if to cement an earlier Protestant tradition with
that of seventeenth-century puritanism, Wallington's son-in-law Jonathan
Houghton signed the volume when he acquired it after Wallington's
death in 1658. Likewise, Henry Newcome drew comfort from reading
about John Careless when he wrote his own diary, a text which was

---

[110] BL, Sloane MS 922 (Nehemiah Wallington, 'Letters on Religious Topics').

treasured in his own family and helped to sustain godly nonconformity. Indeed, Foxe seemed to be aware of the potential cultural value of these works, since he edited many of them in order to preserve the integrity of the Protestant tradition in the new context of the puritan movement.[111] The running title for John Bradford's letters crafted them as his 'ghostly letters', signifying their ability to pass on the message to be read by the godly long after his death.

CONCLUSION

In exploring the prison, this chapter has confronted a space which is defined by confinement and which looms large in the imagination as a place where sociability is denied. But, as we have seen, although many prison-keepers attempted to stop prisoners associating with each other, in practice such a desire was fruitless: godly prisoners sought each other out to engage in the devotional imperatives of collective prayer and social reading. These activities mirrored those they had practised in the household – after all, religious prisoners wanted to demonstrate that their faith would not be broken by confinement or argument or torture. Such collectivity appears to have been the hallmark of prison reading and prison writing. It was both documented in and sustained by key works, notably Foxe's *Actes and Monuments*, which outlined an enduring model of godly prison reading that was continually revisited and refashioned over the long seventeenth century and beyond. In turn, these very printed works also show just how important the reading, writing, copying and circulation of manuscript accounts was in the sustenance of godly religiosity.

At the same time, despite the strength of these modes of collective piety as they were highlighted in collections of lives and martyrologies, prisons were also places of individual piety and reading and prisoners invoked well-known models of solitary piety and reading while inside their walls. Although they might seem incompatible, these starkly divergent ways of worshipping God were in fact practised by the same people – but it is important to note that given the choice and the opportunity (since prisons were hardly stuffed full of godly people) the preference of the godly was

---

[111] The online Variorum edition of Foxe's *Book of Martyrs* includes annotations detailing which letters were changed and how, such as the letters to Lady Elizabeth Fane. See www.hrionline.ac.uk/johnfoxe/.

for sociability in prayer and reading rather than for solitary confinement. However much it diverged from everyday godly practices, the representation of piety and reading in prisons, in combination with that in the seemingly private spaces of the household like the closet, played a crucial part in enabling the crystallization of the stereotype of the individual puritan reader and believer.

CHAPTER 7

Conclusion

THE PRACTICE OF PIETY

At the top of the title page of Lewis Bayly's *The Practise of Pietie* (Figure 12), one of the most frequently published and read of all puritan books throughout the seventeenth century, the duties of the pious man were illustrated in graphic form: he was to read and pray.

This encyclopedic guide to godly living was first published at the start of the seventeenth century. Cheap and accessible, *The Practise of Pietie* was a remarkable bestseller: its impact was felt across England, Europe and North America and its fame continued throughout the long seventeenth century and beyond. It was almost continually in print, with at least fifty-seven editions published in England between 1612 and 1728. As well as gaining a large audience in puritan New England, it was translated into Welsh, French, Hungarian, Romanian, Italian and Dutch. In Germany, where it appealed to pietists, this puritan book achieved spectacular fame, going through at least sixty-nine editions before 1743 and becoming 'the most popular English book in Germany in the seventeenth century'.[1] The continued resonance of Bayly's book can even be seen in an engraving of 1736 by William Hogarth (Figure 13), which depicted a young woman attempting to resist the advances of an aggressive suitor. In the scene, the woman knocks over her dressing table when she tries to escape – from it

---

[1] See Peter Damrau, *The Reception of English Puritan Literature in Germany* (London, 2006), pp. 59–70, quotation at p. 66. On the publication of *The Practise of Pietie* in England, see Ian Green, *Print and Protestantism in Early Modern England* (Oxford, 2000), esp. pp. 348–51 and appendix. For an extended reading of the title page, see Matthew P. Brown, *The Pilgrim and the Bee: Reading Rituals and Book Culture in Early New England* (Philadelphia, PA, 2007), pp. 102–6. Brown contrasts the individuality of the graphic representation of reading with the collectivity of the biblical message at the bottom of the title page, with its reference to Joshua leading the Israelites into battle in Exodus 17.

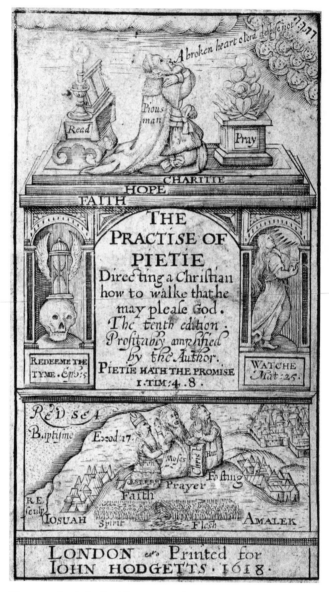

Figure 12. Lewis Bayly, *The Practise of Pietie* (1618 edn), frontispiece.
© Trustees of the British Museum.

Figure 13. William Hogarth, *Before* (1736) (detail). © Trustees of the British Museum.

falls a copy of *The Practise of Pietie*, its descent mirroring the woman's loss of innocence.[2]

In connecting the activities of reading and prayer, Bayly's illustrated title page brings to mind many of the themes which have been discussed in this book, themes which, as I have shown, were somewhere near the heart of the culture of puritanism. It positioned reading alongside prayer as the two uppermost duties of a Christian. It was written by an early Stuart moderate puritan – Bayly was a bishop, a conforming puritan who nevertheless espoused godly modes of piety – yet, despite a brief hiatus in the mid-seventeenth century, it remained a popular book and guide to a godly life until the end of the period, perhaps in part because of a story which suggested that Bayly had not penned the work himself but had taken it in lieu of payment from the widow of the godly minister who had written it.[3] The book was read by individuals as a guide to private prayer and meditation, as well as by families as part of their household piety.

---

[2] William Hogarth, *Before* (1736). See Mark Hallett and Christine Riding, *Hogarth* (London, 2006), pp. 76–9. The other books on the table and in the drawer are labelled 'Novels' and 'Rochester' and presumably also symbolize the corruption of innocence.

[3] See Charles James Stranks, *Anglican Devotion: Studies in the Spiritual Life of the Church of England between the Reformation and the Oxford Movement* (London, 1961), p. 40.

Passed between believers and handed down through families, it helped to shape and structure generations of Protestant piety.

The central argument of this book is that, both in their domestic piety and in more overtly public displays of their religiosity, whether in private or public spaces, puritans read in ways which were for the most part communal in nature and public in orientation. Sustaining such an argument challenges some long-held and deeply cherished historiographical and sociological ideas about puritanism, reading and modernity. These will be discussed below, but the argument also raises an important point about continuity and change in religious history which can be tackled before we move on.

As we have seen, the sorts of social, collective and public reading practised by the godly are illustrative not of a religious culture with significant points of contact with medieval Catholicism, but of one which adopted collective practices for spiritual and political ends. Rather than suggesting that puritan piety had still to be cleansed of the last remnants of traditional religion, such collective reading, when considered in detail, tells us rather more about the godly than some might expect. In particular, by demonstrating that collective reading was a deliberate choice for the godly, the book has highlighted how such reading practices were adopted as a means of displaying their religiosity publicly while at the same time serving to separate the godly community culturally from the population at large.

It was for these reasons that the godly returned again and again to a relatively narrow strand of religious reading material throughout the period covered in this book – this was a canon of early Stuart English puritan devotional literature which arguably fed into a wider corpus of mainstream Protestant literature over the eighteenth century. Rather than developing a strong allegiance towards new books, the godly used those books whose religious and ideological positioning was well known to fashion their religious identity. Thus it is certainly not the case that a nonconformist reading, for instance, Lewis Bayly's book after the Restoration did so in exactly the same way or for exactly the same reasons as those who had read it earlier in the seventeenth century. The reading of old books is not evidence of being hopelessly out of touch and behind the times. Instead – and it is important that such an insight has been gained through the focus upon *how* their reading was practised and by thinking about what the godly were *doing* through their collective reading – I have shown how they could simultaneously be claiming legitimacy for the practice of their piety by deliberately evoking the early Stuart past and, more significantly, how they used such reading to enact their differences culturally from the established Church of England. Such collective reading (particularly of the Bible) served a very useful function in the period after the Restoration since it could provide a platform for distinctly evangelical sorts of piety while at the same time it was relatively easy to defend as orthodox practice.

Interrogating such apparent continuities has two significant consequences. First, historians interested in the impact of books and their reception need to open their eyes to the fact that books have a rather long shelf life. They were picked up and reread by successive generations and their messages constantly reinterpreted, often in significantly changed circumstances. This might seem obvious but it has too often been overlooked by those eager to trace early readers of first editions or to find examples of those who read in the political context in which an author wrote. Without denying the importance of such immediate forms of reception, the reading of old books and of new editions of old books also has a history. Among social and cultural historians, it is fashionable to talk of the recycling, refashioning and reimagining of the past which was emerging in early modern England: historians of reading should take notice of the vast body of information that remains to be tapped of the readership, reception and usage of old books.[4]

The second consequence is a wider one, which applies not only to the study of puritanism but also to that of post-Reformation English religion more generally. Put simply, the historian's job is to identify, explain and describe change. That such changes, the things which distinguish one moment in the past from another, are frequently complicated – the reasons for the early modern witch-craze, say, or the causes of the French Revolution – is well-known. But it is rather less well understood or theorized that continuities might be both as interesting and as important as changes. This book has shown that apparent continuities can be interrogated using categories imported from sociology and the history of the book to show that those apparent continuities had meanings beyond simple inertia.

---

[4] See, for instance, Daniel Woolf, *The Social Circulation of the Past: English Historical Culture 1500–1730* (Oxford, 2003).

Unravelling collective reading as a tool of cultural separation has shown how important these continuities can be, particularly in the context of the evolution of beliefs and practices in the seventeenth century. It builds upon an argument I made with specific reference to the case of John Rastrick – for whom reading was a means of dividing his spiritual friends, whatever their formal religious allegiance, from those he saw as his anti-Christian enemies – that an evangelical subculture after the Restoration used the reading of works of early Stuart piety in order to promote their own distinctive style of evangelical religious identity.[5] This book has shown how such rereading and refashioning of religious identity using a series of key works was characteristic of puritans throughout the period. A similar argument might be made about the apparent continuities in the English Reformation or with regard to arguments about the nature of post-Reformation English Catholicism. Using the tools of the history of the book to interrogate the character of and motivations behind apparent continuities in religious behaviour helps us to move beyond a rather fixed notion that continuity and change are either necessarily opposite or straightforward categories.[6]

THE IMAGE OF THE GODLY READER

In the course of writing this book and of revealing the extent of collective reading among the godly, the need to answer a further related question has become apparent. This is not, given the overwhelming evidence charting social reading among puritans, simply *how* have historians and others got away with characterizing the godly as archetypes of interior piety and individualism, but *why* should commentators wish to focus so strongly on the personal and individualistic elements both of advanced Protestant piety and of reading practices? I have to admit to having no straightforward answer to the evolution of such standpoints – arguably if

---

[5] See Andrew Cambers and Michelle Wolfe, 'Reading, Family Religion, and Evangelical Identity in Late Stuart England', *Historical Journal*, 47 (2004), p. 896.

[6] Admittedly, such an approach would follow the recent post-revisionist strain in studies of the politics and culture of the English Reformation. See, for instance, Ethan H. Shagan, *Popular Politics and the English Reformation* (Cambridge, 2003); and Peter Marshall, *Beliefs and the Dead in Reformation England* (Oxford, 2002). It might, however, also breathe new life into the debate over the nature of post-Reformation Catholicism, and provide a means of revisiting the debate between John Bossy and Christopher Haigh. See John Bossy, *The English Catholic Community 1570–1850* (London, 1975); Christopher Haigh, 'The Fall of a Church or the Rise of a Sect? Post-Reformation Catholicism in England', *Historical Journal*, 21 (1978), pp. 182–6; Christopher Haigh, 'The Continuity of Catholicism in the English Reformation', *Past and Present*, 93 (1981), pp. 37–69.

there was a simple answer the matter might have been dealt with long ago – but rather a series of reflections and suggestions concerning the historiography of puritanism, reading and modernity.

Part of the answer lies in the ways the godly have been represented in graphic form. At odds with the social practices of religious reading outlined in this book, these images consistently presented reading as an individual, solitary and silent enterprise. As such, they helped to solidify the evolution of historiographical assumptions which have linked puritanism, individual and silent reading, and religious interiority. Despite the distance between such representations and actual practice, graphic images of godly readers dovetail neatly with the evolution of a dual tendency to view privacy and individualism as precursors and agents of modernity, as well as with the propensity to connect puritanism with that modernity.

The image of the godly reader was a key licit image in a culture torn between the enthusiastic deployment of graphic images of religious themes (ostensibly for educational purposes) and anxiety about the use of such religious imagery.[7] Although this book has included several images in which godly reading was portrayed as a collective social enterprise, the sheer rarity of these images is striking. While there are significant late medieval examples which represent collective spirituality and collective reading as practically inseparable activities – Holbein's sketch of the More family reading Books of Hours as part of their household piety, for example[8] – there are in fact very few images of godly sociable reading. Images of Protestant sociability are instead generally focused on sermons and prayers. Thus those clergy who were ejected in 1662 were presented collectively in some of the compilations of their farewell sermons in Warhol-esque images which portrayed them as a succession of identikit godly preachers.[9] And those images in Foxe's *Actes and Monuments* which appear to capture moments of collective reading are often better thought of as illustrating a form of religious sociability based around the sermon,

---

[7] For this issue, see Patrick Collinson, *From Iconoclasm to Iconophobia: The Cultural Impact of the Second English Reformation*, Stenton Lecture 1985 (Reading, 1986); and direct and indirect responses in Tessa Watt, *Cheap Print and Popular Piety, 1550–1640* (Cambridge, 1991); and Alexandra Walsham, *Providence in Early Modern England* (Oxford, 1999).

[8] Hans Holbein the Younger, *Design for the More Family Group*, 1526–7, Kunstmuseum Basel, Kupferstichkabinett, 1662.31. For a convincing reading of this sketch, see Eamon Duffy, *Marking the Hours: English People and Their Prayers, 1240–1570* (New Haven, CT, 2006), p. 58.

[9] *The Farewell Sermons of the Late London Ministers, Preached August 17th. 1662. By Mr. Calamy. Dr. Manton. Mr. Caryl. Mr. Case. Mr. Jenkins. Mr. Baxter. Dr. Jacomb. Dr. Bates. Mr. Watson. Mr. Lye. Mr. Mede. Mr. Ash, Fun. Ser.* (London, 1662). For other sets of the 'farewell sermons', published with different titles and different collective portraits, see Wing C243, C5638, E3632, L2905A, and S2257.

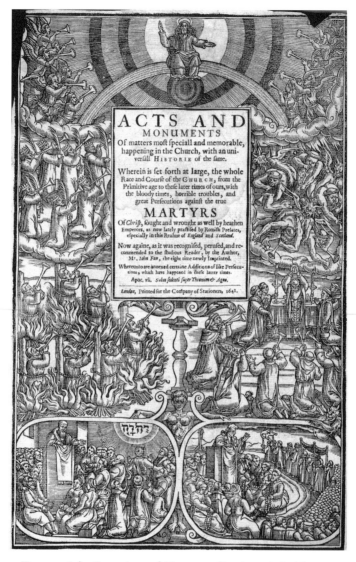

Figure 14. John Foxe, *Acts and Monuments* (London, 1641), title page.
© Trustees of the British Museum.

in which reading formed an essentially subsidiary function. In a detail at
the bottom left of the title page of *Acts and Monuments* [Figure 14] which
was ever-present in the early editions, for example, the members of the
true church listened attentively to the bearded Protestant preacher.

While many of the hearers focused their gaze upon the preacher, for others the sermon was a more dynamic experience: on the right, three men knelt before the light of God, while others had books before them. Two men on the left exchanged words while they held the book open. The woman opposite them held her book open and pointed with her finger to the point in the text, while another woman faced her and perhaps talked a little. And immediately to the preacher's left hand, a man listened attentively while he turned the pages of the book. Although the image clearly tells us something about collective reading, it does so within the context of the sermon: an event which combined preaching, listening, reading, conversation and note-taking.

In fact, the majority of visual representations presented the godly as individual readers. This seems to have been true beyond the confines of the book. To those whose families could afford them, funeral monuments offered opportunities for the representation of godly identity through their presentation as individual readers. Although far from unique to the godly, there are examples of gentry monuments – like that of Sir Thomas Lucy III (d. 1640) – which highlighted their subject's bookishness by showing them leaning on piles of closed books.[10] Others – in particular writers, preachers and book collectors – were represented as readers, entombed with books, whether they reclined with their fingers inside a book, knelt and prayed in front of piles of books or had their coffins depicted as resting upon clasped books.[11] In the vast majority of such monuments, the subject was represented as a solitary reader in a manner which was much more suggestive of individual than of familial piety. The same appears to have been true of the books which chronicled the lives of the godly. Despite the resolute sociability *described* in biographies, how-to books, instructional sermons and so on, in the main the godly were

[10] The monument is reproduced and discussed in Felicity Heal and Clive Holmes, *The Gentry in England and Wales, 1500–1700* (Basingstoke, 1994), pp. 267–8.

[11] See the numerous examples in Nigel Llewellyn, *Funeral Monuments in Post-Reformation England* (Cambridge, 2000). The monument to Thomas Bodley at Merton College, Oxford, is framed by two stacks of clasped books, which resemble pillars. See J. Woodward, 'The Monument to Sir Thomas Bodley in Merton College Chapel', *Bodleian Library Record*, 5 (1954–6), pp. 189–96. Likewise Laurence Humphrey's monument included a ceiling which, on closer inspection, is composed of open books, on which (and for further examples), see Stefanie A. Knöll, *Creating Academic Communities: Funeral Monuments to Professors at Oxford, Leiden and Tübingen 1580–1700* (n.p., 2003). Funeral monuments as imagined in book illustrations continued the theme. The frontispiece to Thomas Fuller's *Abel Redevivus: or, The Dead yet Speaking* (London, 1651), in which he collected biographical sketches of Protestant divines, presented the skeleton of the mortal author underneath a canopy of living books. For further examples, see Dora Thornton, *The Scholar in His Study: Ownership and Experience in Renaissance Italy* (New Haven, CT, 1997), p. 61.

depicted as solitary spiritual travellers, making their way through the post-Reformation landscape alone. Those who had an engraving alongside their biography in Samuel Clarke's compendiums bear witness to this. James Ussher's portrait included an open book on a desk in front of him, along with a pen and skull: the famed author and book collector was shown as a solitary religious writer. John Carter was depicted in action, with book open and hourglass turned, and with his hands slightly raised in prayer. Herbert Palmer was presented with a book open on a cushion in front of him, ready to preach. In these likenesses, the godly were depicted as preachers and their books were props to that image. Such representations are understandable, but they had the effect of isolating the individual with the book and, despite the connection between the reader and the preacher, of suggesting that the practice of reading was individual.[12] Such images were repeated in numerous engravings and woodcuts of the godly throughout the seventeenth century. They became the stock images of godly preachers throughout the seventeenth century, from sober divines like Richard Baxter to radical puritans like Christopher Love.

Indeed, if just one image had to be selected as illustrating the extent to which the puritan was figured as a solitary reader, it would surely be the famous 'sleeping portrait' of John Bunyan in *The Pilgrim's Progress*.[13] In this engraving, the premise of the book was illustrated in graphic form: Bunyan sleeps and dreams, his vision being that of a man walking, holding open a book, and questioning his own salvation. After the fifth edition of 1680, the work was embellished with further illustrations which faithfully depicted scenes from the book and highlighted the picture of the spiritual traveller as an individual reader. And these images have endured, helping to shape the representation of the godly reader ever since.[14]

The image of the godly reader presents something of a paradox: individuals described as standard-bearers of collective piety were frequently depicted as though their faith and their reading were purely solitary endeavours, designed to communicate with God rather than with other mortals. Such representations, although influential in shaping our

---

[12] See Samuel Clarke, *The Lives of Thirty-Two English Divines Famous in their Generations for Learning and Piety, and most of them Sufferers in the Cause of Christ etc.* (London, 1677), pp. 132 (Carter), 183 (Palmer), 277 (Ussher).

[13] John Bunyan, *The Pilgrim's Progress* (3rd edn, London, 1679), frontispiece.

[14] See, for example, William Blake, 'Christian Reading in His Book' (c.1824), in John Bunyan, *The Pilgrim's Progress* (Limited Editions Club edn, New York, 1941). The reproduction of Blake's watercolour on the cover of John Coffey and Paul C. H. Lim (eds.), *The Cambridge Companion to Puritanism* (Cambridge, 2008), for instance, helps to perpetuate such associations.

picture of puritan piety, fail to give depth to reading as a social practice. Interestingly, it seems that – with a few exceptions – the styles of piety as they have been described throughout this book were not represented in graphic form until they had passed out of common practice, if we are to judge from the likes of Alexander Carse's famous depiction of a rural family reading the Bible at home on a Sunday morning.[15]

PURITANISM, SILENT READING AND MODERNITY

The image of puritanism in graphic form is arguably among the reasons which have allowed commentators to characterize it as an individual, personal and otherworldly faith. But there is clearly more to any full answer to the evolution of such settled historiographical standpoints. For some, true faith – the relationship between the individual and God – is necessarily an individual thing. On this reasoning, the growth of individualism is a logical consequence of reformed religiosity, enshrined in the Reformation's twin rallying cries *sola fide* and *sola scriptura*, neither of which left much room for the mediation of the clergy or of society. The Reformation created models of spirituality which might seem irrevocably individual in both the Catholic and Protestant worlds, whether based upon a bibliocentric theology or on revelatory experiences of conversion. The process by which religion turned from being essentially a social matter to a personal or an individual one might even be seen to have taken physical form in the shape of the confessional box.[16]

This book has looked beyond such ideals to try to reveal something about religious and textual practice. While it has used books like Foxe's *Actes and Monuments*, it has not ascribed to Foxe some sort of automatic position at the top of the list of things which transformed the socially dominated world of medieval Catholicism into the recognizably modern atomized world of reformed Protestantism. Instead, it has used Foxe's book to display the opposite of what it is frequently thought to have achieved – it has shown how models of collective religiosity and spiritual sociability were perpetuated through the *Actes and Monuments*, at least as much as models of spiritual alienation and interiorization. This is in stark contrast to those twentieth-century historians who accorded Foxe's book

---

[15] Alexander Carse, *Sunday Morning (Bible Reading at the Cottage Door)*, n.d., National Galleries of Scotland, Edinburgh.
[16] See John Bossy, 'The Social History of Confession in the Age of Reformation', *Transactions of the Royal Historical Society*, 5th ser., 25 (1975), esp. pp. 27–33.

transformative powers, assuming that those who read it did so as part of a recognizably modern and individualistic form of religious belief.[17]

The tendency to connect a modernity which emerged from the era of the Reformation with puritanism and individual religious belief also has roots in nineteenth-century historiography. Although eighteenth-century historians had spent plenty of time evaluating the impact of puritanism in relation to England's history, it was only over the course of the nineteenth century that puritanism became more widely appreciated in anything like a positive light. Where nonconformist, internalist histories had long appreciated the spiritual debt they owed to seventeenth-century puritanism – most obviously in books like Daniel Neal's *History of the Puritans* (1738) – and the key works of puritan piety played a significant (but still underappreciated) role in the growth of evangelical piety in the eighteenth century, it was only in the nineteenth century that works of history more generally – from Macaulay to Carlyle – saw puritanism as anything more than religious fanaticism. Key puritans, notably Oliver Cromwell and John Milton, became lauded as national heroes.[18]

But the Victorians did not simply rediscover puritanism or treat it more sensitively, they also recast it in their own image. In the eighteenth century, puritanism had tended to be written off as a fanatical doctrine which belonged in the past. In the nineteenth century, it was seen as a largely progressive force which pointed the way to the modern age. Puritanism was praised for its moral characteristics – puritans were seen as sober, serious in their private devotion, intolerant of immorality and in favour of liberty of conscience. Non-sectarian and pluralistic, puritanism was inscribed with the characteristics of progress and modernity. Victorian puritanism was overwhelmingly individualistic. Perhaps, in the era

---

[17] It seems that the tendency to ascribe to the various editions and abridgements of Foxe's book this kind of weight in explaining momentous changes in history says at least as much about the historians who make such claims as it does about the actual impact of Foxe's work. See, for example, William Haller, *Foxe's Book of Martyrs and the Elect Nation* (London, 1963). However ill-documented, such claims in turn become axiomatic. See, for instance, how otherwise excellent studies like Linda Colley, *Britons: Forging the Nation 1707–1837* (New Haven, CT, 1992), Chapter 1, afford Foxe, together with Bunyan, a transformative role in the creation of British Protestant patriotism in the eighteenth century.

[18] On the rise of puritanism's fortunes, I have found the following useful: Raphael Samuel, 'The Discovery of Puritanism, 1820–1900: A Preliminary Sketch', in Jane Garnett and Colin Matthew (eds.), *Revival and Religion since 1700: Essays for John Walsh* (London, 1993), pp. 201–47; Timothy Lang, *The Victorians and the Stuart Heritage* (Cambridge, 1995); and John Coffey, 'Puritan Legacies', in John Coffey and Paul C. H. Lim (eds.), *The Cambridge Companion to Puritanism* (Cambridge, 2008), pp. 327–45. Blair Worden, *Roundhead Reputations: The English Civil Wars and the Passions of Posterity* (London, 2001), Chapters 8–10, is excellent on the fortunes of puritanism as well as on the reputation of Oliver Cromwell.

of Darwin and of Samuel Smiles's *Self-Help* (1859), it could not have been otherwise.

Such a present-centred picture of individualistic puritanism came to endure as it slipped so easily into the gloves provided by the master narratives of the age. Among them, two particular examples – one historical, one sociological – linked individualism with modernity and puritanism with progress. If the examples seem obvious, it is for good reason: although they do not stand alone, their influence upon our understanding of the past, the ways we conceive of the structures of historical development, has been spectacular. The first is Jacob Burckhardt's *The Civilization of the Renaissance in Italy* (1860), a book which, although written by a Swiss Calvinist, ostensibly has nothing whatsoever to do with puritanism. What the book did, however, was establish a seemingly incontrovertible link between individualism and modernity and locate these changes in the Renaissance period. Part II of *The Civilization of the Renaissance in Italy* carried the grand title 'The Development of the Individual'. The book's message was encapsulated in its most famous passage, which was cited so frequently that it might have permeated collective scholarly consciousness on its own. It was the Balinese cockfight of its day:

In the Middle Ages both sides of human consciousness ... lay dreaming or half awake beneath a common veil. The veil was woven of faith, illusion, and childish prepossession, through which the world and history were seen clad in strange hues. Man was conscious of himself only as a member of a race, people, party, family, or corporation – only through some general category. In Italy this veil first melted into air; an objective treatment of the state and of all the things of this world became possible. The subjective side at the same time asserted itself with corresponding emphasis; man became a spiritual individual, and recognized himself as such.[19]

Although Burckhardt clearly drew upon the ideas and language of other historians and philosophers – most obviously, in his discussions of individuality, objectivity and subjectivity, upon Hegel – he expressed his thesis with clarity: individualism, in short, was the child of the Renaissance. This was a transformation seen through the 'strange hues' of the nineteenth century and it found a ready audience in Victorian and early twentieth-century England: the book was translated in 1878, there

---

[19] Jacob Burckhardt, *The Civilization of the Renaissance in Italy*, trans. S. G. C. Middlemore, introduction by Peter Burke (London, 1990), p. 98.

were two new editions before the end of the century, and four more in the first half of the twentieth century.[20]

The second master narrative comes from Max Weber's *The Protestant Ethic and the Spirit of Capitalism*, first published in 1905 and translated into English by the American sociologist Talcott Parsons in 1930. Even if his general argument is frequently misrepresented – he was proposing a philosophy of history whereby spirituality was put back into Marxist interpretations of change – a specific element of Weber's thesis is so well known that it sounds like a caricature: his claim that the Calvinist theology of English and American puritans bred 'inner loneliness' and 'the inner isolation of the individual', a sort of holy anxiety which facilitated the growth of the 'spirit of capitalism' at the heart of modern Western culture. Historians had long since claimed a natural connection between Protestantism and progress but Weber, using a thin strand of source material, claimed an intrinsic connection between Calvinism and individual belief. The enduring significance of Weber's thesis in twentieth-century historiography and sociology (regardless of whether the intention has been to refute or to defend Weber's claims) has meant that much of the debate about modernity has revolved around the concepts of puritanism, individualism and progress. The puritanism of the twentieth century was born of nineteenth-century ideas and ambitions.[21]

These two master narratives, in which a series of more widely held ideas crystallized, have had enormous influence in connecting puritanism, individualism and modernity. But it is significant for the purposes of this book that, although they have provided the bedrock of theories which place print and silent reading as vectors in this transformation, they actually say very little about printing as such. Instead, the importance of silent reading of printed books has been grafted onto these theories about individualism and modernity: if modernity is to be judged by the self-consciousness of the individual, then silent reading seems to bolster such a transformation. Thus Elizabeth Eisenstein, making the case for the revolution occasioned by printing, returns to the theories of Burckhardt and Weber and suggests that printing supports their arguments.[22] Similarly,

---

[20] Ibid., p. 12.

[21] Max Weber, *The Protestant Ethic and the Spirit of Capitalism*, trans. Talcott Parsons (1930; repr. London, 1992), citations at pp. 104, 105.

[22] Elizabeth L. Eisenstein, *The Printing Press as an Agent of Change: Communications and Cultural Transformations in Early Modern Europe* (2 vols., continuously paginated, Cambridge, 1979), esp. pp. 225–8 (on Burckhardt), 228–30 (on individualism) and 378–403 (on Weber). It is telling that Eisenstein relies in part on 'historical common sense' (p. 389) in sustaining the link between the

although describing an earlier transformation, Paul Saenger argues that the emergence of silent reading is evidence of a transition towards modernity, a theory which again rests at least in part upon nineteenth-century ideas about individuality and progress.[23] Even Adrian Johns's *The Nature of the Book*, which sets out to repudiate just about every claim in Elizabeth Eisenstein's book, concentrates exclusively upon silent reading in the making of modernity.[24] In contrast, this book has argued that it is only when we put aside nineteenth-century ideas of progress and individualism that we can begin to unravel the importance of communal reading in its own right.

CONCLUSION

This book has attempted to delineate something like an ethnography of godly reading in the long seventeenth century and to evaluate its impact upon how we think about both puritanism and reading in the early modern period. Setting aside, as far as possible, the ingrained habits of thought brought about through settled historiographical assumptions, it has shown not only the extent of collective, social and public forms of reading among the godly but also how analysing such reading might tell us something of the character of the culture of puritanism more generally. To do this, it has eschewed thinking about communal reading principally in the framework of the dissemination of religious knowledge and the skills of literacy, as many previous studies have done. Although a discussion of the extent of communal reading might in theory shed light upon religious and intellectual culture further down the social spectrum, in practice thinking about collective reading in this way tends towards rather unhelpful discussions of elite and popular culture and towards assessing such reading in terms of who performed it rather than of how it was done.[25] Consciously or not, such work has confirmed social reading as at

Reformation and modernity. Her discussion of Bible-reading in the section on 'Aspects of the New Book Religion' (pp. 422–50, esp. at p. 428) is heavily weighted towards internalized silent reading.

[23] Paul Saenger, *Space between Words: The Origins of Silent Reading* (Stanford, CA, 1997), esp. Chapter 15.

[24] See Adrian Johns, *The Nature of the Book: Print and Knowledge in the Making* (Chicago, IL, 1998), Chapter 6.

[25] This way of assessing social reading has in part flowed from (the reception of) R. W. Scribner, *For the Sake of Simple Folk: Popular Propaganda for the German Reformation* (Cambridge, 1981). Despite challenging some of Scribner's assumptions (and in particular the assumptions of those who have appropriated his work), Andrew Pettegree continues to give prominence to questions of social dissemination in his *Reformation and the Culture of Persuasion* (Cambridge, 2005), esp. p. 119. The social setting of such reading and the social hierarchies of the time, he argues, made it much more

best a second-rate activity which was performed primarily for the education of the semi-literate.

In contrast, this book has demonstrated how misleading a way this is to think about collective godly reading. It has shown that collective reading was chosen as the preferred means of textual engagement by the godly. Rather than thinking about collective reading as a means of confirming a picture of puritanism as a popular religious culture (albeit a culture which shared much with the religious cultures against which it defined itself, thus making puritans seem much less 'rational' and forward-thinking than they are sometimes made out to be), this study has demonstrated the level of spiritual agency in the choice of such reading for the godly. Collective reading was a style of textual engagement which was deliberately chosen to fit in with a mode of puritan religiosity. Whether with friends, family or the wider religious community, collective reading was a key part of experimental puritanism, a practical method by which the godly tried to channel the Holy Spirit into believers and through which they hoped to be able to discover whether they had been saved.

At the same time, such reading was also a ritual of separation from the perceived enemies of the godly, a form of cultural praxis which enabled them to enact their difference from the rest of society. But while the cultural separation enacted through communal reading might be thought to have isolated the godly within early modern society, it also had a more positive outcome. The reading of a core group of puritan texts – a canon of early Stuart puritan practical divinity – helped to solidify the religious and cultural identity of godly people. Communal reading thus fostered the idea of an imagined community of godly people who articulated their shared identity through their engagement with books. It helped puritanism to survive and change shape long after its political star had faded.[26] Incidentally, one of the unexpected by-products of the focus on such communal and public forms of reading has been to detach the theological ideas of puritan 'interiority' from the daily world of religious practice.

---

likely that those who listened were already readers and, since it was almost always the case that social inferiors would read to their social superiors, there is little evidence that such occasions broadened the impact of print and literacy.

[26] Interpretive communities have been better conceptualized either side of the early modern period. See, for instance, Benedict Anderson, *Imagined Communities: Reflections on the Origin and Spread of Nationalism* (London, 1983); Brian Stock, *Listening for the Text: On the Uses of the Text* (Baltimore, MD, 1990); and Adrian Hastings, *The Construction of Nationhood: Ethnicity, Religion and Nationalism* (Cambridge, 1997). A similar case – that religious and ideological coherence was fostered primarily through engagement with the text – might also be made for post-Reformation Catholicism.

It seems that such ideas, which emerged over the period, were largely theological arguments for otherworldliness which had little effect upon the spiritual lives of the godly. Communal reading reveals puritan 'interiority' to have been essentially a myth of the long Reformation.

At the same time, the prevalence of communal reading in puritan culture provides a forceful reminder of the intersection and mutual interaction of orality and literacy in this period – of the word spoken and the word read.[27] The interactions are evident in the cross-over between communal reading and prayer and in particular in the mutual interaction of the book and reading and the broader sermon culture which is often presented as the defining characteristic of puritanism. Not only did the godly attend sermons as a matter of urgent soteriological necessity, they took notes there, circulated them and bought printed versions of the sermons which in turn they read, often in the context of their family piety. This interplay between orality and literacy was frequently deliberate and cultivated. This was certainly the case with the reading of sermons and of the Bible, where the voice had to be employed to give spiritual life to the word of the written text. The living Word of God had a power which was best channelled not through private reading and contemplation but through collective reading and ecstatic spirituality.[28]

The book has also shown how far methods and styles of reading were influenced by the spaces in which they took place. By sharpening the focus upon godly reading, the great variety of styles of reading that could be performed by a single individual or a family – from reading and praying with penitential tears in the closet to reading with pen in hand in the study or with friends and family in the household hall – have come to light. While others have suggested that space might have been an important factor in determining styles of reading and a few studies have outlined such an approach, this book has demonstrated just how much material can be uncovered which specifies the location of reading while showing the extent to which early modern readers were aware that the

---

[27] Walter Ong, *Orality and Literacy: The Technologizing of the Word* (London, 1982); Jack Goody, *The Interface between the Written and the Oral* (Cambridge, 1987); Adam Fox, *Oral and Literate Culture in England, 1500–1700* (Oxford, 2000).

[28] It should be noted that while internalist histories define puritanism as a religion of the word, the anthropologically minded historian should reconstruct puritanism as a religion of the book. See Margo Todd, *The Culture of Protestantism in Early Modern Scotland* (New Haven, CT, 2002), p. 24 ('Protestantism is above all a religion of the book'). It is noteworthy that those Muslims who wrote about their encounters with European Christians also described them (following the Koran) as 'the People of the Book'. See Nabil Matar, *Europe through Arab Eyes 1578–1727* (New York, 2009), pp. 9, 14, 32.

space they chose to read in made a difference to how they read. In this, books themselves have given up rather less information than hoped for, while diaries and autobiographies have been much more revealing. Perhaps we might question the pathology of those who constantly remarked not only on what they had read but also on where they had read it (although in the age of blogging and Twitter the recording of even the tiniest details of everyday life has become commonplace). But for the godly, reading and recording what one had read served interlinked religious purposes – to read was to attempt to channel the Holy Spirit into one's heart as a believer, while to make a record of such reading was to provide material from which to judge whether you were indeed one of the elect. This perhaps explains why so many Calvinists made such full records of their religious reading and rereading throughout their lives. To their enemies this made for a particularly self-conscious and showy form of religiosity, which preached the importance of inward spirituality but expressed it everywhere in outward form.

Importantly, the focus on space also shows us how many of the same individuals often read in starkly divergent ways depending on context. In contrast to a historiography which has tended towards categorizing types of reader – as active readers 'poaching' for information, or as passive readers led by the text and its apparatus – the framework of the spaces of reading has revealed how the same individuals would read in different ways. Of course, the space of reading was not the only factor in determining how it was done, nor was each style of reading particular to a specific place. But even if styles of reading sometimes overlapped between places, the approach can be revealing. Focusing on space shows, for example, how far domestic reading and religiosity mimicked the reading and religiosity of the church. In this, reading was part of a strategy whereby the godly brought the church into their homes, a 'spiritualization of the household' with potentially radical consequences.[29] In particular, this approach sheds light on how a seemingly conservative, patriarchal form of spirituality which resonates with the picture of the quiescent godly painted by Patrick Collinson and others might actually be the same setting for a more radical form of semi-separatism, where the home became the forum for a voluntary form of true spirituality, much more in line with the theology and cultural practices of puritanism as described by Peter Lake and David Como.

---

[29] Christopher Hill, 'The Spiritualization of the Household', in his *Society and Puritanism in Pre-Revolutionary England* (London, 1964), pp. 382–416.

This perspective upon puritanism has been enabled by thinking about it as a form of religious culture. The focus on reading as a key part of this culture might have been expected to privilege doctrinal issues in the understanding of puritanism and, certainly, when we consider what puritans read, the importance of scriptural reading and Calvinist theology, including the doctrine of predestination, is never far from the surface. But such issues were part of a broader religious culture: they took their place in a culture in which theological issues were expressed through (and sometimes modified by) other forms of activity, notably the hearing of sermons, praying and reading. At the same time, the focus upon how such reading was performed has highlighted the social dimension of puritanism, its practice as a collective faith strengthened through communal activity. If this has challenged some of the cruder portraits of puritanism as an inward-looking and deeply personal form of religiosity, it has also told of the strange survival of puritanism in the longer term. What Christopher Hill once called the 'secret victory of puritanism' is evident in the daily religious reading of nonconformists after the Restoration, of family and household religiosity across the long seventeenth century.[30] Puritanism may have died as a political force but its cultural consequences were long-lived and they were sustained through a series of religious practices among which reading had a doubly important role: it was at once a vital part of puritan religiosity and a means of transmitting such forms of devotion across generations. Reading remained at the heart of the culture of puritanism. Indeed, perhaps the key finding of this book has been that intertwining the two divergent historiographies of the history of reading and the history of puritanism has resulted in a richer and more nuanced understanding of both.

---

[30] Hill, *Society and Puritanism in Pre-Revolutionary England*, p. 441.

Bibliography

MANUSCRIPTS

Bodleian Library, Oxford
　MS Rawlinson D.1289
British Library, London
　Additional MSS
　Egerton MSS
　Harley MSS
　Lansdowne MSS
　Sloane MSS
　Stowe MSS
Brotherton Library, Leeds University, Leeds
　MS Lt q 17
Cambridge University Library, Cambridge
　MS Add 8499
Cheshire Record Office, Chester
　EDC 5
　Z D/Basten/8
Chetham's Library, Manchester
　MS A.2.21
　MS A.2.125
　MS A.3.123
Dorset History Centre, Dorchester
　D 413/22/1
Guildhall Library, London
　MS 204
John Rylands Library, Manchester
　Eng MS 524

Lambeth Palace Library, London
  Sion College MS, ARC L40.2/E29
  Sion College MS, ARC L40.2/E.64
Lincoln Cathedral Library, Lincoln
  Lincoln MSS 256
Lincolnshire Archives, Lincoln
  MS 2 Cragg 4/7
London Metropolitan Archives, London
  DL/C/362
The National Archives, Public Record Office, London
  PROB 11
  STAC 5
  STAC 8
Norfolk Record Office, Norwich
  Will Register, Kirke, 82–4
Dr Williams's Library, London
  Morrice MS M
  Morrice MS X
  MS 24.7
  MS 24.8
  MS 28.2
York Minster Archives
  Add MS 214
Trinity College Library, Dublin
  MS 709, vols I–II
Beinecke Rare Book and Manuscript Library, Yale University, New Haven, CT
  Osborn MS b.236
Folger Shakespeare Library, Washington, DC
  MS V.a. 284–99
  MS V.a. 436
Henry E. Huntington Library, San Marino, CA
  MS HA 9211
  MS HM 6131
  MS EL 5965
Princeton University Library, Princeton, NJ
  MS RTC01 (no. 62)

PRINTED PRIMARY SOURCES

An Account Of The Life and Death Of Mr Philip Henry, Minister of the Gospell, near Whitchurch in Shropshire. Who Dyed June 24; 1696 in the Sixty fifth Year of his Age. With Dr Bates's Dedication (2nd edn, London, 1699).

[Alstree, Richard], *The Whole Duty of Man* (London, 1684).

Aubrey, John, *Brief Lives*, ed. Richard Barber (Woodbridge, 1982).

Augustine, St, *Confessions*, trans. Henry Chadwick (Oxford, 1992 edn).

The Autobiography of Mrs Alice Thornton, of East Newton, co. York, Surtees Society, **62** (Durham, 1875 for 1873).

Bagshaw, Edward (d. 1671), *The Life and Death of Mr Vavasor Powell* (London, 1671).

B[agshaw], E[dward] (d. 1662), 'The Life and Death of the Author', in *The Workes of the Reverend, Truly Pious, and Judiciously Learned Robert Bolton* (London, 1641).

Bauthumley, Jacob, *The Light and Dark Sides of God or A Plain and Brief Discourse, of the Light Side God, Heaven and Earth, the Dark Side Devill, Sin, and Hell. As also of the Resurrection and Scripture. All which are Set Forth in their Severall Natures and Beings, according to the Spirituality of the Scripture* (London, 1650).

Baxter, Richard, *Rich: Baxter's Confesssion [sic] of his Faith* (London, 1655).

The Worcester-Shire Petition . . . Defended (London, 1653).

Beadle, John, *The Journal or Diary of a Thankful Christian. Presented in Some Meditations upon Numb. 33. 2.* (London, 1656).

Beard, Thomas, *The Theatre of Gods Judgements* (London, 1597).

Bernard, Nicholas, *The Penitent Death of a Woefull Sinner. Or, The Penitent Death of John Atherton Executed at Dublin the 5. of December 1640. With Some Annotations upon Severall Passages in it* (Dublin, 1641).

The Case of John Atherton (London, 1710).

Bibliotheca Charnockiana, sive, Catalogus librorum selectissimae bibliothecae clarissimi, doctissimiq; viri domini Steph. Charnock, S.T.B. nuperrime defuncti (London, 1680).

Bibliotheca Jacombiana, sive, Catalogus variorum librorum plurimis facultatibus insignium instructissimae bibliothecae Rev. Doct. Thomae Jacomb, S.T.D. . . .: quorum auctio habebitur Londini in aedibus Nigri Cygni ex adverso australis porticus ecclesiae Cathed. Paulin. in Caemiterio D. Paul (London, 1687).

Bibliotheca Oweniana, sive, Catalogus librorum plurimis facultatibus insignium, instructissimæ bibliothecæ Rev. Doct. Vir. D. Joan Oweni (London, 1684).

Bodin, Jean, *On the Demon-Mania of Witches*, trans. Randy A. Scott (Toronto, 1995).

Bovet, Richard, *Pandaemonium: or, The Devil's Cloyster. Being a Further Blow to Modern Sadduceism, Proving the Existence of Witches and Spirits* (London, 1684).

Boyle, Robert, *Some Motives to the Love of God, better known as Seraphick Love*, in Robert Boyle, *Works*, ed. Michael Hunter and Edward B. Davis (7 vols., London, 1999).

Bray, Thomas, *An Appendix to the Discourse upon the Doctrine of our Baptismal Covenant being a Method of Family Religion* (London, 1699).

Bibliotheca Parochialis (London, 1697).

An Essay towards Promoting all Necessary and Useful Knowledge ... both at Home and Abroad (London, 1697).

Proposals for the Encouragement and Promoting of Religion and Learning in the Foreign Plantations (London, 1696).

Brewer, J. S., *et al.* (ed.), *Letters and Papers, Foreign and Domestic, of the Reign of Henry VIII* (23 vols., London, 1862–1932).

A Brief Discourse of the Christian Life and Death, of Mistris Katherine Brettergh (London, 1602).

Brookes, Thomas, *The Privie Key of Heaven; or, Twenty Arguments for Closet-Prayer: in a Select Discourse on that Subject* (London, 1665).

Bruce, John (ed.), *Diary of John Manningham, of the Middle Temple, and of Bradbourne, Kent, Barrister-At-Law, 1602–1603, Camden Society*, old ser., **99** (London, 1868).

Bull, Henry (ed.), *Certain most Godly, Fruitful and Comfortable Letters of such True Saintes and Holy Martyres* (London, 1564).

Bunyan, John, *Grace Abounding: with Other Spiritual Autobiographies*, ed. John Stachniewski with Anita Pacheco (Oxford, 1998).

The life and death of Mr. Badman (London, 1696).

The Pilgrim's Progress (2nd edn, London, 1678).

The Pilgrim's Progress (3rd edn, London, 1679).

The Pilgrim's Progress (Limited Editions Club edn, New York, 1941).

Butler, Samuel, *Hudibras* (London, 1663).

Carlisle, Nicholas, *A Concise Description of the Endowed Grammar Schools in England and Wales* (2 vols., London, 1818).

Catalogue of Library March 18 1697 (London, 1697).

Catalogus librorum in bibliothecis selectissimis doctissimorum virorum viz., D. Georgii Lawsoni, Salopiensis, D. Georgii Fawleri, Londinensis, D. Oweni Stockdoni, Colcestriensis, D. Thomæ Brooks, Londinensis (London, 1681).

Catalogus variorum & insignium librorum instructissimæ bibliothecæ clarissimi doctissimiq; Viri Thomæ Manton, S.T.D. (London, 1678).

Catalogus variorum & insignium librorum instructissimæ bibliothecæ clarissimi doctissimiq[ue] viri Lazari Seaman, S.T.D. Quorum auctio habebitur Londini in ædibus defuncti in area & viculo Warwicensi, Octobris ultimo. Cura Gulielmi Cooper bibliopolæ (London, 1676).

Catalogus variorum librorum bibliothecae selectissimae Rev. Doct. Viri D. Tho. Lye B.D. nuperrime Londinensis, defuncti cui accessit bibliotheca Anglica non minus elegans & copiosa, M. Tho. Jennings civis Londinensis ingeniosissimi (London, 1684).

Catalogus variorum librorum ex bibliothecis selectissimis doctissimorum virorum, viz. R.D. Johan. Bradford, D.D., R.D. Gulielmi Cooperi, A.M. londinensium (London, 1686).

Catalogus variorum librorum in selectissimus bibliothecis doctissimorum virorum; viz. D. Hen. Stubb nupperrime Londdinensis D. Dillinghami de Oundle

Northamptoniensis D. Thomæ Vincent Londinensis D. Cautoni Westmonasterieusis (London, 1680).

Catalogus variorum librorum instructissimae bibliothecae doctissimi viri D. Thomae Watson, A.M. Scholae Suttonianae apud Charter-House, Londini nuperrime archididaschali (London, 1680).

Chillingworth, William, *The Religion of Protestants a Safe Way to Salvation* (Oxford, 1638).

Christie, R. C. (ed.), *The Diary and Correspondence of Dr John Worthington, Chetham Society*, 1st ser., **114** (Manchester, 1886).

Clarke, Samuel, *A Generall Martyrology ... Whereunto are Added, The Lives of Sundry Modern Divines etc.* (London, 1651).

The Lives of Sundry Eminent Persons in this Latter Age (London, 1683).

The Lives of Thirty-Two English Divines Famous in their Generations for Learning and Piety, and most of them Sufferers in the Cause of Christ etc. (London, 1677).

The Marrow of Ecclesiastical History (3rd edn, London, 1675).

Clifford, D. J. H. (ed.), *The Diaries of Lady Anne Clifford* (revised edn, Stroud, 2003).

C[ollinges], J[ohn], *Par Nobile. Two Treatises. The One, Concerning the Excellent Woman, ... the Lady Frances Hobart ... The Other, ... the Lady Katharine Courten etc.* (London, 1669).

Comber, Thomas, *A Companion to the Temple and Closet* (London, 1672).

Comenius, Joannes Amos, *Orbis sensualium pictus*, ed. James Bowen (Sydney, 1967).

Constitutions and Canons Ecclesiasticall: Treated upon by the Bishop of London, President of the Convocation for the Province of Canterbury, and the Rest of the Bishops and Clergie of the Said Province (London, 1604).

Cooke, Alexander, *The Abatement of Popish Braggs, Pretending Scripture to be theirs. Retorted by the Hand of Alexander Cooke* (London, 1625).

More Worke for a Masse-Priest (London, 1621).

Pope Joane. A Dialogue Betweene a Protestant and a Papist (London, 1625).

Pope Joane. A Dialogue Betweene a Protestant and a Papist (London, 1610).

Saint Austins Religion Wherein is Manifestly Proued out of the Works of that Learned Father, that he Dissented from Popery, and Agreed with the Religion of the Protestants in all the Maine Points of Faith and Doctrine (London, 1624).

The Weather-Cocke of Romes Religion: with her Severall Changes. Or: The World Turn'd Topsie-Turvie by Papists (London, 1625).

Worke, More Worke, and a Little More Work for a Masse-Priest Reviewed and Augmented by the Authour (London, 1628).

Worke for a Masse-Priest (London, 1617).

Yet more Worke for a Masse-Priest (London, 1622).

[Corbett, Thomas], *Bibliotheca Sturbitchiana, &c. A Catalogue of Curious Books, Selected out of Several Libraries and Parcels Bought at Sturbitch-Fair ... with an Uncommon Collection Belonging to the Late Famous Mr. Winstanley of Littlebury* (London, 1722).

Cotton, John, *Milk for Babes. Drawn out of the Breasts of both Testaments. Chiefly, for the Spirituall Nourishment of Boston Babes in Either England: But May be of Like Use for any Children* (London, 1646).

Crakanthorpe, Richard, *Defensio ecclesiae Anglicanae* (London, 1625).

Davenport, Robert, *A Pleasant and Witty Comedy: Called, A New Tricke to Cheat the Divell* (London, 1639).

Dell, William, *The Tryal of Spirits both in Teachers and Hearers. Wherein is held forth the Clear Discovery, and Certain Downfal of the Carnal and Antichristian Clergie of these Nations* (London, 1653).

Dent, Arthur, *The plaine mans path-way to heaven* (London, 1601).

Digby, Kenelm, *Observations Upon Religio Medici* (London, 1643).

Digitus Dei. A Faithful Relation and Collection of Seven Wonderful and Remarkable Judgements, Lately Inflicted by God on Several Persons using Execrations and Wicked Wishes to Themselves (London, 1677).

Dunsford, Martin, *Historical Memoirs of the Town and Parish of Tiverton in the County of Devon Collected from the Best Authorities, with Notes and Observations* (Exeter, 1790).

Dunton, John, *The Life and Errors of John Dunton Late Citizen of London; Written by Himself in Solitude* (London, 1705).

Dyke, Daniel, *The Mystery of Self-Deceiving. Or a Discourse ... of the Deceitfulnesse of Man's Heart* (London, 1615).

Dyke, Jeremiah, *A Worthy Communicant: or, A Treatise, Shewing the Due Order of Receiving the Sacrament of the Lords Supper. By Jer. Dyke, Minister of Epping, in Essex* (London, 1636).

Edwards, Thomas, *Gangraena* (3 Parts, London, 1646).

Equiano, Olaudah, *The Interesting Narrative and Other Writings*, ed. Vincent Carretta (Penguin Classics revised edn, London, 2003).

Evans, Arise, *To the Most High and Mighty Prince, Charles the II. By the Grace of God, King of Great Britain, France and Ireland, Defender of the Faith, &c. An Epistle Written and Humbly Presented for His Majesties Use, and Enlightning of the Nation* (London, 1660).

Everard, John, *Some Gospel-Treasures Opened: Or, The Holiest of all Unvailing* (London, 1653).

Eyre, Adam, 'A Dyurnall, or Catalogue of all my Accions and Expences from the 1st of January, 1646–[7]', in *Yorkshire Diaries and Autobiographies in the Seventeenth and Eighteenth Centuries*, Surtees Society, **65** (Durham, 1875).

Fairfax, Edward, *Daemonologia: a Discourse on Witchcraft as it was Acted in the Family of Mr. Edward Fairfax, of Fuyston, in the County of York, in the Year 1621*, ed. William Grainge (Harrogate, 1882).

The Farewell Sermons of the Late London Ministers, Preached August 17th. 1662. By Mr. Calamy. Dr. Manton. Mr. Caryl. Mr. Case. Mr. Jenkins. Mr. Baxter. Dr. Jacomb. Dr. Bates. Mr. Watson. Mr. Lye. Mr. Mede. Mr. Ash, Fun. Ser. (London, 1662).

Farmer, John S. (ed.), *National Ballad and Song: Merry Songs and Ballads, Prior to the Year 1800* (5 vols., [London], 1897).

Favour, John, *Antiquitie Triumphing over Noveltie* (London, 1619).

Featley, Daniel, *The Dippers Dipt* (1646).

Fishwick, Henry (ed.), *The Note Book of the Rev. Thomas Jolly, A.D. 1671–1693. Extracts from the Church Book of Altham and Wymondhouses, 1649–1725. And an Account of the Jolly Family of Standish, Gorton, and Altham, Chetham Society*, new ser., **33** (Manchester, 1895).

Fourth Report of the Royal Commission on Historical Manuscripts (2 vols., London, 1874).

Foxe, John, *Actes and Monuments of these Latter and Perillous Dayes* (London, 1563).

   Actes and Monuments of Matters most Speciall and Memorable, Happenyng in the Church, with an Uniuersall History of the same (London, 1583).

   Acts and Monuments of Matters most Speciall and Memorable, Happening in the Church, with an Universall Historie of the Same (London, 1641).

Fuller, Thomas, *Abel Redevivus: or, The Dead yet Speaking* (London, 1651).

Goldie, Mark, *et al.* (eds.), *The Entring Book of Roger Morrice 1677–1691* (6 vols., Woodbridge, 2007).

Goodwin, Philip, *Religio Domestica Rediviva: or, Family-Religion Revived. Or A Treatise as to Discover the Good Old Way of Serving God in Private Houses: so to Recover the Pious Practice of those Precious Duties unto their Primitive Platform* (London, 1655).

Hall, Thomas, *Vindiciae Literarum, the Schools Guarded* (London, 1654).

Henry, Matthew, *A Church in the House. A Sermon Concerning Family-Religion* (London, 1704).

   A Sermon Concerning the Catechizing of Youth (London, 1713).

Heywood, Oliver, *Closet-Prayer, a Christian Duty: Or a Treatise upon Mat. vi. 6* (London, 1671).

   A Narrative of the Holy Life, and Happy Death of that Reverend, Faithful and Zealous Man of God, and Minister of the Gospel of Jesus Christ, Mr. John Angier (London, 1683).

Heywood, Thomas (ed.), *The Diary of the Rev Henry Newcome, from September 30, 1661, to September 29, 1663, Chetham Society*, 1st ser., **18** (Manchester, 1849).

Hinde, William, *A Faithfull Remonstrance of the Holy Life and Happy Death, of John Bruen of Bruen Stapleford* (London, 1641).

Hobbes, Thomas, *Leviathan*, ed. Richard Tuck (Cambridge, 1991).

Holland, John, *The Smoke of the Bottomlesse Pit or, A More True and Fuller Discovery of the Doctrine of Those Men which Call Themselves Ranters: or, The Mad Crew* (London, 1651).

Horner, Craig (ed.), *The Diary of Edmund Harrold, Wigmaker of Manchester 1712–15* (Aldershot, 2008).

Houghton, John, *A Collection for the Improvement of Husbandry and Trade*, vol. 6, no. 129, 18 January 1694/5.

A Hundred Godly Lessons. That a Mother on her Death-Bed Gave to her Children, whereby They may Know how to Guide Themselves towards God and

Man, to the Benefit of the Common-Wealth, Joy of their Parents, and Good of Themselves (London, c.1674–9).

Jackson, C. (ed.), *Diary of Abraham de la Pryme*, Surtees Society, **54** (Durham, 1869).

[James, Thomas], *Catalogus librorum bibliothecae publicae quam vir ornatissimus Thomas Bodleius nuper instituit* (Oxford, 1605).

Jessop, Augustus, *The Oeconomy of the Fleete*, Camden Society, new ser., **25** (London, 1879).

Johnson, G. W., *The Fairfax Correspondence: Memoirs of the Reign of Charles the First* (2 vols., London, 1848).

Jones, David, *A Sermon Of the Absolute Necessity of Family-Duties* (London, 1692).

Latham, R. C., and Matthews, W. (eds.), *The Diary of Samuel Pepys* (11 vols., London, 1970–83).

The Lawfulnesse of our Expedition into England Manifested (n.p., 1640).

Lechford, Thomas, *New-Englands Advice to Old-England* ([London], 1644).

Lee, Matthew Henry (ed.), *Diaries and Letters of Philip Henry of Broad Oak, Flintshire, 1631–1696* (London, 1882).

London Gazette, no. 1140, 19 October, 1676.

Macfarlane, Alan (ed.), *The Diary of Ralph Josselin, 1616–1683* (Oxford, 1976).

Massie, R. M., *A Catalogue of Books in the Library at Wisbech in the Isle of Ely* (Wisbech, 1718).

Mather, Cotton, *The Wonders of the Invisible World: Being an Account of the Tryals of Several Witches Lately Executed in New-England* (repr. of 1693 edn, London, 1862).

Middleton, Thomas, *A Game at Chæss* (London, 1625).

Moody, Joanna (ed.), *The Private Life of an Elizabethan Lady: The Diary of Lady Margaret Hoby, 1599–1605* (Stroud, 1998).

The Morning-Exercise at Cripple-Gate (London, 1661).

Moryson, Fynes, *An Itinerary* (London, 1617).

Naudé, Gabriel, *Advis pour dresser une bibliothèque* (Paris, 1627) [trans. as Evelyn, John, *Instructions Concerning Erecting of a Library* (London, 1661)].

A Necessary Doctrine and Erudition for any Christen Man (London, 1543).

Nichols, John, *The History and Antiquities of the Countie of Leicester* (4 vols., London, 1795–1815).

Literary Anecdotes of the Eighteenth Century (9 vols, London, 1812–15).

(ed.), *Narratives of the Days of the Reformation: Chiefly from the Manuscripts of John Foxe the Martyrologist*, Camden Society, old ser., **77** (1859).

Old Mr Dod's Sayings (London, 1667).

Orme, William, *The Life and Times of the Rev. Richard Baxter: with a Critical Examination of his Writings* (2 vols., London, 1830).

Our Demands of the English Lords Manifested, being at Rippon Octob. 8. 1640 (n.p., 1640).

Palmer, Samuel (ed.), *The Nonconformist's Memorial* (3 vols., London, 1802 edn).

Parkinson, R. (ed.), *The Autobiography of Henry Newcome*, Chetham Society, **26**, **27**, (2 vols., paginated continuously, Manchester, 1852).

The Life of Adam Martindale, Written by Himself, and now First Printed from the Original Manuscript in the British Museum, Chetham Society, 1st ser., **4** (Manchester, 1855).

Patrick, Simon, *The Hearts Ease, or A Remedy against all Troubles. To which is Added a Consolatory Discourse against the Loss of our Friends and those that are Dear unto us* (London, 1660).

Payne, William, *Family Religion: Or, The Duty of Taking Care of Religion in Families, And the Means of Doing it. Recommended in A Sermon Preached at Guild-Hall Chappel Before the Lord Mayor And Court of Aldermen, On Sunday February 22th 1690/91* (London, 1691).

Pearse, Edward, *The Great Concern* (London, 1671).

Peck, Dwight C. (ed.), *Leicester's Commonwealth: the Copy of a Letter Written by a Master of Art at Cambridge (1584) and Related Documents* (Athens, OH, 1985).

Perkins, William, *A Discourse of the Damned Art of Witchcraft* (Cambridge, 1608).

The Foundation of Christian Religion Gathered into Six Principles (London, 1591).

Prynne, William, *The Lyar Confounded* (London, 1645).

Quakers are Inchanters, and Dangerous Seducers. Appearing in their Inchantment of one Mary White at Wickham-skyeth in Suffolk, 1655. (London, 1655).

Questions to be Disputed in Counsell of the Lords Spirituall after their Returne from their Visitation (London, 1641).

Reading, William, *The History of the Ancient and Present State of Sion College . . . and of the Library there* (London, 1724).

Resbury, Nathaniel, *Of Closet-Prayer. A Sermon Preach'd before the Queen at Whitehall* (London, 1693).

Reynolds, John, *The Triumph of Gods Revenge, against the Crying and Execrable Sinne of Murther* (London, 1622).

Rost, John, *The Swearer's Doom; Or, A Discourse Setting Forth the Great Sinfulness and Danger of Rash and Vain Swearing* (London, 1695).

Rudierd, Edmund, *The Thunderbolt of Gods Wrath against Hard-Hearted and Stiffe-Necked Sinne[r]s, or An Abridgement of the Theater of Gods Fearefull Judgements Executed Upon Notorious Sinners* (London, 1618).

Sandys, George, *A Relation of a Journey* (London, 1615).

S[eagar], F[rancis], *The Schoole of Vertue and Booke of Good Nurture* (London, 1557).

Shakespeare, William, *Titus Andronicus* (London, 1594).

Shawe, John, *Two Clean Birds: Or, The Cleansing of the Leper* (York, 1644).

Sherlock, William, *A Practical Discourse Concerning Death* (London, 1689).

Shower, John, *Family Religion in Three Letters to a Friend* (London, 1694).

Sir Thomas St. Serfe, *Tarugo's Wiles: or, The Coffee-House. A Comedy. As it was Acted at his Highness's, the Duke of York's Theater* (London, 1668).

Slater, Samuel, *A Discourse of Closet, or Secret Prayer* (London, 1691).

An Earnest Call to Family-Religion, or, A Discourse Concerning Family Worship being the Substance of Eighteen Sermons (London, 1694).

Strype, John, *A Survey of the Cities of London and Westminster ... By John Stow* (2 vols., London, 1720).

Swan, John, *A True and Breife Report, of Mary Glovers Vexation, and of her Deliverance by the Meanes of Fastinge and Prayer* (London, 1603).

Sylvester, Matthew (ed.), *Reliquiæ Baxterianæ: or, Mr. Richard Baxter's Narrative of the Most Memorable Passages of his Life and Times* (London, 1696).

Tany, Thomas, *My Edict Royal* ([London], 1655?).

Theauraujohn High Priest to the Jewes, his Disputive Challenge to the Universities of Oxford and Cambridge, and the whole Hirach. of Roms Clargical Priests ([London], 1652).

Taylor, Alexander (ed.), *The Works Of Symon Patrick, D.D. Sometime Bishop of Ely, Including His Autobiography* (9 vols., Oxford, 1858).

Thoresby, Ralph, *Vicaria Leodiensis* (London, 1724).

Tillotson, John, *Six Sermons, I. Of Steadfastness in Religion. II. Of Family-Religion. III. IV. V. Of Education of Children VI. Of The Advantages of an Early Piety* (London, 1694).

Tomkins, Thomas, *Lingua: or the Combat of the Tongue* (London, 1607).

Toulmin, Joshua, *An Historical View of the State of the Protestant Dissenters in England* (London, 1814).

A True and Fearefull Vexation of One Alexander Nyndge: Being Most Horribly Tormented with the Devill, from the 20. Day of January, to the 23. of July. At Lyeringswell in Suffocke: with his Prayer after his Deliverance. Written by his Owne Brother Edward Nyndge Master of Arts, with the Names of the Witnesses that were at his Vexation (London, 1615).

Turner, J. H. (ed.), *The Rev. Oliver Heywood, B.A. 1630–1702, his Autobiography, Diaries, Anecdote and Event Books, Illustrating the General and Family History of Yorkshire and Lancashire* (4 vols., Brighouse, 1881–5).

Two Wise Men and All the Rest Fooles: or A Comicall Morall, Censuring the Follies of this Age (London, 1619).

Underhill, Edward Bean (ed.), *Records of the Churches of Christ, Gathered at Fenstanton, Warboys and Hexham. 1644–1720*, Hanserd Knollys Society (London, 1854).

Vicars, John, *A Prospective Glasse to Looke into Heaven* (London, 1618).

A Looking-Glasse for Malignants: or, Gods Hand against God-Haters. Containing a Most Terrible yet True Relation of the Many Most Fearefull Personall Examples (in these Present Times, Since the Yeere, 1640.) of Gods Most Evident and Immediate Wrath against our Malevolent Malignants (London, 1643).

The Looking-Glasse for Malignants, Enlarged. Or, The Second Part of Gods Hand against God-Haters (London, 1645).

Vincent, Thomas, *An Explicatory Catechism, Or, An Explanation Of The Assemblies Shorter Catechism* (London, 1680).

Vox Borealis, or the Northern Discoverie: by Way of Dialogue between Jamie and Willie (n.p., 1641).

W., J., *A Booke Declaringe the Fearfull Vexasion, of One Alexander Nyndge: Beynge Moste Horriblye Tormented wyth an Euyll Spirit. The xx. Daie of Januarie. In the Yere of our Lorde. 1573. At Lyeringswell in Suffolke* (London, ?1573 [= modern 1574]).

Walker, Anthony, *Eureka, Eureka. The Virtuous Woman Found her Loss Bewailed, and Character Exemplified in a Sermon Preached at Felsted in Essex, April, 30, 1678. At the Funeral of that most Excellent Lady . . . Mary, Countess Dowager of Warwick* (London, 1678).

Walker, George, *A Sermon Preached in London by a Faithfull Minister of Christ. And Perfected by him: and Now Set Forth to the Publike View of all, for the Justification of the Truth, and Clearing the Innocencie of his Long Suffering for it* (London, 1641).

Walker, John, *The English Pharise, or Religious Ape* (n.p., 1616).

Webster, John, *The White Devil* (London, 1612).

Webster, Tom, and Shipps, Kenneth (eds.), *The Diary of Samuel Rogers 1634–1638* (Woodbridge, 2004).

Weston, William, *The Autobiography of an Elizabethan*, trans. Philip Caraman (London, 1955).

Wetenhall, Edward, *Enter into thy Closet* (London, 1666).

Whitaker, T. D., *Loidis and Elmete* (Leeds, 1816).

Wild, Robert, *The Benefice: a Comedy* (London, 1689).

A Poem upon the Imprisonment of Mr. Calamy (London, 1663).

Williams, J. B. (ed.), *Memoirs of the Life and Character of Sarah Savage* (London, 1821).

Winstanley, Ian (ed.), *The Diary of Roger Lowe of Ashton-in-Makerfield, Lancashire. 1663–1678. Including a Record of Burials at Winwick Church 1666–71* (Wigan, 1994).

Wolfe, Heather (ed.), *Elizabeth Cary Lady Falkland: Life and Letters* (Cambridge, 2001).

Young, Samuel, *Vindiciæ Anti-Baxterianæ: or Some Animadversions on a Book, Intutuled Religueæ Baxterianæ; or The Life of Mr. Richard Baxter* (London, 1696).

SECONDARY SOURCES

Ahnert, Ruth, 'Writing in the Tower of London during the Reformation, ca. 1530–1558', in William H. Sherman and William J. Sheils (eds.), *Prison Writings in Early Modern England*, themed issue of *Huntington Library Quarterly*, **72** (2009), pp. 168–92.

Altick, Richard, *The English Common Reader: A Social History of the Mass Reading Public 1800–1900* (Chicago, IL, 1957).

Anderson, Benedict, *Imagined Communities: Reflections on the Origin and Spread of Nationalism* (London, 1983).

Atherton, Ian, and Como, David, 'The Burning of Edward Wightman: Puritanism, Prelacy and the Politics of Heresy in Early Modern England', *English Historical Review*, **120** (2005), pp. 1215–50.

Baines, Paul and Rogers, Pat, *Edmund Curll, Bookseller* (Oxford, 2007).

Barnard, J., and Bell, M., 'The Early Seventeenth-Century York Book Trade and John Foster's Inventory of 1616', *Proceedings of Leeds Philosophical and Literary Society, Literary and Historical Section*, **24** (2) (1994), pp. 17–132.

Barnard, John and McKenzie, D. F. (eds.), *The Cambridge History of the Book in Britain: Volume IV, 1557–1695* (Cambridge, 2002).

Barnes, Geraldine, 'Curiosity, Wonder, and William Dampier's Painted Prince', *Journal for Early Modern Cultural Studies*, **6** (2006), pp. 31–50.

Barr, Bernard, 'The Minster Library', in G. E. Aylmer and R. Cant (eds.), *A History of York Minster* (Oxford, 1977).

Barry, Jonathan, 'The Press and the Politics of Culture in Bristol, 1660–1775', in Jeremy Black and Jeremy Gregory (eds.), *Culture, Politics and Society in Britain 1660–1800* (Manchester, 1991).

Beedham, B. H., *Notices of Archbishop Williams* (London, 1869).

Bell, Bill, Finkelstein, David, and McCleery, Alistair (eds.), *The Edinburgh History of the Book in Scotland* (4 vols., Edinburgh, 2007).

Bell, Maureen, 'Elizabeth Calvert and the "Confederates"', *Publishing History*, **32** (1992), 5–49.

'"Her Usual Practices": The Later Career of Elizabeth Calvert, 1664–75', *Publishing History*, **35** (1994), 5–64.

Bell, Richard, '"Our People Die Well": Deathbed Scenes in John Wesley's Arminian Magazine', *Mortality*, **10** (2005), pp. 210–23.

Bellany, Alastair, 'Libels in Action: Ritual, Subversion and the English Literary Underground, 1603–42', in Tim Harris (ed.), *The Politics of the Excluded, c. 1500–1850* (Basingstoke, 2001).

'A Poem on the Archbishop's Hearse: Puritanism, Libel, and Sedition after the Hampton Court Conference', *Journal of British Studies*, **34** (1995), pp. 137–64.

'"Raylinge Rymes and Vaunting Verse": Libellous Politics in Early Stuart England, 1603–1628', in Kevin Sharpe and Peter Lake (eds.), *Culture and Politics in Early Stuart England* (London, 1994).

Bendall, Sarah, Brooke, Christopher, and Collinson, Patrick (eds.), *A History of Emmanuel College, Cambridge* (Woodbridge, 2000).

Bennett, Judith M., 'Feminism and History', *Gender and History*, **1** (1989), pp. 251–72.

Bernard, George, 'The Church of England, c. 1529–c. 1642', *History*, **75** (1990), pp. 183–206.

Berry, Helen, 'An Early Coffee House Periodical and Its Readers: the *Athenian Mercury*, 1691–1697', *The London Journal*, **25** (2000), pp. 14–33.

Gender, Society and Print Culture in Late-Stuart England: the Cultural World of the Athenian Mercury (Aldershot, 2003).

Bigsby, Robert, *Historical and Topographical Description of Repton, in the County of Derby* (London, 1854).

Blair, Ann, *The Theater of Nature: Jean Bodin and Renaissance Science* (Princeton, NJ, 1997).

Blatchly, J., *The Town Library of Ipswich* (Woodbridge, 1989).

Bossy, John, *Christianity in the West, 1400–1700* (Oxford, 1985).

The English Catholic Community 1570–1850 (London, 1975).

'The Social History of Confession in the Age of Reformation', *Transactions of the Royal Historical Society*, 5th ser., **25** (1975), pp. 21–38.

Bourdieu, Pierre, *Distinction: A Social Critique of the Judgement of Taste* (London, 1984).

The Field of Cultural Production, ed. Randal Johnson (Cambridge, 1993).

Bourdieu, Pierre, and Chartier, Roger, 'La Lecture: Une pratique culturelle', in Roger Chartier (ed.), *Pratiques de la lecture* (Marseille, 1985).

Braddick, Michael J., (ed.), *The Politics of Gesture: Historical Perspectives* (*Past and Present* supplement no. 4, Oxford, 2009).

Brayman Hackel, Heidi, *Reading Material in Early Modern England: Print, Gender, and Literacy* (Cambridge, 2005).

Bremer, Francis J., *John Winthrop: America's Forgotten Founding Father* (Oxford, 2003).

Brigden, Susan, *London and the Reformation* (Oxford, 1989).

Brown, Matthew P., *The Pilgrim and the Bee: Reading Rituals and Book Culture in Early New England* (Philadelphia, PA, 2007).

Bryan, Jennifer, *Looking Inward: Devotional Reading and the Private Self in Late Medieval England* (Philadelphia, PA, 2008).

Burckhardt, Jacob, *The Civilization of the Renaissance in Italy*, trans. S. G. C. Middlemore, introduction by Peter Burke (London, 1990).

Bush, Sargent, and Ramussen, Carl J., *The Library of Emmanuel College, Cambridge, 1584–1637* (Cambridge, 1986).

Calvino, Italo, *If on a Winter's Night a Traveller*, trans. William Weaver (London, 1983).

Cambers, Andrew, '"But Where Shall My Soul Repose?" Nonconformity, Science and the Geography of the Afterlife, c. 1660–1720', in Peter Clarke and Tony Claydon (eds.), *The Church, the Afterlife and the Fate of the Soul*, Studies in Church History, **45** (Woodbridge, 2009), pp. 268–79.

'Demonic Possession, Literacy, and "Superstition" in Early Modern England', *Past and Present*, **202** (2009), pp. 3–35.

'Pastoral Laudianism? Religious Politics in the 1630s: A Leicestershire Rector's Annotations', *Midland History*, **27** (2002), pp. 38–51.

'Readers' Marks and Religious Practice: Margaret Hoby's Marginalia', in John N. King (ed.), *Tudor Books and Readers: Materiality and the Construction of Meaning* (Cambridge, 2010).

'Reading, the Godly, and Self-Writing in England, circa 1580–1720', *Journal of British Studies*, **46** (2007), pp. 796–825.

Cambers, Andrew, and Wolfe, Michelle, 'Reading, Family Religion, and Evangelical Identity in Late Stuart England', *Historical Journal*, **47** (2004), pp. 875–96.

Carley, James (ed.), *The Libraries of King Henry VIII* (London, 2000).

Carlson, Leland H., *Martin Marprelate, Gentleman: Master Job Throckmorton Laid Open in His Colors* (San Marino, CA, 1981).

Champion, Justin, *Republican Learning: John Toland and the Crisis of Christian Culture, 1696–1722* (Manchester, 2003).

Chartier, Roger, *The Cultural Uses of Print in Early Modern France*, trans. Lydia G. Cochrane (Princeton, NJ, 1987).

'Culture as Appropriation: Popular Cultural Uses in Early Modern France', in S. Kaplan (ed.), *Understanding Popular Culture* (Berlin, 1984).

The Order of Books: Readers, Authors, and Libraries in Europe between the Fourteenth and Eighteenth Centuries, trans. Lydia G. Cochrane (Stanford, CA, 1994).

'*The Order of Books* Revisited', *Modern Intellectual History*, **4** (2007), pp. 509–19.

Chartier, Roger, and Martin, Henri-Jean, *Histoire de l'édition française* (4 vols., Paris, 1982–6).

Clark, Stuart, *Vanities of the Eye: Vision in Early Modern European Culture* (Oxford, 2007).

Claydon, Tony, 'The Sermon, the "Public Sphere" and the Political Culture of Late Seventeenth-Century England', in Lori Anne Ferrell and Peter McCullough (eds.), *The English Sermon Revised: Religion, Literature and History, 1600–1750* (Manchester, 2001).

Clegg, Cyndia Susan, 'Burning Books as Propaganda in Jacobean England', in Andrew Hadfield (ed.), *Literature and Censorship in Renaissance England* (Basingstoke, 2001).

Coffey, John, and Lim, Paul C. H. (eds.), *The Cambridge Companion to Puritanism* (Cambridge, 2008).

Cogswell, Thomas, 'Underground Verse and the Transformation of Early Stuart Political Culture', *Huntington Library Quarterly*, **60** (1998), pp. 303–26.

Cohen, I. Bernard, (ed.), *Puritanism and the Rise of Modern Science: The Merton Thesis* (New Brunswick, NJ, 1990).

Revolution in Science (Cambridge, MA, 1985).

Colley, Linda, *Britons: Forging the Nation 1707–1837* (New Haven, CT, 1992).

Collins, Wilkie, *The Moonstone* (London, 1868).

Collinson, Patrick, 'Books of the People', *Times Literary Supplement*, 29 June 2001.

'Cranbrook and the Fletchers: Popular and Unpopular Religion in the Kentish Weald', in P. N. Brooks (ed.), *Reformation Principle and Practice: Essays in Honour of Arthur Geoffrey Dickens* (London, 1980).

'Ecclesiastical Vitriol: Religious Satire in the 1590s and the Invention of Puritanism', in John Guy (ed.), *The Reign of Elizabeth I: Court and Culture in the Last Decade* (Cambridge, 1995).

'Elizabethan and Jacobean Puritanism as Forms of Popular Religious Culture', in Christopher Durston and Jacqueline Eales (eds.), *The Culture of English Puritanism, 1560–1700* (Basingstoke, 1996).

The Elizabethan Puritan Movement (London, 1967).

From Iconoclasm to Iconophobia: The Cultural Impact of the Second English Reformation, Stenton Lecture 1985 (Reading, 1986).

'Lectures by Combination: Structures and Characteristics of Church Life in Seventeenth-Century England', *Bulletin of the Institute of Historical Research*, **48** (1975), pp. 182–213.

'"A Magazine of Religious Patterns": An Erasmian Topic Transposed in English Protestantism', in his *Godly People: Essays on English Protestantism and Puritanism* (London, 1983).

The Religion of Protestants: The Church in English Society, 1559–1625 (Oxford, 1982).

'Shepherds, Sheepdogs, and Hirelings: The Pastoral Ministry in Post-Reformation England', in W. J. Sheils and D. Wood (eds.), *The Ministry: Clerical and Lay*, Studies in Church History, **26** (Oxford, 1989), pp. 185–220.

'The Theatre Constructs Puritanism', in David L. Smith, Richard Strier and David Bevington (eds.), *The Theatrical City: Culture, Theatre and Politics in London, 1576–1649* (Cambridge, 1995).

Collinson, Patrick, Craig, John, and Usher, Brett (eds.), *Conferences and Combination Lectures in the Elizabethan Church: Dedham and Bury St Edmunds 1582–1590* (Woodbridge, 2003).

Como, David R., *Blown by the Spirit: Puritanism and the Emergence of an Antinomian Underground in Pre-Civil-War England* (Stanford, CA, 2004).

'Secret Printing, the Crisis of 1640, and the Origins of Civil War Radicalism', *Past and Present*, **196** (2007), pp. 37–82.

Como, David, and Lake, Peter, 'Puritans, Antinomians, and Laudians in Caroline London: The Strange Case of Peter Shaw and Its Contexts', *Journal of Ecclesiastical History*, **50** (1999), pp. 684–715.

Condren, Conal, 'More Parish Library, Salop', *Library History*, **7** (1987), pp. 141–62.

Connor, T. P., 'Malignant Reading: John Squier's Newgate Prison Library, 1642–46', *The Library*, 7th ser., **7** (2006).

Coster, Will, *Baptism and Spiritual Kinship in Early Modern England* (Aldershot, 2002).

Cowan, Brian, 'The Rise of the Coffeehouse Reconsidered', *Historical Journal*, **47** (2004), pp. 21–46.

The Social Life of Coffee: The Emergence of the British Coffeehouse (New Haven, CT, 2005).

Craig, John S., 'The Bury Stirs Revisited: An Analysis of the Townsmen', *Proceedings of the Suffolk Institute of Archaeology and History*, **37** (1991), pp. 208–24.

'Forming a Protestant Consciousness? Erasmus' *Paraphrases* in English Parishes, 1547–1666', in Hilmar Pabel and Mark Vessey eds., *Holy*

Scripture Speaks: Studies in the Production and Reception of Erasmus'
Paraphrases on the New Testament (Toronto, 2002).

'The Marginalia of Dr Rowland Taylor', *Historical Research*, **64** (1991),
pp. 411–20.

Reformation, Politics and Polemics: The Growth of Protestantism in East Anglian
Market Towns, 1500–1610 (Aldershot, 2001).

Cressy, David, 'Book Burning in Tudor and Stuart England', *Sixteenth Century*
Journal, **36** (2005), pp. 359–74.

'Books as Totems in Seventeenth-Century England and New England',
Journal of Library History, **21** (1986), pp. 92–106.

England on Edge: Crisis and Revolution, 1640–1642 (Oxford, 2006).

Literacy and the Social Order: Reading and Writing in Tudor and Stuart
England (Cambridge, 1980).

Cross, Claire, *Magistrates and Ministers: Religion in Hull and Leeds from the*
Reformation to the Civil War, Borthwick Papers, **67** (York, 1985).

The Puritan Earl: The Life of Henry Hastings, Third Earl of Huntingdon, 1536–
1595 (London, 1966).

'The Third Earl of Huntingdon's Death-Bed: A Calvinist Example of the "Ars
Moriendi"', *Northern History*, **21** (1985), pp. 80–107.

Curtis, T. C., and Speck, W. A., 'The Societies for the Reformation of Manners:
A Case Study in the Theory and Practice of Moral Reform', *Literature and*
History, **3** (1976), pp. 45–64.

Damrau, Peter, *The Reception of English Puritan Literature in Germany* (London,
2006).

Daniell, David, *The Bible in English: Its History and Influence* (New Haven, CT,
2003).

Darnton, Robert, *The Great Cat Massacre: And Other Episodes in French Cultural*
History (New York, 1984).

The Kiss of Lamourette: Reflections in Cultural History (London, 1990).

Davies, Robert, *A Memoir of the York Press: With Notices of Authors, Printers, and*
Stationers, in the Sixteenth, Seventeenth, and Eighteenth Centuries (Facsimile
reprint, York, 1988; original edition Westminster, 1868).

Davis, Natalie Zemon, 'Beyond the Market: Books as Gifts in Sixteenth-Century
France', *Transactions of the Royal Historical Society*, 5th ser., **33** (1983), pp.
69–88.

De Certeau, Michel, *Culture in the Plural*, ed. Luce Giard, trans. Tom Conley
(Minneapolis, MN, 1997).

'Reading as Poaching', in his *The Practice of Everyday Life*, trans. Steven
Rendall (Los Angeles, CA, 1984).

Dickens, A. G., *Reformation and Society in Sixteenth-Century Europe* (London,
1966).

Dijkgraaf, Hendrik, *The Library of a Jesuit Community at Holbeck,*
Nottinghamshire (1679) (Nijmegen and Cambridge, 2003).

Dillon, Anne, *The Construction of Martyrdom in the English Catholic Community,*
1535–1603 (Aldershot, 2002).

Douglas, Mary, *Purity and Danger: An Analysis of Concepts of Pollution and Taboo* (London, 1966).

Duffy, Eamon, *Marking the Hours: English People and Their Prayers, 1240–1570* (New Haven, CT, 2006).

The Stripping of the Altars: Traditional Religion in England c. 1400–c. 1580 (New Haven, CT, 1992).

The Voices of Morebath: Reformation and Rebellion in an English Village (New Haven, CT, 2001).

Durston, Christopher, and Eales, Jacqueline (eds.), *The Culture of English Puritanism, 1560–1700* (Basingstoke, 1996).

Eales, Jacqueline, *Puritans and Roundheads: The Harleys of Brampton Bryan and the Outbreak of the English Civil War* (Cambridge, 1990).

'A Road to Revolution: The Continuity of Puritanism, 1559–1642', in Christopher Durston and Jacqueline Eales (eds.), *The Culture of English Puritanism, 1560–1700* (Basingstoke, 1996).

'Thomas Pierson and the Transmission of the Moderate Puritan Tradition', *Midland History*, **20** (1995), pp. 73–102.

Eco, Umberto, *The Name of the Rose*, trans. William Weaver (London, 1983).

Edwards, Edward, *Memoirs of Libraries* (2 vols., London, 1859).

Edwards, Mark U. Jr, *Printing, Propaganda, and Martin Luther* (Berkeley, CA, 1994).

Eisenstein, Elizabeth L., *The Printing Press as an Agent of Change: Communications and Cultural Transformations in Early Modern Europe* (2 vols., Cambridge, 1979).

Ekirch, Roger A., 'Sleep We Have Lost: Pre-industrial Slumber in the British Isles', *American Historical Review*, **106** (2001), pp. 343–86.

Eliot, George, *Middlemarch: A Study of Provincial Life* (Edinburgh and London, 1871–2).

Ellis, Markman, 'Coffee-House Libraries in Mid Eighteenth-Century London', *The Library*, 7th Ser., **10** (2009), pp. 3–40.

Elton, G. R., *The Sources of History: Studies in the Uses of Historical Evidence. England 1200–1640* (London, 1969).

Engelsing, Rolf, *Der Bürger als Leser: Lesergeschichte in Deutschland 1500–1800* (Stuttgart, 1974).

Erler, Mary C., *Women, Reading and Piety in Late Medieval England* (Cambridge, 2002).

Evenden, Elizabeth, *Patents, Pictures and Patronage: John Day and the Tudor Book Trade* (Aldershot, 2008).

Evenden, Elizabeth, and Freeman, Thomas S., *Religion and the Book in Early Modern England: The Making of John Foxe's 'Book of Martyrs'* (Cambridge, forthcoming).

Febvre, Lucien, and Martin, Henri-Jean, *L'apparition du livre* (Paris, 1971), trans. David Gerard as *The Coming of the Book: The Impact of Printing 1450–1800* (London, 1976).

Fehrenbach, Robert, and Leedham-Green, Elisabeth (eds.), *Private Libraries in Renaissance England* (Binghamton, NY, 1992–).

Ferch, David L., '"Good Books Are a Very Great Mercy to the World": Persecution, Private Libraries, and the Printed Word in the Early Development of the Dissenting Academies, 1663–1730', *Journal of Library History*, **21** (1986), pp. 350–61.

Ferguson, James P., *The Parochial Libraries of Bishop Wilson* (Douglas, Isle of Man, 1975).

Fincham, Kenneth, *Prelate as Pastor: The Episcopate of James I* (Oxford, 1990).

Fish, Stanley, *Is There a Text in This Class? The Authority of Interpretive Communities* (Cambridge, MA, 1980).

Fissel, Mary E., *Vernacular Bodies: The Politics of Reproduction in Early Modern England* (Oxford, 2004).

Flather, Amanda, *Gender and Space in Early Modern England* (Woodbridge, 2007).

Fleming, Juliet, *Graffiti and the Writing Arts of Early Modern England* (London, 2001).

Foley, Henry, *Records of the English Province of the Society of Jesus: Historic Facts Illustrative of the Labours and Sufferings of Its Members in the Sixteenth and Seventeenth Centuries* (7 vols., London, 1877–82).

Ford, Alan, *James Ussher: Theology, History, and Politics in Early-Modern Ireland and England* (Oxford, 2007).

Foucault, Michel, *Discipline and Punish: The Birth of the Prison*, trans. Alan Sheridan (London, 1977).

Fox, Adam, 'Ballads, Libels and Popular Ridicule in Jacobean England', *Past and Present*, **145** (1994), pp. 47–83.

Oral and Literate Culture in England, 1500–1700 (Oxford, 2000).

Francis, Jane, 'The Kederminster Library: An Account of Its Origins and a Reconstruction of Its Contents', *Records of Buckinghamshire*, **36** (1996), pp. 62–85.

Francois, M. E., 'The Social and Economic Development of Halifax, 1558–1640', *Proceedings of the Leeds Philosophical and Literary Society: Literary and Historical Section*, **11** (1964–6), pp. 217–80.

Freeman, Thomas S., 'Dissenters from a Dissenting Church: The Challenge of the Freewillers, 1550–1558', in Peter Marshall and Alec Ryrie (eds.), *The Beginnings of English Protestantism* (Cambridge, 2002).

'Publish and Perish: The Scribal Culture of the Marian Martyrs', in Julia Crick and Alexandra Walsham (eds.), *The Uses of Script and Print, 1300–1700* (Cambridge, 2004).

Friedman, Alice, *House and Household in Elizabethan England: Wollaton Hall and the Willoughby Family* (Chicago, IL, 1989).

Gawthrop, Richard, and Strauss, Gerald, 'Protestantism and Literacy in Early Modern Germany', *Past and Present*, **104** (1984), pp. 31–55.

Geertz, Clifford, *The Interpretation of Cultures: Selected Essays* (London, 1973).

Gentles, Ian, 'The Iconography of Revolution: England 1642–1649', in Ian Gentles, John Morrill and Blair Worden (eds.), *Soldiers, Writers, and Statesmen of the English Revolution* (Cambridge, 1998).

Gillespie, Raymond, *Reading Ireland: Print, Reading and Social Change in Early Modern Ireland* (Manchester, 2005).

Gilmont, Jean-François (ed.), *The Reformation and the Book*, trans. Karin Maag (Aldershot, 1998).

Gingerich, Owen, *The Book Nobody Read: Chasing the Revolutions of Nicolaus Copernicus* (New York, 2004).

Ginzburg, Carlo, *The Cheese and the Worms: The Cosmos of a Sixteenth-Century Miller*, trans. John and Anne Tedeschi (London, 1980).

Girouard, Mark, *Life in the English Country House: A Social and Architectural History* (New Haven, CT, 1978).

Goody, Jack, *The Interface between the Written and the Oral* (Cambridge, 1987).

Grafton, Anthony, *Commerce with the Classics: Ancient Books and Renaissance Readers* (Ann Arbor, MI, 1997).

Green, Ian, *The Christian's ABC: Catechisms and Catechizing in England c. 1530–1740* (Oxford, 1996).

Print and Protestantism in Early Modern England (Oxford, 2000).

Gregory, Brad S., *Salvation at Stake: Christian Martyrdom in Early Modern Europe* (Cambridge, MA, 1999).

Griffiths, Paul, and Jenner, Mark S. R. (eds.), *Londinopolis: Essays in the Cultural and Social History of Early Modern London* (Manchester, 2000).

Habermas, Jürgen, *The Structural Transformation of the Public Sphere: An Inquiry into a Category of Bourgeois Society*, trans. Thomas Burger with the assistance of Frederick Lawrence (Cambridge, 1989).

Haigh, Christopher, 'The Continuity of Catholicism in the English Reformation', *Past and Present*, **93** (1981), pp. 37–69.

English Reformations: Religion, Politics, and Society under the Tudors (Oxford, 1993).

'The Fall of a Church or the Rise of a Sect? Post-Reformation Catholicism in England', *Historical Journal*, **21** (1978), pp. 182–6.

The Plain Man's Pathways to Heaven: Kinds of Christianity in Post-Reformation England, 1570–1640 (Oxford, 2007).

Hall, David D., *Worlds of Wonder, Days of Judgment: Popular Religious Belief in Early New England* (New York, 1989).

Cultures of Print: Essays in the History of the Book (Amherst, MA, 1996).

(ed.), *A History of the Book in America* (5 vols, Cambridge, 2000–).

Haller, William, *The Rise of Puritanism* (New York, 1938).

Foxe's Book of Martyrs and the Elect Nation (London, 1963).

Hanson, T. W., 'Halifax Parish Church Library', *Transactions of the Halifax Antiquarian Society*, (1951), pp. 37–47.

Harkness, Deborah E., *The Jewel House: Elizabethan London and the Scientific Revolution* (New Haven, CT, 2007).

Harris, Frances, *Transformations of Love: The Friendship of John Evelyn and Margaret Godolphin* (Oxford, 2002).

Harris, J, 'A Rare and Precious Room: The Kederminster Library, Langley', *Country Life* (1977), pp. 1576–9.

Harvey, Karen, and Shepard, Alexandra, 'What Have Historians done with Masculinity? Reflections on Five Centuries of British History, circa 1500–1950', *Journal of British Studies*, **44** (2005), pp. 274–80.

Hastings, Adrian, *The Construction of Nationhood: Ethnicity, Religion and Nationalism* (Cambridge, 1997).

Heal, Felicity, *Reformation in Britain and Ireland* (Oxford, 2003).

Heal, Felicity, and Holmes, Clive, *The Gentry in England and Wales, 1500–1700* (Basingstoke, 1994).

Hessayon, Ariel, *'Gold Tried in the Fire': The Prophet TheaurauJohn Tany and the English Revolution* (Aldershot, 2007).

Hessayon, Ariel, and Keene, Nicholas (eds.), *Scripture and Scholarship in Early Modern England* (Aldershot, 2006).

Heyworth, P., *James Forbes, Nonconformist: His Library* (Toronto, 1968).

Hill, Christopher, *Society and Puritanism in Pre-Revolutionary England* (London, 1964).

The World Turned Upside Down: Radical Ideas during the English Revolution (revised edn, London, 1975).

Hindmarsh, D. Bruce, *The Evangelical Conversion Narrative: Spiritual Autobiography in Early Modern England* (Oxford, 2005).

Hoare, Peter (ed.), *The Cambridge History of Libraries in Britain and Ireland* (3 vols., Cambridge, 2006).

Hoggart, Richard, *The Uses of Literacy: Aspects of Working-Class Life with Special Reference to Publications and Entertainments* (London, 1957).

Holden, William P., *Anti-Puritan Satire, 1572–1642* (New Haven, CT, 1954).

Hoppe, Harry R., 'John Wolfe, Printer and Publisher, 1579–1601', *The Library*, 4th ser., **14** (1933), pp. 241–88.

Hopper, Andrew, *'Black Tom': Sir Thomas Fairfax and the English Revolution* (Manchester, 2007).

Houlbrooke, Ralph, *The English Family, 1450–1700* (London, 1984).

Death, Religion, and the Family in England, 1480–1750 (Oxford, 1998).

Hughes, Ann, *Gangraena and the Struggle for the English Revolution* (Oxford, 2004).

Hunt, Arnold, *The Art of Hearing: English Preachers and Their Audiences, 1590–1640* (Cambridge, forthcoming).

'The Lord's Supper in Early Modern England', *Past and Present*, **161** (1998), pp. 39–83.

Hunter, Michael, Mandelbrote, Giles, Ovenden, Richard, and Smith, Nigel (eds.), *A Radical's Books: The Library Catalogue of Samuel Jeake of Rye, 1623–90* (London, 1999).

Ingram, Martin, 'Reformation of Manners in Early Modern England', in Paul Griffiths, Adam Fox and Steve Hindle (eds.), *The Experience of Authority in Early Modern England* (Basingstoke, 1996).

Isaac, P. C. G., An Inventory of Books Sold by a Seventeenth-Century Penrith Grocer, *History of the Book Trade in the North*, **53** (1989).

Isaac, Rhys, *The Transformation of Virginia, 1740–1790* (Chapel Hill, NC, 1982).

Iser, Wolfgang, *The Act of Reading: A Theory of Aesthetic Response* (Baltimore, MD, 1978).

The Implied Reader: Patterns of Communication in Prose Fiction from Bunyan to Beckett (Baltimore, MD, 1980).

Israel, Jonathan I., *Radical Enlightenment: Philosophy and the Making of Modernity 1650–1750* (Oxford, 2001).

Jackson, H. J., *Marginalia: Readers Writing in Books* (New Haven, CT, 2001).

Romantic Readers: The Evidence of Marginalia (New Haven, CT, 2005).

Jacob, W. M., 'Provision of Books for Poor Clergy Parochial Libraries in the British Isles and the North American Colonies, 1680–1720', in R. N. Swanson (ed.), *The Church and the Book,* Studies in Church History, **38** (Woodbridge, 2004), pp. 257–67.

Jagodzinski, Cecile M., *Privacy and Print: Reading and Writing in Seventeenth-Century England* (Charlottesville, VA, 1999).

James, A. T. S., 'The Forbes Library Southgate Chapel, Gloucester', *Transactions of the Congregational Historical Society,* **10** (1927–9), pp. 100–4.

Jardine, Lisa, and Grafton, Anthony, '"Studied for Action": How Gabriel Harvey Read His Livy', *Past and Present,* **129** (1990), pp. 30–78.

Jayne, Sears, *Library Catalogues of the English Renaissance* (2nd edn, Winchester, 1989).

Johns, Adrian, *The Nature of the Book: Print and Knowledge in the Making* (Chicago, IL, 1998).

Johnson, Trevor, 'Gardening for God: Carmelite Deserts and the Sacralisation of Natural Space in Counter-Reformation Spain', in Will Coster and Andrew Spicer (eds.), *Sacred Space in Early Modern Europe* (Cambridge, 2005).

Ker, N. R., 'Oxford College Libraries in the Sixteenth Century', *Bodleian Library Record,* **6** (1959), pp. 459–515.

(ed.), *The Parochial Libraries of the Church of England* (London, 1959).

King, John. N., *Foxe's Book of Martyrs and Early Modern Print Culture* (Cambridge, 2006).

Knights, Mark, *Representation and Misrepresentation in Later Stuart Britain: Partisanship and Political Culture* (Oxford, 2004).

Knöll, Stefanie A., *Creating Academic Communities: Funeral Monuments to Professors at Oxford, Leiden and Tübingen 1580–1700* (n.p., 2003).

Krivatsky, N., and Yeandle, L., 'Books of Sir Edward Dering of Kent, 1598–1644', in Robert Fehrenbach, and Elisabeth Leedham-Green (eds.), *Private Libraries in Renaissance England: A Collection and Catalogue of Tudor and Early Stuart Book-Lists* (Binghamton, NY, 1992–), vol. 1.

Lake, Peter, *The Boxmaker's Revenge: 'Orthodoxy', 'Heterodoxy' and the Politics of the Parish in Early Stuart London* (Manchester, 2001).

'"A Charitable Christian Hatred": The Godly and Their Enemies in the 1630s', in Christopher Durston and Jacqueline Eales (eds.), *The Culture of English Puritanism, 1560–1700* (Basingstoke, 1996).

'Deeds against Nature: Cheap Print, Protestantism and Murder in Early Seventeenth-Century England', in Kevin Sharpe and Peter Lake (eds.), *Culture and Politics in Early Stuart England* (London, 1994).

'Defining Puritanism – Again?', in Francis J. Bremer (ed.), *Puritanism: Transatlantic Perspectives on a Seventeenth-Century Anglo-American Faith* (Boston, MA, 1993).

'The Historiography of Puritanism', in John Coffey and Paul C. H. Lim (eds.), *The Cambridge Companion to Puritanism* (Cambridge, 2008).

Moderate Puritans and the Elizabethan Church (Cambridge, 1982).

'Moving the Goal Posts? Modified Subscription and the Construction of Conformity in the Early Stuart Church', in Peter Lake and Michael Questier (eds.), *Conformity and Orthodoxy in the English Church, c. 1560–1660* (Woodbridge, 2000).

'Popular Form, Puritan Content? Two Puritan Appropriations of the Murder Pamphlet from Mid-Seventeenth-Century London', in Anthony Fletcher and Peter Roberts (eds.), *Religion, Culture and Society in Early Modern Britain: Essays in Honour of Patrick Collinson* (Cambridge, 1994).

'Puritanism, Arminianism and a Shropshire Axe-Murder', *Midland History*, **15** (1990), pp. 37–64.

Lake, Peter, and Como, David R., '"Orthodoxy" and Its Discontents: Dispute Settlement and the Production of "Consensus" in the London (Puritan) "Underground"', *Journal of British Studies*, **39** (2000), pp. 34–70.

Lake, Peter, and Pincus, Steven, 'Rethinking the Public Sphere in Early Modern England', *Journal of British Studies*, **45** (2006), pp. 270–92.

(eds.), *The Politics of the Public Sphere in Early Modern England* (Manchester, 2007).

Lake, Peter, and Questier, Michael, 'Agency, Appropriation and Rhetoric under the Gallows: Puritans, Romanists and the State in Early Modern England', *Past and Present*, **153** (1996), pp. 64–107.

'Margaret Clitherow, Catholic Nonconformity, Martyrology and the Politics of Religious Change in Elizabethan England', *Past and Present*, **185** (2004), pp. 43–90.

'Puritans, Papists, and the "Public Sphere" in Early Modern England: The Edmund Campion Affair in Context', *Journal of Modern History*, **72** (2000), pp. 587–627.

Lake, Peter, with Questier, Michael, *The Antichrist's Lewd Hat: Protestants, Papists, and Players in Post-Reformation England* (New Haven, CT, 2002).

Lamb, Mary Ellen, 'The Agency of the Split Subject: Lady Anne Clifford and the Uses of Reading', *English Literary Renaissance*, **22** (1992), pp. 347–68.

'Margaret Hoby's Diary: Women's Reading Practices and the Gendered Reformation Subject', in Sigrid King (ed.), *Pilgrimage for Love: Essays in Honor of Josephine A. Roberts* (Tempe, AZ, 1999).

'The Sociability of Margaret Hoby's Reading Practices and the Representation of Reformation Interiority', *Critical Survey*, **12** (2) (2000), pp. 17–32.

Lamont, William, *Puritanism and Historical Controversy* (London, 1996).

Lang, Timothy, *The Victorians and the Stuart Heritage* (Cambridge, 1995).

Laslett, P., and Wall, R. (eds.), *Household and Family in Past Time* (Cambridge, 1972).

Leedham-Green, E., and Webber, T. (eds.), *The Cambridge History of Libraries in Britain and Ireland. Volume I. To 1640* (Cambridge, 2006).

Lehmberg, Stanford, *The Later Parliaments of Henry VIII, 1536–1547* (Cambridge, 1977).

Lepore, Jill, *The Name of War: King Philip's War and the Origins of American Identity* (New York, 1998).

Levy, F. J., 'How Information Spread among the Gentry, 1550–1640', *Journal of British Studies*, **21** (1982), pp. 11–34.

Linnell, N., 'The Catalogues of Lincoln Cathedral Library', *Library History*, **7** (1985).
  'Michael Honywood and Lincoln Cathedral Library', *The Library*, 6th ser., **5** (1983), pp. 126–39.

Llewellyn, Nigel, *Funeral Monuments in Post-Reformation England* (Cambridge, 2000).

Love, Harold, 'Preacher and Publisher: Oliver Heywood and Thomas Parkhurst', *Studies in Bibliography*, **31** (1978), pp. 227–35.
  Scribal Publication in Seventeenth-Century England (Oxford, 1993).

MacCulloch, Diarmaid, 'The Myth of the English Reformation', *Journal of British Studies*, **30** (1991), pp. 1–19.

McCullough, Peter, 'Print, Publication, and Religious Politics in Caroline England', *Historical Journal*, **51** (2008), pp. 285–313.

MacDonald, Michael, '"The Fearful Estate of Francis Spira": Narrative, Identity and Emotion in Early Modern England', *Journal of British Studies*, **31** (1992), pp. 32–61.

McDonald, Peter D., 'Implicit Structures and Explicit Interactions: Pierre Bourdieu and the History of the Book', *The Library*, 6th ser., **19** (1997), pp. 105–21.

McElligott, Jason, *Royalism, Print and Censorship in Revolutionary England* (Woodbridge, 2007).

Macfarlane, Alan, and Martin, Gerry, *The Glass Bathyscape: How Glass Changed the World* (London, 2002).

McKenzie, D. F., *Bibliography and the Sociology of Texts* (London, 1986).
  Making Meaning: 'Printers of the Mind' and Other Essays, ed. Peter D. McDonald and Michael F. Suarez, SJ (Amherst, MA, 2002).
  'Speech – Manuscript – Print', in D. Oliphant and R. Bradford, eds., *New Directions in Textual Studies* (Austin, TX, 1990).

McKenzie, D. F., McKitterick, David, and Willison, I. R. (eds.), *The Cambridge History of the Book in Britain* (7 vols., Cambridge, 1999–).

McLachlan, Herbert, *English Education under the Test Acts: Being the History of the Non-Conformist Academies, 1662–1820*, University of Manchester publications no. 213, Historical series no. 59 (Manchester, 1931).

McLuhan, Marshall, *The Gutenberg Galaxy: The Making of Typographic Man* (Toronto, 1962).

McRae, Andrew, *Literature, Satire, and the Early Stuart State* (Cambridge, 2004).
  (ed.), *'Railing Rhymes': Politics and Poetry in Early Stuart England*, themed issue of *Huntington Library Quarterly*, **69** (2006).

Maggs Bros Ltd, Catalogue 1350: STC and Wing Books Printed in England 1500–1700 from the Library of James Stevens-Cox (1910–1997) (London, 2003).

Mandelbrote, G., and Manley, K. A. (eds.), *The Cambridge History of Libraries in Britain and Ireland. Volume II 1640–1850* (Cambridge, 2006).

Manguel, Alberto, *A History of Reading* (London, 1996).

Mankell, Henning, *Before the Frost*, trans. Ebba Segerberg (London, 2005).

Manley, K. A., 'The SPCK and English Book Clubs before 1720', *Bodleian Library Record*, **13** (1989), pp. 231–43.

Marchant, R. A., *The Puritans and the Church Courts in the Diocese of York 1560–1642* (London, 1960).

Marsh, Christopher W., *The Family of Love in English Society, 1550–1630* (Cambridge, 1994).

Marshall, Peter, *Beliefs and the Dead in Reformation England* (Oxford, 2002).

Mother Leakey and the Bishop: A Ghost Story (Oxford, 2007).

Mascuch, Michael, *Origins of the Individualist Self: Autobiography and Self-Identity in England, 1591–1791* (Cambridge, 1997).

Matar, Nabil, *Europe through Arab Eyes 1578–1727* (New York, 2009).

Matthew, H. C. G., and Harrison, Brian (eds.), *The Oxford Dictionary of National Biography* (60 vols., Oxford, 2004).

Matthews, A. G., *Calamy Revised: Being a Revision of Edmund Calamy's Account of the Ministers and Others Ejected and Silenced, 1660–2* (Oxford, 1934).

Mayo, C. H. (ed.), *The Municipal Records of the Borough of Dorchester, Dorset* (Exeter, 1908).

Morgan, Edmund S., *The Puritan Family: Religion and Domestic Relations in Seventeenth-Century New England* (revised edn, New York, 1966).

Morgan, J., *Godly Learning: Puritan Attitudes towards Reason, Learning and Education 1540–1640* (Cambridge, 1986).

Morley, H. (ed.), *The Earlier Life and the Chief Earlier Works of Daniel Defoe* (London, 1889).

Morrill, John, 'William Dowsing, the Bureaucratic Puritan', in John Morrill, Paul Slack and Daniel R. Woolf (eds.), *Public Duty and Private Conscience in Seventeenth-Century England* (Oxford, 1992).

Morris, John (ed.), *The Troubles of Our Catholic Forefathers Related by Themselves* (3 vols., London, 1872–7).

Mortimer, J. E., 'The Library Catalogue of Anthony Higgin, Dean of Ripon (1608–1624)', *Proceedings of the Leeds Philosophical and Literary Society, Literary and Historical Section*, **10** (1962), pp. 1–75.

Mullan, David George, *Narratives of the Religious Self in Early-Modern Scotland* (Aldershot, 2010).

Munby, A. N. L., and Coral, L., *British Book Sale Catalogues 1676–1800* (London, 1977).

Murray, Molly, 'Measured Sentences: Forming Literature in the Early Modern Prison', in William H. Sherman and William J. Sheils (eds.), *Prison Writings in Early Modern England*, themed issue of *Huntington Library Quarterly*, **72** (2009), pp. 147–67.

Myers, Robin, Harris, M., and Mandelbrote, Giles (eds.), *Under the Hammer: Book Auctions since the Seventeenth Century* (London, 2001).

Nelles, Paul, 'The Library as an Instrument of Discovery: Gabriel Naudé and the Uses of History', in Donald R. Kelley (ed.), *History and the Disciplines: The Reclassification of Knowledge in Early Modern Europe* (Rochester, NY, 1997).

Nuttall, Geoffrey F., *The Holy Spirit in Puritan Faith and Experience* (revised edn, Chicago, IL, 1992).

'A Transcript of Richard Baxter's Library Catalogue', *Journal of Ecclesiastical History*, **2** (1951), pp. 207–21; 3 (1952), pp. 74–100.

Oldenburg, Ray, *The Great Good Place: Cafés, Coffee Shops, Community Centers, Beauty Parlors, General Stores, Bars, Hangouts and How They Get You Through the Day* (New York, NY, 1989).

Oldham, J. B., 'Shrewsbury School Library', *The Library*, 6th ser., **14** (1959), pp. 81–99.

Ong, Walter, *Orality and Literacy: The Technologizing of the Word* (London, 1982).

Orlin, Lena Cowen, *Locating Privacy in Tudor London* (Oxford, 2007).

Palmer, Richard, 'In the Steps of Sir Thomas Bodley: The Libraries of Lambeth Palace and Sion College in the Seventeenth Century', *Lambeth Palace Library Annual Review* (2006), pp. 53–67.

Palmes, William, *The Life of Mrs Dorothy Lawson, of St Anthony's, near Newcastle-on-Tyne* (London, 1855).

Parker, K. L., and Carlson, E. J. (eds.), *'Practical Divinity': The Works and Life of Reverend Richard Greenham* (Aldershot, 1998).

Pearce, E. H., *Sion College and Library* (Cambridge, 1913).

Perkin, Michael (ed.), *A Directory of the Parochial Libraries of the Church of England and the Church in Wales* (London, 2004).

Perry, Sir Erskine (ed.), *The Van den Bempde Papers: The Bibliographical and Historical Miscellanies of the Philobiblion Society*, Vol. XII (London, 1868–9).

Peters, Kate, *Print Culture and the Early Quakers* (Cambridge, 2005).

Pettegree, Andrew, *Reformation and the Culture of Persuasion* (Cambridge, 2005).

Petti, Anthony, 'Stephen Vallenger (1541–1591)', *Recusant History*, **6** (1962), pp. 248–64.

Pincus, Steven, '"Coffee Politicians does Create": Coffeehouses and Restoration Political Culture', *Journal of Modern History*, **67** (1995), pp. 807–34.

Pollard, A. W., and Redgrave, G. R., *A Short-Title Catalogue of Books Printed in England, Scotland, and Ireland and of English Books Printed Abroad 1473–1640* (2nd edn, London, 1976–91).

Porter, Roy, 'Reading: A Health Warning', in Robin Myers and Michael Harris (eds.), *Medicine, Mortality and the Book Trade* (Folkestone, 1998).

Porter, Roy, and Teich, Mikuláš, *The Scientific Revolution in National Context* (Cambridge, 1992).

Postles, David A., *Social Geographies in England (1200–1640)* (Washington, DC, 2007).

Pounds, N. J. G., *A History of the English Parish: The Culture of Religion from Augustine to Victoria* (Cambridge, 2000).

Rambuss, Richard, *Closet Devotions* (Durham, NC, 1998).

Raven, James, *The Business of Books: Booksellers and the English Book Trade 1450–1850* (New Haven, CT, 2007).

Raymond, Joad, *Pamphlets and Pamphleteering in Early Modern Britain* (Cambridge, 2003).

Reynolds, David (ed.), *Christ's: A Cambridge College over Five Centuries* (London, 2005).

Richardson, R. C., *Puritanism in North-West England: A Regional Study of the Diocese of Chester to 1642* (Manchester, 1972).

Roberts, Sasha, 'Shakespeare "Creepes into the Womens Closets about Bedtime": Women Reading in a Room of Their Own', in Gordon McMullan (ed.), *Renaissance Configurations: Voices/Bodies/Spaces, 1580–1690* (New York, 1998).

Robson, Lynn, '"Now Farewell to the Lawe, too Long Have I Been in thy Subjection": Early Modern Murder, Calvinism and Female Spiritual Authority', *Literature and Theology*, **22** (2008), pp. 295–312.

Roper, Lyndal, *The Holy Household: Women and Morals in Reformation Augsburg* (Oxford, 1989).

Rose, Jonathan, *The Intellectual Life of the British Working Classes* (New Haven, CT, 2001).

Rosecrans, Jennipher Allen, 'Wearing the Universe: Symbolic Markings in Early Modern England', in Jane Caplan (ed.), *Written on the Body: The Tattoo in European and American History* (London, 2000).

Rostenberg, Leona, *Literary, Political, Scientific, Religious and Legal Publishing, Printing and Bookselling in England, 1551–1700: Twelve Studies* (2 vols., New York, 1965).

Rowse, A. L., *The England of Elizabeth*, ed. Christopher Haigh (Basingstoke, 2003; first published London, 1950).

Saenger, Paul, 'Silent Reading: Its Impact on Late Medieval Script and Society', *Viator*, **13** (1982), pp. 367–414.

Space between Words: The Origins of Silent Reading (Stanford, CA, 1997).

St Clair, William, *The Reading Nation in the Romantic Period* (Cambridge, 2004).

Samuel, Raphael, 'The Discovery of Puritanism, 1820–1900: A Preliminary Sketch', in Jane Garnett and Colin Matthew (eds.), *Revival and Religion since 1700: Essays for John Walsh* (London, 1993).

Schaffer, Simon, '"On Seeing Me Write": Inscription Devices in the South Seas', *Representations*, **97** (2007), pp. 90–122.

Schücking, L. L., *Die Familie im Puritanismus. Studien über Familie und Literatur in England im 16. 17. und 18. Jahrhundert* (Leipzig and Berlin, 1929) (English edn L. L. Schücking, *The Puritan Family: A Social Study from the Literary Sources*, trans. Brian Battershaw (London, 1969)).

Schurink, Fred, 'Like a Hand in the Margine of a Booke': William Blount's Marginalia and the Politics of Sidney's Arcadia', *Review of English Studies*, **59** (2008), pp. 1–24.

Scott, Jonathan, *England's Troubles: Seventeenth-Century English Political Instability in European Context* (Cambridge, 2000).

Scott-Warren, Jason, *Sir John Harrington and the Book as Gift* (Oxford, 2001).

Scribner, R. W., *For the Sake of Simple Folk: Popular Propaganda for the German Reformation* (Cambridge, 1981).

'Incombustible Luther: The Image of the Reformer in Early Modern Germany', *Past and Present*, **110** (1986), pp. 38–68.

Seaver, Paul S., *Wallington's World: A Puritan Artisan in Seventeenth-Century London* (London, 1985).

Shagan, Ethan H., *Popular Politics and the English Reformation* (Cambridge, 2003).

Sharpe, James A., '"Last Dying Speeches": Religion, Ideology and Public Execution in Seventeenth-Century England', *Past and Present*, **107** (1985), pp. 144–67.

Sharpe, Kevin, *The Personal Rule of Charles I* (New Haven, CT, 1993).

Reading Revolutions: The Politics of Reading in Early Modern England (New Haven, CT, 2000).

Sir Robert Cotton, 1586–1631: History and Politics in Early Modern England (Oxford, 1979).

Sharpe, Kevin, and Lake, Peter (eds.), *Culture and Politics in Early Stuart England* (London, 1994).

Sheils, W. J., *The Puritans in the Diocese of Peterborough 1558–1610* (Northampton, 1979).

'"The Right of the Church": The Clergy, Tithe, and the Courts at York, 1540–1640', in W. J. Sheils and D. Wood (eds.), *The Church and Wealth,* Studies in Church History, **24** (1987), pp. 231–55.

Sheils, William, and Sheils, Sarah, 'Textiles and Reform: Halifax and Its Hinterland', in Patrick Collinson and John Craig (eds.), *The Reformation in English Towns, 1500–1640* (Basingstoke, 1998).

Sher, Richard B., *The Enlightenment and the Book: Scottish Authors and Their Publishers in Eighteenth-Century Britain, Ireland and America* (Chicago, IL, 2006).

Sherman, William H., *John Dee: The Politics of Reading and Writing in the English Renaissance* (Amherst, MA, 1995).

Renaissance Libraries (forthcoming).

Used Books: Marking Readers in Renaissance England (Philadelphia, PA, 2008).

Slights, William W. E., *Managing Readers: Printed Marginalia in English Renaissance Books* (Ann Arbor, MI, 2001).

Smith, Nigel, *Perfection Proclaimed: Language and Literature in English Radical Religion, 1640–1660* (Oxford, 1989).

Smyth, Adam, *Autobiography in Early Modern England* (Cambridge, 2010).

Spufford, Margaret, *Contrasting Communities: English Villagers in the Sixteenth and Seventeenth Centuries* (Cambridge, 1974).

'First Steps in Literacy: The Reading and Writing Experiences of the Humblest Seventeenth-Century Spiritual Autobiographers', *Social History*, **4** (1979), pp. 407–35.

Small Books and Pleasant Histories: Popular Fiction and Its Readership in Seventeenth-Century England (London, 1981).

Spurr, John, *English Puritanism, 1603–1689* (Basingstoke, 1998).

Stachniewski, John, *The Persecutory Imagination: English Puritanism and the Literature of Religious Despair* (Oxford, 1991).

Stallybrass, Peter, 'Books and Scrolls: Navigating the Bible', in Jennifer Anderson and Elizabeth Sauer (eds.), *Books and Readers in Early Modern England: Material Studies* (Philadelphia, PA, 2002).

Stock, Brian, *After Augustine: The Meditative Reader and the Text* (Philadelphia, PA, 2001).

Stranks, Charles James, *Anglican Devotion: Studies in the Spiritual Life of the Church of England between the Reformation and the Oxford Movement* (London, 1961).

Stewart, Alan, 'The Early Modern Closet Discovered', *Representations*, **50** (1995), pp. 76–100.

Close Readers: Humanism and Sodomy in Early Modern England (Princeton, NJ, 1997).

Stewart-Brown, R., 'The Stationers, Booksellers and Printers of Chester to about 1800', *Transactions of the Historic Society of Lancashire and Cheshire*, **83** (1932), pp. 101–52.

Stock, Brian, *Listening for the Text: On the Uses of the Text* (Baltimore, MD, 1990).

Summit, Jennifer, *Memory's Library: Medieval Books in Early Modern England* (Chicago, 2008).

Tadmor, Naomi, 'The Concept of the Household-Family in Eighteenth-Century England', *Past and Present*, **151** (1996), pp. 111–40.

Family and Friends in Eighteenth-Century England: Household, Kinship, and Patronage (Cambridge, 2001).

Taylor, Andrew, 'Into His Secret Chamber: Reading and Privacy in Late Medieval England', in James Raven, Helen Small, and Naomi Tadmor (eds.), *The Practice and Representation of Reading in England* (Cambridge, 1996).

Thomas, Keith, *Man and the Natural World: Changing Attitudes in England 1500–1800* (Harmondsworth, 1983).

'The Meaning of Literacy in Early Modern England', in Gerd Baumann (ed.), *The Written Word: Literacy in Transition* (Oxford, 1986).

Religion and the Decline of Magic: Studies in Popular Beliefs in Sixteenth- and Seventeenth-Century England (revised edn, London, 1973).

Thornton, Dora, *The Scholar in His Study: Ownership and Experience in Renaissance Italy* (New Haven, CT, 1997).

Tite, Colin, *The Early Records of Sir Robert Cotton's Library: Formation, Cataloguing, Use* (London, 2003).

Todd, Margo, *The Culture of Protestantism in Early Modern Scotland* (New Haven, CT, 2002).

'Puritan Self-Fashioning: The Diary of Samuel Ward', *Journal of British Studies*, **31** (1992), pp. 236–64.

Tribble, Evelyn B., 'Godly Reading: John Foxe's *Actes and Monuments* (1583)', in Sabrina Alcorn Baron (ed.), *The Reader Revealed* (Washington, DC, 2001).

Margins and Marginality: The Printed Page in Early Modern England (Charlottesville, VA, 1993).

Tyacke, Nicholas, *Anti-Calvinists: The Rise of English Arminianism, c. 1590–1640* (Oxford, 1987).

(ed.), *England's Long Reformation 1500–1800* (London, 1998).

The Fortunes of English Puritanism, 1603–1640 (London, 1990).

'Popular Puritan Mentality in Late Elizabethan England', in Peter Clark, Alan Smith and Nicholas Tyacke (eds.), *The English Commonwealth 1547–1640: Essays in Politics and Society Presented to Joel Hurstfield* (Leicester, 1979).

Underdown, David, *Fire from Heaven: Life in an English Town in the Seventeenth Century* (London, 1992).

Vernet, André, Jolly, Claude, Varry, Dominique, and Poulain, Martine (eds.), *Histoire des bibliothèques françaises* (4 vols., Paris, 1988–1992).

Vickery, Amanda, *Behind Closed Doors: At Home in Georgian England* (New Haven, CT, 2009).

Viles, David R., *The Revd. Dr Robert Wilde 1615–1679: Poet, Preacher, Provider of Bibles by Dicing in His Native St Ives* (Hemingford Grey, 2003).

Walker, W. J. (ed.), *Chapters on the Early Registers of Halifax Parish Church, from the Local Archaeological Collection of the Late E. J. Walker* (Halifax, 1885).

Wall, Cynthia, *The Literary and Cultural Spaces of Restoration London* (Cambridge, 1998).

Walsham, Alexandra, '"Domme Preachers"? Post-Reformation English Catholicism and the Culture of Print', *Past and Present*, **168** (2000), pp. 72–123.

'The Godly and Popular Culture', in John Coffey and Paul C. H. Lim (eds.), *The Cambridge Companion to Puritanism* (Cambridge, 2008).

Providence in Early Modern England (Oxford, 1999).

'The Reformation and "The Disenchantment of the World" Reassessed', *Historical Journal*, **51** (2008), pp. 497–528.

The Reformation of the Landscape: Religion, Memory and Legend in Early Modern Britain and Ireland (Oxford, forthcoming).

Walter, John, '"The Poormans Joy and the Gentlemans Plague": A Lincolnshire Libel and the Politics of Sedition in Early Modern England', *Past and Present*, **203** (2009), pp. 29–67.

Watt, Tessa, *Cheap Print and Popular Piety, 1550–1640* (Cambridge, 1991).

Weber, Max, *The Protestant Ethic and the Spirit of Capitalism*, trans. Talcott Parsons (1930) (London, 1992).

Webster, Charles, *The Great Instauration: Science, Medicine and Reform, 1626–1660* (London, 1975).

Webster, Tom, *Godly Clergy in Early Stuart England: The Caroline Puritan Movement c.1620–1643* (Cambridge, 1997).

'Writing to Redundancy: Approaches to Spiritual Journals and Early Modern Spirituality', *Historical Journal*, **39** (1996), pp. 33–56.

Welsford, Anne, 'Mr Newte's Library in St Peter's Church, Tiverton', *The Devonshire Association for the Advancement of Science Literature and Art. Report and Transactions*, **106** (1974), pp. 17–31; **107** (1975), pp. 11–20.

Withington, Phil, 'Public Discourse, Corporate Citizenship, and State Formation in Early Modern England', *American Historical Review*, **112** (2007), pp. 1016–38.

Wing, Donald, *Short-Title Catalogue of Books Printed in England, Scotland, Ireland, Wales and British America and of English Books Printed in Other Countries 1641–1700* (2nd edn, New York, 1972–88).

Woodward, J., 'The Monument to Sir Thomas Bodley in Merton College Chapel', *Bodleian Library Record*, **5** (1954–6), pp. 189–96.

Woolf, Daniel, *Reading History in Early Modern England* (Cambridge, 2000).

The Social Circulation of the Past: English Historical Culture 1500–1730 (Oxford, 2003).

Worden, Blair, *Roundhead Reputations: The English Civil Wars and the Passions of Posterity* (London, 2001).

Wrightson, Keith, *Earthly Necessities: Economic Lives in Early Modern Britain* (New Haven, CT, 2000).

Wrightson, Keith, and Levine, David, *Poverty and Piety in an English Village: Terling, 1525–1700* (New York, 1979).

Zaret, David, *Origins of Democratic Culture: Printing, Petitions, and the Public Sphere in Early-Modern England* (Princeton, NJ, 2000).

Zwicker, Steven N., 'Habits of Reading and Early Modern Literary Culture', in David Loewenstein and Janel Mueller (eds.), *The Cambridge History of Early Modern English Literature* (Cambridge, 2002).

UNPUBLISHED THESES AND PAPERS

Benger, J. S., 'The Authority of Writer and Text in Radical Protestant Literature 1540 to 1593 with Particular Reference to the Marprelate Tracts' (unpublished DPhil thesis, Oxford University, 1989).

Best, Graham, 'Books and Readers in Certain Eighteenth-Century Parish Libraries' (unpublished PhD thesis, Loughborough University, 1985).

Black, Laurence, 'Pamphlet Wars: The Marprelate Tracts and "Martinism", 1588–1688' (unpublished PhD thesis, University of Toronto, 1996).

Cambers, Andrew, 'Print, Manuscript, and Godly Cultures in the North of England, c. 1600–1650' (unpublished DPhil thesis, University of York, 2003).

Hetet, J. S. T., 'A Literary Underground in Restoration England: Printers and Dissenters in the Context of Constraints, 1660–1689' (unpublished PhD thesis, University of Cambridge, 1987).

Newton, J. A., 'Puritanism in the Diocese of York (excluding Nottinghamshire) 1603–1640' (unpublished DPhil thesis, University of London, 1955).

Robson, Lynn, ' "No Nine Days Wonder": Embedded Protestant Narratives in Early Modern Prose Murder Pamphlets 1573–1700' (unpublished PhD thesis, University of Warwick, 2003).

Schildt, Jeremy, ' "God Put It into His Heart to Record It": Domestic Encounters with Scripture in Post-Restoration England', paper given at the Institute of Historical Research, London, 29 June 2006.

Spinks, Mary C., 'The Cranston Library: An Eighteenth Century Parish Library at Reigate, Surrey' (unpublished postgraduate diploma in librarianship, University of Sheffield, 1966).

Southcombe, George, 'The Responses of Nonconformists to the Restoration in England' (unpublished DPhil thesis, Oxford University, 2005).

Thomas, Samuel S., 'Individuals and Communities: Religious Life in Restoration England' (unpublished PhD thesis, Washington University, St Louis, 2003).

Wolfe, Michelle, ' "Sacred Imployments": Gendering Spiritual Space and Labour in the Clerical Household' (unpublished paper).

Index